Un-Disciplining Literature

Studies in the Postmodern Theory of Education

Joe L. Kincheloe and Shirley R. Steinberg
General Editors

Vol. 121

PETER LANG
New York • Washington, D.C./Baltimore • Boston • Bern
Frankfurt am Main • Berlin • Brussels • Vienna • Canterbury

Un-Disciplining Literature

Literature, Law, and Culture

Edited by
Kostas Myrsiades
and Linda Myrsiades

PETER LANG
New York • Washington, D.C./Baltimore • Boston • Bern
Frankfurt am Main • Berlin • Brussels • Vienna • Canterbury

Library of Congress Cataloging-in-Publication Data

Un-disciplining literature: literature, law, and culture /
[edited by] Kostas Myrsiades and Linda Myrsiades.
p. cm. — (Counterpoints; vol. 121)
Includes bibliographical references and index.
1. English literature—History and criticism. 2. Law in literature. 3. Shakespeare, William, 1564–1616—Knowledge—Law. 4. American literature—History and criticism. 5. Legal stories—History and criticism. 6. Law and literature. 7. Culture and law. I. Myrsiades, Kostas. II. Myrsiades, Linda S. III. Series: Counterpoints (New York, N.Y.); vol. 121.
PR408.L38U5   809'.93355—dc21   99-15500
ISBN 0-8204-4541-X
ISSN 1058-1634

Die Deutsche Bibliothek-CIP-Einheitsaufnahme

Un-disciplining literature: literature, law, and culture /
ed. by Kostas Myrsiades and Linda Myrsiades.
–New York; Washington, D.C./Baltimore; Boston; Bern;
Frankfurt am Main; Berlin; Brussels; Vienna; Canterbury: Lang.
(Counterpoints; Vol. 121)
ISBN 0-8204-4541-X

A number of the essays printed here first appeared
in College Literature 25.1 (Winter 1998) and 26.1 (Winter 1999)

Cover design by Nona Reuter

© 1999 Peter Lang Publishing, Inc., New York

All rights reserved.
Reprint or reproduction, even partially, in all forms such as microfilm, xerography, microfiche, microcard, and offset strictly prohibited.

CONTENTS

Linda Myrsiades	Introduction	1
Jane B. Baron	Storytelling and Legal Legitimacy	13
Michael Brooks	Stories and Verdicts: Bernard Goetz and New York in Crisis	28
Anne E. Shaw and Alane C. Spinney	Rhetoric, Repetition, and Violence: A Case Study of Clinic Conflict in Milwaukee	47
Jennifer K. Wood	Refined Raw: The Symbolic Violence of Victim's Rights Reforms	72
Frances J. Ranney	Posner on Legal Texts: Law, Literature (Economics), and "Welcome Harassment"	94
Lesley Higgins and Marie-Christine Leps	"Passport Please": Legal, Literary, and Critical Fictions of Identity	117
Theron Britt	Narrative Pragmatics and the Genius of the Law in Lyotard's *Just Gaming*	169
Richard H. Weisberg	Antonio's Legalistic Cruelty: Interdisciplinarity and *The Merchant of Venice*	180
Dennis R. Klinck	Shakespeare's *Richard II* as Landlord and Wasting Tenant	190
Richard Clarke Sterne	The Trial in *A Passage to India*: "Justice" Under Colonial Conditions	206

Contents

Linda Myrsiades	Law, Medicine, and the Sex Slave in Margaret Atwood's *The Handmaid's Tale*	219
Paula Jean Reiter	Husbands, Wives, and Lawyers: Gender Roles and Professional Representations in Trollope and the Adelaide Bartlett Case	246
Patrick Colm Hogan	Fictive Tales, Real Lives: Problems With Reading Law as Literature	271
	Contributors	291
	Index	295

INTRODUCTION

Un-Disciplining Literature:
Literature, Law, and Culture
by Linda Myrsiades

If the rush of new books that have appeared in recent years examining the relationship of literature and law is any indication,[1] the usefulness of an interdisciplinary approach to literature and law is not at issue in terms of its potential contribution to cultural studies. What remains at issue, however, is what interdisciplinarity is and why it is useful. One response to that query is that concepts of interdisciplinarity became necessary once differentiation and specialization of knowledge in discrete categories became a law of being in the eighteenth century. This categorization destroyed the holistic view of knowledge more characteristic of the classical heritage, in which all knowledge was related and classifying was convenient rather than categorical. Interdisciplinarity has basically been viewed in one of two ways: law as literature and law in literature (Ward). Klein ("Crossing," "Interdisciplinarity"), nevertheless, contends that purportedly interdisciplinary research has in practice not been integrative but additive: the relation of the disciplines "may be mutual and cumulative but not interactive," for the participating disciplines are left unchanged by their interaction ("Interdisciplinarity" 56). That state of affairs is, however, far too limiting. Law, for example, can operate not only through doctrine but "by the light of local knowledge" absorbed in "seeing broad principles in parochial fact" (Geertz 167). By means of such a light, literature and law studies can address the disorder of vigilantism (Abrahams) and the rhetoric of prostitution (Day), looking for law in everyday life (Sarat and Kearns), folk law (Dundes Renteln and Dundes), or the kind of order without "law" that occurs where the informal and the extralegal act to regulate disputes (Ellickson). Taking issue with the non-integrative view of contemporary interdisciplinary studies, the present book considers a variety of methodological approaches that allow us to rethink the interactivity of literature and law through a diverse range of techniques. In the present collection, we find storying, rhetorical analysis, "readings" of such diverse legal texts as passports, Supreme Court opinions, and victim impact statements, interpretive critique of legal theory, postmodern narrative pragmatics analysis, as well as traditional literary criticism. The content of such studies as they affect the present collection ranges from Berhard Goetz's subway crimes, sexual harassment law, King Solomon and adoption law, theory in the literature and law movement, videotaping as viewed by trial juries, violence and rhetoric at abortion clinics, and legal fictions of personal and national identity to the commodification of women's bodies in Margaret Atwood, tenant law and trial legalism in Shakespeare, trials in Trollope related to the nineteenth-century Pimlico murder case, and British colonial justice in E. M. Forster.

A critical issue in interdisciplinary study is whether it has truly integrated the material of two or more disciplines into a newly coherent entity or whether it has merely achieved a questionable eclecticism that we might refer to as indiscriminate interdisciplinarity. What one looks for in an interdisciplinary approach is mutual integration of organizing concepts and the use of a common language. In a soft sense, one might illustrate in one discipline what is already clear in the discipline to which it is being related. In a hard sense, one might make use of the materials or methods of the target discipline with which a source discipline is being integrated. At base, however, is the idea of an interaction that creates of two or more disciplines a new synthesis that could be considered metadisciplinary. Theoretically, interdisciplinarity demonstrates that place where the two disciplines have achieved a singularity of focus so that boundaries are busted and disciplinary paradigms are subordinated to the interests of a particular issue.

Nevertheless, there remains a diversity of understandings relative to interdisciplinarity. Without appearing too restrictive, some labeling (adapted from the work by Klein, "Interdisciplinarity") might prove useful here, with the understanding that no single approach is necessarily to be valued more than another as if some absolute criterion of interdisciplinarity existed. Indeed, to think the latter is in some sense to have conceived of interdisciplinarity in a disciplinary sense. To apply a limited use of labeling, we could refer, for example, to the Baron and Brooks essays as concept interdisciplinarity, in this instance involving a technique in which storying techniques construct and read law. Here, a literary concept that shares techniques with those available in legal analysis is used to interpret legal cases, opinions, and trials. A second form of interdisciplinarity, linear interdisciplinarity, can be said to characterize Britt's use of a Lyotardian narrative pragmatics. This approach "legalizes" one discipline by means of a law belonging to another discipline. Here,

Lyotard's language game methodology opens to us the literary moment of law as a means of grounding narrative expression. Restrictive interdisciplinarity is exemplified by Higgins and Leps's piece on passports. Restricted interactions between passport law and an understanding of identity and nationism narrow the focus of the researcher to concentrate on a concrete project. Weisberg on *The Merchant of Venice*, Klinck on *Richard II*, and Sterne on *A Passage to India* use what can be described as a supplemental interdisciplinarity that addresses overlappings along the borderlines between two disciplines. Tenant law explains *Richard II*'s understanding of property and interpersonal relations, while legalism in trial law and property law explains *The Merchant* and postcolonialism *A Passage to India*. A related form, border interdisciplinarity, is exemplified by Ranney's essay on Posner where the shared interpretive interests of law and literature are demonstrated to have created a liminal zone between the two disciplines where mutual concepts and methods can be applied.

The first essay of the book, Jane B. Baron's "Storytelling and Legal Legitimacy," establishes the parameters for a methodology that has contributed importantly to the literature and law movement. Baron makes it clear that, faced with a crisis of legitimacy, the law finds in storying methodology a useful tool to address "the public's loss of respect for the law [as well as] the profession's loss of confidence in itself." Law has been successfully challenged internally through stories, many of them highly personal. Referencing Susan Estrich's work in rape law, Patricia Williams in race and the law, and Richard Delgado in critical legal theory, Baron introduces "what really happened" stories, "what if" stories, and what she calls "many realities" stories to offer a window into the legal profession as it critiques itself through new, as-yet imperfectly heard voices representing themselves. Law is critiqued here for its "purported objectivity and neutrality," capitalizing on narrative and cognitive theories emanating from other disciplines. At the same time, as Baron makes clear, a certain looseness in borrowing undermined the use of storytelling in law so that it engendered resistance to the tellers (who had previously been disempowered) and to the message of its "newness" (the stories, some contended, looked a lot like what litigators had been doing all along). Using the 1993 Baby Jessica case, and relating it to the image of King Solomon's justice in threatening to split a contested child, Baron argues that stories are often more crucial than purely legal tools in understanding a case. In the case studied here, the stories told introduced issues of judicial delay, manipulation of the court system, the dehumanization of parties to the case, as well as social and biological questions, none of which surfaced in either of the two allowable legal issues (adoption rights and custody rights). In storying methodology, in sum, stories provide the heart, the life, the people of law, reminding us, as Baron tells us, of "the trauma, tragedy, and heartache of a case," the very thing that has been "so often sucked out of the law."

Michael Brooks's "Stories and Verdicts: Bernhard Goetz and New York in Crisis" provides us with a case contextualized by the life of the New York subway, itself a sub-culture that serves as a synechdoche for the city. Goetz, known as the "subway killer," shot four black teenagers on a subway car in 1984 and went on to be represented in the press as a New York vigilante. Brooks tells Goetz's story as one among many storytellers he believes constructed that story, among them, of necessity, his lawyers and the press, but also, importantly, films, novels, and the subway itself which were "already written" like a scenario into which Goetz himself slipped somewhat unwillingly. Brooks takes us along "a path which leads from the social reality of New York City into the realm of private fantasy" and then outward again into the public world of popular culture and the press. He takes us through Larry Peerce's 1967 film *The Incident* (which treats an event similar to Goetz's but features knife-wielding white "punks" on the IRT), Tom Wolfe's New York novel *The Bonfire of the Vanities* (which opens with what Wolfe considers an obligatory initiating subway scene), Brian Garfield's 1972 urban New York vigilante novel *Death Wish* (subsequently a film), as well as nonfiction works by Rubin and by Kaminsky specific to the Goetz case itself. The essay culminates in a version of the story constructed from trial transcripts, videotape, and press reports.

Anne E. Shaw and Alane C. Spinney's "Rhetoric, Repetition, and Violence: A Case Study of Clinic Conflict in Milwaukee" examines the impact of post-*Roe* law on sidewalk counseling at abortion clinics, given the failed "human life" amendment to the Constitution and the gradual exhaustion of legal limits to abortion rights through waiting periods and consent provisions. Obstructionist efforts to establish a law beyond the law exemplify an assertion of a natural law of motherhood supported by the Old Testament law of the father. Here, the rhetoric of abortion reads "choice" as "murder," an act for which disobedient mothers will be punished and for which redemption must be sought under the natural order of male dominance. The Apocalypse—figured in lurid sidewalk displays and performances as well as clinic bombings—calls the fetus forth as witness to testify at Judgment Day. Justice is thereby enacted by the innocent on the guilty in a reversal of the earlier act of abortion, taking its authority from the doctrine of antiabortion texts. Law without order results in the disorder that attends each Remembrance Day (the anniversary date of *Roe v. Wade*) when shootings, arson, and acid attacks certify a vigilantism that chooses its own informal, local law over a formal, official law that has ceased to respond to its call for retribution. We either open closed discourse, as the authors claim, or we must reconceptualize free speech using tools (like the RICO law) meant to corral what has become an "organized" crime.

Jennifer Wood's "Refined Raw: The Symbolic Violence of Victim's Rights Reforms" takes us directly into the courtroom to examine how legal rituals and symbolic violence operate to affect jury verdicts. Speaking as a rhetorician, Woods looks back to the Rodney King videotape and the 1991 *Payne* decision—which provides for the victim's right to testify during the penalty phase of a capital murder trial—to gauge the effect on jury verdicts that result from both videotapes and victims' stories. She considers the construction of crime narratives in Supreme Court opinions and how they enact the victim's story as well as how such a story operates to "misrecognize" the violence exercised through it. Indeed, Wood considers that the criminal trial itself and its formalities constitute rituals that themselves exercise legal violence in formal terms. Such rituals "grant some the authority to act and to speak in the name of others" as a sort of "usurpatory ventriloquism" that she considers has clear racial- and gender-based implications.

Frances J. Ranney's "Posner on Legal Texts: Law, Literature, (Economics), and 'Welcome Harassment'," provides a strong interpretive reading of the work of Richard Posner, a figure who has had a formative influence in the law and literature movement. Posner's interjection of an economic perspective into law and literature studies is examined in Ranney's piece through sexual harassment law, using *Carr v. Allison* (1994) as a case in point. As Judge of the Seventh Circuit Court of Appeals, Posner himself wrote the majority opinion in *Carr*, which allows Ranney both to examine that opinion in light of Posner's critical writing on law and literature and to take up Posner's challenge that judicial opinions "are the only legal texts appropriate for literary analysis." Ranney provides, in addition, an analysis of what she calls Posner's "eclectic New Critical" theory, considering it in relation to the work of the feminist legal/literary critic Robin West and that of one of Posner's strongest critics and the third of the founding triad of literature and law studies (along with Posner and Richard Weisberg, represented in this volume), James Boyd White. Ranney pursues Posner like a deer caught in the twin headlights of West and White to give us an original reading of what she considers "oxymoronic 'welcome harassment'," the logically implied tautological cousin of "unwelcome harassment."

Lesley Higgins and Marie-Christine Leps's "'Passport Please': Legal, Literary, and Critical Fictions of Identity" presents us with an innovative examination of passports that elevates this identification document, initially designed for security, to the status of a "power-knowledge matrix." This piece uses a Foucauldian framework to explore fictions of identity and their response to a "shift from cultural homogeneity to heterogeneity." The piece pursues a historical account of the World War II emergence of the passport that is followed by critical discussion of perspectives offered in literature by Henry James, T.S. Eliot, Virginia Woolf, and Michael Ondaatje. It goes on to consider selected Supreme Court decisions, innovations in literary forms, and questions of identity politics and cross-border citizenship. Taking an approach that puts the passport at the center of disciplinary practices, the authors recognize in this travel document a tool in the relations of power that is emblematic of one form of power, governmentality. Ranging broadly in its long reach across "the contiguities and divergences, the correlations and contradictions existing among different discursive practices," this piece nevertheless keeps a tight rein on the questions it raises by focusing on the passport as a singular legal tool. Using *The American Scene* (1906), "The Waste Land" (1922), *Mrs. Dalloway* (1925), and *The English Patient* (1992), Higgins and Leps illustrate the different scenes across the century in which the passport strategically constructs community, citizenship, nationalism, and identity in literary as well as legal fictions, using its power as a key instrument in negotiating state security to administer new ways of understanding and knowing ourselves as a nation.

Theron Britt's "Narrative Pragmatics and the Genius of Law in Lyotard's *Just Gaming*" introduces a postmodern approach to justice that highlights "the inherent 'literary' moment of the law." Law's objectivity is reinvented here to un-repress its "figural fluidity" and expose the indeterminacy it shares with literature. In what way, Britt asks, does law inhabit or constitute the literary? He denies one possibility (that it resides as a "paradoxical law of textuality" or "indeterminate figurality") to prefer another (attention to the other side of "the oscillation between a moment of grounding and its undoing," that is, to a grounding that is as totalitarian a repression as any). Britt uses *Just Gaming* as his text and begins by engaging Lyotard's loss of faith in criteria as a central problem of justice. Indeed, judgments made without criteria come down to judgments that rely on feelings. Drawing an analogy to Kant's rule-giving figure, Britt looks further for the source of the ability to judge without criteria or, alternately, to judge by inventing criteria. He arrives at a "timeless repetition that is always original," which, he finds, Kant and Lyotard share. It both denies prescriptions and provides them in what the author regards as a "quintessentially postmodern Paradox" that totalizes discourse in the name of democratic pluralism. Lyotard's "next move" is thus instituted in "a type of 'totalitarian' movement" rather than as an idealized image of abstract justice. In this way, Britt concludes, the unavoidable violence of law marks literature with an aggressive totalitarian violence.

Richard Weisberg's piece "Antonio's Legalistic Cruelty: Interdisciplinarity and *The Merchant of Venice*" represents the work of a central figure in the literature and law movement. Weisberg introduces us to the vigorous debate on interpreting Shakespeare through a literature and law perspective as well as to traditional literary/legal criticism of the type for which the field has become justly renowned. Weisberg considers *The Merchant* a "well-worked 'legalistic' story" comparable only to Melville's legalistic *Billy Budd* in terms of the debate it has aroused. Weisberg examines the disposition of Shylock's estate, his trust, and his will, Portia's use of an "Alien Statute," and Christian mercy in law. He draws the conclusion that the property arrangements, Shylock's conversion, and the mercy he is shown are no justice at all but plunder assisted by a legalistic reading of the law. Ultimately, he posits that a thoughtful member of the audience will find neither the merchant Antonio nor the Jew Shylock completely in the right and that Portia must in the end feel herself compelled to try whether "Jewish ethical modes might be less formalistic and less cruel than Christian 'mercy' of the Antonio variety."

Dennis R. Klinck's "Shakespeare's *Richard II* as Landlord and Wasting Tenant" focuses on property law to examine the king as both landlord and perpetrator of waste. Using period legal materials, Klinck holds Shakespeare up to the scrutiny of his legal contemporaries. He provides a close reading of Shakespeare's intentions in creating *Richard II* as a character who threatens royal dignity and the state itself, sacrificing both to his own ends. Klinck's insightful use of the metaphor of the king's body as both natural (mortal) and political (historical) leads us to conceive of a severed Richard who paradoxically performs at odds with himself, that is, as both a landholder and a landwaster. Liability issues and private as opposed to public harms are explored carefully and at length to play out the paradox both figuratively and legally in an imaginative balance of the contrary provisions of waste and caretaking.

In "The Trial in *A Passage to India*: Justice Under Colonial Conditions," Richard Clark Sterne provides a reading of E. M. Forster's novel of British rule in India that probes the administration of colonial justice. In his reading, the fortuitous justice produced by such rule is informed by ethnic, religious, and caste antagonisms that would ultimately lead to the dissolution of the British raj and end in war and massacres. The validity of the trial itself had to be endorsed not only by the ruling British and the dominant Hindu population, but by Moslems as well, each of which maintained its own legal philosophy and political interests. The legal machine of the British legal system, in a position of having to implement justice between antagonistic ethnic and national communities, was in the business of negotiating ethnic prejudice and guilt at the same time that it operated under its own religious and ethnic biases. The risks it ran were thus of potentially losing control of the trial as well as undermining its own legitimacy as a court of law. Closely text-based, Sterne's approach is to see the legal world of the raj through Forster's eyes as a construction informed by the perspectives of the characters he has created. It is a world both contextualized by a vast political panorama on the verge of abjecting British colonial rule and, at the same time, reduced to a personalistic view of law that defines the limited interests of its immediate players and their own psychological and social agendas.

Linda Myrsiades's "Law, Medicine, and the Sex Slave in Margaret Atwood's *The Handmaid's Tale*" views reproductive woman as triangulated by literature, medicine, and law and locates how representations diverge and converge to construct her in these discourses. Using the frame image of the judgment of Solomon, she ties her understanding of Atwood's novel to recent feminist legal analysis in which surrogacy and abortion rights are addressed in relation to woman's autonomy. Myrsiades tells five tales of woman as she is presented in Atwood's cult classic. In "The Tale of Separability" women are examined in medicine as absented from a central place in the pregnancy process. "The Judge's Tale" unpacks the role of Solomon the Judge as a figure who establishes superordinate male authority in the law. In "The Economic Tale," the handmaid Offred is marked as a designated breeder assigned to "labor" for the state as a commodity of exchange and a home for the "seeds" of state. "The Tale of Property" extends the discussion to view woman as property "inhabited" by the state while the final tale, "Composing her 'Tail'," introduces the handmaid's effort to reclaim her property by composing herself and taking possession of her body.

Paula J. Reiter's "Husbands, Wives, and Lawyers: Gender Roles and Professional Representation in Trollope and the Adelaide Bartlett Case" compares a wife accused of forging her husband's will in Trollope's *Orley Farm* to a wife accused in the infamous 1886 Pimlico Case of poisoning her husband. Reiter's piece examines gender assumptions and legal tactics in the construction of female roles in late nineteenth century England. In Lady Mason, *Orley Farm* presents us with a female figure whose forgery leaves her at the mercy of three men in her life (her lawyer, a suitor, and her son). Unable to represent herself in her trial, she becomes silent and dependent upon those who take up the responsibility of representing her. A comparable strategy of representation becomes the strategy of choice in the Pimlico case. To gain her acquittal, Adelaide Bartlett's defense successfully constructs her as a woman incapable of sufficient planning or self-direction to commit such a crime. Although she takes the stand in her own defense, her self-presentation embraces the logic of passivity and silence characteristic of middle-class women of her period. In reality, she and Lady Mason reject the construction imposed upon them, so that the forgery and murder of which they are accused come to stand as secret statements of refusal and realignment of power in their relations with men. At the same time, their "acquittals" essentially rely upon their willingness to perform the submissive roles designed by men for them.

Finally, in the last essay, "Fictive Tales, Real Lives: Problems With Reading Law as Literature," Patrick Colm Hogan challenges us to rethink the entire literature/law enterprise. Hogan takes on its use of "narrative study as a model for legal study, selecting a particularly influential reading of the narrative approach for his critique—Richard Delgado's "Storytelling for Oppositionists and Others," which he unpacks as a Romantic misconception. He holds that the mere fact that a given methodology leads us to reflect more thoughtfully about a field is an insufficient rationale for regarding it as good in itself. To admit that stories humanize us is no more, in Hogan's view, than to acknowledge that they accomplish what any manifestation of the human spirit is capable of accomplishing. He objects, more particularly, to a dichotomization of science and art that opposes narrative to logic, the creative to the mechanistic. In this regard, he takes issue with the use of personal anecdotes in narrative understandings of law, which he considers coercive in their rejection of careful argument. He finds that whereas their intent is to counter oppression by expanding the diversity of testimony, personal anecdotes contribute to racism as essentially an irrefutable set of feelings to which one is unable effectively to respond. Thus, he stands Delgado's defense of personal stories on its head, for he concludes that, granting such stories their value, "they are not intrinsically valuable because they are personal stories." Hogan would require narrative theorists to define what, indeed, they mean by "narrative," other than in the most "vacuous" terms. Here, he takes on Robert Cover and rejects his grand or master narrative approach to thinking about what Hogan would consider principles rather than narratives. Hogan's standard, by contrast, would be to question legal narratives in terms of the extent to which issues in law are determined "according to stereotyped plot structures or standard character prototypes," an approach that Robin West has somewhat adopted, but in a general way insufficient to convince Hogan. Finally, Hogan addresses the issue of social construction as a theory describing reality and how that theory affects the truth or falsity of claims (presumably the work of the law). For Hogan, "factual plausibility and the completeness of descriptive and explanatory accounts relative to governing laws" have no parallel in narrative per se, while they are critical to legal adjudication. A narrative approach, in sum, is in his view no substitute for empirical study as an explanatory tool and is likely, in a worst-case scenario (here he conducts an analysis of the *Bakke* case), to obscure more likely explanations with greater empirical validity.

What this book, indeed the field of literature and law, has tried to demonstrate is that disciplinarity, a form of traditional academic nationalism, is showing signs of age and that restless research/critic adventurers along the frontier territory between disciplinary lands have chipped away at the great wall that separates them to create demilitarized zones and border traffic that will allow them to fish in each others' waters. Lining each other up in the intellectual cross-hairs of the interdisciplinary bow, literature and law may together yield new outlooks and solve old problems. They may, to switch metaphors, remedy hardening of the categories and create collateral circulation to strengthen the heart-beat of academic research. Where the narrowly specialized, highly codified, high paradigm approaches characteristic of the field of law interface with the configurational, eclectic, broad specialism emanating from the less codified, lower paradigm field of literature, both admittedly risk the dangers inherent in interdisciplinarity—that is, the risk of becoming undisciplined or the risk that there might be no concrete payoff. But they have at least the opportunity to explore the relation of divergent and convergent thinking. They still profit from learning what new questions can be asked and what new concepts, skills, or languages might be profitably borrowed. Disciplinary leaves of absence get authorized and taken-for-granted assumptions get taken out for air. Hierarchies are more likely to become inverted, dominance get challenged, and new voices get to speak. The periphery gets to play center, and marginalized questions get pushed in from the boundaries. In this way, boundary busting and boundary blurring shake up the disciplinary enterprise to produce fresh angles of vision, such as we hope we have provided in this volume.

NOTES

[1] Elizabeth Villiers Gemmette has clearly assisted the process with the publication of *Law in Literature: An Annotated Bibliography of Law-Related Works*, a work that includes 250 annotated entries compiled by thirty contributors in the field. Even more to the point is her three-volume *Law in Literature*, an anthology of works with legal themes in drama, short stories, and novellas, the most extensive such work to appear and, to this writer's knowledge, the only in-print anthology for ready use in literature and law classrooms. It is not just the availability of such literature that figures into our more refined understanding of both the interstices and the interfaces between the two disciplines, for several cultural studies come to mind, including not only the Series in Law, Jurisprudence, and Social Thought begun in 1993 and edited by Austin Sarat and Thomas R. Kearns (including such relevant titles as *The Rhetoric of Law* and *Law in Everyday Life*) but Jane M. Gaines's *Contested Culture: The Image, The Voice, and The Law*, Richard H. Weisberg's *Vichy Law and the Holocaust in France*, Sarat's edited essays *Race, Law, and Culture*, and, particularly, Saidiya V. Hartman's starkly evocative *Scenes of Subjugation: Terror, Slavery, and Self-Making in Nineteenth-Century America*.

Related to Hartman's work, Sandra Gunning's *Race, Rape, and Lynching: The Red Record of American Literature, 1890-1912* in the Race and American Culture series edited by Arnold Rampersad and Shelley Fisher Fishkin is itself a powerful cultural analysis of race, law, and literature. Treating much the same period but with a strong reading of social contract and the literature of Twain, James, Chesnutt, Howells, and Chopin is Brook Thomas's *American Literary Realism and the Failed Promise of Contract*. Other works worth noting in their treatment of legal themes in American literature include Ann M. Algeo's *The Courtroom as Forum: Homicide Trials by Dreiser, Wright, Capote, and Mailer* and Barry R. Schaller's *A Vision of American Law: Judging Law, Literature, and the Stories We Tell*. An especially useful work, John Denvir's edited collection of essays *Legal Reelism: Movies as Legal Texts*, addresses American cinema and its use of legal themes.

Two works that integrate philosophy into the equation deserve notice—Costas Douzinas and Ronnie Warrington's *Justice Miscarried: Ethics, Aesthetics and the Law* and Wai Chee Dimock's *Residues of Justice: Literature, Law, Philosophy*—not only for their coverage of classical literature (*Antigone*) and American literature (Melville, Whitman, and Fenimore Cooper, in particular) but for their treatment of foundational issues related to theories of justice. Taking a broader view of the range of literature open to discussion using a literature and law perspective, Theodore Ziolkowski in *The Mirror of Justice: Literary Reflections of Legal Crises* takes us through Greek, pagan, Roman, German, French, and English literature from the classical period to the twentieth century. (For additional sources see Myrsiades "Law," "Interdisciplinarity.")

WORKS CITED

Abrahams, Ray. "Vigilantism: Order and Disorder on the Frontiers of the State." *Inside and Outside the Law: Anthropological Studies of Authority and Ambiguity*. Ed. Olivia Harris. New York: Routledge, 1996.

Day, Sophie. "The Law and the Market: Rhetorics of Exclusion and Inclusion Among London Prostitutes." *Inside and Outside the Law: Anthropological Studies of Authority and Ambiguity*. Ed. Olivia Harris. New York: Routledge, 1996.

Ellickson, Robert C. *Order Without Law: How Neighbors Settle Disputes*. Cambridge: Harvard UP, 1996.

Geertz, Clifford. *Local Knowledge: Further Essays in Interpretive Anthropology*. New York: Basic Books, 1983.

Klein, Julie Thompson. *Crossing Boundaries: Knowledge, Disciplinarities, and Interdisciplinarities*. Charlottesville: UP of Virginia, 1996.

———. *Interdisciplinarity: History, Theory, and Practice*. Detroit: Wayne State UP, 1990.

Myrsiades, Linda. "Interdisciplinarity, Law, Language, and Literature." *College Literature* 23.1 (Winter 1996): 204-16.

———. "Law and Literature: A Review Essay. *College Literature* 21.1 (Winter 1994): 164-71.

Renteln, Alison Dundes, and Alan Dundes, eds. *Folk Law: Essays in the The-*

ory and Practice of Lex Non Scripta. 2 Vols. Madison: U of Wisconsin P, 1995.

Sarat, Austin, and Thomas R. Kearns, eds. *Law in Everyday Life*. Ann Arbor: U of Michigan P, 1995.

Sterne, Richard Clark. *Dark Mirror: The Sense of Injustice in Modern European and American Literature*. New York: Fordham UP, 1994.

Ward, Ian. "Responsibility in Critical Legal Theory: An Interdisciplinary Investigation." *Studies in the Humanities* 20.1 (June 1993): 49–62.

Weisberg, Richard. *Poethics and Other Strategies of Law and Literature*. New York: Columbia UP, 1992.

CHAPTER ONE

Storytelling and Legal Legitimacy[1]
by Jane B. Baron

Anyone who has not slept through the last few years will have observed that a tremendous rift has grown up between the legal profession and the lay public. When rodeo style "great lawyer roundups" can be used to sell beer; when the burning question following the acquittal verdict in the lengthy O. J. Simpson trial is still "did he actually do it?"; when people who have never read a play by Shakespeare suggest "the first thing we do, let's kill all the lawyers"—when these kinds of things happen, you know the public has lost confidence in your profession.

But more interesting, in some ways, than the public's loss of respect for law is the profession's loss of confidence in itself. Especially from within the legal academy, the legitimacy of law has come under intense criticism. This criticism goes beyond the perennial calls for reforms such as higher ethical standards, increased public service, or an end to suits asserting frivolous claims. The critique of which I am speaking is, at bottom, not that our legal system is operating less fairly than it should, but rather that it is *incapable* of operating fairly. And, curiously, though it is an internal critique, it relies on and has been fueled by theoretical developments in fields outside of law, most notably in the areas of narrative and epistemological theory. So the crisis of legitimacy is, paradoxically, both internal and interdisciplinary. This challenge from within is my subject. My thesis is that scholars have employed the seemingly innocent device of storytelling to challenge the objectivity and neutrality of law.

But I cannot explain the crisis of legitimacy without stepping backwards to explain important aspirations and ideals that lie behind the idea of the rule of law.[2] Necessarily, I will oversimplify here, but to get at the essentials I ask you to consider the following rather odd hypothetical based on the biblical story of Solomon (1 Kings 3). In this story, you may recall, two women approach Solomon, then King of Israel, and each alleges that she is the mother of the living child who is with them. (Each alleges that the other's child died.) As the story is written in the Bible, only Solomon was asked to resolve this dispute—which seems more than reasonable given the historical time and his position.

But imagine several possible decision makers: possibility no. 1 is Mr. T (of television "A-Team" fame); possibility no. 2 is the husband of one of the two claimants; and possibility no. 3 is Solomon. When my students have this choice, they always go with Solomon (and I think they are right to do so). But it is worth examining why.

What's with Mr. T? He is known for his brute strength (and his gold jewelry), not his good judgment or brilliance. And while he might be an extremely gentle and a very intelligent giant, he equally well might not be, in which case he just might rely on force or strength alone to resolve the dispute. And *this* would contradict our sense that part of the reason we have law is to protect the weak against the strong, so that something other than might makes right. In other words, part of our understanding of fairness in law is that, while strength may be used to enforce law, law should be based on something other than mere strength. Law, that is, should be backed by reason.

OK, this will eliminate Mr. T. But what about letting the husband decide this dispute? Well, we can all see the problem here: the husband is likely to be biased, whereas in our eyes justice is not interested but disinterested. In the ideal, a decision maker should be neutral. At the least, he should not be already partisan toward or against one of the claimants. They, in turn, should have an equal chance to win, and not be advantaged by something other than the "merits" of their respective claims.

All this does seem to leave us rather firmly with Solomon as our decision maker. But notice that we might not be equally happy to leave the judgment to some other person, even some other king, like Jordan's King Hussein or fight promoter Don King. Solomon's judgment was self-evidently wise. We don't trust all individuals, even all kings, to be wise.

But why do we need to "trust" judicial decision makers? Consider for a moment a contemporary variation on the problem Solomon was asked to solve. Many of you read about the Baby Jessica case, involving the child given up for adoption at birth by her biological mother without the consent of her biological father.[3] She was raised for almost three years by her adoptive parents before her father won his battle to rescind the adoption and regain custody of the child. Now in this case, unlike the Bible story, we had proof of the child's actual biological ancestry. But the ultimate question in the modern variation is the same as in the original story: What qualities define a parent? How do we determine who will love a child?

It is possible to approach this question from dramatically divergent assumptions. We can assume, on the one hand, that biological or genetic connection exerts a claim regardless of the quality of the actual emotional relationship between people. Or we can assume, on the other hand, that once an adult truly assumes the parental functions of love and care, that person is a child's parent, regardless of biological ties.

I am quite confident that not everyone would make the same assessment of which assumption should prevail. (Indeed, I am fairly confident that not everyone will even accept my formulation of the alternatives.) But I think this case, like the Solomon case itself, helps to bring to the surface a notion deeply seated in legal thinking, the notion that part of what makes us individuals, and defines our identity, is our choices about values. These choices are understood in our liberal legal culture to be deeply personal, individual choices that each person makes for him or herself (Unger; Singer 40-46). There may be such things as "shared values," as, for example, that torturing babies is wrong. But these values are shared only in the sense that many individuals happen to have made the same choice.

So where values are in conflict, as in the Baby Jessica case, there is nothing to tell us how to "rank" them, which value to put first. Without criteria for ranking, any choice will "just" be a value judgment. It is then subject to the critique that it merely reflects the decision maker's personal values and is not necessarily in any way "right."

In this light, we need to consider what to do if Solomon is not around to decide our adoption dispute. Some more "ordinary" judge is going to have to make a ruling. But the judge in an American courtroom is envisioned more or less as the antithesis of Solomon. He (and only recently would the judge in an American court plausibly have been a she, so I'll use the male pronoun here)—he, this more ordinary judge, is considered someone who, if free to decide the case on the basis of his own insight and inclination, would probably get things wrong, either by implementing his personal preferences as the law or by somehow favoring one side over the other. For this reason, the judge must be *constrained* from deciding the case on the basis of his own inclinations. That constraint may take numerous forms, but the most important takes the form of a rule, previously given to the judge as the basis for decision. In other words, our legal and political culture demands that a *rule*, not a person, decide. This is why we are a government of laws and not of "men."[4]

Summarizing, then, the aspirations of the rule of law can be understood as attempts to deal with identifiable dangers, things we fear: decisions based purely on brute strength, decisions based on personal interest, decisions based on individual, idiosyncratic preferences. The rule of law can be understood as an attempt to respond to these dangers by placing various *constraints* on various actors within the legal system. To prevent or constrain judges from imposing their own values in the guise of law, we deprive them of the power to make legal rules, reserving that power to the legislature. The legislature, by the way, is constrained, too: by the obligation to make laws that are "rational." The judge's role is then limited to merely *applying*, rather than making, legal rules. This process, in the ideal, is nonpartisan and more or less mechanical: as in, here is the law, here are the facts, press the law down, squeeze out the result. Ideally, results are decisions that are determinate (in the sense of being demanded by and in accord with the rules) and objective (i.e., not based on anyone's personal preferences or whims, but rather based on neutral criteria perceivable by reason). The fancy name for all these constraints is well known to you: it is "due process of law." Justice in this vision is most just when it is most mechanical and leaves least to individual discretion. The Supreme Court of Iowa expressed this ideal in the Baby Jessica case, saying:

> As tempting as it is to resolve this highly emotional issue with one's heart, we do not have the unbridled discretion of a Solomon. Ours is a system of law, and adoptions are solely creatures of statute. [W]ithout established procedures to guide courts in such matters, they would be engaged in uncontrolled social engineering. This is not permitted under our law. (*In re* B.G.C., 496 N.W.2d 239, 241 [Iowa 1992])

Now how did this vision of justice come to be challenged? The answer is that it has been challenged from a number of directions and for a very long time, but I will skip over some of the earlier efforts in order to focus on the challenges that have been most influential of late. In a nutshell, the challenges I wish to describe take the form of stories. Quite simply, legal scholars began to tell stories—often true stories—that gave readers reason to question the law's objectivity and neutrality.

Some of these stories were surprisingly personal, and for that reason extremely powerful. Among the first to use this technique was Susan Estrich, who already had a national reputation when she entered the legal academy because she had been, in 1977, the first woman President of the *Harvard Law Review*. After clerking for Justice John Paul Stevens on the United States Supreme Court, Estrich returned to Harvard Law School as a professor. Among her first articles was an exhaustive historical and critical treatment of the law of rape which appeared in the *Yale Law Journal* in 1986. The article focused particularly on the way the legal definition of rape, especially the requirement that the intercourse be nonconsensual, turned attention to the conduct of the female victim rather than the male perpetrator, and it argued persuasively that existing doctrine tended to identify as real rape only those instances of compelled sexual intercourse that occurred between strangers. The depth and quality of the article's analysis would have alone made it noteworthy, but it was even more remarkable for its introduction, which begins as follows: "Eleven years ago, a man held an ice pick to my throat and said: 'Push over, shut up, or I'll kill you.' I did what he said, but I couldn't stop crying. A hundred years later, I jumped out of my car as he drove away" (1087).

The power of this disclosure, and of Estrich's description of the remainder of the events of the night she was raped, were undeniable. But the next 100 pages of the article were, as I have said, well within the mainstream of traditional legal scholarship. Others, however, took the storytelling strategy farther, not just using stories to introduce their articles, but interweaving stories throughout their more conventional analysis, or sometimes leaving the conventional part out altogether, and writing the entire article in story form.

Now what were these stories offered to show? How did they challenge the rule-of-law ideals I described earlier? What is the reason to tell, as Estrich did, a story of something that really happened? Let me take some examples.[5] Let's say that litigation and judicial decision-making in cases of severe domestic violence reflect the assumption that violence against women is rare or exceptional. But let's say also that we can produce stories of women from all walks of life who have been subjected to such violence. If, as these stories suggest, battering occurs with great frequency, then the assumption of exceptionality is just wrong. Moreover, to the extent that the assumptions underlying the law applicable to battering contradict women's actual experience of battering relationships, those assumptions may silence the very women the law is meant to help. To those who are silenced by legal assumptions that bear little connection to the reality in which they live, the law seems anything but objective and neutral. Rather, it seems part of the very structure of oppression into which they feel locked.

We can be even more specific here. One question that consistently lurks behind the legal analysis of issues that arise in connection with battering is the question, "why didn't she leave him?" But the stories told by women in battering relationships demonstrate that it is *when* women seek to leave that they face the greatest physical danger, from what has been called separation assault—assaults by which batterers seek to retain the power which they might lose if the woman leaves. Stories about these assaults show that the reality of violence and danger that battered women face is quite unlike the "reality" governing the courts' framing and resolution of the legal issues posed by domestic violence, for in the courts' view the reality is that the woman puts herself at risk by staying and could remove the danger by leaving.

Let me give one more example of a "what really happened" story. Within the legal academy, this one is quite famous. It is told by Patricia Williams, an

African-American professor of law at Columbia Law School. Williams tells of seeing a sweater in the window of a Bennetton store in New York City and deciding that the sweater would make a good Christmas gift for her mother. When she went to enter the store, however, she learned that the door was controlled by a buzzer lock system. The gum-chewing teen-aged white clerk at the desk refused to buzz Williams in on the ground that the store was closed, but Williams knew this was a lie because she could see other shoppers, all white of course, in the store. Williams describes at some length her rage and humiliation at being excluded, but the story is about more than hurt feelings. It demonstrates powerfully how the formal equality offered by existing antidiscrimination laws fails to reach or remedy the awful and pervasive consequences of racism.

"What really happened" stories tell of events and responses that genuinely occur in the "real" world.[6] The point of these stories, in many instances, is to demonstrate the gap between the reality of the described experiences, on the one side, and existing legal doctrine, on the other. The gap shows that the perspective of the law is just that—a perspective, a viewpoint—and that it is not a neutral one either, but one with the potential to oppress and injure those whose stories don't fit the authorized reality. Ideally, exposing this gap points the way to change: reformed and transformed law will better reflect the reality of the experiences of those subject to it.

But there is another kind of storytelling that poses a different sort of challenge to the rule of law ideal of justice as objective, neutral, and mechanical. This kind of storytelling—which I will call "many realities" storytelling—emphasizes the multiplicity of ways in which a single event might be perceived and experienced. An excellent example appears in the work of Richard Delgado, one of the pioneers of what has come to be called critical race theory. In an early article exploring the potential of stories to transform conventional beliefs and attitudes, Delgado presented several versions of a story of a minority applicant seeking an entry-level faculty position at a more or less typical law school ("Storytelling"). The first story, told by the school itself, describes the school's benevolent motivation, meritocratic selection criteria, and procedural fairness. To this story, Delgado counterposes the stories of other actors in the drama, especially the story of the applicant himself. The applicant experiences not benevolence but a wicked combination of hostility and inattention, not procedural fairness but a stacked deck. The judge, asked to pass on the applicant's antidiscrimination claim, produces yet a third story, one devoid of the emotions felt by any of the actors in the process. Minority students who have no real voice in the hiring process generate still another story, this one of anger and cynicism.

"Many realities" stories raise questions about objectivity and neutrality that differ somewhat from those raised by "what really happened" stories.

"Many realities" stories question not whether any account is actually objective or true but rather whether there can be a single objective account. Perhaps all that exists are competing stories, each true for the particular actor, but none representing the whole truth. Perhaps there is no perspective that is impartial, and all we can ever have is a multitude of partial accounts. The point of these "many realities" stories, then, is to demonstrate that the story legal doctrine tells is but one among many that could be told. The choice of stories could be remade. Reformed law, in this view, will not reflect reality better. Nor will it become less partial; "many realities" stories reveal the futility and impossibility of impartiality as an idea. Rather, law reformed in reaction to "many realities" stories will, at best, be conscious of itself as someone's particular story and sensitive to its suppression of other possible accounts.

Before I further explore storytelling's challenge to law's purported objectivity and neutrality, I want to spend a moment on the interdisciplinary aspects of the interest in storytelling. In general, the law school curriculum is, putting it mildly, light on subjects that are not "law," and so those arguing that stories have the potential to change established ways of thinking needed to borrow from other fields. They relied, in general, on cognitive and literary theories that assert that we tend to understand our world in terms of stories.

But the borrowing was hardly systematic or, if you'll pardon the pun, disciplined. Theories of narrative and cognition were treated as a kind of grab bag out of which supporting ideas and citations could be drawn. Not much attention was paid to theories that were not immediately perceived as being helpful. Nor was much care put into using terms from literary theory; words like story, narrative, rhetoric, account, ideology, and myth were often used as if they meant the same thing. Here is an example, from a different article by Richard Delgado:

> It is now almost a commonplace that we construct the social world. We do this through stories, narratives, myths, and symbols—by using tools that create images, categories, and pictures. Over time, through repetition, the dominant stories seem to become true and natural, and are accepted as "the way things are." Recently, outsider jurisprudence has been developing means, principally "counterstorytelling," to displace or overturn these comfortable majoritarian myths and narratives. A well-told counterstory can jar or displace the dominant account. ("Shadowboxing" 818)

When words get thrown around, concepts can easily get confused. Is law *itself* a story? Is law *a way* of telling stories? Or are stories one thing and law another, so that stories can serve as a *corrective* for the distinguishable entity "the law"? Not much effort has been spent sorting out these very different claims.[7]

A similar confusion or looseness has characterized legal scholars' use of epistemological theory. Many storytellers would claim to be "postmodernists" in some respect or other, but—as I hope my earlier description made clear—the epistemological premises of "what really happened" stories and "many realities" stories differ. "What really happened" stories present themselves as factual, true in the sense of being empirically verifiable (at least, if you had been there at the time to witness the events in question). They aim to demonstrate the real fact of the matter, and in assuming that there can be such a thing, they reflect what might be called a foundationalist perspective. "Many realities" stories, in contrast, aim to highlight the absence of any neutral position from which we could ever discover the fact of the matter. In raising questions about whether objectivity is possible, these stories reflect what might be called an antifoundationalist perspective. But the claim "law is just a story" is perfectly ambiguous as between these two perspectives. It could mean that law fails to take account of important experiences and facts and has therefore gotten things wrong. Or the claim that law is just a story could mean that in law, as elsewhere in life, there is no unmediated way to know the truth, i.e., to get things right, so that law can never do more than reflect some particular points of view and, necessarily, suppress others. As with legal borrowing from narrative theory, very little effort has been made to clarify these potentially conflicting claims.

The lack of rigor in the use of nonlegal theory has been unfortunate. Ransacking other academic disciplines without taking those disciplines seriously seems to illustrate just the sort of arrogance that has traditionally justified lawyer-bashing in the public mind. But even more, the sloppiness of some of the borrowing has provided ammunition to legal academics hostile to the storytelling movement, who have relied on the ambiguity of some of the storytellers' claims to mount vicious critiques both of storytelling as scholarship and of individual storytellers.[8]

The viciousness and energy of these attacks do not arise, in my view, from the desire of traditional legal scholars to protect narrative or epistemological theory from the depredations of the undisciplined. Rather, it arises from resistance to the message, if you will, of the storytelling movement. The notion that we cannot go on thinking about law in the same old ways is not easy to swallow.

And I think this really *is* the message. For both antifoundationalist and foundationalist stories do challenge the viability of the rule of law ideal. Let us begin with stories written from a foundationalist perspective. These stories, in effect, offer experiences for what has been called their "informational value" (Eskridge 614). Presumably, the data thus provided could be used to correct errors in existing law. So, for example, if stories like Williams's tell of harms that the antidiscrimination laws as presently drafted do not reach, the law can be amended to reach the newly discovered harms.

But let's examine who tells these stories. We will see that it is primarily women, people of color, and poverty lawyers who represent clients with little political power (Baron 266). When we see that it is traditionally disempowered groups who have hit upon the storytelling strategy, and when we see also that their stories are so structurally similar, pointing to systemic blindness to certain kinds of harms—these facts suggest that existing defects are not accidents or mistakes awaiting correction. That is, it is not that the system fails to be impartial in a few isolated instances, but rather that the system is positively tilted in a way not likely to be reformed any time soon. And this tilt contradicts the premise of neutrality.

Now let's take the stories written from the perspective of antifoundationalism. These stories are meant to challenge the idea that if we just look carefully and hard enough, we can discover the important facts about a dispute. The stories reveal that if we look at events from different perspectives—perhaps asking a wider universe of people what they saw, or examining incidents that occurred earlier in time—we will encounter not a single account of the events, but multiple plausible accounts. If this is true, then law cannot be objective in the traditional sense of that word. Rather, seen from this perspective, law inevitably participates in a process of suppression and silencing by selecting among conflicting accounts.

In light of the overall message, it would actually have been surprising if there *hadn't* been negative or disparaging reactions, at least from some quarters. That there hasn't been even more criticism of the storytelling movement stems, in my view, from at least three factors. First, this movement originated largely within the legal academy; indeed, even the poverty lawyers writing about storytelling tend to be clinicians at law schools. The gulf between legal academicians and practicing lawyers is, to be quite honest, huge.

Second, to the extent that practitioners notice what law professors write, their reaction has been something along the lines of, "This is *new*?" Practitioners specializing in litigation have long understood that presenting an effective case requires telling a persuasive, credible story that explains the evidence in a way favorable to their clients (Ohlbaum). They tend to read the storytelling scholarship as an endorsement of what they are already doing. "Stories?," they ask. "You want stories? Come see me try a case!" They tend to ignore the larger critiques.

Finally, the legal storytelling movement has not encountered even more resistance because it resonates with a vein of deep dissatisfaction that many practitioners feel when they engage in conventional law practice. I am not going to attempt here any sort of full analysis of the causes of discontent among lawyers. But I can describe the way in which conventional legal analysis can rob cases of their interest and life and the way storytelling may serve as an antidote.

I want to return, for my example, to the modern-day Solomon dispute: the case of Baby Jessica. Baby Jessica was known legally as "Baby Girl Clausen" or, even more colorfully, as BGC, but I will nonetheless call her by her name. Jessica was born to Cara Clausen in Iowa on February 8, 1991. Cara signed a release terminating her parental rights to the child less than 48 hours later, on February 10. Two weeks later, on February 25, 1991, a Michigan couple, Roberta and Jan DeBoer filed a petition to adopt Jessica. While that petition was pending, the DeBoers were awarded temporary custody of Jessica, and the baby lived with them until the United States Supreme Court declined their final appeals in July of 1993. Throughout this entire period, Daniel Schmidt—who was conclusively proven to be Jessica's biological father—and the DeBoers, who had exclusive custody, clawed at each other through the courts, each side seeking to be adjudicated the child's legal parents. The case garnered national media attention, including over 15 articles in *The New York Times* alone. Most people who followed the case, including several of the judges who heard various stages of it, saw the dispute as raising serious issues about the relative strength of biology as opposed to other qualities in making a family and in serving the best interests of a child.

But this was decidedly NOT the legal issue in the case. The legal questions, of which there were two, were both entirely statutory. The first involved the Iowa adoption statute, which provides quite simply that an adoption petition cannot be filed "until a termination of parental rights has been accomplished." Since Daniel had not been named on any legal papers as the father, and had not signed any papers releasing his parental rights, it did not seem that his rights had been terminated. The DeBoers nonetheless argued that it would be in the baby's best interest to bypass the statutory termination requirements and grant their adoption petition. The Iowa Supreme Court's response was simple, and typical. The court found that the statute did not permit consideration of the child's best interest, but that it did require proper termination of parental rights before adoption. In this case, proper termination had simply not occurred (*In re* B.G.C., 496 N.W.2d 239, 245 [Iowa 1992]). End of adoption, end of story.

The second legal issue arose when the DeBoers refused to comply with the Iowa court's order and instead filed a separate lawsuit in Michigan seeking to retain custody of Jessica. This gambit succeeded initially, producing a lower court judgment that Jessica's best interests required her remaining with the DeBoers. But that judgment was quickly appealed, on the legal ground that the Michigan courts lacked jurisdiction to intervene in the dispute. I will spare you a summary of the Michigan Supreme Court's intricate analysis of such statutes as the Uniform Child Custody Jurisdiction Act and the Parental

Kidnapping Prevention Act. I'll just give you the exciting conclusion: "Iowa continues to have jurisdiction, it has not declined to exercise that jurisdiction, its jurisdiction is, therefore, exclusive, and Iowa's exclusive continuing jurisdiction precludes the courts of this state from exercising jurisdiction to modify the Iowa order" (*DeBoer v. Schmidt*, 442 Mich. 648, 673, 502 N.W.2d 649, 659 [1993]). Thrilling stuff, eh?

The desiccation and dehumanization of the court's treatment of the issues is, I am sorry to say, not at all unusual. But the limitation of the issues is all the more remarkable if we consider some additional facts of the case—facts of which the courts were aware and which appear in the opinions.[9] From the DeBoers' side, lots of information suggested that Jessica's biological parents were not to be trusted. To begin with, Cara lied on all the legal papers she signed in the period immediately following Jessica's birth, naming another man as the father and procuring his signature on a parental release form. As for Daniel, he already had two other children, but he had largely failed to support and almost never seen either of them. It was hard to see why two individuals who previously showed such scant interest in being parents should now be so eager to gain custody of this child.

But from the Schmidts' side—Daniel and Cara did ultimately marry—the DeBoers were not the innocent victims the media were busy presenting. The DeBoers made much of the fact that they had had exclusive custody of Jessica almost from birth, and they traded on the disruption a change would cause after Jessica's prolonged stay in their home. But they knew within a month of beginning adoption proceedings that their claim to Jessica would be contested. Indeed, Cara sought to revoke her release of custody just one week after the DeBoers filed their adoption petition. A week after that, Daniel filed an affidavit of paternity alleging that he, and not the man named on Cara's release-of-custody form, was Jessica's biological father. And two weeks later, just one month after the DeBoers took Jessica home, Daniel filed formal objections to the adoption. It was the DeBoers elaborate legal maneuvering that prolonged Jessica's stay in their home. Since the DeBoers created the delay, it seemed hardly seemed fair for them to rely on the attachment Jessica then formed with them as a reason for denying a change in custody.

There is still a third story here—a story of judicial delay. This story was implicit in the Baby Jessica case and became explicit in the case of Baby Richard—a 1993 Illinois case with almost identical facts. In Baby Richard, the court identified yet a third possible wrongdoer—the legal system itself. "Richard's story," the court wrote—and these words apply directly to Baby Jessica as well—

> is the account of a helpless child caught in the quagmire of a judicial system that in attempting to resolve his problem became part of his problem. It has taken two years and five months for this case to slug-

gishly move through our judicial system. In a case of this nature, where plainly time is critical, it is a sad commentary on our judiciary.[10]

But the judges carefully noted that they did not alone create the problem: "The attorneys are not blameless for the delay. No attorney in this case has ever filed a motion to advise the court of the exigent nature of the case. . . . As a result, this case just 'hung around' on the court's case calendar" (254 Ill. App. 3d at 417 n.5, 627 N.E. 2d at 655 n. 5). The story here is of a system in disrepair, too cumbersome and slow in its operations to produce just results.

Now you can see why people might become unenthusiastic about a professional life in which stories of greedy parents, manipulative adopters, and systemic failure are all considered irrelevant to the actual legal issue in the case, which turns out to be the interpretation of fairly dry and uninteresting statutes. The fledgling lawyer's thrill at winning "on a technicality" can quickly turn to boredom when even the most controversial of cases boils down to the definition of a word such as "termination." Nor is it sufficient to note that the result—the return of Baby Jessica to her biological parents, one of whom never consented to her release, and the other of whom consented in a petition she hastily retracted—might be consistent with the conclusion that might have been reached had the "stories" been given a central role. Central to the competing stories are competing visions of parenting and the basis of family, not to mention the role of fault or blame in custody determinations. These visions and the complicated moral questions that accompany them are elided when courts frame the legal issue in the narrow, technical manner adopted by the various jurisdictions that heard the Baby Jessica case.

So why are the stories so often sucked out of the law so that we need a new storytelling movement to bring them back? What could be worse than the tedium produced by defining the legal issues in a way that makes the fewest possible facts relevant?

The answer, in my view: responsibility. What do I mean? Let's examine the reaction of the Iowa district court, the very first tribunal to confront the Baby Jessica case and the only one to hear live testimony from the parties. Here is what that court said:

> Th[is] court had an opportunity to observe [the DeBoers] at the time of hearing and the court is under no illusion that this tragic case is other than an unbelievably traumatic event. While cognizant of the heartache which this decision will ultimately cause, this court is presented with no other option than that dictated by the law in this state. Purely equitable principles cannot be substituted for well-established principles of law. (Quoted in *In re* B.G.C., 496 N.W.2d at 246)

Notice how law is here presented as a refuge from the trauma, tragedy, and heartache of the case. The judge will not inflict the pain that the parties will suffer; nor can he by resort to "purely equitable principles" avert the heartbreak. The judge is as helpless as the parties themselves before the power of the law.[11]

It is, I think, no accident that this language was quoted by each court that subsequently heard the case. No legal actor wished to take responsibility for Baby Jessica. And in some ways no one did—by the end the issue was narrowed to a point of jurisdiction that hardly seemed to involve human beings at all. The courts may have attained the highest ideals of the rule of law, but paradoxically in avoiding brute strength, bias, and idiosyncrasy, they avoided responsibility as well.

This evasion contrasts rather unfavorably with Solomon. But then again, he had help. The story of the two mothers follows another story, one that tends not to be told nearly as often. In that story, Solomon, who has just become king, has a dream in which the Lord appears before him and asks "what shall I give thee?" Noting how young and inexperienced he is compared to his father King David, Solomon asks for "an understanding heart to judge thy people, that I may discern between good and bad: for who is able to judge this thy so great a people?" This request pleases God, who had anticipated being asked for long life, riches, and the death of Solomon's enemies. And so God gives Solomon a wise and understanding heart. It is after Solomon awakens from this dream that the two women approach him. No wonder he confidently exercised his own judgment, without seeking a rule to protect him.

Those of us in the legal profession who must go it alone, without assurance that we will be able to be wise, will probably continue to try and evade responsibility for the troubles we cause or cannot cure. We will continue to seek shelter in the notion that the law, and not some fallible human, magically resolves emotionally complex problems. But when this fiction breaks down, as it so often does, so that we lawyers cannot pretend that we do not affect the outcome of our cases, few of us turn for guidance to the blindfolded, scale-bearing goddess of Justice. We are more apt to turn, I think, to stories—including the Solomon story itself. For while not every story is persuasive, moving, or effective, stories can recall us to what is at stake in legal decision-making, remind us of the human consequences of legal judgments, and teach us that we cannot escape from judging and responsibility. And only by accepting responsibility can law retain its legitimacy.

NOTES

[1] This paper is drawn from a lecture, originally entitled "What Makes Arguments Legal? Fact, Fiction, or the 'Real Story,'" delivered at Haverford College on September 17, 1996. I thank Professor Julia Epstein, of Haverford's Comparative Literature Department, for inviting me to give the lecture, and I thank

Professor Barry McCarthy, of Temple University School of Law, for editorial assistance in turning the remarks into this paper.

[2] For more detailed statements and critiques of the concept of the rule of law, see Michelman, Resnick, and Singer.

[3] For reasons explained in the text, there were multiple judicial opinions in the Baby Jessica case. The most relevant are *In re* B.G.C., 496 N.W.2d 239 (Iowa 1992); *DeBoer v. Schmidt*, 199 Mich.App. 10, 501 N.W.2d 193 (1993), *aff'd in part* 442 Mich. 648, 502 N.W.2d 649 (1993). The Supreme Court of the United States declined to stay the orders entered in the courts below. *DeBoer v. DeBoer*, 509 U.S. 1301 (1993).

[4] For a detailed treatment of the problem of constraint, see Balkin.

[5] Many of the examples which follow are drawn from Mahoney.

[6] The ideas in this and the following two paragraphs are developed at greater length in Baron "Resistance."

[7] The ideas in this and the next paragraph are developed at greater length in Baron and Epstein.

[8] See Coughlin, Farber and Sherry, and Tushnet.

[9] The "stories" that follow in the text were included in the opinions in the sense that the courts recited these facts in their statement of the case. But the courts' framing of the legal issues made these stories immaterial, as they had no bearing on the jurisdictional and statutory issues central to the courts' analysis. So the stories appeared, but were rendered marginal.

[10] *In re* John Doe, 254 Ill. App.3d 405, 417, 627 N.E.2d 648, 655 (1993). This case moved up and down the Illinois courts for several years. The final opinion is *In re* Kirchner, 164 Ill.2d 468, 649 N.E.2d 324 (1995).

[11] Surely, someone would experience heartbreak no matter how the case was decided. The question is whether the decision to impose that heartbreak on the DeBoers or the Schmidts presented as a choice that *the judge* makes or whether it is presented, instead, as the inevitable result of impersonal and implacable forces.

WORKS CITED

Balkin, J. M. "Ideology As Constraint." *Stanford Law Review* 43 (1991): 1133-169.

Baron, Jane B. "Resistance to Stories." *Southern California Law Review* 67 (1994): 255-85.

Baron, Jane B., and Julia Epstein. "Is Law Narrative?" 45.1 *Buffalo Law Review* (1997): 141-87.

Coughlin, Anne M. "Regulating the Self: Autobiographical Performances in Outsider Scholarship." *Virginia Law Review* 81 (1995): 1229.

Delgado, Richard. "Shadowboxing: An Essay on Power." *Cornell Law Review* 77 (1992): 813-24.
———. "Storytelling for Oppositionists and Others: A Plea for Narrative." 87 *Michigan Law Review* 87 (1989): 2411-441.
Eskridge, William. "Gaylegal Narratives." *Stanford Law Review* 46 (1994): 607-46.
Estrich, Susan. "Rape." 95 *Yale Law Journal* 95 (1986): 1087-184.
Farber, Daniel A., and Suzanna Sherry. "Telling Stories Out of School: An Essay on Legal Narratives." *Stanford Law Review* 45 (1993): 807-55.
Mahoney, Martha R. "Legal Images of Battered Women: Redefining the Issue of Separation." *Michigan Law Review* 90 (1991): 1-94.
Michelman, Frank I. "Justification (And Justifiability) of Law in a Contradictory World." 28 *Nomos* (1986): 71-99.
Ohlbaum, Edward D. "Basic Instinct: Case Theory and Courtroom Performance." *Temple Law Review* 66 (1993): 1-122.
Resnick, Judith. "On the Bias: Feminist Reconsiderations of the Aspirations for Our Judges." *Southern California Law Review.* 61 (1988): 1877-944.
Singer, Joseph William. "The Player and the Cards: Nihilism and Legal Theory." *Yale Law Journal* 94 (1984): 1-70.
Tushnet, Mark. "The Degradation of Constitutional Discourse." *Georgetown Law Journal* 81 (1992): 251-311.
Unger, Roberto. *Knowledge and Politics.* New York: Free P, 1975.
Williams, Patricia J. *The Alchemy of Race and Rights.* Cambridge: Harvard UP, 1991.

CHAPTER TWO

Stories and Verdicts:
Bernard Goetz and New York in Crisis
by Michael Brooks

Few real-life crime stories present a more coherent narrative than the shooting by Bernhard Goetz of four black teenagers on a New York City subway train. It has almost all that a good novel requires: a compelling setting, sharp contrasts of character, and a sudden moment of crisis. Trials often present good material for fiction, but they usually require the shaping hand of a novelist. The Goetz case seemed to be a coherent narrative from the beginning.

This, however, was not an accident. The Goetz story was created not by one storyteller but by several. It was born amid the tensions and anxieties of the urban crisis. It took shape as folk narratives do—first in private fantasies, next in anecdotes told around the water cooler, and then in short paragraphs that began to appear in the newspapers. The emerging story was developed into a popular novel and then into a highly successful film. When the actual Bernhard Goetz arrived on the scene, he stepped into a story that had already been told.

The victorious lawyers at his criminal and civil trials recognized this. Barry Slotnick drew on the popular narrative to create sympathy for his client as a decent citizen who had been pushed too far. He won an acquittal. Ron Kuby, at the civil trial, used repugnance toward the *Death Wish* shooter to present Goetz as a virulent racist. In part, the difference between the two verdicts resulted from purely legal matters—the different standards of proof required in criminal and civil trials, for example. But it also resulted from the different ways in which the Goetz story was told and the quite different audiences that heard it.

The facts of the case are comparatively simple. A few days before Christmas in 1984, Bernhard Goetz boarded a southbound Seventh Avenue express near his home at 14th Street. There were four teenage boys in the car—Barry Allen, Troy Canty, James Ramseur, and Darrell Cabey. They were sprawling across the seats and generally behaving in a rowdy manner. Goetz may not have noticed it as he entered, but the other passengers had moved to the far end of the car. One of the boys, lying stretched out on the bench opposite, asked casually "How are ya?" Then either one or two of the boys approached Goetz and asked for five dollars. Goetz, interpreting this behavior as the prelude to a mugging, took a gun from his pocket and fired five bullets. He may have fired all five in rapid succession, or he may have paused after the fourth and said "You seem to be all right; here's another." He then went to the platform between the subway cars, unfastened the safety chain, and escaped into the tunnel. On December 31, he surrendered to the police in Concord, New Hampshire.

The events immediately monopolized newspaper headlines and talk shows. Telephone switchboards of newspapers and television stations were lit up by calls of support. There was even a song, "Subway Vigilante" recorded by Ronny and the Urban Watchdogs.

Bernhard Goetz has not faded from public memory. George P. Fletcher, author of *A Crime of Self Defense; Bernhard Goetz and the Law on Trial*, comments that when people noticed what he was writing about they invariably wanted to discuss the case. I have had the same experience. Passions remain both intense and bitterly divided. Some Goetz admirers were potential vigilantes—I could almost see their trigger fingers moving as they talked. Some of his detractors were passionately hostile. I am not likely to forget the mild and friendly bookstore clerk who burst out with passionate delight when I mentioned that Goetz was suffering from testicular cancer.

The Goetz case fascinated so many New Yorkers because it expressed their deep-seated emotions. The trial in Judge Stephen Crane's courtroom dealt with very specific questions: Did Goetz reasonably interpret the youths' approach as a threat? Did he pause after the fourth shot and fire the fifth with cold-blooded intent? Was Darrell Cabey standing and menacing Goetz when he was shot or was he cowering in his seat? But these questions were tangential to the public drama. The story that monopolized newspaper headlines and talk shows in the days after the shooting, by contrast, was a symbolic drama, one that utilized the events in the subway to crystallize the feelings of New Yorkers about their city.

I. BERNHARD GOETZ AND THE URBAN CRISIS

To understand this drama, we need follow a path which leads from the social reality of New York City into the realm of private fantasy and then outward again into the public expressions of novel, film, and journalism. In the nineteen-sixties, New Yorkers began to fear that their city was in decline. Goetz's New York differed dramatically from the optimistic metropolis of earlier decades. It was a city in which the crime-victim narrative could become a recognized category of urban folklore. Eleanor Wachs's study of these stories does not list "revenge" in its index, and it does not figure as a motive in any of her tales.[1] Nevertheless, newspapers, films, and novels show fantasies of revenge gaining power during the sixties and seventies. The Goetz story was waiting to erupt.

From the sixties on, we see a growing literature which insists that despite the vast amounts of money being made there, New York was in decline. The city's traditional rhetoric of booming optimism was increasingly replaced by a language of impotence: the city was "not livable," it was a "hassle," it was "not working," its only hope was in "planned shrinkage." In 1965 the *Herald Tribune* ran a five-month series of articles under the standing head "City In Crisis." The same year Richard Whalen published his angry polemic *A City Destroying Itself*. In 1971 Miles Donis published *The Fall of New York*, a futuristic novel set in the late nineteen-seventies which portrayed a world where gangs of thirteen-year-olds roamed the streets shooting adults for sport. Jules Feiffer's play (1967) and film (1971) *Little Murders* showed the city as a place where the besieged middle-class could save itself from the violence in the streets only by gleefully joining the punks and murderers.

Anxieties about the city tended to focus on the subway. New Yorkers have long used their transit system as a synechdoche—the essential part which stands for the urban whole.

It is not surprising that a fear of random violence in the city as a whole should have focused on subway crime in particular. What is surprising is that the association of the subways with violence is so recent. During the first fifty years of the subway's existence, New Yorkers complained about its crowding, its heat, and its schedules. It was only in the late nineteen-fifties that they began to suspect that it might be dangerous.

This fear accompanied the rising proportion of teenagers in the population. In several well-publicized incidents, gangs of high school students rioted on the cars, breaking windows, pulling up seat cushions, bending fan blades, and terrifying passengers.

Newspapers fanned public alarm. HIGH SCHOOL GANGS ARE TURNING TRAINS INTO HELL ON WHEELS read a 1958 headline in the *Daily News* (Hanson 48). Other aspects of subway crime began to command attention. In 1963 the *Journal-American* sent reporter Joan Hanauer into the trains to experience the danger to women. She reported back under such headlines as TERROR LURKS IN THE DARK, LONELY HOURS (Hanauer 13). In 1964 the *World-Telegram and Sun* told readers that TERROR RIDES ALONG WITH

YOU WHEN YOU TRAVEL AT NIGHT (Kessler and Savelson 1). The next year the *Post* ran a series on TERROR IN THE SUBWAYS (Katz and Cashman).

It was only in 1965 that New Yorkers were transfixed by the story of an actual murder on the subway. Seventeen-year-old Andrew Mormile boarded an IND train in Brooklyn. Two other teenagers, apparently drunk, came on board the train in East New York. They began harassing two girls and generally behaving in a way that indicated danger. Some passengers moved to the next car, others buried themselves in their newspapers. When Mormile tried to walk to the next car, one of the boys shoved him. He shoved back. The boy drew a knife. Two of the stabs were strong enough to fracture his skull and a third went four inches into it.

Since crime had not been a major threat in the system, no one had designed an effective means of calling for help. The year of the Mormile killing, the Transit Authority experimented with a pathetic system in which a tollbooth attendant, aware of a crime in progress, would press a pedal with his or her foot, thus setting an amber light blinking on the street level which, it was hoped, would be noticed by a passing pedestrian "who, it is expected, will then call the police" (Grutzner 23:8). Lacking even this Rube Goldberg device, the motorman of the train on which Mormile lay dying had to blow loud whistle blasts at each station he passed in an effort to summon aid.

Crime continued to increase. The Mormile stabbing had been the first subway murder in over a year. In 1981 there were fourteen murders in the system. Crime stories appeared almost daily in the newspapers while anecdotes of small indignities became a normal feature of New York conversation.

The Transit Authority insisted, with absolute accuracy, that crime was growing more slowly in the subways than it was in the streets above. "The perception of crime is much greater than actual crime," said a TA spokesperson in 1978. "Of 3,000 rapes in the city, on the subway system there are eight. Of 1,500 homicides, there are six in our system" (Lichtenstein B12:3).

That, however, was no comfort to anyone. The subway stands for the city. To most New Yorkers, a murder at the corner of Westchester Avenue and Castle Hill Avenue happens in a far distant place, but one on the Pelham Bay line is next door. Even articles minimizing subway crime do not avoid the mythology of danger. In 1985 and 1987 the *New York Times* published two reports under the headlines "Statistically, At Least, It Is Rather Safe Down There" (Rangel E7:1) and "The Numbers Say Subways Are Safer Than They Seem" (Levine E6:4). Each article was accompanied by a photo—a policeman peering nervously out of a graffiti-marked car, a dark subway entrance yawning like an open grave—which dramatically undercut the content of the text.

The new equation of a violent city with a menacing subway found expression in Larry Peerce's 1967 film *The Incident*. Adapted from a 1963 DuPont Hour television show titled "Ride With Terror," it featured an impressive number of the city's best actors and actresses—Martin Sheen, Tony Musante, Jack Gilford, Thelma Ritter, Ed McMahon, Donna Mills, Brock Peters, Ruby Dee, Robert Bannard, Diana Van Der Viis, Jan Sterling, and Beau Bridges, among others. Nicholas Baehr's script shows a selection of middle-class New Yorkers terrorized by two giggling, knife-wielding punks on a late-night train.

Worried by the possibility that the film would provoke copycat incidents, the Transit Authority refused permission to film *The Incident* in actual stations. Instead, the crew worked with a very convincing replica of an IRT train in the old Biograph studios and used stock footage. Gerald Hirschfeld's camera work fills the screen with menacing shots of the Lexington Avenue-Woodlawn train roaring above garbage-strewn streets and through narrow tunnels.

The punks in *The Incident*, like most of those involved in early subway rampages, were white. But increasingly, as New York's demographics changed, middle-class subway riders were confronted with black teenagers whose swagger seemed to violate the decorum of a public place. As the novelist Wesley Brown put it, "a display of bravado by a young, indigo-skinned black male, moving through a crowded subway car like a point guard bringing the ball up the court, sporting a haircut that makes the shape of his head resemble a cone of ice-cream, and wearing barge-size sneakers with untied laces thick as egg noodles, is immediately considered a dangerous presence whether he is or not" (Brown 482).

The trains in *The Incident* are also not marked by graffiti. That did not appear until the early seventies. When it did, it added a powerful new element to many New Yorkers' feelings of anger and frustration. It was almost inevitable that middle-class New Yorkers would interpret the outburst of graffiti in terms of a power struggle between them and us. "Them" was a young male, probably Puerto Rican or Black. "Us" was the average, productive, law-abiding citizen, the person who ought to be served and protected by the city authorities.

But the spread of graffiti showed how little protection law-abiding citizens could expect. Riders quickly linked the tags and air-sprayed patterns on the train walls to the damaged doors, the delayed arrivals, and all the other signs of breakdown that they encountered daily. Mayors Lindsay and Koch called for attack dogs to protect the train yards and long jail terms for offenders, but their rhetoric swelled in exact proportion to their helplessness. Graffiti became a symbol of the city's inability to solve even the most visible of its problems.

The emotional response to the Goetz shooting grew out of a double experience of hope and anguish. New Yorkers looked for a dramatic improvement in their city and instead saw spreading poverty, rising crime, and growing racial tension. For millions of New Yorkers, these fears were dramatized each day in the subway. And it was all too clear that things would get worse. Five months before Bernhard Goetz boarded that southbound IRT, the *New York Times* published a survey of the prospects for the subway system under the headlines "GREATER WOES LIE AHEAD FOR CITY'S TRANSIT RIDERS" (July 30), INEFFICIENT WAYS OF THE PAST STILL HAMPER TRANSIT SYSTEM (July 31), and TRANSIT SYSTEM IS FACING A TROUBLED FUTURE (August 1). The subway, which had once been a cause of the city's growth, had now become its pre-eminent symbol of urban collapse.

II. STRIKING BACK

Feelings of helplessness bred fantasies of resistance. Let me make a digression that I hope is relevant. In 1983 I was mugged, not in the subway but in a far more dangerous place—the entrance vestibule of a New York City apartment building. The door to the inner lobby was locked while I waited for someone to buzz me in. Three young men approached rapidly from behind. One caught me in a chokehold. When I regained consciousness, I had lost the usual items—a watch, a wallet, some money, various credit cards.

When I told people this story over the ensuing weeks, their response was invariable: "You should have had a gun." It was clear from my telling that I was approached from behind, taken by surprise, and that my gun would have fallen into very bad hands. It didn't matter. "You should have had a gun." The implication was not simply that I was entitled to protect myself but that I was entitled to inflict justice.

During the eighties, this fantasy of striking back became widespread among New Yorkers. One of its oddest and most striking forms was found not in the movies but on the subways themselves.

In February 1979, a young man named Curtis Sliwa, night manager of the McDonald's on East Fordham Road in the Bronx, organized a group of friends into an informal and completely unauthorized anticrime patrol. First calling themselves "The Magnificent Thirteen Subway Safety Patrol," they soon became the Guardian Angels.

Sliwa had a genius for publicity. Guardian Angel patrols were in fact few and infrequent, but many a subway rider felt a thrill when a well-muscled young man, wearing a white tee-shirt and sporting a red beret, stepped into a subway car and took up his position near the door. Newspapers and television stations carried frequent reports on Guardian Angel patrols. The fact that the police so obviously resented the Angels' presence only added to their glamour. A careful study reported in Dennis Jay Kenney's *Crime, Fear, and the New York City Subways* (1987) failed to substantiate any Guardian Angel impact on actual crime rates, but the organization had a major presence in the consciousness of ordinary New Yorkers.

In November 1992, Sliwa, by this time a radio talk-show host, admitted that several of the group's earliest exploits had been faked. Soon other Angels joined in with more stories of manufactured bravery. In the early 1980s, public appetite for resistance to crime had been so great that Sliwa could depend on a credulous press.

In this environment, Bernhard Goetz-like incidents began to occur. In October 1971, a fifty-eight-year-old real estate salesman, faced with two young men attempting to rob him in the Astor Square station, drew a licensed .38 caliber revolver and shot them. The *Times* called this unexpected turn of events "implausible" and "improbable" ("Urban Jungle" 30:2). On October 31, 1979, a passenger shot an assailant dead on the Lexington Avenue IRT and disappeared into the crowd. In February 1984, seventy-one-year-old Lop B. Lee drew a licensed revolver in the East Broadway station and shot seventeen-year-old Darrius Cox. These incidents received little press attention, though the 1979 Lexington IRT shooting inspired Jerry Oster's detective novel *Sweet Justice* (1985), begun before the Goetz shooting though published after, in which the police search for a man acclaimed in the tabloids as the "Subway Samaritan."

The fantasy of striking back received vivid expression in Bradley J. Steiner's self-defense manual *Subway Survival!* (1980). Its author selects the best moves from British and Canadian Commando Systems, Kenpo-Ju-Jitsu, Karate, Combat Judo, Box, and Street-Fighting in order to show the ordinary transit rider how he or she can use chin-jab attacks, hand-axe chops, knee attacks, elbow blows, concussion blows, front kicks, side kicks, and back-stamp kicks against the punks, the scum, the low-lifes, the savages, and the street rats who terrorize the subways "thanks to liberal, scum-sympathizing laws, gun control, and a corrupt juridical and police establishment" (Steiner 5).

Tom Wolfe, setting out to portray the quirks and tensions of New York life in *The Bonfire of the Vanities*, very nearly gave this revenge fantasy the mocking it deserves. As he explains in his essay "Stalking the Billion-footed Beast," he began his novel with the knowledge that any big book on New York City required a subway scene. An assiduous researcher, he began riding the subways looking for material and quickly struck gold. He found a distinguished looking broker commuting through the South Bronx to Manhattan in a dirty raincoat and moldy orthotic running shoes. He had been mugged once and feared being mugged again. Once safely arrived at his Wall Street office, he would exchange his shabby coat and shoes for properly distinguished equivalents. Then, when the day was finished, he would revert to protective shabbiness for the journey home.

Wolfe wrote the first version of his novel in monthly installments for *Rolling Stone*. In the July 19–August 2, 1984, issue, a Puerto Rican woman named Julia Noganz looks across the aisle on the D train and is astonished at the man sitting opposite. He appears to be in disguise with a greasy poplin rain hat pulled down over his eyes and the *New York Post* held nervously in front of his face. What Julia Noganz especially notices is that he has a pair of long, thin, charcoal-gray socks rising above his cheap, purple and white stripped running sneakers. His incongruous clothes and his nervous glances about the train make him appear deranged. Julia Noganz easily decides that he is just another nut on the subway.

Then the train stops and three teenage boys get on. Julia knows their type. She knows them from their striped sneakers and their black thermo jackets. They are "the animals."

She sees that the man opposite has seen them as well and is clearly frightened. He pulls the newspaper around his face and shoulders, trying so conspicuously to disappear that he becomes an advertisement for disaster: "Either the animals will go to work on him or he'll just snap. Julia gets up and walks down to the other end of the car" (Wolfe).

This is Wolfe's first, magazine version of Assistant District Attorney Lawrence Kramer, a man so terrorized by an earlier brutal mugging that he rides the subway in fear, carrying his dress shoes in an A&P shopping bag and wearing Nike sneakers as a disguise. The synopses in several succeeding issues of *Rolling Stone* mention Kramer's mugging. It was clearly preparation for a major plot development.

The parallels between this scene from the early, serialized version of *The Bonfire of the Vanities* and the Goetz case that broke four months later are astonishingly close: the white man traumatized by an earlier mugging, the teenagers, the passenger who avoids trouble by moving to the other end of the car. New York life was proving more sensational than anything a novelist could imagine, and Wolfe at once saw that his fearful Assistant D.A. with dreams of striking back would cut a pale figure next to the real Bernhard Goetz who was appearing in the daily headlines. In the book version of *The Bonfire of the Vanities,* Kramer steps into the D train wearing a worn raincoat and Nike running shoes, with his own leather dress shoes concealed in an A&P shopping bag, but the subsequent flashback describing his mugging remained unwritten. This strand of the action was simply dropped.

A pity. Instead of a satire of the revenge fantasy, New Yorkers were treated to the real thing in its most blatant form. As soon as the news of the mysterious young man on the IRT reached them, the editors of the *New York Post* realized that they were confronting a story which was basically a repetition of one that had already seized the public imagination.

Death Wish was both a 1972 novel by Brian Garfield and a series of films starring Charles Bronson. The outlines of the plot were certainly familiar to all New Yorkers and had no doubt entered the fantasy lives of many. Four aspects of Garfield's novel are directly relevant to the *New York Post*'s coverage of the Goetz case:

1) The protagonist, Paul Benjamin, is a mild-mannered New York liberal who, driven mad by crimes against his wife and daughter, turns into a pitiless vigilante.

2) The subway is used to signify all that Benjamin hates in New York City.

3) Paul Benjamin arms himself, frequents high crime areas, and then turns murderously on the punks and muggers who try to harm him. In the course of his progress from New York liberal to self-appointed executioner of punks, Garfield's protagonist finds himself aboard a lurching Broadway express: "He found he was looking from face to face along the rows of crowded passengers, resentfully scanning them for signs of redeeming worth: if you wanted to do something about overpopulation this was the place to start. He made a head-count and discovered that of the fifty-eight faces he could see, seven appeared to belong to people who had a right to survive. The rest were fodder" (86).

4) Though he realizes his murderousness, Paul Benjamin does not repent. On the last page of the novel, he realizes that he has the barely concealed sympathy of the police. In the last scene of Michael Winner's extremely popular 1974 film version, Charles Bronson, with a mischievous glint in his eye, transfers operations from New York to Chicago—thus making possible a series of popular sequels.

III. GOETZ STORIES AND COUNTERSTORIES

Though all New York newspapers put the Goetz case in their headlines, it was the *New York Post* that established the dominant interpretation. The *Post*'s strategy was simple. It merely slapped the *Death Wish* scenario on top of the few known facts about the incident in the IRT. The still anonymous gunman, said its first front-page headline on December 24, 1984, was the "*Death Wish* Shooter" (1).

The *Post* had to work the *Death Wish* theme especially hard during the opening phase of the story because for the first week no one knew who the gunman was. Coverage on December 24 featured a photo of Charles Bronson firing his pistol directly at the reader, and a Transit Authority police officer was quoted as conceding reluctantly that "the corollary between this and *Death Wish* is there" (2).

The paper began identifying its Goetz stories with a small drawing showing a dark subway tunnel, a hand holding a pistol, and the words "*Death Wish* Vigilante." It published a psychological profile by Dr. Joyce Brothers, who explained that "ectomorphs are very sensitive people" and concluded that the unknown gunman was imitating the *Death Wish* films (December 27 1984, 2) On December 28, the paper interviewed Brian Garfield himself, who explained that sometimes people feel they have no choice: "They are back up against a wall and feel a need to lash out. I don't blame them" (2).

Once Goetz's identity was revealed on January 1, 1985, the *Post* (as well as every other paper and TV station in town) was relentless in tracking down the smallest detail of its hero's life. It revealed that Goetz had a security clearance from the federal government and that he had once written to the city Planning Commission about a zoning matter. It published a photo of a toy fire engine which it claimed to be the same kind of toy fire engine that Goetz had purchased at a Toys 'R' Us store in Union, New Jersey.

Trivial as they are, these details serve a vital purpose. They present Goetz as an average man but a firm one. They put us in his shoes and make it easier for us to act out our secret desires through daily retellings of his actions. When the *Post* finally tracked down Goetz in person, it reported:

> His voice was whisper-quiet and he seemed awed by the five people around him.
> Somehow he wished it would all go away.
> But the quiet-spoken Goetz was giving a signal: He had been bullied once too often. (January 10, 1985, 5)

Like Paul Benjamin in Brian Garfield's novel, the *Post*'s Goetz is driven to act by the madness of the city, not by any demons within. He is simply a man who fights back, a hero for decent citizens.

In the year and a half that followed, as Goetz faced two grand juries and a criminal trial, the *Post* continued to present him as the subway rider who fought back. On March 4, 1985, it even interviewed him aboard a Seventh Avenue southbound train, quoting his conversations with fellow riders. When a transit police officer asked him to leave the train ("I don't want a riot on my hands"), a black teenager quickly replied: "Come on, man, we dig the guy. Ain't nothing wrong with old Bernie. Nobody is gonna touch that guy. Wow." Two white women, on the other hand, were angered by the sight of him:

> They approached Goetz and one of them said: "We don't think you are a hero. We think you are a racist."
> Goetz looked at them and smiled: "Believe what you want. But I hope you never get raped. I hope you never get attacked. If you do, I hope you have a weapon to protect yourself."
> The other woman yelled back: "I have been raped."
> Goetz told her: "I'm sorry to hear that. Then I can't understand why you attack me. Most victims of violence know what I'm talking about."
> "I wish the whole thing didn't happen but I'm never going to be a victim again if I can help it. And I hope you won't ever be a victim again." (Dunleavy 5:5)

The *Post* implied that Goetz had inspired the entire New York region to a frenzy of effective self-defense. The front page headline on January 22, 1985, for example, read 75-YR-OLD ROUTS TEEN MUGGERS. Below was a photo of plucky Nunzio Motola next to the subway headline: "Subway Drama: 'I kicked like hell.'" Inside was another story about a Long Island delicatessen owner who killed a bandit with a licensed pistol. At the top of page four was a ribbon containing the words "We're fighting back . . . we're fighting back . . . we're fighting back!" ("Deli Owner" 5). A *Post* cartoon showed a subway stand selling Bernie Goetz face masks. None of the Goetz lookalikes are getting mugged.

Not surprisingly, a great many people were alarmed at this prospect of imitation vigilantes patrolling the city. Accordingly, they set out to construct counternarratives to the *Post* story.

The *Daily News*, the city's other tabloid, was much more critical of Goetz than the *Post*. Jimmy Breslin, its leading columnist, stressed Goetz's psychological quirks. He pointed out that, contrary to published reports, the four boys had not shown sharpened screwdrivers. He calculated that lifetime medical expenses for Darrell Cabey—half to be paid by the federal government, twenty-five per cent each by the state and city—could come to well over two million dollars: "The medical care for Darrell Cabey comes out of the paychecks of the people who said 'At last!' when they heard of his shooting" (6).

An angrier counternarrative was presented by Harlem's *Amsterdam News*, which insisted Goetz represented not all New Yorkers against crime but only white New Yorkers determined to strike back violently at teenage blacks. The editors suggested a thought experiment: "Paint Goetz Black or Puerto Rican. Name him Jones or Suarez. Give him the college degrees and a similar life style. Let him shoot four whites, two of them in the back, for any reason. See what happens to him. You can be sure that it will not be applause" ("Vigilante" 12).

The *Post*, which had many African-American readers, anticipated this interpretation and worked hard to counter it. The editors made sure that Goetz stories appeared in close proximity to those of African-Americans who had used similar violence to prevent crime.

On March 1985, for example, the IRT gunman shared the front pages with the IND candy man. This was Andy Frederick, a black ex-marine who attempted to prevent a theft from a subway candy vendor and stabbed the would-be thief to death in the ensuing struggle. On January 8, 1986, while the Goetz case was still before a Grand Jury, the paper highlighted James Grimes, a black token clerk who had shot a potential bandit with an unlicensed gun.

Another counternarrative was offered by the *New York Times* which was explicit in its distaste for the *Post*'s treatment. Columnist Sidney Schwanberg attacked it, and several op-ed articles worried about the public's apparent support for vigilante justice.

Many of its readers believe that the *Times* does not tell stories as the tabloids do. It would be more accurate to say that it tells tales for the managerial class. It embodies the world view of a person constantly asking "What institution should deal with this social problem?" and "What procedures should be followed?" Accordingly, its news stories gave us the problems and dilemmas that the Goetz case presented to the Governor, the Mayor, the Police Commissioner, and the District Attorney. Its reporters carefully described the processes of extradition, weighed the pros and cons of granting witnesses immunity, and went into great detail on the strategies of prosecution and defense lawyers.

The *Times* editorials deplored the outpouring of enthusiasm for self-defense but at the same time exemplified to the point of parody the intelligent liberal's impotence in the face of rising crime rates. Conceding that dramatically increasing the number of transit policemen had not worked, the paper urged that the officers be better trained. A Police Corps would do the trick, offering young men college scholarships in exchange for three years of service ("Why Surrender" A26:1). The *Times* showed an invincible conviction that there was a bureaucratic solution to every social problem.

Two books, Lillian Rubin's *Quiet Rage: Bernie Goetz in a Time of Madness* and Alice R. Kaminsky's *The Victim's Song*, demonstrate polar responses to the Goetz shooting. Rubin's book is a psychotherapist's effort to explain the event by tracing its roots in the past. Bernhard Goetz, it appears, had a cold and demanding father. Worse, his father had been charged with sexually molesting young boys. Still worse and very significantly, he had attempted to buy a boy's silence with five dollars—the very same amount that Troy Canty had asked for on the subway.

Rubin makes a brave attempt to calm the passions that the Goetz shooting aroused, but this explanation of Goetz's action reads like a parody of therapeutic liberalism. She does better with Darrell Cabey. His father had been a truck driver who bought his own truck and struck out on his own. He was murdered resisting a thief who was trying to steal his truck. His widow was left raising her children on her own, a task she performed with some success. Darrell was the son who was hard to control, the one who, without the guidance of his hard-working father, got into trouble. Rubin puts a face on Darrell Cabey, and it turns out to be the face of a crime victim.

If Lillian Rubin wants to calm the violent passions that New York's crime wave aroused, Alice Kaminsky insists on shouting them out. Her son Eric had moved to New York where he was studying to be a concert pianist. One morning two young men, Jose Deltejo and Furman Urena, stopped him in the subway station at 181st Street. They first took his wallet, then stabbed him, cutting his aorta, and pushed him onto the subway tracks where he bled to death.

Alice Kaminsky wants to inundate the reader with anger and repugnance for the evil of her son's death. She rages against those who commit crimes and those who accept them. She denounces the token clerk who saw Deltejo and Urena enter the station without paying but did nothing. She is furious against the witnesses who saw her son pushed onto the tracks and ran from the station but didn't bother to call a policeman. She is bitter against the judge who reminded a slightly aggressive prosecutor that this was "only a murder case." Above all, she denounces the indifference of the city which sees a crime wave and does nothing. Her longest chapter is titled "The Rotten Apple," and it contains a long list of crimes in the subway.

Alice Kaminsky reminds us that while one portion of the sympathy for Goetz was politically suspect and morally trashy, another very large portion was honestly motivated and rooted in bitter experience. She is all too typical of the contemporary climate of feeling, however, in her inability to move from a hatred of crime to a social program for resisting it. Describing a seventy-three-year-old subway rider who shot his would-be robber with a licensed .38 revolver, she asks: "If all the muggers knew that all the passengers on the subway carried guns, would the miserable, bullying thieves continue to do so" (163). It is a heart-felt statement. That Kaminsky is not frightened by the spectacle of "all" the passengers on the subway carrying guns shows how thoroughly passion was sweeping away prudence.

IV. GOETZ'S OWN STORIES

In the days immediately after the shooting when Bernhard Goetz became bitterly aware that others were manufacturing his story, he became eager to tell it himself. He did so three times. First he talked for an hour and twenty minutes to Officer Warren Foote of the Concord, New Hampshire, police department. Then he gave an hour and a half audiotaped statement to Officer Foote and Detective Christopher Domian. Then he went over the ground again in a two and a half hour videotaped statement to Assistant District Attorney Susan Braver and two New York City detectives. Each version reveals essentially the same facts, the same angers, and the same confusions.

The audiotaped and videotaped confessions are among the most remarkable documents of America's urban crisis. An exhausted and emotionally drained Goetz alternates between precise, rational analysis and emotional tirades. At some points he is self-righteously confident that he has acted justly. By this time the press has reported that all four boys had been in trouble with the law before the shooting and were on their way to rob video parlors at Pace University when they approached him. He has no reason to think they weren't threatening violence.

Yet although he doesn't think the shooting was wrong, he thinks the entire experience was disgusting. He has trouble finishing sentences when he tries to describe it. He expresses dismay, regret, horror, and rage. He is trying to construct a story that will make sense of his own experience, and he is succeeding only in part.

Goetz is sure that he is a crime victim who has turned on his victimizers. He had suffered an earlier mugging on Canal Street, and that had prompted him to buy guns. Although the police refused him a permit, he bought several weapons. He bought a quick release holster and refused to wear gloves in winter because they slowed his draw. He had thwarted muggers while walking along Central Park North, and when he boarded the downtown Express on December 22 he was psychologically primed and physically ready.

Like Alice Kaminsky, Goetz assails an uncaring city that permits criminals to roam freely through its subway. His rage at the city on the audiotape is astonishing. "In the business world in New York," he says in attempting to explain how he could go about the city armed, "you have to hide—you know, to hide the person you are."[2] His failed attempt to get a gun permit had taught him that "the city doesn't care what happens to you." The city is lawless, and its subway system is a disaster. Its bureaucracy is a sham, a disgrace, a joke. He admits that his shooting was cold-blooded, but says "You have to think in a cold-blooded way in New York." "In New York," he says, "you have to have a gun." "In New York," he says later, "people do crimes all the time and get away with them."

He is even more furious with the city on the videotape. He explodes in anger at the mere sound of Susan Braver's New York accent: "Oh, God, you know, just when I hear New Yorkers speak, I don't even want to—." Later he exclaims: "I can't stand it. Just the sound. It's—It's, uh—It's all, you know." New York City, he is sure, "doesn't give a damn about violence" (*Confessions*).

It would be easy for Goetz to match his story to the *Death Wish* pattern, but he refuses to do so. For all the justification he finds in his past mugging and the moral laxness of the city, Goetz is appalled at his own inner rage. He knows how the *Post* is portraying him, and he explicitly repudiates the paper's version of the story.

The *Death Wish* gunman is a fairly jaunty figure. Brian Garfield's hero grieves at the violence done to his wife and daughter but recovers his equilibrium once he becomes a vigilante. Charles Bronson is positively dapper by the end of the film version, even cracking one of his few cinematic smiles. Goetz, by contrast, expresses a sick, helpless anguish at what he has done even while he tries to justify it. He is at once dismayed and dismaying.

An explicit repudiation of the *Post* version of the story comes near the end of the videotaped confessions when Goetz says:

> People are looking for a hero, or they're looking for a villain, and neither is . . . nothing is the truth. What you have here, what you have here is nothing more, what you have here is nothing more than a vicious rat. That's all it is. It's not Clint Eastwood. It's not, uh, who's this guy in the shooting around people, and uh, that one movie *Death Wish*, whatever it was, it's not what the cops said.

If the *Post*'s staffers were embarrassed by this discovery in private, they didn't bat an eyelash in public. When reporter Mike Pearl gave an account of Goetz's words, he simply shortened them. In the *Post* version of the passage quoted above, Goetz says: "This means I'll never escape this. Some people are looking for a hero, some people are looking for a villain. I'm not Clint Eastwood"

(52). There was no hint that the *Post*'s urban hero had repudiated its version of his life as soon as he heard about it.

V. THE HAPPY ENDING OF YOUR CHOICE

In the trial of Bernhard Goetz, as George P. Fletcher observes, "most people were inclined to see the case as standing for something more" (87). One function of a trial is to reduce the role of this something more, to silence the angry voices of public debate and to focus the attention of twelve dispassionate citizens on determining what actually happened and why. It is difficult to examine the Goetz trial without gaining respect for the ways in which legal procedures calm passions and focus attention on questions of fact that can be decided by objective standards. At the same time, it is not hard to see that the popular narrative that had been developing in New York City for twenty years provided jurors with the framework in which Goetz's actions could be judged. Both prosecuting attorney Gregory Waples and defense attorney Barry Slotnick constantly referred to the *Death Wish* interpretation of the shooting. Waples presented the hard version in which Goetz became a self-appointed avenging angel. Slotnick presented a more sympathetic account in which Goetz was an ordinary guy who had been pushed too far and who, with his back against the metal subway wall, did what the law allows.

Slotnick had the advantage of an audience that shared an important area of experience with his client. A startling proportion of the jury members had been crime victims. The foreman had experienced a subway mugging. Another member had successfully resisted a mugging in the subway. A third had been pickpocketed in the subway. A fourth had been the victim of several burglaries. A fifth had seen her mother mugged while walking in the street. A sixth was a bus driver who had worried about being surrounded by delinquent teenagers. A seventh believed that she had never been mugged because she always walked in the center of the street where it was well lighted.

Even with this sympathetic audience, Barry Slotnick had a difficult task. He had to defend a client who had confessed three times in great and damaging detail. Slotnick succeeded in part because he was able to challenge the most potent item in the anti-Goetz story—the widely held belief that Goetz paused after firing the fourth shot, made a hostile statement to Darrell Cabey, and then fired again. Goetz himself confessed that he had done this, and witness Jack Boucher testified to it. But on the videotape Goetz becomes curiously vague and inconclusive on this point. He might be fantasizing out of his rage. And Slotnick presented eight witnesses from the subway car who testified that the shots were fired in rapid succession. Only Boucher claimed to hear the pause, and, since there were other inconsistencies in Boucher's account, the jury just didn't believe him.

With this damaging question of fact out of the way, the jury could concentrate on the motives and actions of the persons inside the subway car. Waples had conceded in his opening statement that all four boys had been in trouble with the law before the shooting and that two of them had been convicted of felonies, a chain snatching and a rape, after it. Slotnick was quick to follow up on these admissions. He constantly referred to the four boys as "vultures," "savages," a "gang of four." When it came time to demonstrate the positions of Goetz and his victims in the subway car, he arranged to have the four boys represented by four tough-looking Guardian Angels wearing their street clothes. He provoked (not much provocation was needed) James Ramseur into a snarling, threatening performance before the jury. He arranged to have the jury members visit an actual subway car so that they could have the experience of feeling "trapped like a rat" (Fletcher 128). It was an experience that at least one juror, Mark Lesly, later said had "a definite effect on me" (218).

The jury could understand that Goetz was afraid of criminals and alarmed by the crime rate in the city. To convict him, they would have had to feel that his reactions were so extreme that they could no longer be called reasonable. Gregory Waples told the jurors in his opening statement that Goetz was not "a reasonable person such as yourselves" but was instead an emotionally troubled individual" (Fletcher 102-03). He argued that Goetz was deeply suspicious and paranoid, seething inside with suppressed, self-righteous anger—an "individual who is obsessed with crime and his own solutions to the problems of crime and disorder in our cities" (Lesly 257). But clearly the jury members shared Goetz's concerns, and after extended scrutiny they didn't find his actions beyond the limits of reasonableness. If Goetz had really been an emotional powderkeg, one of them wanted to know, how had he managed to carry a gun every day for over three years before using it? "In New York that constitutes a pretty long fuse" (317).

By the time the civil trial took place, the context in which Goetz's stories were told had changed dramatically. Before the criminal trial, stories in the newspapers frequently dealt with crimes occurring in the subway. Now crime in the city had fallen significantly. Shortly before the civil trial began, a headline on the first page of the *New York Times* read: "New York's Violent Crime Rate Drops to Lows of Early 70s" (December 31, 1995 1:4-5). Now the headlines dealt with crimes that had happened far away—the O. J. Simpson trial, the bombing of the Oklahoma Federal Office Building, the Freemen standoff, and the Unibomber. The newspapers were no longer much interested in Goetz. They treated him like some eccentric old relative who had unexpectedly come back to visit.

The immediate audience for the lawyers had also changed dramatically. The first jury had been largely white and from Manhattan. The jury now consisted of six blacks and six Puerto Ricans, all from the Bronx.

And it was surely bad luck for Goetz that the story tellers had changed. Prosecutor Gregory Waples and Defense Attorney Barry Slotnick were evenly matched. At the second trial Ron Kuby was organized, forceful, and eloquent while Goetz's lawyer, Darnay Hoffman, was conducting only his second trial and doing so in a remarkably unassertive, confused manner.

Kuby had the advantage of focusing his case where Goetz was weakest. Slotnick had been able to deal with a sequence of shots which started with two young men who were, it is very easy to believe, threatening him. Start the sequence there and it is very easy to follow it through to the end with Goetz shooting on what Slotnick called automatic pilot.

But Kuby started with the fourth victim, who was positioned across the car and who, by Goetz's own account, was not engaging in overtly threatening behavior. Barry Slotnick successfully convinced the first jury that Christopher Boucher could not be trusted and that there had never been a pause before the final shot—that Goetz was acting on automatic pilot. Boucher had died between the two trials, but Kuby had his testimony read by an actor. The result was that Boucher, who had been found untrustworthy by the first jury, now emerged as the only witness to what happened.

Ironically, the only important piece of evidence in Goetz's favor was provided by columnist Jimmy Breslin. He had been one of the most eloquent voices countering the *Death Wish* narrative in the eighties, but at the civil trial he could not be shaken from his insistence that in the course of an interview after the shooting a lucid, coherent Cabey had told him that his friends went after Goetz because he looked like "easy bait." That wasn't enough. The jury concluded, as one member told a television interviewer, "I mean Mr. Goetz came over to him again and he asked him, 'Oh, you look O.K.' So he shot it again . . . . That was unfair" ("Bronx Jury" B4:1).

The jury awarded $18 million for past and future suffering and $25 million in punitive damages. That moves the case into a new phase. Goetz has declared bankruptcy and legal moves are underway to garnish 10% of his wages for the rest of his life. Like Tom Wolfe's Sherman McCoy, Goetz has become a permanent defendant.

NOTES

[1] See especially Wachs Chapter 5. Wachs notes that Goetz's refusal to submit to an offender's power distinguishes his story from most of those that she has collected. I suspect that her informants were too decent and civilized to express a desire for revenge but that it was festering unacknowledged in their minds. Otherwise, it is difficult to explain the Goetz story's extraordinary burst of popularity.

² Quotations from the audiotape are my own transcriptions from videotapes of the civil trial provided by Court TV.

WORKS CITED

"Bronx Jury Orders Goetz to Pay $43 Million to Man Paralyzed on Train." *New York Times* 24 April 1996, B4:1.

"Deli Owner Guns Down Holdupman on L.I." *New York Post* 25 January 1985, 5.

Breslin, Jimmy. "Bite the Bullet for Subway Corner." *New York Daily News* 27 December 1984, 6.

Brown, Wesley. "Where Pluralism and Paranoia Meet." *Dissent* (Fall 1987), 482.

Confessions of Bernhard Goetz, The. MPI Home Video (MP 1379). 1987.

"'Death Wish' Shooter." *New York Post* 24 December 1984. 1-2.

Dunleavy, Steve. "Goetz Rides Again." *New York Post* 4 March 1985, 5:5.

Fletcher, George P. *A Crime of Self Defense: Bernhard Goetz and the Law on Trial*. Chicago: U of Chicago P, 1988.

"Guardian Angel Training Inadequate, Critics, Say." *New York Times* 29 November 1992. 43:5-6.

Garfield, Brian. *Death Wish*. New York: Mysterious P, 1985.

Grutzner, Charles. "Blinker to Fight Crime in Subways." *New York Times* 13 February 1965, 23:8.

Hanauer, Joan. "Terror Lurks in the Dark, Lonely Hours." *Journal-American* 23 October 1963, 13.

Hanson, Kitty. "In the Rumble of the Subways—High School Gangs Are Turning Trains into Hell on Wheels." *Daily News* 3 December 1958, 48.

Kaminsky, Alice R. *The Victim's Song*. Buffalo: Prometheus, 1985, 163.

Katz, Leonard, and John Cashman. "Terror in the Subways." *New York Post* 8-12 March 1965.

Kessler, Felix, and Erwin Savelson. *World-Telegram and Sun* 27 January 1964, 1.

Lesly, Mark with Charles Shuttleworth. *Subway Gunman*. New York: British American, 1988.

Levine, Richard. "The Numbers Say Subways Are Safer Than They Seem." New York Times 28 June 1987, E6: 4.

Lichtenstein, Grace. "New Funds Unlikely to Alter New York's View on Subway." *New York Times* 8 May 1978, B12:3.

New York Post 10 January 1985, 5.

"New York's Violent Crime Rate Drops to Lows of Early 70s." *New York Times* 31 December 1995, 1: 4-5.

Pearl, Mike. "Goetz: I Wanted to Kill." *New York Post* 29 April 1987, 52.

"Portrait of Death Wish Gunman." *New York Post* 27 December 1984, 2.

Rangel, Jesus. "Statistically, At Least, It Is Rather Safe Down There." *New York Times* 10 February 1985, E7:1.
"Sliwa Admits Faking Crimes for Publicity." *New York Times* 25 November 1992, B1:6.
Steiner, Bradley J. *Subway Survival!* Mason: Loompanics Unlimited, 1980, 5.
"Vigilante Did What Was Natural." *New York Post* 28 December 1984, 2.
"Urban Jungle, The." *New York Times* 16 October 1971, 30:2.
"Vilgilante, The." *New York Amsterdam News* 19 January 1985, 12.
Wachs, Eleanor. *Crime-Victim Stories; New York Cities Urban Folklore*. Bloomington: Indiana UP, 1988.
"Why Surrender on the Subway?" *New York Times* 4 January 1985, A26:1.
Wolfe, Tom. "The Bonfire of the Vanities." *Rolling Stone* 19 July–2 August 1984.

CHAPTER THREE

Rhetoric, Repetition, and Violence:
A Case Study of Clinic Conflict in Milwaukee
by Anne E. Shaw and Alane C. Spinney

> Want to see what a picture of a
> dead baby looks like?
> Jim, Milwaukee sidewalk-counselor

On January 16, 1997, two bombs, spaced an hour apart, exploded outside a family planning clinic in Atlanta. The same day, the Feminist Majority Foundation held a press conference to announce that acts of clinic violence had decreased in 1996. Despite the drop, the group warned, potential for violence was high. Moreover, the intensity of violent acts was likely to increase. "I have noticed a general trend of escalation," commented President Eleanor Smeal (Bragg 6). Smeal's observations were borne out the next day when a second set of bombs exploded at the Reproductive Services clinic in Tulsa, Oklahoma, and again in February, when an arsonist caused over $100,000 worth of damage at a Virginia clinic.

According to the National Abortion Federation (NAF), the incidence of clinic bombings and arsons rose 38% in 1997 (NAF 2). NAF also noted that abortion-related violence was becoming more sophisticated. The Federation reported "increasing links between anti-abortionists and paramilitary organizations" (2), noting that "bombings in particular have become linked with other causes" (3). In February 1997, Atlanta suffered a second bombing—this time of a gay and lesbian nightclub. After investigating, law enforcement officials stated that the similarity of the explosive devices used made it likely that the two bombings were connected to one another and to the 1996 bombing of Atlanta's Olympic Centennial Park. A paramilitary organization known as the Army of God later claimed responsibility for the clinic and nightclub bombings. The group, whose underground membership has a record of extreme antiabortion violence, had also been responsible for kidnapping a doctor and his wife in 1982 (3).

As clinic violence intensified in 1997, picketing, hate mail, and harassing phone calls at women's health facilities reached their highest levels ever. A NAF survey reported 7,651 incidents of picketing in that year alone, with clinics in 43 states reporting daily or weekly picketing (3). The NAF report concluded that abortion-related violence and disruption "have not subsided over time" and that, to the contrary, "there have been dramatic increases in all categories of violence and disruption" since 1977 (2). Thus, antiabortion violence and picketing appear to be related phenomena, both of which are currently on the rise.

PREVIOUS STUDIES OF ABORTION CONFLICT

Despite a 1985 survey revealing that all but one clinic subjected to bombing or arson had been heavily picketed (Blanchard and Prewit 246), the connection between clinic violence and sidewalk protest remains largely unexplored. Scholarly investigations of the abortion debate have tended to fall into two categories. The first may be broadly characterized as sociopolitical, focusing on particular historical events and groups. Foremost among these is Kristin Luker's seminal study, in which Luker provides demographic profiles of California abortion activists on both sides of the issue. Sociopolitical approaches often make use of case studies, and have tended to focus on extreme acts of clinic violence, such as bombings and shootings.[1] The second approach is rhetorically based, focusing on the linguistic devices abortion activists use to convey their message. In general, scholars using this approach have focused either on the history of the abortion conflict or on mass-produced materials such as pamphlets, photographs, and films.[2] A few investigators have addressed themselves to both approaches, attempting to trace the social effects of antiabortion rhetoric. Among these is Celeste Condit, who explores the development of the public abortion debate, tracing the history of particular rhetorical devices and their roles in effecting social change.[3]

While scholars using a sociopolitical approach have tended to ignore the role that rhetoric plays in large-scale acts of violence, those using the rhetorically based or combined approach have tended to ignore violence in favor of political debate. Investigators in both areas have also tended to disregard antiabortion demonstrators, perhaps because their behavior appears moderate. In this paper, we focus on the rhetoric of antiabortion demonstrators and the ways in which it may contribute to clinic violence. Using examples drawn from three Milwaukee clinics, we propose that the highly repetitive nature of demonstrators' rhetoric normalizes cultural conflict around clinics, establishing a backdrop against which clinic violence can occur.[4] Thus, while leaning toward the rhetorical, our analysis combines aspects of both approaches, attempting to provide a partial explanation for the interconnected phenomena of violent rhetoric and violent action in the antiabortion movement.

A BRIEF HISTORY OF THE ANTIABORTION MOVEMENT

In order to understand the significance of Milwaukee's antiabortion movement, it is useful to be familiar with the sociological and historical context of the movement as a whole. The pivotal year for reproductive rights in the United States was 1973: this was the year that the Supreme Court handed down its landmark *Roe v. Wade* decision legalizing abortion. However, abortion opponents had begun organizing even before the Court made its ruling. In the summer of 1971, an ad hoc committee of the Family Life Division of the U.S. Catholic conference assembled for an organizational meeting. As Luker notes, most members of this small group were middle-aged Catholic men with successful careers in fields such as medicine and law (128). Drawing on their legal talent, the group drafted an amicus brief in the *Roe v. Wade* case. After the Supreme Court handed down its ruling, the committee separated from the Catholic Conference, and, in a move reflecting its subsequent rhetorical focus on the abortion issue, renamed itself National Right To Life. The ruling itself mobilized a different group of abortion opponents. Unlike pre-Roe activists, those propelled to activism by the Court's decision were primarily women with a high-school level education. Most were married, had children, and did not work outside the home (Luker 138). Like the pre-Roe activists, these women were devout Catholics who had been largely insulated from the practice of abortion. In conjunction with their male counterparts, these women became the core of the early antiabortion movement.[5]

This movement, supported by the Catholic hierarchy, evolved a two-pronged strategy to eliminate legalized abortion. Both parts of the strategy called for activism to be focused at the legislative level. The first called for overturning the *Roe* decision through a "human life" amendment to the Constitution. The second entailed eroding abortion rights through laws requiring waiting periods, parental consent for minors, and other restrictions. Despite major differences in their groups' social agendas, the Catholic bishops also formed antiabortion coalitions with groups such as the Moral Majority—largely Protestant organizations that came to be part of the neoconservative movement known as the New Right. The 1976 Republican Party platform supported a human life amendment that was pushed by neoconservatives as well as Catholics.

It was this somewhat unlikely coalition that initiated the antiabortion movement into its second, more radical phase. In this phase, direct action was to become the third major component of the strategy to end legalized abortion. Instead of focusing primarily on legislative work, the leaders of the new direct-action wing encouraged activists to take their opposition to abortion clinics. Activists were not only encouraged to engage in picketing, but were also trained in the use of illegal tactics, such as blocking driveways, blockading entrances, and invading clinics in order to destroy medical equipment. This approach aimed to end legalized abortion by forcing clinics to close one at a time, either temporarily, as a result of blockades, or permanently, as a result of the damage inflicted by long-term campaigns of picketing and harassment.

In 1980, a former newspaper reporter named Joseph Scheidler emerged as the leader of this new, direct-action wing of the movement. Scheidler, often referred to as "the godfather" of the antiabortion movement, set out to create what he later referred to as a "pro-life mafia."[6] Drawing on the Catholic neoconservative coalition that already existed at the level of party politics, Scheidler formed an umbrella organization known as the Pro-Life Action Network (PLAN). PLAN established close ties with both Catholic and Protestant direct-action groups and helped form new groups (NAF 2).

A distinctive feature of Scheidler's direct-action movement was that national leaders tended to work alongside local activists. Nationally known figures, including Scheidler himself, provided important leadership by appearing at clinics to confront patients, train activists, and encourage blockades that would result in arrest and incarceration. Although the leaders themselves were infrequently arrested, their presence at local blockades allowed them to form important relationships with local protesters. In addition, both the leaders and their supporters tended to be working class, and new national leaders were often recruited from the ranks of committed local activists.

In 1985, Scheidler published a direct-action guidebook entitled *Closed: 99 Ways to Stop Abortion*; the book became another important link between national leadership and local supporters and played a key role in disseminating information on direct-action tactics. Although national leaders did not publicly advocate violence, the number of clinic arsons and bombings reached a new high as these direct-action tactics became more widespread (NAF 2). In late November 1986, Scheidler held a meeting in Pensacola, Florida, with two of his colleagues: a newly recruited young activist named Randall Terry and a second associate named Joseph Foreman. Together, the three of them founded Operation Rescue (OR), a group that was to become famous for staging massive clinic blockades in Atlanta, Wichita, and Buffalo.

THE ANTIABORTION MOVEMENT IN MILWAUKEE

Milwaukee's antiabortion movement began in 1988, the year a young activist named Matthew Trewhella founded a branch of Operation Rescue in the city. Trewhella, a convicted arsonist, was not Milwaukee's first antiabortion leader: Monica Migliorino Miller, a Catholic associate of Scheidler's and founding member of PLAN, was already leading city activists. While Miller worked with conservative Catholics, Trewhella began organizing evangelical Protestants. Working in tandem, the two were able to organize around the same issue in much the same way that Catholic bishops and the New Right had formed their coalition a decade earlier. Although they have never joined forces officially, Miller and Trewhella have maintained Milwaukee's antiabortion movement for the past ten years. Both leaders have become nationally known among antiabortion activists while continuing to work closely with their local supporters.

In 1990, Joseph Foreman, now the Field Director for Operation Rescue, came to Milwaukee and began working with Trewhella. The standard OR tactic called for targeting a city for blockades, blockading intensively, and then moving on, but Foreman felt that this method was ineffective. Instead, he favored a long-term approach to wear down local clinics. With this in mind, Foreman and Trewhella established a new group called Missionaries to the Preborn (MTP). From 1990 to 1992, the group conducted almost daily blockades of Milwaukee women's clinics. In 1992, MTP, OR, and Youth For America targeted the city for a summer of clinic blockades. During the blockades, thousands of protesters lined the streets and attempted to block clinic entrances. Children as young as six were encouraged to participate because they faced little, if any, chance of criminal prosecution. The blockades subsided in 1993, due largely to the implementation of a permanent injunction.[7] In 1994, the Freedom of Access to Clinic Entrances Act (FACE) made it a felony to prevent entry into clinics and brought the blockades to a halt.

These legal restrictions had the effect of honing Milwaukee's antiabortion movement. While many recently recruited protesters fell away, the most committed activists remained. For the past five years, daily protests have been staged by a group of about a dozen full-time activists. This core group, in conjunction with fifty to seventy-five other protesters, continues to follow the long-term strategy originally laid out by Foreman. Each morning, protesters line the sidewalks outside Milwaukee's clinics, where they accost patients with pamphlets, placards, and poster-size photographs of "aborted" fetuses. They shout accusations at patients, confront their companions, and yell through the doors and windows of clinics. Much of this behavior violates Milwaukee's permanent injunction, but it has become routine due in large part to the District Attorney's office, which has repeatedly failed to prosecute injunction violations.

Organizationally, Milwaukee's antiabortion movement descends directly from Joseph Scheidler and reflects his emphasis on hard-hitting, direct-action tactics. Demographically, it reflects the national movement's Catholic roots and the ascendancy of the New Right. Approximately two-thirds of Milwaukee's protesters attend non-denominational Protestant churches; the remaining third are conservative Catholics. Unlike the activists interviewed by Luker in 1984, the majority of the clinic protesters are men. Like Luker's activists, most are white and in their mid-to-late thirties, but few are professionals. The majority of the protesters are working class, with a high school diploma and some post-secondary education. As the NAF report suggests, many of these activists align themselves with other right-wing causes and groups, including citizens' militias and the U.S. Taxpayers Party.[8] Thus, Milwaukee's antiabortion movement reflects a national demographic shift in the movement. While the direct-action movement is still overwhelmingly white and working class, its predominantly female base has become a predominantly male base with strong ties to secretive, right-wing organizations.

THE RHETORICAL CONTEXT OF MILWAUKEE'S MOVEMENT

In addition to having organizational links to the direct-action wing of the antiabortion movement, Milwaukee's activists situate themselves within the rhetorical and organizational context of a broader conservative movement. One force that links Milwaukee's antiabortion activists to this larger movement are VCY/America, a Christian radio and television network. VCY has stations in Wisconsin, Kansas, and South Dakota and broadcasts its programs nationwide. Theologically, the network's positions are consistent with those of a movement known as Christian Reconstructionism. Reconstructionists seek to establish a theocracy run according to Old Testament law. In this society, the nuclear family would be the central unit, women would be subservient to men, and capital punishment would be the penalty for numerous crimes including homosexuality, adultery, heresy, and striking a parent (Blanchard and Prewitt 243-45; Clarkson 77-96). Consistent with this agenda, VCY programming combines support for state enforcement of "God's Word" with a desire for minimal government involvement within "Christian families." Typical programming on VCY voices strong opposition to assisted suicide, gay rights, birth control, and gun regulation, stressing the importance of parents' rights, home-schooling, and political involvement. Abortion is discussed on nearly every program; many of Milwaukee's antiabortion activists make regular appearances. Thus, VCY acts as an important tool for framing and disseminating antiabortion rhetoric in Milwaukee, linking it to a larger right-wing agenda.

THE RHETORIC OF THE ANTIABORTION MOVEMENT

The rhetoric commonly used to discuss abortion on VCY, and in the antiabortion movement as a whole, is absolutist. This rhetoric insists that there is only one way of viewing abortion and dismisses all opposing arguments as trivial in comparison. In her 1990 study, Condit identifies the use of such rhetoric as "over-weighing." Using this strategy, she writes, speakers "attempt to show that the values and interests on their side [outweigh] those of the opposition" (159). By far the most important example of over-weighing in antiabortion rhetoric is the slogan of Operation Rescue: "If you think abortion is murder, act like it." This call to action has become a central tenet of the sidewalk "rescue" movement and has had enormous impact on the public abortion debate. Indeed, personhood of the fetus is a claim that typically goes unrefuted, even by individuals who identify themselves as pro-choice (Condit 82).

The slogan "abortion is murder" frames antiabortion discourse in two important and closely related ways. First, it articulates a defining equation: abortion equals murder. Second, it creates a closed system that eliminates competing definitions. According to this equation, abortion can be viewed as nothing *but* murder. The claim that the fetus is a person functions similarly, categorically excluding other definitions. Beneath Operation Rescue's moral imperative, then, lies an epistemological one—one must not only take action if one believes in the abortion/murder equation: one must accept the equation (indeed, there is no alternative to it) and *then* take action. Within this constricted epistemology, the course of action is left unspecified, opening a range of possibilities from political protest to reciprocal violence.

While antiabortion rhetoric consists largely of the iteration of these defining equations ("abortion is murder"; "the fetus is a person"), the behavior of sidewalk protesters ranges from quiet prayer vigil to aggressive physical and verbal behavior toward patients and clinic staff. Among Milwaukee's antiabortion activists, the most common activity is a form of aggressive verbal behavior known as "sidewalk counseling." As one how-to manual defines it, sidewalk counseling is "a highly intense verbal interaction between you [the counselor] and a mother who is about to deliver her unborn child over to death" (*Sidewalk Counseling*). The manual further defines sidewalk counseling as a process in which the counselor engages the patient verbally, offers written material, and exchanges information with her in an attempt to "persuade her to keep the baby."[9] As in Operation Rescue's slogan, embedded in this rhetoric are the dual assertions that abortion constitutes murder and that it creates a moral imperative to act.

THE RHETORIC OF SIDEWALK COUNSELING

By allowing the arguments and general humanity of one's opponents to be dismissed, over-weighing contributes to the formation of closed ideologies. Closure may occur in public discourse, as seen in the widespread acceptance of the "abortion is murder" equation, or in private rhetoric, as manifested by the group responsible for a series of clinic bombings in Pensacola, Florida. This group, already committed to conservative Christianity, isolated itself from discourse with others and subsequently developed a set of beliefs in which violent action became a moral imperative.[10]

Over-weighing and discursive closure also occur in the rhetoric of sidewalk counseling. In practice, most sidewalk counselors do not adhere to the model of persuasive counseling described in the manual. Instead, they accost patients with aggressive statements that are repeated verbatim from one patient to the next. Counselors may make the same statement or set of statements hundreds of times over the course of an average morning. "That's your son or daughter," a sidewalk counselor named Mary is likely to say, "that little baby's heart is beating." "Want to see what a picture of a dead baby looks like?" asks a second counselor named Jim. In most of these encounters there is no attempt at discourse with the patient. Patients who attempt to explain their decision or discuss extenuating circumstances are met with standard responses: "You don't have to kill your baby." After the woman has entered the clinic, counselors shout repetitive speeches through the clinic doors. Between patients, counselors such as Jim occupy themselves by rereading antiabortion pamphlets or accosting pedestrians with lines that are repeated over and over: "Pray for the babies who are scheduled to die here today"; "You know this is an abortion clinic where they murder babies?"

Integral to the sidewalk counseling environment is a backdrop of tracts and placards. At the Summit clinic in Milwaukee, protesters stand on both sides of the sidewalk with photographic enlargements, some as much as six feet in height, of *in utero* and "aborted" fetuses.[11] The rhetorical processes at work in these images have been detailed by previous authors, who argue that the "self-evident" nature of the photographs is constructed within the context of the abortion debate.[12] In the context of sidewalk counseling, the images function as non-verbal iterations of the "abortion is murder" equation. Over-weighing and repetition thus intersect in counselors' rhetoric, establishing and maintaining discursive closure.

Within this rhetorically constricted environment, the repetitive statements of individual protesters are undergirded by the repetition of a common post-abortion narrative. This narrative, which is similar to the motif of order and disorder identified by Lake, consists of the *assertion* of a reconstructionist world view, articulated through over-weighted equations; the *prescription* for compliance, based on the implementation of traditional sex roles; and the *prediction of punishment* for failure to obey these directives. This pattern of assertion, prescription, and prediction is exemplified by a sidewalk counselor named Mary:

> You've already got a son or daughter. That little baby's heart is beating. There are people out here who care about you and can help you today. You don't have to choose death for your child. Give your child a hope and a future. You are going to live with this forever. There's going to come a day when you want to have children, and you're

going to regret this little child whose life you took in his place. (Videotape)[13]

In this speech, Mary repeats both over-weighing antiabortion equations, referring to the fetus as "a son or daughter," "that little baby," and "your child" and to the abortion procedure as "death." As Luker observes, emphasis on motherhood as the natural state of women is integral to the antiabortion world view. Here, Mary prescribes motherhood as the appropriate course of action ("Give your child a hope and a future"). It is not merely the appropriate female role, however; failure to comply with her directive will result in punishment. Because the woman's maternal instincts will inevitably awaken ("there *will* come a day *when* you want to have children"), her disobedience will eventually usher her into a state of remorse that will last "forever." As Mary portrays it, the inevitability of motherhood is rewarding for obedient women, but punitive for disobedient ones.

The insistence that women accept motherhood is accompanied by a prescription for male dominance and traditional family structures.[14] In the speech quoted above, Mary goes on to elaborate her view of appropriate sex roles: "If this man really loves you, he'll help you, support you, and you can have your child. He won't be taking you to an abortion clinic to kill your child." The directive for male dominance is made more explicit by another sidewalk counselor named Drew, who counseled a patient's partner to take control of the situation:

You know it's wrong. She needs a man to take charge. Grab her hand. Take her home. Most of the women come in here drive their man. You're the man. Grab her by the hand. Pray with her. Take her home. Do what's right, sir. Protect that little child. (Videotape)

Like Mary, Drew assumes knowledge of the couple's relationship. Both counselors also assert that the "natural order" of male dominance and female subservience has been upset. Within the context of their assumptions ("If this man really loves you," "You know it's wrong"), both map a course of redemptive action. Redemption here is equated with the implementation of restrictive sex roles, that is, a new relationship in which the man is financially, physically, and theologically dominant. Drew emphasizes this as he urges the partner to "take charge," linking the exertion of physical control ("grab her hand," "take her home") to the establishment of the male partner's theological authority ("pray with her," "do what's right"). It is this restriction of the woman's autonomy, her coercion into motherhood, that results in the "protection" of the fetus, "that little child."

Intertwined with the prescription of these restrictive sex roles are dire predictions about what will happen to patients and partners if they fail to comply. These predictions include threats of infertility, breast cancer, and "post-abortion syndrome" (*Sidewalk Counseling* "Preparing for Sidewalk Counseling"; Hopkins, Reicher, and Saleem 544). As one counselor put it,

> Sometimes, psychologically, [women] can't get over these babies and so they commit suicide. Sometimes they end up in a mental institution. So many things happen because of these abortions. Not to mention they're going to Hell. (Videotape)

Whether they emphasize fertility problems, mental illness, or damnation, counselors invariably predict forms of punishment in which the patient revisits the abortion experience. Vivid re-experiencing is not only a defining characteristic of "post-abortion syndrome" (Hopkins, Reicher, and Saleem 544) but a key component of counselors' apocalyptic warnings. As Dan illustrates, some counselors envision a second confrontation with the patient, one in which the "murdered baby" acts as a vengeful mouthpiece for God:

> It's your own son or your own daughter. That baby will point at you on Judgment Day and say, "That was my mother, she had me killed." Don't mock God. What about that baby's life? That baby's going to point at you. . . . God says, "Thou shall not kill, thou shall not bear false witness." There's a holy God in Heaven, and your baby will stand there on Judgment Day and say, "That was my mother, that had me killed." (Videotape)

In each revisitation scenario, the patient has no alternative but to accept both her own punishment and the epistemological "truth" that "abortion is murder." Indeed, it is acceptance of this epistemology that constitutes the patient's punishment, for the realization causes her everlasting remorse that is fitting retribution for the "murder" of her "baby."

In counselors' punishment scenarios, the concerns and justifications of the patient—the reasons behind the abortion decision—are either entirely obscured or portrayed as so trivial that they can barely be said to exist at all. The same is true of the woman herself, who is eradicated in the narratives by the force of what she has done. A woman suffering from "post-abortion syndrome" is not only portrayed as obsessed with "the abortion death trauma," and consequently afflicted by guilt, self-hatred, and the loss of personal relationships; she also experiences the eradication of her female identity through a body that is portrayed as sterile and cancerous. Similarly, in the Judgment Day scenarios, the positions of fetus and woman are reversed, as the patient is condemned to "spiritual death" by her own "murdered" fetus, now elevated to a state of complete autonomy.

Although counselors portray God as the agent of this punishment, their rhetoric also attempts to punish women by forcing them to "know the truth." "Counseling" techniques such as standing outside clinics with posters of "aborted babies," calling patients "baby killers" and chasing them from their cars to the door of the clinic rest on the assumption that patients can be forced to the experiential realization that "abortion is murder." As the line between persuasion and punishment becomes blurred, counseling techniques that upset patients become more and more acceptable. Justification for aggressive "counseling" is provided by the sidewalk-counseling manual, which advises: "A mother who is crying does not want the abortion. You must redouble your efforts with her because she is very close to choosing life. Do not let up on her no matter how tired you are" (*Sidewalk Counseling* "Special Situations"). Thus, counselors approach tearful, young, or frightened-looking patients even more aggressively and may view bringing a patient to tears as evidence that they have succeeded in "getting through to her."

Not all aggressive tactics can be justified on the basis of preventing abortion. Despite periodic claims of sidewalk "saves" or "turn-arounds," it is extremely rare for women to leave as a result of having been "counseled."[15] Some counselors view the abortion as a foregone conclusion and focus instead on delivering what "murderers" deserve. Repetitive rhetoric becomes especially important in this type of counseling, for it subjects patients to a punitive and seemingly relentless barrage of "truth." Dan provides an illuminating example:

> [These women] should be upset, because they're killing their babies. They know what they're doing, they're killing their babies. They're going to be upset, because they know what they're doing. They know the reality of what's going on. They know that they pay a doctor money to have their babies killed. (Videotape)

Dan's counseling techniques, in this case yelling through the doors of the clinic, suggest that he views the abortions as an accomplished fact. Although he cannot prevent them, he can continue to expose patients to the idea that "abortion is murder" in the hope that what they already "know" will be experientially realized.

REPETITIVE RHETORIC AND DISCURSIVE CLOSURE

Thus far, we have outlined two types of repetition in the rhetoric of sidewalk counseling: repetition of the assertion-directive-warning pattern, or narrative repetition, and repetition of distinct words and phrases, or formal repetition. We now turn to the latter, which is perhaps the most striking and pervasive feature of sidewalk counseling. It was this type of repetition that led us to formulate our original research question: since it is not an effective means of persuasion, what function does repetition serve in sidewalk counselors' discourse? As discussed above, repetition of over-weighted rhetoric is used by some counselors as a form of punishment. In Dan's example, it serves another function as well; it precludes competing discourse by monopolizing the rhetorical arena. His repetition of the phrase "they're killing their babies" not only over-weighs the patients' justifications; it seems to push them out of his discursive space.

Counselors are especially likely to use formal repetition when their beliefs are challenged. One argument we witnessed provides an illustrative example. In this case, a pedestrian took issue with KC's sign, a 3 x 5-foot photographic enlargement of an "infant's" head. The head, which was covered with blood, was held in a pair of forceps and appeared to be screaming. Although he agreed with Dan and KC on their moral position, the pedestrian took issue with their rhetorical strategy. As this example illustrates, Dan and KC interpreted his objection as a rejection of their entire belief system:

PED. I agree abortion is wrong.

KC. No, you don't.

PED. I agree with that. Yes, I do. But what I also think is wrong is you imposing and forcing these images on innocent people.

DAN. [But] that's the truth. That's the truth.

PED. Innocent people.

KC. [Pointing toward the clinic.] What about them?

PED. You want to stop abortion, you preach Jesus. Get people saved—

DAN. Tell them the truth.

PED. -and they won't be thinking about having no abortion.

DAN. Tell them the truth. You've got to tell the truth to people. [Gesturing toward the sign.] That's the truth. That's what goes on here. (Videotape)

Here, Dan uses formal repetition of the phrase "that's the truth" to avoid addressing the argument that abortion should not over-weigh the concerns of "innocent people." When the pedestrian persists, raising the possibility that abortion can be prevented by "preaching Jesus," Dan refuses to address his objection directly. As reassertion of the original, over-weighted equation fails to end the debate, Dan substitutes a second formal element for the first:

PED. Ok, well maybe that's the truth. But imagine some fragile young mind coming along here and seeing that image and they say, "Oh Mommy, what's that?" "Oh, that's a baby, honey." She's never going to want to have one of them inside of her.

> DAN. What about the Judgment of God? What about the Judgment of God? (Videotape)

As the argument progresses, the pedestrian responds to this emphasis on judgment by challenging what he perceives as inconsistencies in the reconstructionist viewpoint.

> PED. You want a law to say that you can't kill babies, but you've got laws to say that people can be put to death for a crime.
>
> DAN. That's different. That's God's Law.
>
> PED. Don't try to be dictating public policy in the name of the Lord.
>
> KC. He dictated public policy to Israel. He said, "You shall execute the murderers. You shall execute adulterers."
>
> PED. Well, that's the Old Testament.
>
> DAN. Oh, no. That's God's Law. (Videotape)

As this example demonstrates, both Dan and KC used formal repetition to avoid discussing the ideological ambiguities introduced by their opponent. Their repetition served an important defensive function, enabling the narrative repetition of reconstructionist assertions ("That's the truth"), directives ("You shall execute the murderers"), and warnings ("the Judgment of God"). To the counselors, this repetition became analogous to the discourse itself, and thus to the enforcement of "God's Law."

Closely related to the defensive function of formal repetition is its ability to narrow the terms of an already closed discourse. In the context of sidewalk counseling, formal repetition of words and images limits the terms of debate. It may also reinforce counselors' justifications as they counsel. Repetition met with silence seems to contribute to counselors' perceptions that their assertions are morally unanswerable. As one self-appointed pastor proclaimed,

> Those of you that are against God's word and God's truth, you've got nothing to say. You tell your lies in a secret place. You tell your lies in quiet. You tell your lies in a dark place, where you think nobody's watching, where nobody can hear. Well, I've got news for you: God hears every word. God sees it all. God knows what's going on down here today. And you, sir, or lady, you, are without excuse, that's what the Bible says. (Videotape)

Feelings of moral certainty and superiority may account for counselors' persistence in yelling through clinic doors, pursuing patients who ask to be left alone, and approaching pedestrians, most of whom are unresponsive or hostile. Ritual monologues and unreciprocated "counseling" may then strengthen these feelings, acting as a positive feedback mechanism and resulting in more repetition.

REPETITIVE SPECTACLE AND BEHAVIORAL ESCALATION

As the presence of placards and signs suggests, the narrative and formal repetitions of sidewalk counseling occur in the larger context of repetitive public displays. On Saturdays, the sidewalk counselors outside Milwaukee's clinics are joined by prayer groups, guerrilla actors, and sidewalk evangelists. The presence of these individuals helps to transform the displays into public spectacles. In addition to large placards, props for Saturday activities include religious icons, a six-foot wooden rosary, a seven-foot crucifix, pink and blue balloons, baby clothes, musical instruments, "bloody" dolls, and a portable podium with amplification. In addition, protesters sometimes bring their own children as illustrations of the "abortion is murder" argument. The resulting spectacles are a chaotic mix of counseling, singing, witnessing, and preaching combined with readings from the Bible and antiabortion texts.

These more dramatic forms of protest reinvigorate the counselors, resulting in rhetorical and behavioral escalation. As they are repeated, the spectacles become ritualized and tend to increase in frequency. The escalation they have engendered then comes to be accepted as a "normal" part of the protest arena. The presence of repetitive spectacle is thus a significant contributing factor to the escalation of clinic conflict, and one that accounts for its current high levels in Milwaukee.

AFFILIATED MEDICAL SERVICES: PRAYER AS SPECTACLE

The Rosary Society is one group that provides insight into the historical escalation of Milwaukee's protest activities. This group of Catholics has assembled on a weekly basis to pray the Rosary since 1992. Originally, the group prayed at the Wisconsin Women's Health Center in Brown Deer, a suburb of Milwaukee. Here, members of the group began interrupting the litany to shout at incoming patients: "Mom!" "Grandma!" and "[Make] a good choice!" The exclamations developed into a permanent feature of their vigil, despite the fact that they were separated from patients by a large parking lot and were nearly drowned out by the noise of nearby traffic. When the clinic closed temporarily, the Rosary group moved to Affiliated Medical Services, a clinic in downtown Milwaukee. Here they lined the sidewalk, shouting as patients walked past them. The group was also joined by Charlie, a sidewalk counselor known for chasing patients and pushing the volunteer escorts who walk them in. When Wisconsin Women's Health reopened, the group remained at Affiliated, where it began to pray the "Rosary for Life."

In combination with the ritualized "counseling" of patients, the use of the Rosary for Life helps to obscure the distinction between prayer vigil and sidewalk counseling. The following transcript shows the reaction of group members (including Ron, Paul, John, and Charlie) to an entering patient. Standing near the group is a counselor named Jan.

> RON. [Leading the group.] As it was in the beginning, is now, and ever shall be, world without end. Amen.
>
> PAUL. Oh, my Jesus, forgive us our sins. Save us the fires of hell.
>
> RON. Lead all souls to heaven, especially those who are in most need of thy mercy.
>
> [A patient walks by.]
>
> JAN. Bring her back out.
>
> GROUP. [Singing.] Ave, Ave—
>
> CHARLIE. Let us help you.
>
> GROUP. –Ave Maria—
>
> CHARLIE. [Yelling.] Is that your baby you're taking in there? Let us help you save your baby.
>
> GROUP. –Ave, Ave, Ave Maria.
>
> PAUL. Second sorrowful mystery, the scourging at the pillar. As Christ was scourged, his skin was torn. The pain was agonizing upon his innocent flesh. May the merits of Christ's suffering bring an end to legalized abortion.
>
> CHARLIE. [Leading the group.] Our Father who art in Heaven, hallowed be thy name. . . . (Videotape)

In this example, Charlie moves easily from his roles as sidewalk counselor to the position of group leader. The "abortion is murder" argument is thus integrated into the litany, where it is reinforced by the prayer to "end legalized abortion." The idea that abortion demands direct action as well as prayer is introduced as group members yell at patients and attempt to impede them. Thus, the group reinforces the notion, held by sidewalk counselors, that direct action is a moral imperative. The group's litany provides a point of reference for counselors, who, in turn, behave more aggressively than members of the "prayer group."

In this way, the Rosary group sets a baseline for counseling behavior. The group's performance also adds to the confusion outside the clinic. The noise of the litany, overlaid by repetitions of "Mom!" "Grandma!" and "A good choice!" competes with the message of individual sidewalk counselors, who yell "Thou shalt not kill!" and "Escorts to the executioner!" This rhetorical crowding is accompanied by physical crowding. Group members line the space outside the door with religious statues and signs. In the press of people, it is not uncommon for protesters to push, shove, and commit other "minor" assaults on patients and escorts. The interaction between the Rosary Society and sidewalk counselors thus sanctions and creates opportunities for behavioral escalation. Since their move and the addition of Charlie, group members and sidewalk counselors have both become increasingly aggressive.

SUMMIT WOMEN'S HEALTH CENTER: THE DEVIL ABORTIONIST

Without the infusion of new formal elements through which the overall sidewalk counseling narrative can be articulated, counselors' rhetoric might reiterate itself to the point of obliteration.[16] In addition to establishing visible reference points and contributing to the melee, spectacle redramatizes the "abortion is murder" equation, articulating it with new urgency. Spectacle therefore plays an important role in perpetuating sidewalk protest.

Some of the most dramatic forms of spectacle are brought to the local scene by itinerant protesters. Like Milwaukee's "missionaries to the preborn," these protesters have committed themselves wholly to the antiabortion movement. They travel from city to city, where they establish ties with local protesters. Because they are willing to use extreme tactics and are among the most vocal proponents of violence, they play an important role in revitalizing and escalating local protest. In February 1997, an itinerant counselor named Jimmy came to Milwaukee from clinic blockades in Englewood, New Jersey. He was quickly accepted into Milwaukee's sidewalk counseling scene where his own form of spectacle has become a routine practice.

Although he also sidewalk counsels and preaches, Jimmy creates the most impact when he performs guerrilla theater. On these days, he appears outside the clinic dressed in green surgical scrubs, which are covered in dried red "blood." The plastic legs of a baby doll hang from a string around his neck. Jimmy also brings two naked and "bloody" baby dolls, which he props on the rim of an aluminum trashcan. Completing the costume is a gray plastic machete, which from a distance appears real. Like the other props, the machete is covered in "blood." Jimmy hacks at the dolls with the machete; he also bites them and pounds them against his trashcan. During these performances, Jimmy plays off the rhetoric of local sidewalk counselors by adopting the persona of a "devil abortionist,"

> JIMMY. Ma'am, it's that baby's fault. It's that baby's fault. You kill that baby. You get that baby in there and you kill it. You know it's the baby's fault you got pregnant. You get in there and you get that baby killed.

DAN. The Word of God says, "Thou shalt not kill."

JIMMY. Don't worry about God. Worry about Satan. Satan'll have a fit if you don't kill that baby. You get in there and kill that baby. Get that baby murdered. Get him tortured. Get his arms cut off, get his legs cut off. Get his heart cut out. Get him decapitated. Yes ma'am, we'll take care of your baby. You're special to us. Why, you don't have to worry a thing about that baby. We'll take good care of him. (Videotape)

During these performances, Jimmy's shouting can be heard inside the clinic and along the street for more than a block. He creates further disruption by dragging his trashcan across the sidewalk and yelling "Legalized murder!" at passing cars. This yelling has no perceptible effect on its "audience" and can hardly be intended to "persuade" passing drivers. Rather, the yelling seems intended to maintain a high level of disruption around the clinic, increasing the sense of urgency felt by other protesters.

When he is not yelling, Jimmy dons a red and black devil mask, and returns to "butchering babies." Through the repetition of his "butcher-doctor" spectacle, Jimmy reinscribes the "abortion is murder" equation. As Condit observes,

> Once a set of activists decides that the opposition's values are outweighed by its own, and can therefore be totally ignored, they can easily depict opponents as devil figures and supporters as saints. One's own grounds become the sole values; therefore, any means are justified to secure those ends. (Condit 160; emphasis in original)

Jimmy's embodied discourse falls between rhetoric and direct action. At times, his "performances" include physical acts such as impeding patients, hitting volunteer escorts, and trespassing on clinic property to confront doctors and staff. As Jimmy behaves more disruptively, other sidewalk counselors also escalate. Since Jimmy's arrival in Milwaukee, there has been an overall increase in the intensity of "counseling," the noise level of protesters, and the number of contacts between protesters and police.

As of this writing, Jimmy's behavior and the accompanying escalation are also becoming ritualized. The doctor costume has begun to appear on other veteran protesters, one of whom was arrested for brandishing a real knife. According to Jimmy, he is training local counselors in guerrilla theater so that he can be free to engage in his other activities. Rhetorical closure is also establishing itself as Jimmy's language becomes integrated into the speeches of local counselors. The iteration of this spectacle has thus resulted in the normalization of more violent rhetoric and the assimilation of more extreme forms of protest.

PLANNED PARENTHOOD:
ORATORY, AUDIENCE, AND THE WIDER COMMUNITY

Repetitive spectacle can also be used to draw attention to clinics, disseminating the rhetoric of sidewalk counseling to a wider than normal audience. Two Milwaukee area pastors, both affiliated with suburban antiabortion groups, have introduced repetitive oratory to the sidewalk counseling scene. This spectacle is unique in that the pastors bring with them ten to twenty people who serve as protesters and provide an audience for the sermons. Unlike pedestrians and passing cars, members of this audience are predisposed toward antiabortion activism. However, most are new to the sidewalk counseling environment; their experience of it is framed, shaped, and interpreted by the pastors' sermons.

These oratories combine television-style evangelism with medical descriptions from antiabortion texts; they are preached over microphones from a full-sized, portable podium. In their sermons, Pastors Dave and Dale paint visions of a cold, futuristic society centered on "the culture of death." The pastors' main focus, however, is on their role in exposing the agents of "murder." These include doctors, staff, escorts, and the patients themselves. Escorts and clinic workers who pass the podium are singled out as examples of "killers." Patients may also be "counseled" directly from the pulpit:

> How many [women] for three hundred dollars will turn their child over to a man whose sole purpose is to kill? He's been instructed in medicine not for the saving of lives but the taking of lives. The machine, in this place today, will go inside of this woman's uterus. This woman's baby, who's alive today—the heart's beating right now ma'am, the heart's beating! That device will go inside your womb and that beating heart, that child, that child that was made in the image of God, that child will be ripped limb from limb, that child will die today, that baby will die if you don't turn around right now. Turn around sir, and bring your wife out of there. Bring your girlfriend out! Save your child. (Videotape)

In this example, Pastor Dave makes a rhetorical shift, signaled by the use of the word "ma'am"—from the use of argument and persuasion to the repetitive language of counseling. While the first part of his speech locates culpability with the doctor ("trained not for the saving of lives but the taking of lives") and medical technology (in the form of "the machine"), the second half focuses on the entering couple. The course to redemptive action is for the man to seize headship, to "bring your wife out of there." This form of public "counseling" not only seems calculated to frighten and humiliate the patient, it serves also the additional function of drawing her to the attention of sidewalk counselors. During his speech, Pastor Dave pointed his finger at the couple, who were immediately surrounded by protesters and followed to the door.

Like Jimmy, Pastor Dave has also used physical means to dramatize the "abortion is murder" argument. In one instance, he brought four "aborted" fetuses to Affiliated Medical Services, where they were displayed in child-sized coffins outside the door. These "aborted babies" were then pointed out to patients as they entered the clinic. Such public displays function much like Jimmy's guerrilla theater, giving veteran protesters license to become increasingly loud and aggressive.

During the sermons, other counselors such as Drew use megaphones to shout at patients, who are called "harlots" and "murderers," and to denigrate their male partners, who are told they are "cowards" and not "real men." Drew also wears a green "life escort" vest—an attempt to mislead patients into thinking he is a member of the clinic's staff. Drew's vest attracts the attention of patients, whom he then approaches and "warns" about "what goes on inside." Similarly, Jimmy wears a green vest smeared with streaks of "blood." The inexperienced protesters also escalate by making louder and more aggressive counseling attempts. As a result, the sidewalk counseling scene grows increasingly crowded, noisy, and chaotic.

Because the pastors condone such escalation, the only check on protest behaviors comes from local police who make periodic arrests for disorderly conduct. The counselors and the pastors appear undeterred by these arrests, however. In the past year, the oratories have increased in frequency from once a month to almost every Saturday. Sermons and speakers have become regularized. Some members of this "congregation" have also begun to attend on a regular or semi-regular basis. Several members now have arrest records.

By providing an audience for their spectacles, Pastors Dave and Dale act as important points of connection between sidewalk counselors and the larger antiabortion movement in Milwaukee. In addition to drawing members of their groups and congregations to the clinics, the pastors make frequent appearances on VCY. They use these broadcasts to describe their experiences at the clinics and establish links between abortion and other reconstructionist issues such as homosexuality and birth control. Portraying counselors as heroes and abortion as a "holocaust," Pastors Dave and Dale frame and disseminate over-weighed rhetoric to a highly receptive audience. Stressing that clinic conflict is necessary, they contribute to escalation by urging their listeners to participate.

REPETITIVE VIOLENCE AND SIDEWALK COUNSELING

Like other antiabortion activities, antiabortion violence is repetitive. In the United States, clinic bombings have begun to occur regularly on or around the anniversary of the *Roe v. Wade* decision. In Canada and in New York State, shootings have been timed to coincide with Remembrance Day. Clinic violence also assumes predictable forms—bombing, shooting, arson, and acid attacks. Often, acts of clinic violence are not confined to a single event; they occur in clusters, either in the same city or at the same clinic. Assaults on a given clinic may also be spread out over a long period of time. For example, from 1977 to 1994, the Planned Parenthood clinic in St. Paul was hit 13 times by bombings or arson (Clarkson 139). In many cases, acts of clinic violence are also repetitive in nature. For instance, the Pensacola bombings included three clinics, all of which were bombed on Christmas day, 1984. As mentioned above, the Northside Family Planning clinic in Atlanta was hit by two bombs, which were followed by a double bombing in Tulsa. Individuals may also plan or commit repetitive acts of clinic violence. Prominent examples include Michael Bray who was convicted for conspiring to bomb seven women's clinics, sidewalk counselor Paul Hill, who fatally shot a doctor and his escort, wounding a second escort, and John Salvi, who opened fire at two Boston-area women's clinics and was on his way to a third when he was apprehended.[17]

Inasmuch as they are intended to "send a message" and are accompanied by written statements, bombings, shootings, and arsons are not only acts of destruction, they are also rhetorical acts. Letters such as those issued by the Army of God couch the violence as only one example of what antiabortion forces can or will do unless the law is changed. Large-scale acts of violence therefore differ from sidewalk counseling only to the degree to which they play out reconstructionist narratives of punishment. The underlying assumptions, goals, and rhetoric of the two activities are strikingly similar.

While antichoice leaders may participate in reconstructionist discourse, most are careful to distance themselves from individual acts of violence. Antiabortion leaders as well as the media often portray perpetrators of violence as lone "psychos" or "extremists," contrasting their actions with the "legal" and "peaceful" protests that take place outside local clinics. Most sidewalk counselors are also careful to distinguish their own activities from those of antiabortion "terrorists." At the same time, many continue to argue that such violence is justified if it "saves innocent lives." As Pastor Dave explained, the fact that most protesters do *not* engage in clinic violence is evidence of "remarkable restraint." Thus, sidewalk counselors may admit to sharing the rhetoric of clinic violence but deny direct involvement or institutional connections with its perpetrators.

In addition to sharing over-weighted rhetoric, sidewalk counseling and clinic violence both occupy the same symbolic space outside clinic doors. Within this space, the two interlock to establish a backdrop of "normal" conflict punctuated by acts of seemingly random violence. One example of this protest-violence pattern occurred in Milwaukee in January 1997. That month, the Summit Women's Health clinic experienced a rash of incidents that occurred without warning and was preceded by a long period of routine sidewalk counseling. The vandalism began with an attack by a "patient" who released pepper spray inside the waiting room. This was followed by a lockout, when clinic workers arrived to find superglue in the lock of the back door and a horseshoe bicycle lock around the handles of the front door. The final attack occurred on a day that the clinic was not normally open for procedures. Escorts arrived to find the foyer, doors, and facade of the building covered with large splotches of red enamel paint. None of the regular counselors were present, although Pastor Dave and accompanying protesters had assembled outside the clinic. These protesters expressed surprise, which was soon followed by approval. When police arrived to investigate, the group became angry. In effect, this incident took advantage of variations in the clinic's schedule to break the routine of sidewalk counseling and divert suspicion from regular protesters. No one was arrested for the action.

Following the incident, the clinic remained abnormally calm. Fewer counselors than usual appeared the following week. Within two weeks all had returned and resumed "normal" counseling activities. This period of calm seemed to constitute a cycle of readjustment, during which sidewalk counselors attempted to distance themselves from the action. In the week following the attack, only one protester mentioned it. Other counselors failed to mention either the paint itself or the symbolic significance of the "bloody" building. When questioned about the incident, Dan denied involvement. At the same time, he expressed his approval and attributed the action to "God." Thus, when counselors addressed the action at all, they treated it as a minor incident without threatening implications. None mentioned the fact that the vandalism at Summit coincided directly with the clinic bombings in Atlanta and Tulsa.

As this example illustrates, sidewalk counseling acts as a stabilizing force after acts of clinic violence, re-establishing the idea of "normal" clinic conflict in the public arena. To patients, however, the coercive underpinnings of sidewalk counseling become more evident in the wake of violence. The area outside clinics becomes more frightening as counselors' assertions that "abortion is murder" interact with media images of clinic bombings and shootings justified by the same argument. In the months following a nationally publicized incident of clinic violence, few of the patients seem to distinguish between the work of sidewalk counselors and the work of clinic terrorists. As a result, many think that counselors will shoot or otherwise harm them. Their visible fear evokes more aggressive counseling from local protesters. Despite efforts to distance the two, sidewalk protest and clinic violence help to enable, reinforce, and reconstruct one another.

DISCUSSION: OPENING CLOSED DISCOURSE

As its location outside the doors of clinics suggests, sidewalk counseling occupies a liminal discursive space, connecting moderate to militant members of the antiabortion movement and hovering between repetitive rhetoric and direct coercive action. Within this space, it is easy for moderate protesters to become radicalized and for radical protesters to escalate. Given the spiral of escalation in Milwaukee, what prevents the rhetoric of sidewalk counseling from developing into a large-scale act of clinic violence? We believe that one such check is consistent enforcement of existing legal restrictions on protest behavior. Although failure to enforce the permanent injunction has led to escalation, protesters have been checked when their disruption has reached levels that are covered under the criminal codes for disorderly conduct, assault, trespass, and violations of FACE.

Future research on the abortion issue could benefit from focusing on the social and rhetorical mechanisms that trigger violent acts. In particular, the role of sidewalk counseling needs to be investigated at further length. Such research is necessary to help determine the thresholds for major acts of violence and the likelihood of their occurrence in intensively picketed cities like Milwaukee. A more fundamental question concerns the disruption of discursively closed systems. Once a group has begun to use over-weighing and repetition, how can its discourse be reopened? Further, what is the status of closed discourse in a society that guarantees freedom of speech and religion but also seeks to protect its citizens?

Condit examines these questions when she writes that freedom of speech and religion become problematic "when a group seeks to influence the outside world but refuses to be open to persuasion itself." She suggests that "it may be important to insist that free speech is only possible when it is open speech, constituted by a two-way flow of ideas and argumentation" (163). Although such a "two-way flow of ideas" seems impossible to enforce through legal means, there may be a point at which closed discourse becomes identifiable as dangerous rhetoric. It could therefore become subject to laws such as those that control threats of violence. In any case, it seems likely that the relationship between violence and closed discourse could force a reconceptualization of what constitute speech and the freedom of speech. These are questions to be considered by legislators and judiciaries as well as by researchers of clinic violence.

NOTES

[1] For example, see Blanchard and Prewitt where they analyze the political and social context of a series of bombings that occurred in 1984 in Pensacola, Florida. See also Clarkson and Rizen and Thomas.

[2] For those focusing on the public debate, see also Railsback, Vanderford, and Tribe. For a discussion of leaflets, see Hopkins, Reicher, and Saleem who examine "post-abortion syndrome." For examinations of antiabortion photographs and films, see Newman, Petchesky and Condit (79-95). For themes

and motifs characterizing antiabortion discourse, see Lake and Solomon. For a discussion of antiabortion rhetoric as presented to a medical audience, see Reicher and Hopkins.

3 See also Muir and Petchesky ("Fetal Images").

4 We define clinic violence along a continuum ranging from aggressive physical contact with patients and volunteer escorts to shooting, bombing, and other activities that result in loss of life. In keeping with other investigators, we include vandalism in our definition, since it implies "the use of force against property" (Blanchard and Prewit 178).

5 For extended explanations of the theological, sociological, and personal motivations of antiabortion protesters, see Luker, Blanchard and Prewit, and Rizen and Thomas.

6 See Rizen and Thomas (113), for an example of Scheidler's use of this phrase. Scheidler seems to have used the term "pro-life mafia" on more than one occasion, and it is more than merely descriptive. Indeed, in the case of *N.O.W. et al. v. Scheidler et al.*, the U.S. Supreme Court unanimously ruled that Scheidler and his associates could be prosecuted under the Racketeer and Corrupt Organizations (RICO) Act, a law used to control organized crime. In April 1998, a federal jury found Scheidler, Operation Rescue, and the Pro-Life Action Network guilty under the act. The jury unanimously found that the defendants were part of a nationwide network and had committed more than 120 criminal acts, including physical violence and extortion. One of the plaintiffs was the Summit Women's Health Center in Milwaukee.

7 The injunction took effect in 1993 and covers all Milwaukee clinics. It prohibits sidewalk counseling by more than two people and states that counseling is to cease if the patient refuses or walks away. Protest activity is prohibited within 25 feet of clinic entrances, and people entering or leaving the clinics are not to be crowded or touched.

8 Petchesky has identified two "interlocking themes" in the neoconservative movement ("Antiabortion" 247). The first is opposition to sexual freedom, including abortion, and the second is opposition to social welfare, as signaled by cuts in entitlement programs. The U.S. Taxpayers Party is closely affiliated with the antiabortion movement; its platform advocates legislative reform along both these lines.

9 This use of the term "counseling" is inconsistent with its professional meaning, which implies a contractual, consensual, and confidential relationship. Professional counselors do not foist their services upon others, but rather advertise their services and wait to be sought out by potential clients. Because professional counselors must also be certified by national organizations, the use of this term by antiabortion activists is misleading. For a discussion of the invention and history of "sidewalk counseling," see Rizen and Thomas (112). We use the term "sidewalk counseling" only to distinguish

between this activity, which involves accosting patients, and other, less intrusive forms of protest, such as silent picketing and prayer.

[10] For in-depth discussion of the group's discursive closure, see Blanchard and Prewit. See also Condit (153-63).

[11] Although there is little evidence that these images are authentic, the "abortion is murder" and "fetus is a person" arguments have become so widely accepted that these photographs are rarely questioned.

[12] See Newman, Condit (79-95), and Petchesky ("Fetal Images").

[13] Quotations are transcribed from videotape taken as a part of this study during the summer of 1997.

[14] See Petchesky ("Fetal Images").

[15] The presence of counselors may act as a deterrent to some women, who see the protesters and decide not to leave their cars. These patients may return home, drive to another clinic, or reschedule their appointments. In general, then, counselors' techniques seem to work more as a form of intimidation than a form of persuasion. See also Condit (151).

[16] Despite the persistence of sidewalk counseling as an institution, individual counselors can and do burn out. Some leave the sidewalk counseling scene, only to return a few years later; others drop behind the scenes, working in less visible areas of the antiabortion movement or in other conservative groups.

[17] For further discussion, see Clarkson (139-61).

WORKS CITED

Blanchard, Dallas A., and Terry J. Prewit. *Religious Violence and Abortion: The Gideon Project*. Gainesville: UP of Florida, 1993.

Bragg, Rick. "2nd Atlanta Blast Was Aimed at Police and Rescue Crews." *New York Times* 18 Jan. 1997, 6.

Clarkson, Fredrick. *Eternal Hostility: The Struggle Between Theocracy and Democracy*. Monroe, ME: Common Courage P, 1997.

Condit, Celeste Michelle. *Decoding Abortion Rhetoric: Communicating Social Change*. Chicago: U of Illinois P, 1990.

Hopkins, Nick, Steve Reicher, and Jannat Saleem. "Constructing Women's Psychological Health in Anti-Abortion Rhetoric." *Sociological Review,* 44 (1966): 539-64.

Lake, Randall A. "Order and Disorder in Anti-Abortion Rhetoric: A Logological View." *Quarterly Journal of Speech,* 70 (1984): 425-43.

Luker, Kristen. *Abortion and the Politics of Motherhood*. Berkeley: U of California P, 1984.

Muir, Janette Kenner. "Hating For Life: Rhetorical Extremism and Abortion Clinic Violence." *Hate Speech*. Ed. R. K. Whillock and D. Slayden. Thousand Oaks, CA: Sage Publications, 1995.

National Abortion Federation (NAF). "Anti-Abortion Violence and Disruption, 1997: An Analysis of Trends." Unpublished Report. Washington, D.C., Dec. 1997.

Newman, Karen. *Fetal Positions: Individualism, Science, Visuality*. Stanford: Stanford UP, 1996.

Petchesky, Rosalind Pollack. "The Antiabortion Movement and the Rise of the New Right." *Abortion and Woman's Choice: The State, Sexuality, and Reproductive Freedom*. Rev. ed. Boston: Northeastern UP, 1990.

——. "Fetal Images: The Power of Visual Culture in the Politics of Reproduction." *Feminist Studies*, 13 (1987): 263-92.

Railsback, Celeste Condit. "The Contemporary American Abortion Controversy: Stages in the Argument." *Quarterly Journal of Speech*, 70: (1984) 410-24.

Reicher, Steve, and Nick Hopkins. "Seeking Influence Through Characterizing Self-Categories: An Analysis of Anti-Abortionist Rhetoric." *British Journal of Social Psychology*, 25 (1996): 297-311.

Rizen, James, and Judy L. Thomas. *Wrath of Angels: The American Abortion War*. New York: Basic Books, 1998.

Scheidler, Joseph M. *Closed: 99 Ways to Stop Abortion*. Westchester, IL: Crossway Books, 1985.

Sidewalk Counseling. http://www.webcom.com/sidewalk. 8 June 1998.

Solomon, Martha. "Redemptive Rhetoric: The Continuity Motif in the Rhetoric of Right to Life." *Central States Speech Journal*, 31 (1980): 52-62.

Tribe, Laurence H. *Abortion: The Clash of Absolutes*. New York: Norton, 1990.

Vanderford, Marsha L. "Vilification and Social Movements: A Case Study of Pro-Life and Pro-Choice Rhetoric." *Quarterly Journal of Speech*, 75 (1989): 166-82.

CHAPTER FOUR

Refined Raw:
The Symbolic Violence of Victim's Rights Reforms
by Jennifer K. Wood

The use of videotape evidence in the courtroom has come under a great deal of scrutiny lately, particularly following the acquittal of four Los Angeles police officers accused of beating Rodney King. As is popular knowledge by now, an all-white jury acquitted the police officers despite a videotape of the beating taken by George Holliday on his home video camera. As disturbing as the beating was, also disturbing was the fact that oral testimony during the trial transformed the images of Rodney King on the videotape from the victim of race-based police brutality into a raging, drug-crazed animal. Media critic John Fiske asserts that testimony during the trial "discursively filled [King's body] with drugs and alcohol" (135) and "repeatedly likened [King] to a bear—a neat analogy in which racism could be simultaneously denied and exploited" (141).

A few months following the King beating, a much less noticed event occurred which changed the rules of oral testimony in the courtroom. On June 27, 1991, the U.S. Supreme Court held in *Payne v. Tennessee* (501 U.S. 808) that victim impact testimony presented during the penalty phase of a capital murder trial does not violate the constitutional rights of defendants. This decision overturned the Court's two recent precedents on victim impact testimony, *Booth v. Maryland* in 1987 (482 U.S. 496) and *South Carolina v. Gathers* in 1989 (490 U.S. 805). In Booth, the Court reasoned that victim impact statements risked introducing "arbitrary evidence" about the victims' characteristics into a jury's death sentence decision.[1] According to the Court, death decisions reached arbitrarily violate the defendant's Eighth Amendment right not to be subjected to cruel and usual punishment.[2] In *Gathers*, the

Court extended this reasoning, declaring unconstitutional any statements made by the prosecutor about victim characteristics.[3]

However, just two years after it decided *Gathers*, the majority in *Payne* declared that the defendant's right to be treated as a unique individual when facing a death sentence must be balanced by the victim's right also to be presented as a unique individual to the jury. Indeed, the Court reasoned that during the sentencing phase of a capital trial, a jury facing a death determination could not reach a just sentence without taking characteristics of the victim into account because these characteristics are helpful, if not necessary, in gauging the damage done by the defendant.

As the Rehnquist Court continues to limit the rights of defendants in criminal trials, those concerned about the rights of the accused have been alarmed by the *Payne* decision. "The death sentence is still reserved 99 percent for poor blacks, especially if they kill whites," one public defender remarked. "[*Payne*] will make it even worse" (Sargeant 14). The chair of the American Trial Lawyers Association's Criminal Law Section expressed concern that the decision in *Payne* will increase the "burden on the defendant, who must correct errors like inflammatory testimony through appeals." (Sargeant 85).

Victims' rights advocates and lawmakers (who filed several *amici curiae* briefs in *Payne*, arguing that *Booth* and *Gathers* should be overturned) have heralded this decision for upholding the rights of victims in the courtroom. The Court's ruling in *Payne* should, however, alarm them as well. As antidefendant as the Court's decision is, it is also "antivictim." This paper explores why.

First, I situate this analysis within the context of narrative methodology as it has been applied by scholars of rhetoric, media, and law. Then, I introduce victim impact statements and review their use during the sentencing phase of criminal trials. Third, I analyze the discourse of "innocent victims" in the Court's ruling in *Payne v. Tennessee*. Next, I use Pierre Bourdieu's conception of "symbolic violence" to identify two new masks of state power the Court's decision in *Payne* puts into place. Finally, I examine the "anti-victim impact" of victim impact testimony.

NARRATIVE METHODOLOGY

In the analysis that follows, I attend to the majority opinion's use of a dominant narrative about "innocent victims" in *Payne v. Tennessee* to argue that the opinion restricts the kind of stories about victimization that can be told in legal settings. Although I am sympathetic to the claim that "narratives can create a bridge across gaps in experience and thereby elicit empathic understanding" (Minow 1688), in this analysis I examine the way the Court uses narrative to maintain rather than bridge those gaps. I agree with law professor Jane B. Baron that "stories can recall us to what is at stake in legal decision making, remind us of the human consequences of legal judgments, and teach us that we cannot escape from judging and responsibility" (74-75). However, my aim in this critique is to illustrate how, particularly within the constraints of legal decision-making, narratives can be used to highlight the stakes for some while minimizing or ignoring what is at stake for others. My concern, then, is to examine how the stories of some victims come to be regarded as important stories, worthy of telling in legal settings, while the stories about victimization told by others may be—at best—dismissed as unworthy of legal attention, or—at worst—may become evidence that some victims actually deserve their suffering. In this sense, narrative "is a tool that can be used either to perpetuate the status quo, or to challenge it in order to move the law forward" (Bandes 385). To understand how narratives can maintain rather than challenge the status quo requires an understanding of the role of moral reasoning in legal narratives.

Michael Calvin McGee and John S. Nelson argue for a "functional view of narrative conceived as a moment of argument intrinsic to reason and practiced especially, but not exclusively, in politics" (140). Further, they assert, "To pit a paradigm of narrativity against one of rationality is to repeat the error of the rationalists. What we need is to dispel the dichotomy: to understand and improve the place of narrative in rationality and of the reasoning in storytelling" (145-46). McGee and Nelson, in other words, call for examination of the logic of stories and of the stories inherent in logical reasoning.

W. Lance Bennett, a political scientist writing for communication scholars, examines the logical role narratives play in the courtroom. Bennett is quick to point out that the law privileges logic as the standard for making legal determinations (21). However, he adds, "in no case can 'empirical' standards alone produce a completely adequate judgment," because they fail to account for the context, or story, in which the evidence occurs (21). Moreover, Bennett asserts that "Although the overwhelming emphasis in courtroom procedures and legal discourse is on the determination of facts, it is clear that facts are inherently ambiguous in the absence of a story context" (323). According to Bennett, a legal fact remains indeterminate without narrative to contextualize it and supply its meaning.

James S. Ettema and Theodore L. Glasser also focus on the contextual work of narrative in their examination of the construction of innocence and guilt in Pulitzer Prize-winning newspaper stories. They argue that "innocence must be painstakingly *made real* through narrative" (260, emphasis in original). As they explain: "The moral force brought to bear through each of these [newspaper] reports is, in large measure, the result of skillfully crafted stories of victimization. These reports do not merely identify individuals who apparently have been wronged, but rather define them as victims who are innocent" (260). Ettema and Glasser conclude that the stories they study provide an embodiment and reaffirmation of what we commonly take to be innocence and guilt, but they do not provide a forum for examination of those commonsensical concepts. . . . Thus, although the reality of innocence and guilt in particular cases emerges from these stories, the meaning of innocence and guilt as moral terms submerges into them. (Ettema and Glasser 270)

As such, the stories they analyze invoke moral principles without the need for examining those principles; the principles themselves are assumed within the structure of the story form. In my analysis of the Court's ruling on victim impact statements, I examine the moral principles embedded in the dominant narrative of "innocent victims" that frames the Court's decision.

VICTIM IMPACT TESTIMONY

The Supreme Court's rulings on the constitutionality of victim impact statements (VIS) have dealt exclusively with their use during capital murder trials where a convicted defendant faces a possible death sentence. While courts routinely admit VIS during sentencing hearings in most states, there are important procedural distinctions between capital murder cases and other criminal cases that make analysis of VIS particularly crucial when it comes to death penalty cases. For example, in most states sentencing hearings for noncapital crimes occur before a judge, whose decision about the defendant's penalty usually must conform to sentencing guidelines (and in some cases mandatory minimum sentencing laws). In these instances, VIS generally serve as a formality rather than a basis for determining a convicted defendant's sentence. To illustrate, a study of the effect of victim participation in sentencing hearings suggests that victim impact statements may influence whether a convicted offender receives a prison sentence rather than probation (Erez and Tontodonato 467). However, "once a prison sentence is imposed, . . . the VIS does not significantly affect the length of a prison sentence" (468).

In a capital murder case, however, the jury that found the defendant guilty must also decide whether the defendant will receive a death sentence. Therefore, the stakes are very high, since testimony about the impact of the crime on victims and their relatives can determine whether a defendant lives or dies. The evidentiary rules governing the sentencing phase differ from those applied to the criminal trial. During the trial, the law limits evidence to that which demonstrates the defendant's guilt or innocence. During the sentencing hearing, however, evidentiary rules relax, especially for the defendant.

For capital murder cases, the Supreme Court has consistently held that, because the death penalty is absolute, virtually no limits can be placed on the defendant's presentation of mitigating factors to argue against a death sentence. In *McCleskey v. Kemp* (481 US 279 [1987]), the Court ruled that "States cannot limit the sentencer's consideration of any relevant circumstances that could cause it to decline to impose the death penalty" (306). Alternatively, until its decision in *Payne*, the Court restricted the kinds of aggravating factors prosecutors could present to a jury or judge making a death decision. Before *Payne*, the Court required that aggravating factors address the defendant's "personal responsibility and moral guilt" (*Edmund v. Florida* 458 U.S. 782, 801 [1982]) and that aggravating factors be limited specifically to the "character of the individual [defendant] and the circumstances of the crime" (*Zant v. Stephens* 462 U.S. 862, 879 [1983]). The Court's ruling in *Payne*, however, held that the defendant's right to be treated as a "unique individual" must be balanced by the victim's right also to be presented as a "unique individual" to the jury (*Payne* 825). Indeed, the Court reasoned that a jury making a death determination can come to terms with the defendant's blameworthiness only by full consideration of the victim's characteristics and the impact of the crime on the victim and her/his family (*Payne* 825).

The penalty phase of a criminal trial is the moment when the jury determines what the crime means by deciding the defendant's punishment. Therefore, it is crucial to understand not only who controls the meaning of the crime in this process, but also how meanings are made. As John Fiske asserts, "No truth can speak for itself in a court of law, it always has to be spoken: legal truth is always a product of discourse. Whose discourses are admittable then becomes a crucial question" (132). I turn now to present the facts of *Payne* and examine the discourse of innocent victims the Court's ruling admits.

THE FACTS OF *PAYNE V. TENNESSEE*

Pervis Tyrone Payne, a twenty-year-old borderline retarded black man, was convicted of stabbing to death Charisse Christopher, a twenty-eight-year-old white woman, and her two-year-old daughter, Lacie Jo. Payne was also convicted of assaulting with intent to murder Charisse's three-year-old son, Nicholas. During Payne's sentencing hearing, the prosecutor offered the following aggravating evidence: (1) oral testimony from Mary Zvolanek, the mother and grandmother of the murder victims; (2) two minutes of a videotape taken at the crime scene a little over an hour after discovery of the murders; and (3) the prosecutor's own statements about Nicholas, who had survived the attack by Payne.

The prosecutor called Mary Zvolanek to the stand to answer only one question: "how has the murder of Nicholas's mother and his sister affected [Nicholas]?" Zvolanek replied,

> He cries for his mom. He doesn't seem to understand why she doesn't come home. And he cries for his sister Lacie. He comes to me many times during the week and asks me, Grandmama, do you miss

my Lacie? And I tell yes [sic]. He says, I'm worried about my Lacie. (*State v. Payne* 791 SW 2d 10, 18 [Tenn. 1990])

Following her testimony, the prosecutor showed the jury[4] a videotape of the crime scene. If, as Ronell argues, "Television produces corpses that need not be mourned" (281), Zvolanek's statements and her physical presence as a witness reminded the jury that she and her surviving grandchild mourned the corpses the jury was about to see on a television monitor.

Although the judge indicated that the videotape would not have been admissible evidence during Payne's trial, he reasoned that Tennessee's death penalty statute required admitting it during the sentencing hearing.[5] The video, according to the appeal filed by Payne's attorneys before the Tennessee Supreme Court,

> included the bodies of the two dead victims. Charisse's hands and face revealed the effects of rigor mortis. . . . [T]he tape shows . . . a wide angle shot of Charisse and Lacie Christopher lying on the floor in a pool of blood; . . . a five second close-up of Charisse's blood soaked body with emphasis on the puncture marks in her clothing; a close up . . . of Lacie, emphasizing her eyes and puncture marks on her back. . . . Then it focuses back on Charisse with emphasis upon the effects of death (rigor mortis, swollen limbs, open mouth and eyes). Finally, the tape returns to Lacie, emphasizing the vivid contrast between the large knife and her small foot. (Lathram 8-9)

In showing the video to the jury, the prosecutor argued that it demonstrated Payne's "depravity." The prosecution also explained that, while the video was graphic and in color, it did not convey certain details of the crime as well as had a black and white photograph admitted during the trial.

> Some of the details especially in that picture—in that videotape, you can't see as well as in the black and white picture. For instance, Charisse's right hand all gnarled up in agony. And Lacie Jo's hand and Lacie Jo's eyes and the expression on her face some people refer to as the thousand yard stare because it's just sort of not focused. (Lathram 9-10)

After showing them the video, the prosecutor then argued that while there was nothing the jury could do for Charisse and Lacie Christopher or for the Zvolaneks:

> there is something that you can do for Nicholas. Somewhere down the road Nicholas is going to grow up, hopefully. He's going to want to know what happened. And he is going to know what happened to his baby sister and his mother. He is going to want to know what type

of justice was done. . . . With your verdict, you will provide the answer. (*State v. Payne* 18)

Finally, the prosecutor urged the jury to put themselves in the place of Nicholas Christopher, who had survived the attack:

> You saw the videotape this morning. You saw what Nicholas Christopher will carry in his mind forever. When you talk about cruel, when you talk about atrocious, and when you talk about heinous, that picture will always come to your mind, probably throughout the rest of your life. (*State v. Payne* 18)

The prosecutor placed the jury in the victim's position and urged them to take young Nicholas into account when determining Payne's sentence. He argued, in fact, that the jury should sentence Payne on Nicholas's behalf.

The jury sentenced Payne to death. Payne appealed his sentence to the Tennessee Supreme Court, arguing that Zvolanek's testimony, the videotape, and the prosecutor's statements about Nicholas amounted to a victim impact statement. According to *Booth and Gathers*, testimony about the impact of the crime on victims and their family members violated Payne's Eighth Amendment rights. However, the Tennessee Supreme Court denied Payne's appeal, finding that although the grandmother's statements were "technically irrelevant [they] did not create a constitutionally unacceptable risk of an arbitrary imposition of the death penalty, and [were] harmless beyond a reasonable doubt" (*State v. Payne* 18). Moreover, the Tennessee Supreme Court held that, contrary to *Booth and Gathers*, the prosecutor's statements were "relevant to [Payne's] personal responsibility and moral guilt . . . [because] the physical and mental condition of the boy [Payne] left for dead is surely relevant in determining [Payne's] 'blameworthiness'" (*State v. Payne* 19).

Payne's attorneys appealed his case to the U.S. Supreme Court, which voted 6-3 to grant *certiorari* (Justices Blackmun, Marshall, and Stevens dissenting).[6] Sounding the death-knell for *Booth and Gathers* in its decision to grant *certiorari*, the Court directed that "in addition to the questions presented by the petition, the parties are requested to brief and argue whether *Booth v. Maryland* . . . and *South Carolina v. Gathers* . . . should be overruled" (498 US 1076, *granting cert.* to 791 SW2d 10 [Tenn. 1990]). Referring to the brutality of the Christophers' murders, Berger points out that, in their zeal to overturn *Booth and Gathers*, the dissenting justices in those cases "fish[ed] in the *certiorari* pool . . . [and] hooked a petition from hell" (40).

ANALYSIS OF THE SUPREME COURT'S DECISION IN *PAYNE*

Chief Justice Rehnquist wrote the majority opinion in *Payne*, joined by Justices White, O'Connor, Scalia, Kennedy, and Souter. In a 6-3 ruling, the

Court overturned its precedents in *Booth* and *Gathers* and upheld Payne's death sentence.[7] The first part of the majority opinion relies upon Rehnquist's narrative of the crime as a rationale for the Court's decision to admit victim impact statements during the penalty phase of capital trials. In the second part of the opinion, Rehnquist makes his arguments regarding the doctrine of *stare decisis* ("adherence to what has been decided"; Segal and Spaeth 44) to rationalize the Court's decision to overturn *Booth* and *Gathers*. In *Payne*, the majority had to account not only for its ruling specifically in the case, but also for why it was so quickly overturning the precedents it had established in *Booth* and *Gathers*. In other words, the Court also had to explain why it was changing its mind.[8]

Rehnquist's majority opinion begins with a five-page review of the circumstances of Charisse and Lacie Jo Christopher's murders and Nicholas's assault. According to Robin West (1990), Rehnquist's opening crime story corresponds to the recent practice of the Court to frame its rulings on death penalty cases with a narrative of the crime. West contends that these narratives "have the effect . . . of pushing the reader to assign personal responsibility for the [crime] and its consequences . . . squarely and irrevocably on the defendant" (171).[9]

Rehnquist's majority opinion in *Payne* is, perhaps, a textbook illustration of the narrative process West describes. Beginning with Payne's convictions for the murders and assault, Rehnquist's opinion quickly moves to recount Charisse Christopher's "blood curdling scream" as reported by a neighbor; he then devotes three full paragraphs to describing in detail the Christophers' blood-drenched apartment and the massive extent of their wounds. We learn, for example, that Nicholas sustained several wounds "inflicted by a butcher knife that completely penetrated through his body from front to back" and that he required "a transfusion of 1,700 cc's of blood—400 to 500 cc's more than his estimated normal blood volume" (*Payne* 812). We also learn that,

> Charisse's body was found on the kitchen floor on her back, her legs fully extended. She had sustained 42 direct knife wounds and 42 defensive wounds on her arms and hands. The wounds were caused by 41 separate thrusts of a butcher knife. None of the 84 wounds inflicted by Payne were individually fatal; rather, the cause of death was most likely bleeding from all the wounds. (*Payne* 813)

"Lacie's body," Rehnquist explains, "was on the kitchen floor near her mother. She had suffered stab wounds to the chest, abdomen, back, and head. The murder weapon, a butcher knife, was found at her feet" (*Payne* 813).

The butchered victims' bodies begin, in their loud, bloody silence, to "speak" Payne's monstrous, individual transgressions for Rehnquist. He defines these transgressions through the vulnerability of the individual victims. Rehnquist tells us that the murdered mother sustained as many defensive wounds as she did direct stabs; she did not die without a fight. Lacie Jo's small, mangled body seems even smaller and more vulnerable since she is found lying next to her slain mother with the butcher knife tossed at her feet. The details of Rehnquist's crime narrative "speak" the innocence of the victims as they also shout the defendant's guilt. In other words, the details of the story suggest that the defendant's guilt is determined in part by the victims' innocence. Moreover, for Rehnquist, as for the prosecutor in this case, the survivor of the crime, three-year-old Nicholas, represents the vulnerable innocence of the victims in addition to providing a living memory of Payne's monstrosity, for the memory of Payne's brutality survives in Nicholas's innocence. Rehnquist, therefore, reasons that Nicholas's memories justify the kind of justice to be done.

Rehnquist's crime narrative, which depends upon representation of the Christophers' innocent victimization, also carefully offers a characterization of Payne as a drug-crazed animal. According to Rehnquist, on the day of the murders, Payne "passed the morning and early afternoon injecting cocaine and drinking beer." He also passed the afternoon driving "around the town with a friend . . . each of them taking turns reading a pornographic magazine" (*Payne* 812). When Payne was apprehended, Rehnquist, quoting the arresting officer, notes he had "a wild look about him. His pupils were contracted. He was foaming at the mouth, saliva" (*Payne* 813). Rehnquist's reliance on this image of the perpetrator as a rabid animal that is foaming at the mouth helps to justify the violence of Payne's death sentence while it also obscures that violence.

The majority opinion in *Payne*, like the prosecutor's arguments before the jury, hinges on contrasting little Nicholas to Pervis Payne, juxtaposing Nicholas's smallness and vulnerability to Payne's murderous and inhuman power. The smaller and more innocent the victim, the stronger and more guilty the defendant appears. As such, the state's power hides behind the injured weakness of little Nicholas. As one commentator notes, "The prosecutor in *Payne* urged the jury to make its decision 'for Nicholas.' The power of the state has been erased" (Harris 101). Also erased is the law's own violence inherent in death decisions.[10] Put differently, the Court's decision, as we will now consider, enacts the symbolic violence of victim impact statements.

THE SYMBOLIC VIOLENCE OF VICTIM IMPACT STATEMENTS

Pierre Bourdieu explains "symbolic violence" as "a power which presupposes recognition, that is, misrecognition of the violence that is exercised through it" (209). Symbolic violence is not the "rabid-dog" kind of violence that Payne was convicted of committing. Rather, it is misrecognized as legitimate and justifiable and therefore not recognized as violence at all. Often, symbolic violence is enacted through rituals, such as a criminal trial or the formalities through which the Supreme Court issues its rulings. As Bourdieu explains, "Symbolic violence, of which the realization par excellence is probably law, is a violence exercised . . . in formal terms, and paying due respect to forms" (84–85). Legal rituals themselves can legitimize the state's violence so that it is often misrecognized as something else, such as the state's obligation to protect its citizens. A jury reaches a death sentence, for example, only after a series of ritual events that distinguishes a sentence of death from an act of murder against a citizen. Moreover, symbolic violence "enables those who benefit most from the system to convince themselves of their own intrinsic worthiness, while preventing those who benefit least from grasping the basis of their own deprivation" (Thompson 25). According to Bourdieu, symbolic violence induces those who are dominated by it to comply with the domination: "*Intimidation*, a symbolic violence which is not aware of what it is (to the extent that it implies no *act of intimidation*) can only be exerted on a person predisposed . . . to feel it (51, emphasis in original)." Symbolic violence is effective precisely because those upon whom it acts feel intimidated and constrained by it without recognizing the intimidation and constraint as domination. Rather, in legal rituals especially, domination is often called "justice."

In addition, rituals of legitimization grant some the authority to act and to speak in the name of others, often while denying those others a legitimate voice. According to Bourdieu, this legitimization is a "sort of usurpatory ventriloquism, which consists in giving voice to those in whose name one is authorized to speak" (211). In his majority opinion in *Payne*, Rehnquist speaks on behalf of silenced victims of crime. Yet, he uses a particular conception of crime victims—a "commonsense" conception of victims as small, weak, and vulnerable. This "commonsense" representation of victimization can lead to two masks of the state's power in death sentence decisions. The first is that the victim's innocence conceals the state's power. The second, which depends upon the first, is a scale that balances the innocence of victims against the defendant's guilt. These masks, then, are the mechanisms for exerting symbolic violence.

A. The Symbolic Violence of the "Victim-as-State"

In arguing for the death sentence before the jury, the prosecutor in *Payne v. Tennessee* used the two-minute videotape of the crime scene to show the jurors the image that Nicholas "will carry in his mind forever" (*Payne* 815). Having seen the video images of Nicholas's dead mother and sister, their bloody bodies, their hands gnarled in agony and the "thousand yard stares" on their faces, the members of the jury, who will also carry these images in their minds forever, have no difficulty putting themselves in Nicholas's place. They have no trouble, in other words, standing in for Nicholas. Indeed, they not only sympathize with Nicholas, they empathize with him. As a result, the jurors come to represent young Nicholas in their deliberations. Like little Nicholas, the jurors have also seen these horrible images and will live with them for the rest of their lives.

In a criminal trial, however, the jury does not represent the victim. The jury is not charged with imposing the victim's justice; it is the state's justice that the jury must determine.[11] In fact, one Supreme Court justice[12] raised this concern when questioning Charles Burson, Tennessee's attorney general, during the oral arguments for *Payne*,

> QUESTION: What happened to the old-time theory that the crime was against the state and not the individual? . . . It's about gone, hasn't it? . . . This is the state of Tennessee. Right?
>
> MR. BURTON: With all due respect, I don't think the child was speaking for the state.
>
> QUESTION: Well then, the title says Tennessee v. so-and-so. So-and-so against Tennessee, doesn't it?
>
> MR. BURSON: Yes, sir.
>
> QUESTION: And it's a Tennessee problem. And it's not the child's problem. (Kurkland and Casper 824–25)

As Justice Stevens argued in his dissent in *Payne*, "The Constitution grants certain rights to the criminal defendant and imposes special limitations on the State designed to protect the individual from overreaching by the disproportionately powerful State" (*Payne* 860). However, in *Payne v. Tennessee*, the jury's decision to sentence Payne to death is one made from the position of the victim. All of the power that the state possesses—its power to arrest, try, convict, sentence, and, in capital murder cases, execute—is hidden behind Nicholas, whose mind the jury embodies. Hence, a powerful yet subtle switch has occurred: Payne is not sentenced to death for a crime against the state, which represents the interests of the community; he is sentenced to death for a crime against Nicholas, who begins to represent the state's interest in this case. We move, then, from a representation of the state's interest in punishing crime to a representation of the individual victim's interest in punishment. As one legal commentator argues, "With *Payne*, the Court has disinterred a primitive version of privatized justice . . . that . . . pits the defendant against the victim's family" (Bandes 407). This contest between victims and defendants paves the way for the second mask of symbolic violence that *Payne* puts into place: innocent victims versus guilty defendants.

B. Innocent Victims versus Guilty Defendants

The Supreme Court's ruling in *Payne v. Tennessee* alters the scales of justice. No longer is the adversarial criminal justice system one that balances Payne's rights against the state of Tennessee's power. The case effectively becomes *Nicholas Christopher v. Payne*. This new scale balances representations of the weakened power of the victim against representations of the enormous power of the defendant.

As we have seen, this new balancing act hides the state's power behind the victim's weakness. Just as troubling, however, it masks the defendant's weakened position in the criminal justice system. Indeed, this new scale of justice defies gravity. The weaker, more "innocent" the victim, the heavier the scales of justice weigh on the state's side, and the more powerful the defendant appears. The state in effect exploits the victim's weakness by using it to impose and legitimize the defendant's death sentence. Although the victim's weakness legitimizes the state's power to execute its citizens, rarely is the victim's weakness recognized as an alibi for the power of the state.

One reason for this misrecognition is that representations of the victim's weakness and the defendant's power often depend upon troubling race- and sex-based stereotypes. As Wriggins argues, "the kind of rape that has been treated most seriously throughout this nation's history has been the illegal forcible rape of a white woman by a Black man" (215). According to Fiske, this is an all-too-familiar story to white Americans: "Sexuality and race are inseparable in white American history, and each exerts a different form of power" (142).

We do not have to look very hard in the Supreme Court's opinion to find examples of race- and sex-based stereotypes used to signify the defendant's guilt and the victims' innocence. Rehnquist writes, "Sometime around 3 p.m., Payne . . . entered the Christopher's apartment, and began making sexual advances toward Charisse. Charisse resisted and Payne became violent" (*Payne* 812). In these two sentences, Rehnquist explains while he also condemns Payne's motivation for the crimes. In the story Rehnquist tells, Payne's horrifying and senseless slaughter of Charisse and Lacie Jo Christopher is the brutal act of a black man enraged because he was spurned by a white woman. In order to make sense of this senseless crime, Rehnquist relies upon long-held fears about how black men behave when white women resist their sexual overtures. As Randall Kennedy asserts, one justification for this country's history of lynching black men was the "belief that black men lusted after white women with such powerful longing that ordinary means of control were insufficient" (45). Rehnquist's opinion tacitly relies upon this rationale as well. As such, Rehnquist's "Narrative . . . ultimately validates the assignation of responsibility for the death[s] to the defendant, and by so doing, reestablishes, momentarily, order and meaning in a violently deconstructed world" (West 172).

Moreover, in his account of the circumstances of the crime, Rehnquist includes this description of Payne's arrest: "Payne was apprehended later that day hiding in the attic of the home of a former girlfriend. As he descended the stairs of the attic, he stated to the arresting officers, "Man, I ain't killed no woman" (*Payne* 813). Payne's voice, "Man, I ain't killed no woman,"[13] speaks his race for Rehnquist more clearly yet more subtly than any explicit reference to race could. "The courtroom," explains Fiske, "need[s] to keep race central but unspoken, to exploit its inerasable presence while apparently erasing it" (138).

In addition, Rehnquist tells us, "Three cans of malt liquor bearing Payne's fingerprints were found on a table near [Charisse Christopher's] body" (*Payne* 813). The "malt liquor" and earlier references to residues of cocaine found on Payne at the time of his arrest supply Payne's race in the opinion. These details, presented in the context of Payne's spurned sexual advances as well as the "evidence" that he passed the morning reading a pornographic magazine, inflate his blackness with sexuality; they paint a picture of Payne's depraved, sexualized black power. As Fiske explains in an analysis of the infamous "Willie Horton" campaign ad,

> The ad was widely understood as racist, yet, predictably, its verbal discourse never mentioned race at all: the camera, however, showed Horton's race clearly and had no need to show that of his victims—it could be justifiably confident that the white audience it addressed would align itself with them and supply their missing whiteness. (Fiske 143)

While the camera showed Horton's race to the white audience, leaving them to fill in his victims' whiteness, the prosecution in *Payne* relies on the videotape of Charisse and Lacie Jo Christopher's dead bodies as well as Mary Zvolanek's testimony to fill in the whiteness of Payne's victims. Zvolanek's testimony serves to transform the crime scene video, taken by a police officer, into what sounds like the "authentic voices" of the victims that speak their race and gender as surely as Payne's "Man, I ain't killed no woman" speaks his.

In his analysis of the verdict in the trial of the four Los Angeles police officers acquitted of beating Rodney King, media critic Bill Nichols argues the prosecution erred by assuming that George Holliday's "raw" videotape footage would "speak for itself":

> The videotape debate has been a major obfuscation so far. No image can *show* intent or motivation. Images, whether in real time, slow motion, or freeze frame, can, however, help corroborate a narrative account of what happened. . . . Mr. Holliday's videotape is raw

footage, the latent pearl in the oyster. It does not speak for itself. (Nichols 33, emphasis in original)

Nichols's "raw video" that can be "refined" by discourse (or by video techniques that rely upon certain discourses) corresponds along the lines of economic class to Fiske's "lowtech" and "hightech." "Lowtech," Fiske argues, whether

verbal or visual, is not the exclusive terrain of the weak, for the weak have no territory that is theirs alone, but it is the terrain upon which they can best contest the strong; hightech is more exclusively the terrain of the powerful, not least because hightech needs high capital. (Fiske 136)

The crime scene video shown to the jurors in *Payne* is an example of what Fiske calls "videohigh" (127). The state produced and edited it for evidence at the sentencing hearing. Zvolanek's testimony, however, prepares the jury to see what appears to be an "authentic" videolow: the silent, victimized "thousand yard stares" of Nicholas's murdered mother and baby sister. In this context, Zvolanek's testimony ensures that the crime scene video will not have to "speak for itself" because her testimony provides its meaning. Zvolanek's testimony, reinforced by the prosecutor's closing remarks, guarantees that the images on the video not only signify what Nicholas has lost because of Payne's brutality, but also indicates what Nicholas wants as a result of that loss: Nicholas, who wonders where his mother and baby sister are, "is going to grow up . . . [and will] want to know what type of justice was done" (Lathram 11). This rationale suggests that when he is a man, Nicholas will want to know that Payne's crimes against his mother and sister were properly avenged—that the state will do for Nicholas what he would if he were a man, not a boy.

In other contexts, in other crime stories, this rationale is not as easy to apply. For example, it would be difficult for a jury to rationalize a death sentence for a white man who resisted a black man's sexual advances by beating the black man to death, even if the murdered man's young son testified during the sentencing phase that he missed his father and wanted to be sure justice was done.[14] It is also unlikely that a jury would be tempted to sentence to death a white woman who murdered an African-American man because he refused to have sex with her, even if the man's daughter testified that she witnessed the crime and wanted the woman to be executed. It is even difficult to imagine that a jury would be persuaded to give a death sentence to a white man convicted of murdering a black woman because she resisted his sexual overtures, on the grounds that the murdered woman's young son would grow up to ask what type of justice had been done.[15]

Rehnquist's crime story, gathered from the prosecutor's arguments, the crime scene video, and the grandmother's testimony about the impact of the crime on Nicholas, depends upon a discourse that refines whiteness into what appears as raw victimization and constitutes whiteness as innocence and vulnerability. There are no black victims—feminine or masculine—in this story, of course, nor can there be. And *that* is a story we have heard before. It is, unfortunately, a story we hear all too often. Wriggins explains, "The selective acknowledgment of the existence and seriousness of the rape of white women by Black men has been accompanied by a denial of the rape of Black women that began in slavery and continues today (219)." In addition to denying the rape of black women, this discourse of victimization also minimizes black men's experiences as crime victims. As Harris asserts, "black defendants are consistently thought of as predators, and the extent to which they may be victims is lost" (96).

For example, in her analysis of the Bernhard Goetz case, Patricia Williams points out "the degree to which Goetz's [black] victims were relentlessly bestialized by the public and by the media in New York" (74). Conversely, Williams argues, "young, white urban professionals were mythologized, usually wrapped in the linguistic apparel of lambs or sheep, as the tender, toothsome prey. . . . The meaning of any act by the sheep against the wolves can never be seen as violent in its own right (74)." Just as Goetz's whiteness is refined into what appears as raw victimhood, the vulnerability of Goetz's black male victims is refined into what appears as the raw, animal power of offenders. This is also the same story defense attorneys for the four Los Angeles police officers accused of beating Rodney King used to refine police brutality into what appeared as an expression of fearful, raw victimization. This story, told to and believed by the jurors in this case, also transformed King from victim of brutality into a powerful—and guilty—animal.

When stereotypical race- and sex-based representations of "innocent victims" mask the state's power, these representations also obscure the defendant's weakened position in the criminal justice system. The defendant's weakened position is especially hidden from a jury that faces a determination of death. "The state," as Harris argues, "is not in danger of becoming the underdog in a capital murder case. The difficulty is not in getting the jury to see the humanity in the innocent victims, but the humanity in the killer" (101). This is not the only difficulty, however. Another problem is getting a jury to see the humanity of victims who do not fit the limited categories of victimization as well as Nicholas and his family do.

The Court's decision in *Payne* is clearly hostile to the rights of defendants in the criminal justice system. Less clear, but just as disturbing, is the Court's hostility to most crime victims. *Payne*, as we will now consider, is as "antivictim" as it is "antidefendant."

THE ANTIVICTIM IMPACT OF *PAYNE V. TENNESSEE*

With its decision in *Payne*, the Court risks instituting a narrow set of victim characteristics as evidence of victim impact in a courtroom. In *Payne v. Tennessee* the jury could easily stand in for Nicholas Christopher. As Justice O'Connor wrote in her concurring opinion for this case, "I do not doubt that the jurors were moved by [Mary Zvolanek's] testimony—who would not have been?" (*Payne* 832). The danger, however, is not only that the jury was moved by this testimony. Unless victims can tell a story similar to Nicholas's— unless they can fit themselves into the narrow constraints of victimization that these legal narratives impose—the criminal justice system will remain blind and deaf to their experiences as victims. Unfortunately, hypothetical examples are not necessary to press this point. During a House Judiciary Committee hearing on antigay violence, one witness testified about the murder of a gay man:

> According to the prosecution, the victim was brutally murdered with a sledgehammer by his assailant in Kalamazoo. According to one witness, the defendant was at a party covered with blood bragging about the fact he had kicked in some faggot's head.
>
> The long and short of it, is that the jury recessed, prayed for guidance and 45 minutes later came back with a verdict of not guilty. (U.S. House Subcommittee on Criminal Justice 31)

In this case, the jury's prayers did not lead them to empathize with this murder victim.

Judges' sentencing decisions also can be influenced by perceptions about the victim's worth. As one legal scholar illustrates, citing a trial judge's explanation for his lenient sentence of a man who had killed two gay people: "'I put prostitutes and gays at about the same level . . . and I'd be hard put to give somebody life for killing a prostitute'" (Berger 52-53).

What difference do assumptions about "innocent" victims make? What we know about violent crime in this country is that Nicholas, Lacie Jo, and Charisse Christopher are not very representative of crime victims. According to a 1997[16] U.S. Department of Justice report, males, blacks, Hispanics, the young, the poor, and inner city dwellers were the most vulnerable to violence (4-5). Further, FBI statistics indicate that 77% of murder victims are male, with the majority (28%) being under age twenty-three. In fact, "Individuals age 18-22 represent 15% of murder victims but only 7% of the U.S. population" (U.S. Department of Justice 3). In addition, a 1987 Justice Department report identified lesbians and gay men as "probably the most frequent victims of hate violence in this country" (Vaid 143). These victim characteristics, however, are not likely to be used as evidence of the victim's innocence. More often, they are used to suggest the victim's guilt.

The Court's decision in *Payne* reinforces a dominant narrative that is rife with assumptions about who qualifies as a legitimate victim, which can lead many victims of crime to devalue themselves and negate their experiences. Some, as many victims of sexual assault and harassment, domestic violence, and gay-bashing often do, may even blame themselves for their own victimization. Thus, the symbolic violence exercised through victim impact statements is particularly insidious because it not only can negate the physical violence many crime victims experience, but it also can lead victims of crime to hold themselves responsible for their own suffering. Unfortunately, this could result in countless (and uncountable) victims deciding not to speak precisely because their experiences are not recognized as legitimate forms of victimization. The irony of victim impact statements is that in the interest of giving victims a voice in the legal system in order to tell the stories of their suffering, many victims of crime may be silenced because their stories do not fit the dominant narrative of innocence that the Court's opinion imposes. The Court's reliance on a narrative of innocent victims that is race- and sex-based upholds gaps in understanding the experiences of victims rather than enabling actors in the legal system to offer narratives that can bridge those gaps.

This dominant narrative of "innocent" victimization also quells important debates about criminal justice policy in this country. Well-placed compassion for innocent victims like Nicholas and his family can silence concerns about policies enacted in their name. Vivian Berger, who appeared on ABC's *Nightline* to argue against the use of victim impact statements, provides a clear example of this:

> I felt uneasy contending with victims [who also appeared on *Nightline*] . . . mainly for psychological reasons: my empathy made me feel protective rather than intellectually aggressive. Even apart from such personal sentiments, one tends to pull one's punches for fear of seeming insensitive and, thereby, "turning off" the audience. (Berger 42 n.108)

Even as I conclude this analysis, I worry that I appear callous about the Christophers' suffering and the grief that their family members no doubt continue to endure. Yet, my hope is that this analysis may foster compassion and sensitivity for *all* victims of crime, not only people like the Christophers.

If the degree of the defendant's guilt is determined in part by a contest with the victim's innocence, those who harm "guilty" victims have very little to fear. When the legal system relies upon testimony about the victim's characteristics as a basis for determining whether an offender lives or dies, it further entrenches relations of power between races,[17] sexes, ages, sexualities, and economic classes. The discourse of "innocent victims" the Court uses in

Payne v. Tennessee may benefit some victims like Nicholas Christopher and his family. Unfortunately, it ignores most victims of violent crime by requiring them to establish their innocence—and their worth as human beings—on the basis of their characteristics.

NOTES

[1] During the penalty phase in Booth's trial for the murders of an elderly couple, a probation and parole agent read a report based upon her interviews with the murder victims' family members. The agent stated that the victims were "loving parents and grandparents. . . . Their funeral was the largest in the history of the Levinson Funeral Home. . . . [The victims] were extremely good people who wouldn't hurt a fly" (*Booth* 414-15). Justice Powell wrote in his majority opinion for the Court that "because of the nature of the information contained in a VIS, it creates an impermissible risk that the capital sentencing decision will be made in an arbitrary manner"(*Booth* 506).

[2] Beginning with the 1972 case of *Furman v. Georgia* (408 U.S. 238), the Court has maintained that death decisions reached arbitrarily constitute cruel and unusual punishment. *Furman* abolished the death penalty on the grounds that it was applied arbitrarily on the basis of the race of the defendants. In 1976, in *Gregg v. Georgia* (428 U.S. 153), the Court decided that the death penalty itself was not cruel and unusual, but would be if applied arbitrarily and capriciously. In 1987, in *McCleskey v. Kemp* (483 U.S. 776), the court rejected arguments that death penalty sentences in the state of Georgia were arbitrarily applied on the basis of the victim's race. The Court held in *McCleskey* that the defendant must prove the death sentence was applied arbitrarily in his/her particular case, not on the basis of aggregate data about death decisions. For an overview of the Supreme Court's rulings on the death penalty see Epstein and Kobylka.

[3] During Gathers's sentencing hearing, the prosecutor argued that the murder victim, Richard Haynes, was both a "religious person" and a "good citizen" because at the time of his death, he had in his possession several religious items and a voter registration card (*Gathers* 808). In his majority opinion for the Court, Justice Brennan stated, "While in this case it was the prosecutor rather than the victim's survivors who characterized the victim's personal qualities, the statement is indistinguishable in any relevant respect from that in *Booth*" (*Gathers* 811).

[4] According to the attorney who represented Payne at his trial, the jury consisted of six African Americans and six whites. He could not recollect the gender, age, or economic class composition of the jury (James Garts, telephone interview, 16 January 1998).

⁵ Tennessee Code Ann. § 39-2-203(c) provides: "In the sentencing proceeding, evidence may be presented as to any matter that the court deems relevant to the punishment and may include, but not be limited to . . . [a]ny such evidence which the court deems to have probative value regardless of its admissibility under the rules of evidence" (Lathram 7).

⁶ Although the Tennessee Supreme Court's ruling indicated disagreement with the Court's decisions in *Booth* and *Gathers*, as Stevens argued in his dissent to grant *certiorari*, the Tennessee Supreme Court's decision "rested . . . on the ground that any *Booth* violation that might have occurred was harmless beyond a reasonable doubt" (498 US 1076, *granting cert*. to 791 SW2d 10 [Tenn. 1990]).

⁷ Both *Booth* and *Gathers* had been decided by 5-4 majorities.

⁸ Rehnquist argued "*Stare decisis* is not an inexorable command" (*Payne* 828). He further asserted that "Considerations in favor of *stare decisis* are at their acme in cases involving property and contract rights, where reliance interests are involved" (*Payne* 828). Moreover, he explained, "*Booth* and *Gathers* were decided by the narrowest of margins, over spirited dissents challenging the basic underpinnings of those decisions . . . and have defied consistent application by lower courts" (*Payne* 829-30).

Rehnquist's arguments did not persuade Justice Marshall, who offered his own "spirited" dissent in *Payne*, the last opinion he wrote before he retired. "Neither the law nor the facts supporting *Booth* and *Gathers* underwent any change in the last four years. Only the personnel of this Court did," he opined (*Payne* 844). By the time *Payne* was decided, Powell, who wrote the majority opinion in *Booth*, retired and was replaced by Kennedy, who voted with the majority in *Payne*. Brennan, who authored the opinion in *Gathers*, retired and was replaced by Souter, who also voted with the majority in *Payne*. As Marshall points out, personnel changes are shaky grounds upon which to base a change in the Court's rulings. Justice Benjamin Cardozo, who was a proponent of relaxing the doctrine of *stare decisis*, nonetheless argues: "The situation would be intolerable if . . . changes in the composition of the court were accompanied by changes in its rulings" (150).

⁹ One might ask, especially given the horrifying way the Christophers were slain, who else but the convicted defendant could be held responsible for these crimes? West argues that we all need to be held responsible: "We need to learn once again to recognize [defendants] as human, as 'like us.' We need to be given a stake in their lives, and in the communities from which they come. We need to be made responsible" (174).

If defendants are not "like us," it makes little difference whether they live or die. It also makes little difference if their rights are not protected, since it may be difficult to recognize that "their" rights are "our" rights as well.

¹⁰ Also see Cover and Sarat for analysis of the violence of law.

[11] According to legal scholar Juan Cardenas, "Enlightenment thinkers, most notably Cesare Beccaria, advanced the notion that crime was not a private concern between the aggressor and the victim, but a societal concern" (369). Cardenas adds, "the American system of public prosecution [of criminal trials] was fairly well established by the time of the American Revolution. . . . Crime was to be addressed entirely in terms of an offense against the state" (371).

[12] The transcript does not indicate which justice pursued this line of questioning.

[13] This is an example of what Baugh calls "multiple negation," which, he notes, is often subject to "situational stigma," especially when used by African Americans (82-85).

[14] This is not necessarily a far-fetched scenario: Diana Christensen, Executive Director of the Community United Against Violence in San Francisco, testified during congressional hearings on antigay violence that "what has typically happened in [antigay violence] cases is that either the prosecution hasn't happened or they have put up a homosexual panic defense . . . where the defense suggests that the gay victim had come on to or made sexual advances, and the defendant freaked out and killed him as a result. Those defenses have also worked" (U.S. House Subcommittee on Criminal Justice 29).

[15] As the *amicus* brief filed by the Southern Christian Leadership Conference (SCLC) in the *Payne* case argued, "Only 17 of the first 143 executions that have taken place since *Gregg* were for murders of black people" (Kirkland and Casper 742). Further, according to the SCLC, in Georgia "the death penalty was sought in 48 percent of the cases involving murders of white females, but only 9.4 percent of the cases involving murders of black females" (744-45).

[16] This report provides crime data collected in 1996, the latest year for which statistics are available.

[17] There is some evidence to suggest that the race of the *victim*, according to a study by Baldus, may influence death sentences. Baldus found that "defendants charged with killing white persons received the death penalty in 11% of the cases, but defendants charged with killing blacks received the death penalty in only 1% of the cases." See *McCleskey v. Kemp* 483 U.S. 776.

WORKS CITED

Baugh, John. *Black Street Speech: Its History, Structure, and Survival*. Austin: U of Texas P, 1983.

Bandes, Susan. "Empathy, Narrative, and Victim Impact Statements." *University of Chicago Law Review* 63 (1996): 361-412.

Baron, Jane B. "Storytelling and Legal Legitimacy." *College Literature* 25.1 (1998): 63-76.

Bennett, W. Lance. "Storytelling in Criminal Trials: A Model of Social Judgment." *Quarterly Journal of Speech* 64 (1978): 1-22.

———. "Rhetorical Transformation of Evidence in Criminal Trials: Creating Grounds for Legal Judgment." *Quarterly Journal of Speech* 65 (1979): 311-23.

Berger, Vivian. "*Payne* and Suffering—-A Personal Reflection and a Victim-centered Critique." *Florida State University Law Review* 20 (1992): 21-65. [Quoting Lisa Belkin, "Texas Judge Eases Sentence for Kill of Two Homosexuals." *New York Times* 17 December 1988, 8.]

Bourdieu, Pierre. *In Other Words: Essays Towards a Reflexive Sociology*. Trans. Matthew Adamson. Stanford: Stanford UP, 1990.

———. *Language and Symbolic Power*. Trans. Gino Raymond and Matthew Adamson. Ed. John B. Thompson, Cambridge: Harvard UP, 1991.

Cardenas, Juan. "The Crime Victim in the Prosecutorial Process." *Harvard Journal of Law & Public Policy* 9 (1986): 357-98.

Cardozo, Benjamin N. *The Nature of the Judicial Process*. New Haven: Yale UP, 1921.

Cover, Robert. "Violence and the Word." *Narrative, Violence and the Law: The Essays of Robert Cover*. Ed. Martha Minow, Michel Ryan, and Austin Sarat. Ann Arbor: U of Michigan P, 1995.

Epstein, Lee, and Joseph F. Kobylka. *The Supreme Court and Legal Change: Abortion and the Death Penalty*. Chapel Hill: U of North Carolina P, 1992.

Erez, Edna, and Pamela Tontodonato. "The Effect of Victim Participation in Sentencing on Sentence Outcome." *Criminology* 28 (1990): 451-74.

Ettema, James S., and Theodore L. Glasser. "Narrative Form and Moral Force: Realization of Innocence and Guilt Through Investigative Journalism." *Methods of Rhetorical Criticism: A Twentieth-Century Perspective*. Ed. Bernard L. Brock, Robert L. Scott, and James W. Chesebro. 3rd ed. Detroit: Wayne State UP, 1989. [First published in *Journal of Communication* 38 (Summer 1988): 2-26].

Fiske, John. *Media Matters*. Minneapolis: U of Minnesota P, 1994.

Harris, Angela P. "The Jurisprudence of Victimhood." *The Supreme Court Review* 3 (1991): 77-102.

Kennedy, Randall. *Race, Crime, and the Law*. New York: Vintage, 1997.

Kurkland, Philip B., and Gerhard Casper, eds. *Landmark Briefs and Arguments of the Supreme Court of the United States: Constitutional Law, 1990 Term Supplement*. Vol. 202. Bethesda: U Publishers of America, 1992.

Lathram, J. Brooke. "Petition for a Writ of *Certiorari* to the Supreme Court of the State of Tennessee." *Pervis Tyrone Payne v. State of Tennessee*. No. 90-5721, 1990.

McGee, Michael Calvin, and John S. Nelson. "Narrative Reason in Public Argument." *Journal of Communication* (1985): 139-55.

Minow, Martha. "Words and the Door to the Land of Change: Law, Language, and Family Violence." *Vanderbilt Law Review* 43 (1990): 1665-699.

Nichols, Bill. *Blurred Boundaries: Questions of Meaning in Contemporary Culture*. Bloomington: Indiana UP, 1994.

Ronell, Avital. "Video/Television/Rodney King: Twelve Steps Beyond the Pleasure Principle." *Culture on the Brink*. Ed. Bender and Druckery. Seattle: Bay P, 1994.

Sarat, Austin. "Speaking of Death: Narratives of Violence in Capital Trials." *The Rhetoric of Law*. Ed. Austin Sarat and Thomas R. Kearns. Ann Arbor: The U of Michigan P, 1994.

Sargeant, Georgia. "Victim Impact Testimony Allowed by Supreme Court in Death Penalty Cases." *Trial*, October,1991, 11-12, 14, 85.

Segal, Jeffrey A., and Harold J. Spaeth. *The Supreme Court and the Attitudinal Model*. Cambridge: Cambridge UP, 1993.

Thompson, John B. Introduction. *Language and Symbolic Power*. By Pierre Bourdieu. Trans. Gino Raymond and Matthew Adamson. Cambridge: Harvard UP, 1991.

U.S. Department of Justice. Bureau of Justice Statistics. *Bulletin: Criminal Victimization 1996: Changes 1995-96 with Trends 1993-1996*. Washington, DC: GPO, 1997.

U.S. House. Subcommittee on Criminal Justice of the Committee on the Judiciary. *Hearing on Anti-Gay Violence*. 99th Cong., 2nd sess. Washington, DC: GPO, 1987.

Vaid, Urvashi. *Virtual Equality: The Mainstreaming of Gay and Lesbian Liberation*. New York: Anchor, 1995.

West, Robin. "Narrative, Responsibility and Death: A Comment on the Death Penalty Cases From the 1989 Term." *Maryland Journal of Contemporary Legal Issues* 1 (1990): 161-77.

Williams, Patricia. *The Alchemy of Race and Rights: Diary of a Law Professor*. Cambridge: Harvard UP, 1991.

Wriggins, Jennifer. "Rape, Racism, and the Law." *Rape and Society*. Ed. Patricia Searles and Ronald J. Berger. Boulder: Westview, 1995.

CHAPTER FIVE

> Posner on Legal Texts:
> Law, Literature (Economics), and
> "Welcome Harassment"
> by Frances J. Ranney

> The only exceptionable entry in this catalog is the question about unwelcomeness. "Welcome sexual harassment" is an oxymoron.
> Chief Judge Posner, for the majority
> in Carr v. Allison Gas Turbine Division

> The tinners' conduct, to the extent it may have constituted sexual harassment, was not unwelcome.
> Circuit Judge Coffey, dissenting

I begin with what I see as two important moments in the adjudication of a sexual harassment claim brought against General Motors. Mary Carr was the first and only female tinsmith at GM's Allison Gas Turbine Division. Her male coworkers frequently referred to her by obscene epithets such as "whore," "cunt," and "split tail"; they displayed sexually oriented signs and posters throughout the work area and sabotaged her equipment; and one exposed himself to her on two occasions (*Carr v. Allison Gas Turbine Division* 32 Fed. Rep. 3rd Ser. 1007 [7th Cir. 1994] 1009). Her complaints to supervisors were largely ignored, and she lost her claim at the trial court level because the court believed that she had "invited" the behavior both by her poor work record (she was frequently absent) and by her own use of vulgar language and occasional participation in some of the sexual jokes in the workplace (1010-11). Citing precedent in its own district, the trial court found the tinners' behavior was not "sexual harassment" as the term is legally defined. The case was reversed and remanded by the Seventh Circuit Court of Appeals when Chief Judge Richard Posner, writing for the majority, held that "harassment" is by definition "unwelcome." A strong dissent maintained, however, that "welcome harassment" was a legal reality created by precedent that the majority could not ignore.

I find the *Carr* decision puzzling on two accounts. First, Judge Posner, widely acknowledged as the founder of the law and economics school, has a well-known and frequently published faith in the ability of the market to regulate itself, with a concomitant reluctance to interfere with its activity. Why, then, did his court intervene on Mary Carr's behalf in the operation of General Motors? Second, as the strenuous dissent to the *Carr* opinion demonstrates, we can ignore or dismiss legal oxymorons only at our peril (Ranney 2). Given the strong dissent on this issue, how could Posner peremptorily dismiss "welcome harassment" without refuting the dissent's claim of precedent in his own district?

Of the many useful ways to approach such questions, I have chosen in this essay to use Posner's own theoretical work to examine his judicial practice. I rely on his economic theories of both rhetoric and sexuality to foreground the assumptions and values undergirding Posner's approach to the study of law. For a theory of rhetoric more specifically literary, I turn to Posner's scholarship in law and economics' rival school of legal study, the law and literature movement.

Two major approaches are characteristic of scholarship in law and literature. As Dunlop summarizes it, this scholarship tends to examine either law *in* literature (see for instance Claudia Johnson's study of *To Kill a Mockingbird*, or Daniel J. Kornstein, and Charles Spinosa's studies of "The Merchant of Venice") or law *as* literature (see Robert Weisberg and Ian Ward, among many others). Law *in* literature tends to examine how law, lawyers, or justice are represented in literary works in order to draw historical conclusions about law, explore contemporary legal or social problems, or stimulate discussion about the nature of law itself. Law *as* literature, however, focuses on legal, rather than literary, texts. This approach will sometimes apply literary analysis to such texts, or may discuss how properties such as metaphor, narrative, or interpretation, for instance, function in literary and legal contexts. Posner, like many other students of law and literature, engages in both types of analysis. Because my interest lies in interpreting judicial opinions, which Posner claims are the only legal texts appropriate for literary analysis ("A Relation Reargued" 1351), I focus here on law *as* literature.

There is considerable disagreement, even within the law and literature movement, about the contribution a literary approach to interpretation can or should make to legal interpretation. Therefore, a word of caution is in order here. What is important about Posner's literary theory is not the theory itself, which claims only limited value for law and literature study and which certainly is not typical of the movement in its insistence on an "eclectic New Critical" stance (*A Misunderstood Relation* 222-23). What *is* important about

Posner's theory is its author's stature as a judge and legal scholar. Even if one were to find Posner's theory "uninformed and slipshod," as Stanley Fish has characterized it, Posner himself must be taken quite seriously (310–11).

I begin with a discussion of Posner's economic theories of rhetoric and sexuality before providing a detailed description of what I consider the most important elements of Posner's "eclectic New Critical" theory. I deal very briefly with important criticisms of Posner by Robin West, a feminist legal and literary theorist, before moving to one of Posner's strongest critics, James Boyd White. Often credited as the founder of the law and literature movement, White offers a critique of the language and culture of economics as well as an alternative, though still New Critical, approach to reading legal texts.

Finally, I discuss the *Carr* majority opinion from the perspectives of both Posner and White. In so doing I depart from the method of most law and literature scholars, who tend to examine "great" or "classic" texts from the literary and legal canons. Shakespeare and Kafka receive a great deal of attention from law and literature theorists, as do Oliver Wendell Holmes and John Marshall. However, I am not concerned in this chapter with evaluating the style of what Posner would call "the masters"; instead, I hope to consider how a literary analysis can inform a reading both of *Carr*'s holding and of its dismissal of that legal oxymoron "welcome harassment." I find that Posner's somewhat limited literary theory explains his equally limited view of the oxymoron, while his economic perspective justifies the holding in *Carr*. Those conclusions are considerably aided, however, by the more rhetorically sophisticated literary approach of White. Ultimately, I conclude, law and literature has the most to contribute to our reading of legal texts when it provides the method whereby we may question how rhetorical authority is constructed in those texts.

THE POSNERIAN ECONOMICS OF RHETORIC AND SEXUALITY

To view human behavior from within the framework of economics, Posner explains, is to see human decisions as proceeding according to rational rules. Put into other terms, human beings generally make choices based upon their belief that those choices will accomplish goals that they also believe will be beneficial to them. The assumption behind the economic construal of rationality, then, is that humans will act in their own self-interest. Not all self-interest is "selfish," however; the economic model recognizes that an individual may indeed have altruistic goals. Nor are all goals monetary, but aesthetic, physical, or psychological as well.[1]

From among the many examples that Posner himself has provided, it is most useful for my purposes to draw an illustration from the economic theory of sexuality proposed in Posner's *Sex and Reason*. He begins by debunking what he sees as a commonplace in our culture, that sexuality belongs to the domain of the irrational (4). Instead, his economic model sees sexual activity as governed by a complex balancing of goals and the costs required to attain them in the existing market. For example, Posner contends that the high incidence of male homosexuality among otherwise heterosexual males in prisons may be fairly simply explained by the low opportunity for heterosexual partners. Given the small market of females and the heavy penalties, or costs, attached to acquiring them through such means as assault, smuggling, or escape, homosexual activity incurs comparatively low search and penalty costs while meeting the physical goal of sexual activity, albeit in a potentially less satisfying way (121). In the usual "supply and demand" construction, then, the demand for female sexual partners decreases with the size of the market as the price or penalty associated with acquiring them (through assault on a female prison guard, for instance) increases.

There are numerous possible objections to Posner's economic theory of sexuality, and many feminist theorists have responded to the opportunity it presents (see, for example, Bartlett, Nussbaum "Grey Matter," and West "Sex, Reason"). West, though she praises the contribution Posner makes to the interdisciplinary study of sex, finds that his economic theory ultimately demonstrates the incapacity of its own approach. The model's claim of moral "neutrality," she says, is in fact a deep moral apathy in its insistence on "valuing that which the strong members of a community . . . already value, and hence, designate as 'valuable' in the markets, conflicts, bargains, and transactions which they dominate" ("Sex, Reason" 2416).

To West's objections we may add that Posner conceives of sexual activity rather narrowly as referring to various forms of physical intercourse (vaginal, anal, oral) or activities intended to lead to such intercourse. He does not, then, construe sexual intimidation (including sexual harassment) as sexual "activity" *per se*. This omission of behaviors not strictly physical results from his restriction of the goals of sexual activity to procreation, physical pleasure, and sociability (*Sex and Reason* 111). That power over a sexual object could be a goal of sexual behaviors, even such coercive behaviors as rape, he specifically rejects. Sexual harassment, the "workplace counterpart of date rape," occurs in large part, he explains, because males simply have a difficult time understanding women's goals with respect to sexual activity, a difficulty which Posner identifies as a "search cost" (384, 391-92).

Further, whether we are speaking of sexuality or other areas of human behavior and decision-making, human beliefs can be faulty and their behaviors may be frequently self-destructive or greatly constrained (*Sex and Reason* 254). Our knowledge of our options and their consequences is uncertain, and our decisions—always subject to the contingencies of the communities in which we function—cannot be made as individualistically as the economic model assumes (White, *Justice* 63-4). Our decisions, even rational economic ones, are thus inescapably rhetorical. And though Posner recognizes the role that beliefs can play, and acknowledges that beliefs may be false, he pins the responsibility for this flaw in large part on rhetoric itself. Rhetoric, which Posner sees in the simplest terms as the function whereby one individual attempts to influence the goals or activities of another, is on that account an intrusion into an otherwise rational decision-making process. It also inflicts additional costs, since rhetoric can persuade us to believe a proposition which is false, or disbelieve one which is true (*Overcoming* 500, 529). Far from providing a method whereby individuals may negotiate the inherent uncertainty of their situations, rhetoric in this view actually *creates* uncertainty about propositions, which are viewed as inherently true or false.

Thus the economic model assumes that language is a communicative tool that can be used for good (scientifically, to represent truth) or for ill (rhetorically, to promote either truth or untruth, depending upon the goal of its user). In White's view, this instrumental understanding of language, which assumes that it can be a transparent medium, is a deep commitment of the economic view of life (*Justice* 48). Not surprisingly, it is also the most basic assumption of Posner's more "literary" theory of rhetoric, to which I now turn.

ELIDING THE PROCESS: POSNER'S LITERARY THEORY

Posner outlined the major premises of his approach to law and literature in a 1986 article, "Law and Literature: A Relation Reargued." Though he has refined some of his assumptions since that time, his conclusions—that lawyers *qua* lawyers generally have little to contribute to literary theory, which itself has little to contribute to the understanding of most legal texts—have remained largely the same ("Reargued" 1355, 1361). If anything, they have solidified, as the title of his 1988 book-length work (*Law and Literature: A Misunderstood Relation*) underscores. Therefore, throughout the summary that follows, I will refer to his 1988 work unless otherwise noted.

Posner's literary theory rests on a rather simple taxonomy of texts and approaches to reading them.[2] Texts themselves may be either literary (which he also designates as "rhetorical") or nonliterary ("nonrhetorical"). Nonliterary texts should, in Posner's system, be read "intentionally," meaning the reader is obliged to discern the author's intent in writing the text (and the author is obliged to use language in such a way as to make that intent as apparent as possible). Literary texts, however, are exempt from intentional readings. Here the author's intent is generally irrelevant and often of little utility; such texts should be read primarily for the experience they offer the reader. Posner calls such a reading "New Critical." Most legal texts, according to Posner, fall into the "nonliterary" category (he mentions specifically statutes, constitutions, and contracts). Their nature as directives, he says, requires them to "open a channel to the mind of the author" (221); confronted with "commands," the reader's task is to figure out what the author intended. Authorial intention, of course, may well be problematic in such texts; it may be imperfectly represented through the author's language or, since many statutes and constitutions are jointly written by multiple authors, a text may have multiple and conflicting intentions. The well-written nonliterary text, then, must employ a style that will minimize "noise," or interference, in the transmission of information from writers to readers (212). The "tool" of language must, in other words, work quietly and invisibly.

One legal text, however, falls into Posner's literary category—the judicial opinion. As a literary and hence (in Posner's system) rhetorical text, the opinion becomes exempt from the requirement that its author make his or her intention apparent to the reader. In fact, Posner claims, the intent of the author of a literary text is not only of little importance but even of very little interest, since creative writers have only limited insight into their own work ("Reargued" 1366-67). This is so, Posner claims, because much—if not most—of literary composition takes place unconsciously (231). The author's conscious intention, what Posner calls sometimes the "message," sometimes the "paraphrasable content" of the work, cannot convey the work's "meaning." What makes a literary work distinct and constitutes the only meaning that matters, he says, is the style embodied in the words on the page (what we could call "black letter literature").[3]

We might well question whether Posner really intended such pronouncements to apply to judicial opinions, which create our common law system. That he intends to do so is clear, however, from his analysis of several "classic" judicial opinions written by Supreme Court Justice Oliver Wendell Holmes. In *Buck v. Bell*, Posner tells us, Holmes held that a reputedly mentally incompetent woman could be sterilized against her will, concluding, famously, that "three generations of imbeciles are enough." This, says Posner,

> is beautiful prose—vivid, passionate, topped off by a brilliant aphorism—but it is dubious legal reasoning . . . . *Buck v. Bell* would be a poorly reasoned, brutal, and even vicious opinion even if Carrie Buck really had been an imbecile; but it is a first-class piece of rhetoric. (288-289)

A lengthier analysis of Holmes's dissent in *Lochner v. New York* similarly reflects Posner's criteria for "literary" texts. Here Posner notes Holmes's deceptive use of the "plain" style; the calm assurance with which he states his unsupported opinions and which substitutes for logical proof; his unfair metonymic use of Herbert Spencer's *Social Statics* as representative of the philosophy of laissez-faire economics; and so on (285). He concludes:

> [The dissent] is not logically organized, does not join issue sharply with the majority, is not scrupulous in its treatment of the majority opinion or of precedent, is not thoroughly researched, does not

exploit the factual record, and is highly unfair to poor old Herbert Spencer . . . . It is not, in short, a "good" judicial opinion. It is merely the greatest judicial opinion of the last hundred years . . . . It is a rhetorical masterpiece, and evidently rhetoric counts in law. (285-286)

Clearly, Posner is serious when he tells us that we could understand judicial opinions better if scholars would just stop trying to equate good rhetoric with goodness (289). Rhetoric, he says, is simply style ("Reargued" 1376). Though there is a tendency in current scholarship on rhetoric and law to understand rhetoric more broadly as a mode of reasoning with ethical implications, such a tendency is out of place in discussions of literature (and, by the implications of his theory, "literary" texts such as judicial opinions) because style and content "coalesce" in such texts (271-72). This unity of style and content does not mean, however, that style becomes epistemic. Instead content becomes affective, a text's meaning being a function of its reception by a reader influenced by its rhetoric, defined as the "eloquent or effective use of language" (271). Recent attempts by scholars to make of rhetoric anything grander than style have, says Posner, only retarded the application of literary insights to the study of judicial opinions (290).

Rhetoric or style is thus important in law because legal disagreements frequently cannot be resolved through resort to logical or empirical proof (286). Holmes's rhetoric, like anyone else's, can therefore only be evaluated on the basis of its success or failure leading to its desired result. A more exhaustive reasoning method in *Lochner*, Posner says, would only have diminished the dissent's rhetorical force. Because the issue was a difficult one to reason through, and despite Posner's disagreement with its conclusion, he endorses *Lochner*'s "not wholly creditable" rhetoric as an effective persuasive strategy (288). Whether this strategy is ethical as well as effective is a question that, for Posner, cannot be asked within a "rhetorical" analysis.

Posner's system has serious consequences for both the production and evaluation of judicial rhetoric. Paired with his separation of rhetoric from both knowledge and "truth," Posner's classification of judicial opinions alone among legal texts as "rhetorical" exempts judges from the requirement to make their intentions apparent to their readers and frees them to aim only for effect—in this case, perhaps, to aim only to persuade through whatever means are available. While Posner acknowledges that his view of judicial reasoning may seem "not only 'realistic' but cynical" (287), it is worse than either. His classification of judicial opinions as rhetorical, given his belief that we may read rhetorical texts without searching for authorial intention, denies the authority of judge-made case law. For though Posner acknowledges that prior judicial cases are to the lawyer what data are to the natural scientist, he finds it "a shame that the lawyer's and the judge's database is so often limited to judicial opinions," and argues against confusing "a rhetoric of continuity with a moral obligation to adhere to precedent" (*Overcoming Law* 522-23).

Secure in the knowledge that their "literary" texts are immune from political or ethical evaluation by their readers, judges may use any means to reach conclusions in their texts while eliding the processes by which they were reached from those who read them. In fact, the elision of the reasoning process figures prominently in Posner's evaluation of rhetorical effectiveness, a factor apparent in his criticism of a Cardozo opinion whose rhetoric "fails" because it calls attention to itself (294). Though he concedes that rhetoric can make a serious contribution to reflective thought (299), such a concession is of questionable sincerity if the goal of rhetoric is to persuade invisibly and "obliquely" (274)—surely only the most able readers will be prepared to accept such an invitation to "think hard about important though not fully argued propositions" (298). In the face of such assumptions, Posner's claim (deceptively stated with calm assurance) that Holmes's style in the *Lochner* dissent "invite[s] reflection on the profoundest issues of legal process" (287) is, to say the least, unconvincing.

The contribution of literature to understanding legal texts under Posner's system is thus meager, indeed—what White has called "a very small mouse from a very big mountain" ("What Can a Lawyer Learn" 2032). All that remains in this scheme as the uniquely "literary" contribution one can make to criticizing the judicial opinion is the ability to "understand and improve" the text itself. By "understanding," Posner means knowing what is in the rhetorical bag of tricks; he acknowledges, however, that such insight is of limited value, since it "does not enable the ordinary person to emulate the masters," that is, to improve ("Reargued" 1387). However, Posner contends, realizing that "the importance, one might even say the meaning, of the *Lochner* dissent lies almost entirely in how it says, rather than in what it says . . . . Judges and law clerks might pay more attention to the style of their opinions" (297). The primary contribution of literary criticism should be to make judges "more cautious, more self conscious, more tentative about the process of interpreting legal texts"—in short, to make them "close readers" (260). However, because judges and literary critics read different texts, Posner believes the methods of literary analysis are "promising" only for purposes of analyzing the style of judicial opinions rather than their content. Granting that distinguishing between style and content (or "form" and "meaning") is artificial in the case of literary writing, Posner proceeds to distinguish them for purposes of analysis, maintaining that the meaning of a literary work cannot be exhausted in its "paraphrasable content" but resides in the manner of its expression. A literary analysis of judicial opinions should thus be restricted to the manner in which the opinion is crafted and restrained from evaluating its conclusions of law. Maintaining that understanding the holdings of judicial opinions is rarely problematic, Posner concludes that "the interpretive problem is just not very important" (269).

It is tempting to rest my case here. But Posner's analysis of judicial opinions, though idiosyncratic, inconsistent, and occasionally inexplicable, is not entirely without insight, as we will find when we use his method to "understand" *Carr*. But before testing Posner's method, I turn to James Boyd White's extensive criticism of it, a critique that can expand the Posnerian insights considerably.

JUSTICE AS TRANSLATION: JAMES BOYD WHITE

White prefers to characterize legal discourse as translation, which he defines as "making texts in response to others while recognizing the impossibility of full comprehension or reproduction." Such a view, White claims, provides "a set of practices that can serve as an ethical and political model for the law and, beyond it, as a standard of justice" (*Justice* 258). In White's sense, the judge who reads statutes, legal briefs, and prior judicial decisions synthesizes and responds to those texts in the process of producing another, the judicial opinion. That opinion can then be evaluated ethically based on its fidelity to the original texts, the extent to which it reflects "the competing voices and languages that define the case before it (including those that it ultimately disregards or silences)." By this method the opinion may "expose the ground upon which its own result, its own achievement, can be qualified and criticized" (263).

Posner finds White's metaphor of translation to be of limited utility, of "rhetorical" rather than "analytical" use (*Overcoming Law* 496). A translation can be "good" either through strict adherence to the denotations of the text's words or through a looser commitment to its author's likely manner of expression in the language of translation. White's concept of "fidelity" therefore tells Posner only that writers must make choices between different ways of being faithful to the original text. It thus provides no guidance to judges or attorneys for deciding between strict or loose constructions in law (*Overcoming Law* 495). Similarly, Posner's view of rhetoric as "amoral"—as possessing no inherent moral or truth value and as likely to lead to false beliefs as to true ones (289, 298)—militates against White's claims for the ethical value of viewing justice as translation.

West has also criticized White, claiming that much of his analysis obscures the fact that law is an exercise of power (*Acts of Hope* 182). White has said that this attitude "greatly overstates the connection between law and power" (*Heracles' Bow* 238). Yet White and West agree in many respects. Both are strong advocates of the contribution that literary study can make to a legal education (White, "Can a Lawyer Learn?" 2028). Both recognize metaphor as central to literary method. As "the means by which we come to understand what was initially foreign," metaphor is essential to West's project of developing empathy (West, *Narrative* 259). White, pointing out that translation and metaphor both mean "to carry across," sees metaphor at the heart of the process whereby two texts and voices create their relationship (*Justice as Translation* 235-37).

In marked contrast to both West and White, Posner sees in legal metaphors a "compressed analogy" that allows judges and lawyers "to make things that are unlike in what might appear to be important respects . . . seem as alike as possible, so that an appearance of continuity of legal doctrine is maintained" (*Misunderstood Relation* 3). When a judge, for example, refers to pricing as "the central nervous system of the economy," the metaphor is "undisciplined and misleading," eliding the judge's reasoning process and contributing to obfuscation as it leads literal-minded lawyers to think about antitrust law in terms of inappropriate medical analogies (*Overcoming Law* 524; *Misunderstood Relation* 3). Metaphor thus construed inhibits, rather than enables, the empathic process that West and White consider essential to the production and evaluation of legal texts, at the same time that it contributes to the "success" of a rhetorical text in Posner's system.

As may be expected, White is sharply critical of Posner, seeing in his assessment of the law and literature movement an attempt to marginalize literary studies through a view of language both scientific and economic, "most unliterary in spirit." Economics is not, contrary to Posner's claim, the transparent language through which truth can be stated, and texts are not always propositional, authoritarian, and coercive ("Can a Lawyer Learn?" 2015-17). Because the language we learn to speak within our disciplines shapes our views rather than simply communicates them, our texts are better characterized as practices than as simple directives (*Justice as Translation* 48-51).

Somewhat surprisingly, White's view of literature resembles Posner's in several respects, though in each such respect he reaches markedly different conclusions. White would appear to agree, for example, that there are "right" understandings of texts that result from competent readings. For White, however, a competent reading will ultimately question the text in order "to see it for what it is" ("Can a Lawyer Learn?" 2020), while for Posner a competent reading must only "discover" what it means. White also appears to agree with Posner in his recognition that legal readers are subject to authoritative texts (2021). But where Posner's readers either receive more or less clearly stated instructions from "directive" texts, or are manipulated by the impressive style of "rhetorical" texts, White's legal readers create through translation another text that is a response to, not a duplicate of, the original text, whether it is directive or literary.

Finally, White identifies himself as a New Critic, but his New Criticism is far more eclectic than Posner's, which he criticizes as "caricatured" (2031 n50). In "The Judicial Opinion and the Poem" (*Heracles' Bow* 107-38), he tries to come to terms with the limits of New Criticism while also claiming its unique strengths. Foremost among those strengths, he says, is New Criticism's recognition that a literary work is an artifact, and thus a composition produced by an author who has made decisions about what it should say, and how, and what should be omitted. To understand a text as a composition, he claims, is to recognize the composer (including the judge who creates a judicial opinion) as a person in the process of making decisions that could be made in other ways. This view of texts as "forms of ethical and political action" unveils what Posner would keep under wraps—the productive process whereby the legal reasoner reaches conclusions of law. Posner's view of literary texts as "mere words," evidenced by what for White is his mistaken view of rhetoric, also misunderstands the power of words. Verbal power, "textual, not physical," is the most complete because it is ideological ("Can a Lawyer Learn?" 20-45). An ethical evaluation of literary texts, especially of judicial opinions, is thus not only possible, but imperative.

READING *CARR*: TWO LITERARY PERSPECTIVES

In this section I use the literary theories of Posner and White to analyze Posner's judicial opinion in *Carr*. I should emphasize that, my criticisms of Posner's literary and economic theories notwithstanding, I agree that the behavior of the tinners was unlawful sexual harassment. But I also contend, with White, that the holding of an opinion is "merely substantive" (*Heracles' Bow* 117-18); the ethical "meaning" of an opinion resides instead in its process—in *how* it says rather than in *what* it says, as Posner has also argued (*Misunderstood Relation* 297). In other words, though I agree with the holding in *Carr*, I cannot agree with its method.

In using Posner's literary theory to evaluate his opinion, however, I am immediately confronted with a procedural dilemma. Posner, you will recall, has specifically claimed that rhetoric consists purely of stylistic features applied to language, and that it creates not knowledge or truth, but belief. Yet despite his characterization of judicial opinions as literary (which for him means rhetorical) texts, Posner's literary analysis does evaluate their reasoning, and in a fairly sophisticated rhetorical manner. To avoid claiming more for his method than Posner himself would allow, I have chosen to imitate the analysis Posner himself conducts of opinions authored by Chief Justices Holmes, Marshall, Brandeis, and Cardozo. I therefore attempt to "understand" *Carr* by attending to its diction, the ethos it establishes, and its use of figurative language. I also focus on what Posner calls "arresting propositions," in order to comment on the opinion's reasoning process. In so doing I, like Posner, hope to demonstrate how an analysis limited to specifically stylistic concerns may nevertheless yield insights into the manner in which the opinion persuades, or attempts to persuade, its readers.

POSNER ON *CARR*: ELIDING REASONING THROUGH "RHETORIC"

I have chosen the excerpts from *Carr* appearing in Appendix A to include Posner's comments about unwelcomeness, particularly his declaration that "welcome sexual harassment" is an oxymoron. The excerpts also include a particularly artful passage that represents Posner's style at its best—what he might call its "most rhetorical."

I begin with diction and its contribution to the ethos of the opinion. Posner's vocabulary can be described as varied; he is careful to avoid the unconscious repetition of words that he criticizes in Brandeis (292). It is both intelligent (using words such as "exceptionable," "instigated," and "egregious"); and quaint (a female welder "fends off" offensive males, while a plaintiff's behavior is described as "deportment"). With the exception of the last paragraph, his style exhibits what he has described as Marshall's "voice of reason"—patient, systematic, and unpretentious (290). He does resort to the occasional "vogue word" abhorred by Younger, whose "Persuasive Writing" column in the *ABA Journal* exhibits the nostalgia for time-tested expression that Posner sees as the mark of classic literary writing (Younger 82; Posner, "Reargued" 1355; Posner, *Misunderstood Relation* 298). The description of the female welder "zapping" the males as she "fends" them off, though it may offend some sensibilities, presents an interesting juxtaposition.

As for ethos, we find that the tone is confident throughout. "Of course it was harassment," Posner says of the tinners' behavior. And "no reasonable person" could suppose that General Motors had done all it could to deal with Carr's complaints. Though he cites previous case law extensively for support of legal assertions (such as the definition of "welcomeness"), the refutations of the district court and conclusions of law are original enough that the dissent protests that the court has "seen fit to change the Circuit's law on harassment" by refusing to defer to precedent (10–15). In sum, the style seems similar to what Posner has called Justice Marshall's "voice of reason" (*Misunderstood Relation* 290).

Figurative language is sparse and, in these excerpts, confined primarily to the closing paragraph. GM is personified: it couldn't deal with sexual harassment problems even when they were "rubbed in its face." The personification of corporations, however, is not only a cultural commonplace but also a principle of U.S. law, which recognizes corporations as legal persons. This figure of speech is therefore less artful than conventional.[4] Similarly, the construction of the U.S. Navy as analogous to GM is a conventional move of legal reasoning. Though the Navy seems to serve in some sense as metonymic of all of corporate America, an example of what a corporation should be able to do, its use is again not strikingly figurative.

What *is* striking about this passage is not only its effective use of various schemes and tropes but also its deceptive reasoning. Posner says of GM:

> Its efforts at investigation were lackluster, its disciplinary efforts nonexistent, its remedial efforts perfunctory. The U.S. Navy has been able to integrate women into the crews of warships; General Motors should have been able to integrate one woman into a tinsmith shop. (1012)

The first sentence is stylistically artful, employing parallel structure, ellipsis of the verbs, and asyndeton in its rejection of conjunctions. Though it lacks climactic organization (the middle adjective, "nonexistent," is stronger than either "lackluster" or "perfunctory"; and "disciplinary" and "remedial" efforts seem lateral rather than escalating or sequential actions) the sentence is nevertheless effective and memorable. In the second sentence we see an effective antithesis, as the successful integration of (multiple) women into (mighty and complicated) warships is contrasted with the failure to integrate (one) woman into a (humble) tinsmith shop.

But note the implication that the Navy's integration of women into warships is a model of success. Here Posner uses the legal analogy in a sense that he himself has claimed is specifically nonliterary, yoking together not the "dramatically unlike" in order to produce an effect of vividness and novelty, but instead joining two entities that his readers are likely to accept as quite similar. The purpose of such an analogy, Posner has said, is to create an *appearance* of continuity in legal doctrine (*Misunderstood Relation* 3, my emphasis). This particular analogy encourages Posner's readers to ignore the Tailhook scandal first reported in the press beginning in 1992, two years before the date of the *Carr* opinion. It is hard to say whether Posner's use of the Navy as a paradigm represents hyperbole, irony, ignorance, or legal hairsplitting. (Are aircraft carriers "warships"? Does sexual harassment occur "in the Navy" if it occurs in a hotel but not on board ship?) Whichever it may be, the opinion will not by virtue of this passage violate Posner's standards for greatness if it is "effective" rhetoric—if it is persuasive despite its flaws and "survives" to be quoted throughout the ages. And indeed, the style of this passage, particularly artful, seems also to be particularly effective. Nussbaum refers to it specifically in noting its effective expression of "indignation in a tricolon of ascending condemnation" and "the parallel between the task faced (and accomplished) by the Navy and the task refused by GM" (*Poetic Justice* 1–10). *Carr*'s rhetoric, it appears, may have succeeded in blinding Nussbaum to one of the Navy's more flamboyant failures to integrate women into warships.

How, then, may we "understand and improve" *Carr*? Once having opened its bag of rhetorical tricks, we might simply suggest that Posner continue to polish his style. Despite its own limited claims, the Posnerian method can provide deeper insights. However, before discussing those insights I turn to White for a view of *Carr* as practice.

WHITE ON *CARR*: THE JUDICIAL OPINION AS ETHICAL ACTION

White understands texts as practices, or activities, a focus in which he differs greatly from Posner, whose literary theory views rhetoric as a method whereby a product may mask its creative process. Much of White's analysis is therefore ethically based, asking what relation a text's writer establishes with us, what character the writer seems to have, and what character the text assumes in its readers ("Can a Lawyer Learn?" 2038). Any analysis following White's method is therefore more abstract than the Posnerian analysis. Following White's method of evaluating William Howard Taft in *Justice As Translation*, I ask what texts Posner's opinion recognizes as authoritative and how it views the process of interpreting those texts. I then examine the values implied by the focus of the opinion to see how those values, in turn, define the relationships in the communities under examination, both the work environment at GM and the broader community of employer-employee relationships in general.

AUTHORITATIVE TEXTS AND THEIR INTERPRETATION.

The operative authoritative text in *Carr* is the Civil Rights Act of 1964, which made employment discrimination on the basis of sex an illegal practice. Yet Posner refers to the Act only once, in the first sentence of the decision, which states simply that Carr was bringing suit under that statute. *Carr* is not unusual among sexual harassment decisions in this regard (the dissent, in fact, *never* mentions the Civil Rights Act). Its failure to mention the Act may be due to the brevity of the relevant portion of the Act and to the lack of any explanation in its legislative history as to how the word "sex" was to be interpreted, because it was added at the last minute on the legislative floor. The failure of any opinion to devote itself to discussion of its authorizing texts is troubling, but Posner's literary theory provides a rationale for such an omission. Where a directive text is "inscrutable," he has maintained, the system allows for judicial discretion (*Misunderstood Relation* 248-49). Presumably the lack of legislative history renders the Civil Rights Act "inscrutable" in its application to sex; Posner does not, however, state specifically in *Carr* that he is exercising judicial discretion in refusing to discuss it.

Complex statutes are often clarified by regulations issued by the governing Federal agency, and the Equal Employment Opportunity Commission (EEOC) did issue interpretive language regarding sexual harassment in 1980 and again in 1993. However, that language was issued in the form of "guidelines" rather than as regulations, which makes their use by the courts merely optional. And while many, if not most, courts do refer to the guidelines, *Carr* never does. Instead, Posner grounds his five-page decision in twenty-seven prior judicial opinions. The ambiguity of the relevant statute and the lack of force of the interpretive language issued by the regulatory agency combine to offer Posner the option to ground his opinion primarily in texts that, you will recall, he considers both "rhetorical" and "nonauthoritative." *Carr*, then, exercises considerable interpretive freedom.

Under the terms of Posner's literary theory, judicial opinions are "literary" texts that we are to read without regard to the intention of their authors. *Carr*'s use of these texts as its primary authority means that Judge Posner is doubly released from the obligation to examine the "outside" texts (legislative histories, statutes, and regulatory guidelines) in which those prior opinions grounded their own findings. Because only limited interpretation can be applied to "rhetorical" texts in Posner's system, the judge as reader is free to limit his engagement with the text to its surface features. We can see this method at work as Posner determines whether *Carr* may be distinguished from an earlier Seventh Circuit decision because Carr "provoked" the tinsmiths' behavior rather than giving it an "enthusiastic" reception (10-11). The interpretive process has become what White calls authoritarian, requiring only that the judge engage in a literal reading of purportedly "plain English" ("Judicial Criticism" 400).

FOCUS, VALUES, AND RELATIONSHIPS.

Though *Carr* carefully describes the behavior of the tinsmiths, at times in nearly excruciating detail, the focus of the opinion is on Mary Carr's response to it. Thus it is Carr's behavior, and not the tinsmiths', that is put into question. Posner can make this move for a number of reasons. First, he is working from a text (the trial court decision) that has made the same move and thus to some extent authorizes that strategy. Second, the trial court has nearly conceded the point with respect to harassment, saying that "the tinners' conduct, to the extent it may have constituted sexual harassment, was not unwelcome" (qtd in *Carr* 1011). Third, EEOC guidelines specify that the intent of an accused harasser's behavior is irrelevant; combined with precedent, the guidelines thus place the burden of proof on the accuser (Radford 519).

Nevertheless, it is clear that *Carr*, to paraphrase White, has reached a conclusion that could have been reached in other ways. Posner, for example, says that "welcome harassment" is an oxymoron; he then proceeds to investigate one half of that oxymoron—the nature of "welcomeness," as defined by precedent—rather than investigating the other half—the nature of "harassment," as defined by the EEOC guidelines. As a result, the burden is on Carr to refute a judicial presumption that all behaviors are welcome unless proved otherwise (Radford 524). *Carr* could have reached a finding of sexual harassment by focusing on the inappropriateness of the tinsmiths' behavior rather than on Carr's response, but it chose not to do so. That choice was made possible by the decision's previous choice of textual authority—the judicial precedent that Posner feels free to modify as needed for current circumstances.

Carr focuses as well on the inadequacy of GM's response, which it sees as especially reprehensible in a large, presumably powerful, corporation faced with relatively powerless adversaries ("[w]e do not find the picture of mighty GM helpless in the face of the foul-mouthed tinsmiths remotely plausible") (*Carr* 1012). This effective contrast evinces a faith in the power of scale, organization, and success. A corporation the size of GM, in other words, should be able to control the behavior of workers who are economically dependent upon it. That GM's top-down sexual harassment policy failed is pinned on the failure of its agents (several layers of supervisors) to consult, understand, or communicate it (*Carr* 1012). There is no hint of a suspicion in *Carr* that such a policy might have failed strictly *because* it was conceived as an authoritarian gesture, that workers themselves should be consulted about appropriate or inappropriate workplace behaviors. Such an attitude, indeed, would be highly unusual.

The relationships envisioned in *Carr* are thus both hierarchical and predatory. Employers, we learn, must control their workers. Men, we find, will naturally prey to a greater or lesser extent on women, whose responsibility as prey is to avoid being taken. To do so they must send unambiguous signals to the males in the workforce; perhaps if they did so, men could avoid those extravagant "search costs."

CONCLUSION: *CARR* AS LAW AND ETHICAL PRACTICE

I now return to my opening questions: Why did Judge Posner intervene in the economic and sexual markets at GM by holding for the plaintiff, Mary Carr? Why did he dismiss the legal existence of "welcome harassment" over the protest of the dissent that it had been established by judicial precedent? And what can the literary methods of Posner and White contribute to answering these questions?

I have argued that we can understand Posner's "literary" theory of rhetoric only by also investigating his economic perspectives. The same is true of his holding for Carr against GM. Though, as Warren J. Samuels and Nicholas Mercuro have noted, Posner rarely discusses his economic theories explicitly in his judicial opinions, those theories frequently support his reasoning ("Wealth Maximization" 110). It is thus to the market that I now return, the sexual market, that is, created by the interactions of Carr and the tinsmiths in GM's gas turbine division.

Posner's respect for the market and its self-regulating, wealth-maximizing operation would normally mean that he would not interfere in the balance of powers in the tinshop. However, intervention is permitted in Posner's view when the market is not functioning properly—and sexual harassment is, also in Posner's view, a "market failure" (*Misunderstood Relation* 190). With the sexual market operating dysfunctionally, or inefficiently, worker productivity had decreased (Carr, you will recall, was often absent from work). Meanwhile, women who were less sensitive to harassment than was Carr (the female welder, for instance, who testified that she kept the tinners away by zapping them with her welding arc) had been granted an unfair competitive advantage. And GM, if we accept a claim Posner has made elsewhere, had been forced to pay higher wages than it would have otherwise in order to compensate its female employees for "the unpleasantness of the workplace" (*Misunderstood Relation* 190).

Though we might well wish to quibble with these assumptions, it is useful, if our goal is to evaluate Posner's position, to view the tinshop at GM metaphorically as a sexual marketplace. That market was experiencing a shortage of two commodities: power and women. The tinners were unable to exert much control over their work conditions and saw in Carr's presence the signs of a takeover by niggers [sic] and women (*Carr* 1010). Lacking power to prevent that "takeover," they then sought to exert control where they could—over one scarce and extremely visible female. The search costs were low, and the anticipated benefits high.

We can see Carr's response in economic terms as well. The high cost of working at GM (the constant abuse of the tinners) was not worth the benefits (financial or otherwise) that she received from her job. Put another way, she quit her job because GM just couldn't pay her enough. The market had failed, and Posner made the necessary adjustment by holding the highest level of authority responsible for the failure of its agents, using coercion to promote or simulate the outcome of a well-functioning market ("Wealth Maximization" 132). GM had incurred, and was required by *Carr* to pay, what Posner calls "agency costs" ("Free Choice" 14-41).

As for "welcome harassment," it is relatively easy to see, given Posner's view of rhetoric as stylistic persuasion leading to belief rather than to knowledge or truth, that he would consider this oxymoron to be a rhetorical device of little substantial importance to the case. His view of the role of judicial precedent is also relevant here, since he clearly sees prior judicial opinions as "nonauthoritative" and thus subject to revision. And his "eclectic" method, which allows the judge (or reader of any "literary" text) to decide which "outside" sources to bring to bear on the interpretation of a text also allows him to decide that those prior opinions are irrelevant or should be ignored.

If Posner had questioned the lineage of "welcome harassment," he would have found that the term was apparently created by one of those prior opinions, *Henson v. City of Dundee* (682 Fed Rep 2d Ser. 897 [1982]). The creation appears to have been inadvertent; the language of the opinion, purportedly summarizing the EEOC guidelines governing sexual harassment, changes the EEOC's "*un*welcome sexual *advances*" to "*un*welcome sexual *harassment* (EEOC 1604.11[a], *Henson* 903; my emphasis). The existence of the oxymoronic "welcome harassment" is then implied logically by the existence of its tautological cousin, "*un*welcome harassment." The fact that neither term is specifically authorized by the EEOC guidelines seems to have escaped the attention of over half of the Federal court districts, which quote the *Henson* language in their sexual harassment decisions without comment.

It is possible, of course, that Posner is well aware of the *Henson* amendment to the EEOC language and that he chooses to ignore it by using the oxymoron in the way he believes writers of "rhetorical" texts use all stylistic devices—as a substitute for reasoning. The unquestioned oxymoron is persuasive in this sense and allows Posner either to ignore a controversy he does not care about, or to avoid opening up a rather messy can of worms. Such an attitude may explain how *Carr* can almost casually reject the precedent that establishes "welcome harassment" as a legal concept. Though *Carr* cites the Supreme Court in *Meritor v. Vinson* (477 U.S. Sup. Ct. 57 [1986]) in order to ground its holding in judicial tradition, Posner's eclectic reading of *Meritor* allows him to ignore the precedent cited by the Supreme Court itself (*Henson* and the EEOC language). *Carr* can then represent itself, and see itself, as in keeping with precedent and not at all innovative in its rejection of "welcome harassment." Ironically presenting its departure from tradition as in line with that tradition, *Carr* limits its own authority and claims to be just one more accretion in the growing body of sexual harassment case law. The masking of the reasoning process means that *Carr* will go generally unnoticed, and its challenge of *Henson*'s redefinition of sexual harassment unremarked.[5]

We have already seen that White's literary method insists that judicial opinions reveal their reasoning processes as an element of ethical practice. But another element White sees as part of the judicial task, what he calls "comprehending contraries," can work against the ethical imperative in ways that we see at work in *Carr*'s refusal to discuss "welcome harassment." The judicial opinion, White contends, must represent and integrate the conflicts inherent in a legal dispute into a coherent whole that creates a new meaning by their conjunction. White, of course, is speaking of the opposing positions of the parties to a legal dispute. Yet we have seen how the integration of the legal definitions of welcomeness and harassment have worked in multiple judicial opinions to create a coherent whole—"welcome harassment"—that seems to defy logic. Such opinions have fallen prey to the danger White identifies in the process of comprehending those contraries, that "one will avoid substantive questions about the elements comprehended in the form . . . and focus only on the relation that it gives them" (*Heracles' Bow* 121). This, I think, is also the method employed in *Carr*, which characterizes the relationship between the elements as oxymoronic and thus logically impossible. Given *Carr*'s predilection for masking the reasoning process, the question, necessarily unanswerable, remains: Has Posner reached a "right" conclusion through a "not wholly creditable rhetorical strategy" as he said of Holmes in *Lochner*? Put another way, does Judge Posner see the situation as *Carr* does?

What, then, has a "literary" approach to reading *Carr* been able to tell us? Posner's method delivers more than it promises, its attention to style potentially uncovering the processes by which the judicial voice establishes its authority. Even this weak understanding of rhetoric, equated with the "literary," can lead to useful insights about the reasoning process that the opinion otherwise wishes to keep out of sight. But those insights are considerably expanded when rhetoric is viewed, as it is in White's system, as the method by which a community not only defines itself but conducts its practices—as verbal, hence ideological, power. The literary insights generated by White's method are thus most powerful when they are at their most "rhetorical"—that is, when they question the identities of readers and writers and focus on the joint creation of text within a localized framework.

Questioning the establishment of the judicial voice of authority in *Carr*—questioning Posner—allows us to see that the meaning created by *Carr* is very much an individual exercise, one from which Posner specifically excludes the reader through the effective use of rhetoric as he understands it. Rather than expose the grounds upon which he may legitimately refuse to consider "welcome harassment," a concept created by non-authoritative agency guidelines which he chooses to ignore, he dismisses it as an oxymoron—a rhetorical, hence literary, hence fictive device (*Overcoming Law* 527). Similarly, he does not feel obliged to reveal the economic grounds of his understanding of sexual behaviors but considers himself free to act in accordance with a wealth-maximizing principle that attempts to "make the economic pie as large as possible, irrespective of the relative size of the slices" ("Wealth Maximization" 132). In *Carr* maximizing wealth means adjusting the sexual market in the tinshop so that all the players—male tinners, Mary Carr, and GM—can receive slices of a pie made larger by the more efficient functioning of the workplace. It is consistent with his understanding of the market as optimally free-functioning that he takes the existing distribution of those slices as a given (134), a given that Samuels and Mercuro deplore. And it is consistent with Posner's view of effective rhetoric that the economic basis of the reasoning process underlying his decision in *Carr* remains, as in the 120 decisions that Samuels and Mercuro examine, "passively and relatively inconspicuously displayed" (110).

Even Posner's limited understanding of rhetoric as style can contribute to our understanding of judicial opinions if we accept not only that style and meaning are inseparable, as Posner contends, but also that rhetoric thus construed can lead to knowledge, an implication he denies despite the insights generated by his own method (*Overcoming Law* 528-29). That knowledge, of course, is our understanding of the process by which an opinion generates its conclusions and thus constructs the legal realities that White's theory recognizes as such. A rhetorically grounded literary theory—that is, one that attends to the voices and positions of writers and readers as they combine to create new meanings and realities—has much to offer readers of legal texts. Such a perspective reminds us that a text is a composition jointly constituted by locally situated writers speaking to locally situated readers. It was in much the same spirit that Justice Marshall, as both White and Posner remind us, exhorted the legal community to remember that "it is *a constitution* we are expounding" (qtd in Posner, *Misunderstood Relation* 291; White, *Heracles' Bow* 112). To paraphrase West (*Narrative* 254), we should not need literature to tell us that. But if we do, we should not hesitate to use it.

APPENDIX: EXCERPTS FROM *CARR V. ALLISON GAS TURBINE DIVISION*
[bracketed figures indicate page numbers]

[1008] . . . The district judge believed that in a case such as this in which the harassment is by coworkers rather than by supervisors, the principal questions to be answered are whether the plaintiff was in fact sexually harassed to a degree that could be said to affect adversely the conditions under which she worked, whether it was unwelcome harassment, and whether management knew or should have known about the harassment yet failed to take appropriate remedial action. The only exceptionable entry in this catalog is the question about unwelcomeness. "Welcome sexual harassment" is an oxymoron; if as we concluded in *Reed v. Shepard*, 939 F.2d 484, 486 87 (7th Cr. 1991), the employee demonstrates by word or deed that [1009] the "harassment" is welcome (the plaintiff in that case had instigated sexual pranks—for example, had given one of her male coworkers a softball warmer designed to resemble a scrotum), it is not harassment . . . .

[1010] So the behavior of Carr's coworkers was harassing, yet the district judge concluded that it was not actionable, because it had been "invited." "[S]he was not merely the recipient of crude behavior and crude language—she also dished it out." A female welder, who worked in proximity to the tinsmiths, considered Carr vulgar and unladylike, a "tramp," because she used the "F word" and told dirty jokes. This woman further testified that she herself had no trouble with the men in the shop—though occasionally she did have to zap them with her welding arc to fend them off. Carr indeed used such terms as "fuck head" and "dick head," once placed her hand on the thigh of a young male worker, and, when shown a pornographic picture and asked to point out the clitoris, obliged. Once when her tool bench was moved (apparently not with hostile intent), she got into a shouting match with her coworkers. General Motors' brief describes her as "vulgar, confrontational, profane, lazy and vindictive." The district judge said that "she contributed just as much abusive language and crude behavior as did the male [1011] tinners, and therefore was just as responsible for any hostile sexual environment that consequently arose." "[T]he tinners' conduct, to the extent it may have constituted sexual harassment, was not unwelcome."

Of course it was unwelcome. A plaintiff's words, deeds, and deportment can cast light on whether her coworkers' treatment of her was unwelcome and should have been perceived as such by them and their supervisors, *Meritor Savings Bank v. Vinson, supra,* 477 U.S. at 69, 106 S.Ct. at 2406-07, but we do not understand General Motors to be suggesting that Carr enjoyed or appeared to enjoy the campaign of harassment against her. In this regard the case is different from *Reed v. Shepard, supra,* on which General Motors relies, where the plaintiff had manifested "enthusiastic receptiveness to sexually suggestive jokes and activities." 939 F.2d at 491. Reed, a corrections officer, never complained about sexual harassment, and rather than resigning because the conditions of her employment became intolerable was fired for encouraging two inmates to beat a third. The district judge made no finding of "enthusiastic receptiveness" in the present case, and could not have done so, since Carr's violent resentment of the conduct of her male coworkers toward her is plain. What the judge found, rather, was that Carr had *provoked* the misconduct of her coworkers. Had she been ladylike, he thought, like the welder, they would have left her alone—maybe; for remember that the welder had to use her welding arc to protect herself, and Carr was not so equipped . . . .

[1012] It is difficult for an employer to sort out charges and countercharges of sexual harassment among feuding employees, but we are dealing here with a situation in which for years one of the nation's largest enterprises found itself helpless to respond effectively to an egregious campaign of sexual harassment directed at one woman. No reasonable person could imagine that General Motors was genuinely helpless, that it did all it reasonably could have done. The evidence is plain that it (or at least its gas turbine division) was unprepared to deal with problems of sexual harassment even when those problems were rubbed in its face, and also incapable of improvising a solution. Its efforts at investigation were lackluster, its disciplinary efforts nonexistent, its remedial efforts perfunctory. The U.S. Navy has been able to integrate women into the crews of warships; General Motors should have been able to integrate one woman into a tinsmith shop.

NOTES

[1] See Posner, *Sex and Reason* 85, 88, and 111-45 for a discussion of rationality in economic and sexual terms.

[2] See Posner "Law and Literature" for a discussion of this system.

[3] Legal educators often express dismay at law students' eagerness to learn "black letter" (practical) law rather than the more theoretical doctrinary subjects taught in law schools.

⁴ Nussbaum disagrees, finding in this figure an artful comparison of GM to "an incontinent dog" (*Poetic Justice* 110).

⁵ There has been, in fact, little notice taken of *Carr*, and none of the commentary I have read (other than the dissent to *Carr*) notices that its denial of "welcome harassment" is a significant deviation from precedent, or why (Gregory 379 n88; Nussbaum, "Poets as Judges 1503 n77).

WORKS CITED

Bartlett, Katharine T. "Rumpelstiltskin." *Connecticut Law Review* 25 (1993): 477-90.

Carr v. Allison Gas Turbine Division 32 Fed. Rep. 3rd Ser. 1007 (7th Cir. 1994).

Dunlop, C. R. B. "Literature Studies in Law Schools." *Cardozo Studies in Law and Literature* 3 (1991): 63-110.

Equal Employment Opportunity Commission. "Guidelines on Sexual Harassment." 29 *Code of Federal Regulations* 1604.11 (1980).

Fish, Stanley. *Doing What Comes Naturally: Change, Rhetoric, and the Practice of Theory in Literary and Legal Studies*. Durham: Duke UP, 1989.

Gregory, David L. "Sex discrimination: Continuing clarifications by the Second Circuit." *Brooklyn Law Review* 61 (1995): 363-95.

Henson v. City of Dundee 682 Fed. Rep. 2d Ser. 897 (11th Cir. 1982).

Johnson, Claudia. "Without Tradition and Within Reason: Judge Horton and Atticus Finch in Court." *Alabama Law Review* 45 (1994): 483-510.

Kornstein, Daniel J. "Fie Upon Your Law!" *Cardozo Studies in Law and Literature* 5 (1993): 35-56.

Meritor Savings Bank v. Vinson 477 U. S. 57 (Sup. Ct. 1986).

Nussbaum, Martha C. "Only Grey Matter? Richard Posner's Cost-Benefit Analysis of Sex." *University of Chicago Law Review* 59 (1992): 1689-1734.

———. *Poetic Justice: The Literary Imagination and Public Life*. Boston: Beacon Press, 1995.

———. "Poets as Judges: Judicial Rhetoric and the Literary Imagination." *University of Chicago Law Review* 62 (1995): 1477-1519.

Phelps, Teresa Godwin. "The Margins of Maycomb: A Rereading of *To Kill a Mockingbird*." *Alabama Law Review* 45 (1994): 511-30.

Posner, Richard A. "Wealth Maximization and Judicial Decision-Making." *International Review of Law and Economics* 4 (1984): 131-35.

———. "The Ethical Significance of Free Choice: A Reply to Professor West." *Harvard Law Review* 99 (1986): 1431-48.

———. "Law and Literature: A Relation Reargued." *Virginia Law Review* 72 (1986): 1351-92.

———. *Law and Literature: A Misunderstood Relation*. Cambridge: Harvard UP, 1988.

———. *Sex and Reason*. Cambridge: Harvard UP, 1992.
———. *Overcoming Law*. Cambridge: Harvard UP, 1995.
Radford, Michelle F. "By Invitation Only: The Proof of Welcomeness in Sexual Harassment Cases." *North Carolina Law Review* 72 (1994): 499-548.
Ranney, Frances J. "What's a Reasonable Woman to Do? The Judicial Rhetoric of Sexual Harassment." *NWSA Journal* 9.2 (1997): 1-22.
Samuels, Warren J., and Nicholas Mercuro. "Posnerian Law and Economics on the Bench." *International Review of Law and Economics* 4 (1984): 107-30.
Spinosa, Charles. "Shylock and Debt and Contract in *The Merchant of Venice*." *Cardozo Studies in Law and Literature* 5 (1993): 65-85.
Ward, Ian. *Law and Literature: Possibilities and Perspectives*. Cambridge: Cambridge UP, 1995.
Weisberg, Robert. "Reading *Poethics*." *Cardozo Law Review* 15 (1994): 1103-25.
West, Robin. *Narrative, Authority, and Law*. Ann Arbor: U of Michigan P, 1993.
———. "Sex, Reason, and a Taste for the Absurd." *Georgetown Law Journal* 81 (1993): 2413-56.
White, James Boyd. *Heracles' Bow: Essays on the Rhetoric and Poetics of the Law*. Madison: U of Wisconsin P, 1985.
———. "Judicial Criticism." *Interpreting Law and Literature: a Hermeneutic Reader*. Ed. Sanford Levinson. Evanston: Northwestern UP, 1988.
———. "What Can a Lawyer Learn from Literature?" *Harvard Law Review* 102 (1989): 2014-47.
———. *Justice as Translation: An Essay in Cultural and Legal Criticism*. Chicago: U of Chicago P, 1990.
———. *Acts of Hope: Creating Authority in Literature, Law, and Politics*. Chicago: U of Chicago P, 1994.
Younger, Irving. "Vogue Words are Choking Our Prose." *ABA Journal* (August 1986): 82-3.

CHAPTER SIX

"Passport Please":
Legal, Literary, and Critical Fictions of Identity
by Lesley Higgins and Marie-Christine Leps

THE UNIMAGINABLE MRS. SHIPLEY

(1) Everyone has the right to freedom of movement and residence within the borders of each State.
(2) Everyone has the right to leave any country including his own, and to return to his country.
United Nations Universal Declaration of Human Rights, 1948, Article 13

The right to travel is a part of the 'liberty' of which the citizen cannot be deprived without the due process of law under the Fifth Amendment. . . . Freedom of movement across frontiers in either direction, and inside frontiers as well, was a part of our heritage. Travel abroad, like travel within the country, may be necessary for a livelihood. It may be as close to the heart of the individual as the choice of what he eats, or wears, or reads. Freedom of movement is basic in our scheme of values.
Mr. Justice Douglas, delivering the U.S. Supreme Court's ruling in *Kent v. Dulles,* April 1958.

Every citizen of Canada has the right to enter, remain in and leave Canada.
Canadian Charter of Rights and Freedoms (Canada Act 1982), §6 (1) "Mobility Rights"

In practice, however, this right can only be exercised when one is granted the privilege of a passport—an identification document established during World War I as a temporary security measure that was soon adopted, and never abandoned, around the world. Once again, ideology and practice appear to be in opposition: the hegemonic recognition of individual freedom of movement, its prominent place in the structure of feelings of Western countries (from popular "road movies" to Supreme Court decisions recognizing it as "part of our heritage") is contradicted by the extensive range of government prerogatives where passports are concerned. Each state retains the authority to dispense travel documents (passports, visas, work permits) at will, simply through bureaucratic regulations, and thereby reserves the right to locate and control individuals and peoples according to the changing demands of economic, social, and political contingencies. From the late 1930s to the 1950s, for example, all American applicants were subject to the scrutiny and approval of Ruth B. Shipley, who became Chief of the Passport Division in 1938. A 1941 *New York Times* magazine profile highlighted the extent of her powers: "Although she has ninety assistants in the passport division," Harold Hinton explained, "Mrs. Shipley examines each application personally. Despite this extra work she never seems hurried. The door to her office is always open, and any applicant with a grievance can see that she is there and can walk right in, and people of high and low degree do.... She is completely immovable, however, once a decision has been reached, according to those who have watched her at work for years. She has an inexhaustible fund of patience during the negotiating period, but when she has once said 'no,' the disappointed applicant might as well save himself further conversation" (21). A 1948 news report confirmed her ongoing, "complete discretion to grant or reject [a] request" for a passport (*New York Times* 14). How can an unelected, unknown bureaucrat wield so much power? How can her counterparts operate in consular offices worldwide (Wildes 887-909)? What forms of rationality allow these potentially draconian administrative procedures and instruments to appear so commonsensical and benign? Why, in short, is Mrs. Shipley, or her authority, almost unimaginable and therefore largely unquestioned?

Perhaps because we are accustomed to thinking in universal terms such as the State and the People, Ideology and Practice, Truth and Falsehood—binaries which inevitably exclude the everyday exigencies of actual governmental procedures. Following the work of Michel Foucault, this paper considers power differently, by focusing on a particular instance of its exercise—the passport—and by analyzing this document as a matrix in which specific relations of power (such as control over exit and entry, determination of the individual's status within and without sovereign borders) and domains of knowledge (concerning individual and national identities, citizenship, security, territory) are articulated, and from which other relations are excluded (subjectivity, cultural hybridization). The passport is emblematic of ***governmen-*** ***·lity***, or the "art of government" invented by modernity and implemented as the dominant mode of power in the twentieth century. This method of government—a form of bio-power—targets the *life* of the one and the many, of the population as a whole and of each individual.[1] It works not only through laws and regulations securing the biological, economic, and political health of the nation, but also through the fostering of individual pleasures and passions, desires and ambitions—our very sense of who we are. The passport, as an instrument of governmentality, instantiates some of the mechanisms that *subject* individuals through their *identification*—in terms of nationality, gender, race, class, and the plethora of ever more specifying subcategories such as alienage, partiality, residency, asylum, visitorship. The passport in Western industrialized countries exemplifies one of the many governmental tactics devised to cope with the consequences of nationalism, imperialism, and decolonization in the twentieth century—tactics often justified as measured responses to an unsettling shift from cultural homogeneity to heterogeneity.

But to focus solely on legislation and bureaucratic procedures is to be confined within their realm; what seems so feasible in administrative terms (identification, control, localization) is effectively problematized elsewhere. To apprehend all that has been rendered unimaginable by the discourse of law and the techniques of governance, other discursive practices must be implicated, including debates in the British House of Commons, press reports, League of Nations' conference proceedings, state commissions of inquiry, academic journals, and most of all, for our purposes, literature. Literary texts are especially useful for a discursive critique of the problematic of identity: whereas in legal terms, individuals and nations can be identified through a limited number of fixed markers, literary fictions can display them as discursive processes of elaboration, in which conflicting forces converge, disperse, and even at times annul each other. Examining the intersections and bifurcations of the discourses of law and literature as they elaborate fictions of identity provides a new perspective on the "politics of identity," and its possibilities for resistance and transformation. Our purpose, therefore, is not to present a series of "passport scenes" in order to trace literary representations of social conflicts.[2] Instead, we consider modernist and contemporary texts which reveal, sustain, or counter the processes that make passports "make sense." Stated as broadly as possible, we want to show how the culture that produced the passport as a means to secure the nation and claim its citizens also produced *The Waste Land*: how discussions in the House of Lords decrying the miserable life imposed on British subjects because their neighborhoods were being invaded and disfigured by hordes of "aliens"—a political discourse lamenting the adulteration of the English way of life—must be correlated to the "revolutions" of modernist poetry, which question, parody, and fragment all forms of homogeneity, all the while lamenting its loss. T.S. Eliot's wasteland, in other words, is formed, and feels, like the modern neighborhood—an uneasy assemblage of (at times warring) factions, or, in Foucault's terms, a piecemeal fabrication of alien forms (*Des espaces* 78).

Thus, our method is not to develop a causal argument, teleologically unfolding the necessary imbrications of economics, politics, legislation, and aesthetics in a cause-and-effect chain culminating in literary "expressions." Instead, we demonstrate the contiguities and divergences, the correlations and contradictions existing among different discursive practices, which together produce multiple truths and exert actual relations of force; we trace the varying reiteration of questions of essence, nation, race, homogeneity, adulteration, transformation, and hybridization to map their conditions of possibility and dissemination. Our text interrupts, cites, and enfolds others, to allow intertextual vectors to emerge and discursive remanences in the archive to come to light. Through this enfolding of legal, literary, and critical elaborations of identity, our argument, or critical fiction, takes form.[3] Its purpose is not to reimagine the probability of past historical processes, but to seek their potential for transformation in the future—or now.

The following section, "On alienage," begins a "thin history"of the modern passport, examining its emergence in World War I and its maintenance in peacetime as a particularly prized security measure to ensure (and thereby produce) the integrity of the nation and its citizens, while strengthening the state. Section III, "Who shall remember my house," interrupts this history of legal and governmental tactics to examine their traces in then-contemporary literature. It focuses on texts by Henry James and T.S. Eliot, which address questions of nationhood and citizenship, homogeneity and adulteration, from different angles: while the pre-war *American Scene* (1906) registers the unsettling effects, for the American identity, of immigrant settlements in New York City, the post-war *Waste Land* (1922) can barely contain the fragments and cacophonous voices of the Unreal City. Together, these texts expose the dangers of governmental attempts to normalize and regulate identity, yet nonetheless presuppose the latter's value. Section IV contextualizes the previous legal and literary fictions of identity within the broader theoretical framework of governmentality. Foucault's critique of this mode of power is then correlated to Virginia Woolf's inscription of its effects on the lives of *Mrs. Dalloway* and her circle. Together, these texts reveal the productive aspects of power relations, the ways in which they overdetermine and rarify life rather than merely protect or circumscribe identities. The problem then is not the loss of identity, but the exercise of modern power through its production, at both the individual and national levels. A brief examination of the American government's post-World War II tactical use of the passport as a means to discipline citizens and make them respect foreign policy further documents this point. The fifth section, "On communities," examines how passports are being redeployed and communities reimagined in the 1990s—in legal, economic, and political terms by the European Union (EU), and in historical, narrative terms in Michael Ondaatje's *The English Patient*. The analysis juxtaposes two strategies for building communities after the devastation of war: the top-down, governmental approach taken by member states of the EU, which has established a new legal entity with its own identity and citizenship (including a transnational passport), and the alternate, fragile, anti-national, antiracist communal attempts delineated in Ondaatje's novel. These analysis lead us finally to "Facing governments," which suggests the possibility of an international citizenship of the governed, its rights and duties, and the necessary conditions for its emergence. Thus, rather than trace the evolution of the passport, we begin its genealogy by surveying the different scenes in which it appears in this century to play different roles.

ON ALIENAGE

The modern passport was variously instituted by Western governments during World War I in order to control the traffic of citizens and aliens at their borders, in the interests of national security. Prior to that, travel had been more or less unrestricted, Russia being the great exception.[4] The term "passport," an English adaptation of the French words *passer* and *port*, referred to a range of travel documents and letters of permission which both eased travel for individuals and allowed governments to oversee mobility and control dissidence. The archive of mobility restrictions begins in 1093, when King William I forbade Anselm, a newly appointed archbishop, to travel to Rome to visit Pope Urban II; this incident resulted in a victory of the Crown over the Vatican with the *Constitutions of Clarendon* (Fagen 387-388). In effect, King William was invoking the privilege of *Ne Exeat Regno*. The origins of the writ are obscure, but it was granted statutory basis by Richard II in 1381 (Parker 867); it commands that a man "not go beyond the seas or out of the realm without a license. . . . Because we are given to understand that you design to go privately into foreign parts and intend to prosecute there many things prejudicial to us" (Parker 867). To offset this prerogative, section 41 of the Magna Carta signed by King John in 1215 "granted merchants 'safe and secure exit from England and entry to England,'" and section 42 promised that "'It shall be lawful in the future for anyone (excepting always those imprisoned or outlawed) [t]o leave our kingdom and to return, safe and secure by land and water, except *for a short period in time of war*, on grounds of public policy—reserving always the allegiance due to us'" (Fagen 388; our emphasis). The future of section 42, however, was short-lived: it was omitted by John's successor, Henry III, when he reissued the Magna Carta one year later in 1216. It would take almost four hundred years for the writ of *Ne Exeat Regno* to be repealed; Lansing credits this legal turn to the rise of "the theory of the natural rights of the individual" (16): "by 1607 the writ was no longer in general use except when used as an equity instrument to insure the whereabouts of debtors and defendants" (16; and Parker 867-68).

At the turn of the twentieth century, successive British governments enacted a series of measures to control the movements of aliens across and within their borders (*Aliens Restriction Acts* of 1905, 1914, and 1919, and the *Aliens Order* of 1920). Aliens, for example, could be *required* "to reside and remain within certain places or districts"; they could also be *prohibited* from "residing or remaining in any areas specified in the Order" (*Aliens Restriction Act*, 1914, §1 [d] and [e]). The general effect of such legislation was to transform everyone into a potential alien: "If any question arises on any proceedings under any such Order, or with reference to anything done or proposed to be done under any such Order, whether any person is an alien or not, or is an alien of a particular class or not, the onus of proving that that person is not an alien, or, as the case may be, is not an alien of that class, shall lie upon that person" (*Aliens Restriction Act*, 1914, §4). One year later, passports temporarily became compulsory for anyone landing in or leaving the United Kingdom, as required by regulation 14c of the amended *Defense of the Realm Act*. To this day, British citizens, while not legally required to present a passport to customs officials, must satisfy the latter as to their identity and nationality. And the passport remains the most convenient means of doing so.

> "The Passport Officer"
> This impartial dogs' nose
> scrutinizes the lamppost. All in good
> order.
> He sets his seal on it and
> moves on to the next.
> (The drippings of his forerunners
> convey no information,
> barely a precedent.
> His actions are reflex.)
>   Basil Bunting (109)

Mobility rights were not explicitly mentioned in the American Constitution; subsequent legal opinions have found them to be protected by the First and Fifth Amendments. The first American "passport" was issued on July 8, 1796, "as a letter of introduction to U.S. officials abroad and a request for safe conduct to foreign governments" (Fagen 392). In 1918, however, the Travel Control Act made passports compulsory for anyone either leaving or entering the U.S. (Farber 265-66), measures that went unchanged until 1921.[5] The 1926 *Act to Regulate the Issue and Validity of Passports* (passed by Congress two months after the League of Nations Passport Conference; see below) authorized "the Secretary of State to issue passports under such rules as the President may prescribe. No statutory standards [were] provided" (Farber 266). Title 22 of the Act, "Foreign Relations and Intercourse," included three sections crucial for the definition of power relations, established by the passport, between the government and the governed. Section 211 reaffirmed that the Secretary of State *may*—but need not—grant and issue passports on behalf of the President[6]; Section 212 specified that, "No passport shall be granted or issued to or verified for any other persons than those owing allegiance, whether citizens or not, to the United States"; Section 213 further insists that the passport could not and would not be issued until the applicant had sworn an oath of allegiance (c.4 S.211–227, Stat. 657). Thus travel documents served both to subjectivize individuals who had to swear allegiance to the nation ("whether citizens or not") and to generate new and extensive discretionary powers for the government.

In both Britain and the United States, the passport is a document granted, in the name of a head of state, by an authorized agent, to a named individual. This triadic relation distributes various rights, obligations, and requests. All passports bear the state's request that its subject be granted protection and safe conduct. The passport bearer is obliged to be the person named by the document and has the right to leave and re-enter his or her country of citizenship. The "returnability right" also applies at the governmental level: any country refusing entry to a non-national has the right to return that person to his or her country of origin. Finally, given that the individual does not own the passport, he or she is obliged to surrender it on demand: "This passport remains the property of Her Majesty's Government in the United Kingdom and may be withdrawn at any time"; "THIS PASSPORT IS THE PROPERTY OF THE UNITED STATES GOVERNMENT. IT MUST BE SURRENDERED UPON DEMAND BY AN AUTHORIZED REPRESENTATIVE OF THE DEPARTMENT OF STATE."[7]

But what does the passport identify? Individual bodies as social identities: in addition to the name (is the face presented reiterated in the standardized and countersigned photograph?), primary physical data (sex, age, height, weight), and a history of previous travels (stamps affixed by customs and immigration agents), a series of apparently innocuous entries (photograph, stipulations as to sex and occupation) constructs individual identity according to gender, race, and class. Gender

> "Her Britannic Majesty's Principal Secretary of State for Foreign and Commonwealth Affairs requests and requires in the Name of Her Majesty all those whom it may concern to allow the bearer to pass freely without let or hindrance, and to afford the bearer such assistance and protection as may be necessary."
>
> "The Secretary of State of the United States hereby requests all whom it may concern to permit the citizen/national of the United States named herein to pass without delay or hindrance and in case of need, to give all lawful aid and protection."

implications can only be discovered at the level of administrative and legal measures; in many countries, the privilege of obtaining a passport, or maintaining citizenship, is differently distributed according to sex.[8] Race must be surmised by the photograph; class, by the "occupation" entry. Class also affects the application process itself: the form must be countersigned by a member of the "respectable classes"—a lawyer, a physician, a priest, or a police officer can attest to the truthfulness of the information provided, but not a plumber. University professors qualify in North America, but not in the U.K.[9] Interestingly, the first modern passports redoubled the photograph's burden of proof with verbal descriptions resonant with phrenological and physiognomic implications. As Paul Fussell puts it, "'Forehead' had to be described ('medium' was a favorite), like nose ('straight,' 'normal,' 'hooked,' etc.), mouth ('medium,' 'normal'. . .), chin ('small'), complexion ('fresh,' 'ruddy') and face ('square,' 'round,' 'oval')" (28-29).[10]

While these verbal markers have since been eliminated, the discriminatory processes which they implied have not. As manifested in the minutes of the 1920 and 1926 League of Nations Passport Conferences, the passport system was always entangled with issues of labor, race, immigration, and gender. Trying to keep the issues separate was a recurring problem for the delegates. M. de Gömöry-Laiml of Hungary optimistically maintained that, "If [the delegates] could reach an agreement on passport questions, the emigration questions would settle themselves" (1926 *Minutes* 13). The Hungarian delegation also proposed that any passport and visa restrictions warranted by "internal difficulties of an economic nature (labor market)" should "only be applied in individual cases. They [should] not be applied to whole categories of persons on account of their nationality, race, or any other quality" (1926 *Minutes* 158). But the Conference was warned by Mr. Jenkin that "South Africa would never agree to such a principle" (1926 *Minutes* 52). Jenkin's xenophobic comments, and their racist implications, underline the fervor with which national ontological identities were being reforged—and protected—at that time. A homogenous Englishness, for example, was at stake, a uniqueness for which "race"was the most commonly used (though misapplied) marker. In his May 1924 speech "On England and the West," once and future prime minister[11] Stanley Baldwin praised "the English stock," that "great stock of which we are all members," and lauded "the gifts of that great English race" (Giles and Middleton 102).

In effect, nationalism took a governmental turn in the late nineteenth and early twentieth centuries: the passport was one of a series of *ad hoc* legal measures which defined and controlled aliens while delimiting the nation within. This was not a new phenomenon. In 1793, for example, the British *Aliens Bill* was specifically enacted to prevent the entry or immigration of certain "dangerous" or "objectionable persons" associated with the French Revolution and the massacres of Paris (Sibley 39). But these were always temporary acts responding to immediate circumstances. The 1905 *Aliens Act* was the first *permanent* law which codified the "fact" of alienage as a constitutive national problem. Although, like its predecessors, it was ostensibly targeted at "undesirable aliens" only, in practice it addressed two imperatives: the need to restrict a new influx of Russians (Sibley 14) and to limit the total number of immigrants. In their treatise on the 1905 *Aliens Act*, barristers N. W. Sibley and A. Elias quietly acknowledged in a footnote that

> the numbers of alien immigration, possesses very serious claims to attention. . . . In the House of Lords, the Bishop of London observed that "there were 63,000 aliens in Stepney alone, and 107 streets were said to have been acquired by aliens in six years. This meant a great displacement of British residents. It was estimated that 52,000 English people had left the district during the last decade. With such large numbers of people pouring into the district and making life almost unbearable for those who lived here, he felt that their lordships were justified in passing the [law]." (Sibley and Elias 39–40n)

In 1906, Sibley and Elias noted the "desuetude into which the passport system [was] falling" (44n)—yet within a decade, a new, more refined system had been instigated worldwide. It is as though the passport emerged as the acceptable face, in the midst of crisis, of the racist, anti-Semitic, and xenophobic voices of nationalism that had been resonating, for more than forty years, in discourses as varied as the press, then-emerging "sciences" (criminology, paleoanthropology, sociology, ethnology), literature, popular culture, as well as from segments of the revolutionary right and left (Sternhell). The passport was *the* instrument which gave governments an expedient administrative (as opposed to constitutional or legal) power to restrict immigration—the latter, of course, always being cited as a necessary measure for the security and integrity of national identity.[12]

Interestingly, the problematic of a nationalist essence, homogenous and pure, was contradictorily played out in the fiction of names—the last words for legal and governmental identity—in Britain and the U.S. In 1917, all German-sounding names and titles in the British royal family were expunged: "the House of Saxe-Coburg-Gotha became the House of Windsor; their Serene Highnesses the Prince and Princess of Teck became transformed by the surname Cambridge; and Battenberg—the name of one of the most illustrious families of 19th- and 20th-century Europe—became Mountbatten" (Wier 317).[13] For the sovereign to be "at home," truly representative of his people, King George V had to change his name. But to preserve the integrity of said national home, others were expressly forbidden to do so after the war. The *Aliens Restriction (Amendment) Act* of 1919 categorically stated: "An alien shall not for any purpose assume or use or purport to assume or use or continue after the commencement of this Act the assumption or use of any name other than that by which he was ordinarily known on the fourth day of August nineteen hundred and fourteen [the date when Britain declared war on Germany]" (7.1). The United States adopted exactly the opposite tactic—immigration officers routinely altered the names of immigrants at the border—but to the same end: to ensure the integrity of the American national identity and to protect its "exact essence." Yet, as Foucault suggests in his discussion of Nietzsche and genealogy, essence is pure fabrication:

> Why does Nietzsche challenge the pursuit of the origin (Ursprung)[?]. . . First, because it is an attempt to capture the exact essence of things, their purest possibilities, and their carefully protected identities; because this search assumes the existence of immobile forms that precede the external world of accident and succession. This search is directed to "that which is already there," the image of a primordial truth fully adequate to its nature, and it necessitates the removal of every mask to ultimately disclose an original identity. However, if the genealogist refuses to extend his faith in metaphysics, if he listens to history, he finds that there is "something altogether different" behind things: not a timeless and essential secret, but the secret that they have no essence or that their essence was fabricated in a piecemeal fashion from alien forms. (*Language* 142)

"WHO SHALL REMEMBER MY HOUSE"[14]

In 1906, Henry James found himself in a situation that baffled him: after twenty years of being the American in Europe, he returned to New York City only to find that Europe was already there. *The American Scene* (a narrative of his travels from New England to Florida) is unable to understand the new relations of neighborhood being forged and their implications for the "American" identity.[15] "A Spring Impression" of Manhattan registers "the taste of each dish in the banquet":

> The whole feast affects one as eaten—that is the point—with the general queer sauce of New York. . . . I must confess, notwithstanding, to not being quite ready to point directly to the common element in the dense Italian neighborhoods of the lower East side, and in the upper reaches of Fifth and Madison Avenues; though indeed I did wonder at this inability in recollecting two or three of those charming afternoons of early summer, in Central Park, which showed the fruit of the foreign tree as shaken down there with a force that smothered everything else. The long residential vistas I have named were within a quarter of an hour's walk, but the alien was as truly in possession, under the high "aristocratic" nose, as if he had but three steps to come. If it be asked why, the alien still striking you so as an alien, the singleness of impression, throughout the place, should still be so marked, the answer, close at hand, would seem to be that the alien himself fairly makes the singleness of impression. Is not the universal sauce essentially his sauce, and do we not feel ourselves feed-

ing, half the time, from the ladle, as greasy as he chooses to leave it for us, that he holds out?" (James 114-115)[16]

If each of the incoming foreign identities claims universality, how can a single, true national identity survive and dominate?

"A Spring Impression" is trying to assimilate the effects of a scene described in the book's previous chapter: the arrival of "the million or so of immigrants annually knocking at our official door" at "terrible little Ellis Island" (James 81).[17] The text is not unsympathetic to the "hundred forms and ceremonies" to which they are subjected, to the ways in which they are "marshalled, herded, divided, subdivided, sorted, sifted, searched, fumigated, for longer or shorter periods." Such passages belie any governmental claim that newcomers can be peacefully identified, categorized, and absorbed (or rejected) at the border. Yet "the effect of [this] prodigious process, an intendedly 'scientific' feeding of the mill" is never understood in terms of the immigrants themselves, but is rather limited to the consternation of the American observer: "[it gives] the earnest observer a thousand more things to think of than he can pretend to retail" (James 82). Difficulties extend beyond the problem of classification, however: the place of observation is threatened, and the observer's identity transformed and marked anew (indelibly "stamped," like a passport) by the radical unsettling of established power-knowledge relations.

> I think indeed that the simplest account of the action of Ellis Island on the spirit of any sensitive citizen who may have happened to "look in" is that he comes back from his visit not at all the same person that he went. He has eaten of the tree of knowledge, and the taste will be forever in his mouth. He had thought he knew before, thought he had the sense of the degree in which it is his American fate to share the sanctity of his American consciousness, the intimacy of his American patriotism, with the inconceivable alien; but the truth had never come home to him with any such force. In the lurid light projected upon it by those courts of dismay it shakes him—or I like at least to imagine it shakes him—to the depths of his being; I like to think of him, I positively have to think of him, as going about ever afterwards with a new look, for those who can see it, in his face, the outward sign of the new chill in his heart. So is stamped, for detection, the questionably privileged person who has had an apparition, seen a ghost in his supposedly safe old house. Let not the unwary, therefore, visit Ellis Island. (James 82-83)

Faced with a "houseful of foreigners, physiognomically branded as such" (James 191), the narrator cannot discern any form of collective, let alone national identity; the city—and by extension, the country—is overrun by strangers, marked by the disparate juxtapositions of "queer" differences. The integrity of national and individual identities can only be traced in the past: "There was no escape from the ubiquitous alien into the future, or even into the present; there was an escape but into the past" (James 84). Who is "he" if he is not an American of the America he remembers? Henry James was "naturalized" as a British citizen in July 1915 (Edel 531).

James's "sanctified" childhood memories of a unified, stable, WASP American identity were not shared by T.S. Eliot, who derived no comfort from looking back. Even as a member of the privileged white middle class, he had felt displaced and alienated. As he later informed Herbert Read,

"Someday I want to write an essay about the point of view of an American who wasn't an American, because he was born in the south and went to school in New England as a small boy with a nigger drawl, but who wasn't a southerner in the South because his people were northerners in a border state and looked down on all southerners and Virginians, and so was never anything anywhere?" (qtd in Sigg 110)

> Let us go, through certain half-deserted streets,
> The muttering retreats
> Of restless nights in one-night cheap hotels
> And sawdust restaurants with oyster shells:
> Streets that follow like a tedious argument
> Of insidious intent
> To lead you to an overwhelming question. . .
> Oh, do not ask, 'What is it?'
> Let us go and make our visit.
> T. S. Eliot, "The Love Song of J. Alfred Prufrock"

In the summer of 1914, Eliot, then a Harvard doctoral candidate, went to Germany to pursue his studies in philosophy. Forced out of the country because of the war, he chose not to return to America, but to locate instead in Oxford to complete his degree. Within a year, the publication of "The Love Song of J. Alfred Prufrock" (made possible by Ezra Pound[18]) convinced Eliot that London, the center of literary life in English, was open to him. The cultural imperialism exercised by England made it advantageous for writers to become its subjects. "Anything else," as Pound maintained, was

a waste of time and energy. No one in London cares a hang what is written in America. After getting an American audience a man has to begin all over again here if he plans for an international hearing. He even begins at a disadvantage. . . . The situation has been very well summed up in the sentence: "Henry James stayed in Paris and read Turgenev and Flaubert, Mr. Howells returned to America and read Henry James." (Valerie Eliot 102)

In 1927 Eliot completed the lengthy process of finding an identity by becoming a British citizen, someone who was, in his words, "classicist in literature, royalist in politics, and Anglo-Catholic in religion" (*For Lancelot* 7).[19] Ironically, the only way for Eliot (and James) to attain an *unadulterated* identity was to assume a

> "The population should be homogenous; where two or more cultures exist in the same place they are likely either to be fiercely self-conscious or both to become adulterate."
>
> T. S. Eliot, *After Strange Gods*

prefabricated one. Even more ironically, Eliot's poetry unceasingly decried the very processes of displacement and naturalization that had allowed him to become "himself."

"Gerontion," written in the aftermath of World War I, features an embittered speaker—"an old man in a dry month" with tears "shaken from the wrath-bearing tree" (*Complete Poems* 37-38)—who inveighs against the deracination and other "supple confusions" of the epoch. The allegory of "his house" is venomous in tone, racist in detail; individual identity cannot exist outside of national identities that are becoming "fractured" even as they are cited.

> My house is a decayed house,
> And the Jew squats on the window sill, the owner,
> Spawned in some estaminet of Antwerp,
> Blistered in Brussels, patched and peeled in London.
> The goat coughs at night in the field overhead;
> . . . .
> In depraved May, dogwood and chestnut, flowering judas,
> To be eaten, to be divided, to be drunk
> Among whispers; by Mr. Silvero
> With caressing hands, at Limoges
> Who walked all night in the next room;
> By Hakagawa, bowing among the Titians;
> By Madame de Tornquist, in the dark room
> Shifting the candles; Fräulein von Kulp
> Who turned in the hall, one hand on the door.
> (*Complete Poems* 37-38)

What should and once would have been a communion of citizens has become a debased, unsettling scene of isolated actions. The coherence of home has been supplanted by the squalor of a "rented house," the tenement of the modern urbanized, industrialized city. "Gerontion" asks, "After such knowledge, what forgiveness?" (*Complete Poems* 38). Eliot's texts (like those of James) reiterate the fears expressed in the British House of Lords concerning the "unbearable life" imposed on English (or American) citizens by invading aliens; fourteen years of legislation, war, and the implementation of the passport had inadequately secured the borders and the nation(s) within.

In a very different tone, utilizing antithetical symbolic spaces, Eliot's 1943 contribution to *Queen Mary's Book for India*, "To the Indians who Died in Africa," reaffirms the absolute necessity of cultural homogeneity:

> A man's destination is his own village,
> His own fire, and his wife's cooking;
> To sit in front of his own door at sunset
> And see his grandson, and his neighbour's grandson
> Playing in the dust together.
>
> Scarred but secure, he has many memories
> Which return at the hour of conversation,
> (The warm or the cool hour, according to the climate)
> Of foreign men, who fought in foreign places,
>   Foreign to each other.
>
> A man's destination is not his destiny
> Every country is home to one man
> And exile to another. . . .
> (*Complete Poems* 203)

The speaker assumes a symbiotic relation between country of origin and individual identity; cultural integrity can only be secured when everyone remains in place, at "home," through the generations. "Destiny" may necessitate commerce with "foreign men," but to be elsewhere is always to be in "exile," alienated from one's possessions ("own door," "wife's cooking") and one's being.[20]

But T.S. Eliot is not famous for having written "To the Indians who Died in Africa." Notoriety, fame, and a Nobel Prize for Literature were achieved for *The Waste Land* and other seminal texts characterized by innovations in spatialized form which produce meaning through a montage of disparate elements rather than their alignment in a traditional, teleological narrative. *The Waste Land* (1922) is a resolutely modern space in which nineteenth-century obsessions with time, development, closure, and coherence are gutted and displayed as the "heap of broken images" and "fragments" that can never fulfill the quest for meaning.[21] Temporal linearity is invoked ("April is the cruelest month," "Summer surprised us," "HURRY UP PLEASE ITS TIME"), and yet scenes and quotations are relentlessly juxtaposed, without causal explanation or narrative threading. In spite of these multiple efforts at dislocation, the Eliotic affirmation of singular, essential identities is reiterated throughout *The Waste Land*, nowhere more vividly than in the final collocation of lines, which replicates the overall *techné* of the poem:

> I sat upon the shore
> Fishing, with the arid plain behind me

Shall I at least set my lands in order?
London Bridge is falling down falling down falling down
Poi s'ascose nel foco che gli affina
Quando fiam uti chelidon—O swallow swallow
Le Prince d'Aquitaine à la tour abolie
These fragments I have shored against my ruins
Why then Ile fit you. Hieronymo's mad againe.
Datta. Dayadhvam. Damyata.
   Shantih shantih shantih[.]
(*Complete Poems* 74-75)

Critical discussion is generally divided into two camps: the poem is either viewed as one in which a singular questing figure, the "I," moves between symbolic landscapes,[22] or it is interpreted as a ventriloquist text which actuates a series of voices, all of them clamoring for recognition. Yet both positions assume the integral "I," whether there be one or many. Even the importation of Buddha and his admonitions (*Datta, Dayadhvam, Damyata*; Give, Sympathize, Control) concerns self-regulation in respect to the other ("We think of the key, each in his prison/Thinking of the key, each confirms a prison" [*Complete Poems* 74]).

On every textual plane, the risk to the "I" in *The Waste Land* is self-alienation through displacement; disorders of class, race, gender relations, ethnicity—these are the threats. The difficulty, for example, rests not in being "a true German," not in recognizing the ontological truth of the German identity, but in policing all individual claims to be such: "Bin gar keine Russin, stamm' aus Litauen, echt deutsch" (*Complete Poems* 61).[23] This problem, first presented in the twelfth line of *The Waste Land*, reappears most vividly in Part V, where an unknown, spectral "hooded" "third" materializes and is immediately displaced by the "swarming" of unidentified "hooded hordes":

Who is the third who walks always beside you?
When I count, there are only you and I together
But when I look ahead up the white road
There is always another one walking beside you
Gliding wrapt in a brown mantle, hooded
I do not know whether a man or a woman
—But who is that on the other side of you?

   What is that sound high in the air
Murmur of maternal lamentation
Who are those hooded hordes swarming
Over endless plains, stumbling in cracked earth
Ringed by the flat horizon only
What is the city over the mountains

> Cracks and reforms and bursts in the violet air
> Falling towers
> Jerusalem Athens Alexandria
> Vienna London
> Unreal
> (*Complete Poems* 73)

The intimate community of "you and I together" (not even a "we") on "the white road," menaced by a sexually indeterminate figure "wrapt in a brown mantle," is destroyed by the pressure of the unstoppable movements of peoples, a demographic cataclysm. This is not the quiet, nuanced apprehension of Henry James's "spring impression" (with a chill in his heart) but a traumatized ("April is the cruelest month") understanding of civilization's ruination. What separates Henry James and T.S. Eliot is not just a couple of decades, but the first World War—the war that produced passports and "documents on sight" (*Complete Poems* 68).

Despite Eliot's violent aesthetic of fracture and displacement, the possibility of locating and producing meaning remains. The singular moment of rest in *The Waste Land*, the only time when the City is not "Unreal" but just itself, the city, occurs dead in the middle of the poem, in Part III, when "fishmen lounge" together in homosocial exchange, free of the presence of all others:

> O City city, I can sometimes hear
> Beside a public bar in Lower Thames Street,
> The pleasant whining of a mandolin
> And a clatter and a chatter from within
> Where fishmen lounge at noon: where the walls
> Of Magnus Martyr hold
> Inexplicable splendour of Ionian white and gold.
> (*Complete Poems* 69)

Locals placed near the established church dedicated to the patron saint of fishermen stage the cultural and ontological homogeneity longed for throughout Eliot's poetry. Moreover, the contracted form of "fishmen" links them with Christ and his disciples, the Grail myth, and other ostensible origins of an essential Western civilization ("Ionian white and gold").

In 1917, Eliot argued that "the poet must become more and more comprehensive, more allusive, more indirect, in order to force, to dislocate if necessary, language into his meaning" (*Inventions* 249). The process he is describing is in many ways isomorphic to the process through which legal fictions of identity are produced by the passport, which operates by labeling, specifying, and "dislocating" persons and subjectivities into demographic data to be managed and governed. The following section further documents how the domains of knowledge produced by literary, legal, and governmental discourses are inextricably linked to actual relations of force targeted to the normalization and regulation of individual lives. And one of the most effective and least noticed instruments of enforcement is the passport, which can literally *alienate* one—especially those citizens who question or oppose prevailing truths—from the pursuit of happiness, liberty, and even life.

ON GOVERNMENTALITY

To summarize, the world-wide use of passports has had the definite effect of making all individuals potential aliens who must bear the marks of state identification in order to exercise the *inalienable* human right to mobility. Governmental procedures have so far invaded the practice of living that the identity tag has now become a right to fight for rather than a burden to oppose. By issuing, denying, and revoking passports, governments use their prerogatives in order to control citizens and foreigners through elaborate identification and classification methods. The passport thus emblematizes the necessary interrelations among *sovereign* privileges, *disciplinary* processes, and *governmental* procedures—that is, it presupposes what Foucault has described as the three major models of power relations operating since the Renaissance, while simultaneously confirming the dominance of governmentality in the twentieth century.[24]

But what distinguishes this "art of government" from other modes of power? First, it seeks to manipulate elements, events, and people in order to strengthen the positive and reduce the negative aspects of life as much as possible: "'government is the right disposition of things, arranged so as to lead to a convenient end'" (Gustave de la Perrière, *Miroir Politique* 1567; qtd Foucault, *Foucault Effect* 93). Sovereignty is exercised over a specific territory (inhabited or no); disciplinary mechanisms of surveillance and correction are deployed in controlled spaces (prisons, schools, offices) to ensure specific kinds of conduct. Governmentality, however, manages given sets of circumstances by inserting any phenomenon to be controlled into a series of probable events and instigating security measures accordingly. The modern passport, for example, was instituted as a response to conditions of war to regulate individual mobility, which, when considered within the series of probable dangers posed by espionage and treachery, demanded identification and control. Second, governmentality develops procedures that are both plurifunctional and cost effective. The passport serves many ends; its design and administration must balance the competing interests of state security, economic exchange, immigration, and tourism, to name the most obvious. Third, security mechanisms must be able to handle future occurrences, which are in some part neither measurable nor controllable. Rather than determining an ideal function in a static environment, governmental procedures must be open to aleatory events, and capable of managing them: the visa system, residency requirements, partiality are all examples of such procedures.

Foucault argues that whereas "law and sovereignty were absolutely inseparable . . . with government it is a question not of imposing law on men, but of disposing things: that is to say, of employing tactics rather than laws, and even of using laws themselves as tactics—to arrange things in such a way that, through a certain number of means, such and such ends may be achieved" (*Foucault Effect* 95). This tactical deployment of laws can be discerned in the British government's switch from temporary and specific "Aliens" acts to permanent, future-oriented "Nationality" acts, designed to exclude a wide variety of changing Others. Facing the pressures of a post-imperial order, successive governments (irrespective of party) implemented a series of laws regarding immigration and nationality, beginning with the 1948 *British Nationality Act* and culminating in the *British Nationality Act* of 1981, which modified or nullified the passports held by former colonial British subjects.[25] The 1968 *Commonwealth Immigrants Act*, for example,

> imposed immigration controls for the first time on holders of United Kingdom passports when Asian holders of such passports began to emigrate from East Africa to the United Kingdom. The Act extended immigration controls to the holders of United Kingdom passports issued outside the British Isles unless they or one of their parents or grandparents had been born, naturalised, or adopted in the United Kingdom itself, or had been registered in the United Kingdom or a Commonwealth country already independent or self-governing in 1948. (Thornberry 5)

The 1981 *British Nationality Act* went even further, abolishing "the unqualified right of entry for anyone who could not claim partiality, which meant, effectively, that the majority of black Commonwealth citizens lost their rights while the majority of white Commonwealth citizens retained theirs. It also removed the ancient right of birth on British soil (*jus soli*) as the basis of citizenship and replaced it with that of descent (*jus sanguinus*)" (Baimbridge 422-23).[26] Rather than operating from the legal binary of the permissible and the forbidden, governmentality proceeds first by determining an optimal mean and then fixing the limits beyond which deviations can no longer be tolerated: immigration numbers, for example, can be set at a percentage of the population as a whole, in accordance with calculations of economic costs, and quota systems established depending on the ethnic composition of the population—and passport, visa, residency requirements, etc., can then be adjusted appropriately.

The art of government arose as a problematic in the sixteenth century, Foucault notes, at the crossroads of two great processes: the shift from feudalism to the great "territorial, administrative, and colonial states," and the Reformation and Counter-Reformation.

> There is a double movement, then, of state centralization on the one hand and of dispersion and religious dissidence on the other: it is, I believe, at the intersection of these two tendencies that the problem comes to pose itself with this peculiar intensity, of how to be ruled, how strictly, by whom, to what end, by what methods, etc. There is a problematic of government in general. (*Foucault Effect* 88)

Listing several factors which impeded the full exploration of this problematic in the seventeenth century, Foucault identifies the emergence of the "population" in the eighteenth century as a key factor in its acquiring a new prominence. We would argue that a similar conjuncture exists in the twentieth century, with the consolidation and centralization of a global capitalist system on the one hand and the great dispersions and dissent caused by world wars, wars of national liberation, and the international movements of peoples on the other. Furthermore, the development of information technologies during and after World War II for the first time made the gathering and computation of data necessary for the government of the one and the many possible in practice to a degree unattainable in previous periods. If governmentality became an important problematic in the eighteenth century, it became a way of life in the twentieth.

First described as the "police," governmental security mechanisms target the life and happiness of the entire population (through

> "The sole purpose of the police is to lead man to the utmost happiness to be enjoyed in this life."
> Delamare, *Compendium* (qtd Foucault, *Omnes* 2: 250)

adequate economic, social, and political infrastructures and institutions) as well as foster the desires, ambitions, securities, knowledges (*connaissances*) of each individual.[27] This form of bio-power works to encompass every aspect of life and claims the survival of the population, and the nation, as its field of intervention. As Foucault summarizes, "In seeing to health and supplies, it [the police] deals with the preservation of life; concerning trade, factories, workers, the poor and public order, it deals with the conveniences of life. In seeing to the theatre, literature, entertainment, its object is life's pleasures" (*Omnes* 2:250). The effects of this power are double-edged, as by cultivating individual lives, the state ensures its own: "the aim of the modern art of government, or state rationality . . . [is] to develop those elements constitutive of individuals' lives in such a way that their development also fosters that of the strength of the state" (*Omnes* 2:252).[28] Almost half a century before Foucault's critical fictions, the literary fictions and essays of Virginia Woolf were demonstrating just that.

Mrs Dalloway (1925) shows that individual identity is actually relational: it can only be understood in terms of broader national and international forces and the pressures of sexism, racism, and class domination. The novel purportedly tells the story of an ordinary June day when an upper-class woman prepares to host a large party. But the privileged life of Clarissa Dalloway, ostensibly undamaged by the recently ended war, is continually juxtaposed with that of Septimus Smith, a shell-shocked World War I veteran who can only reaffirm that "life is good" (Woolf 132) by killing himself. Tied to this life-death tandem are a series of characters whose lives and positions instantiate the major institutional forces of governmentality which operate in the state: the judiciary, the army (and the Empire), the industrial middle class, the church, mental and physical health, and academia.[29] By moving from one consciousness to another, from the present to the past, from quotidian observations to daydreams and hallucinations, the narrative demonstrates the extent to which "'the utmost happiness to be enjoyed in this life'" (qtd Foucault, *Omnes* 2:250) serves only to strengthen the state.

Peter Walsh, the imperial administrator, feels "hollowed out, utterly empty within" (Woolf 45), yet is so effectively subjectivized that the predictable string of failures which constitute his life (as student, socialist, lover, husband, bureaucrat) does not prevent him from maintaining his love for "the triumphs of civilization" (Woolf 165). "He was not old, or set, or dried in the least," he reassures himself:

> Striding, staring, he glared at the statue of the Duke of Cambridge. He had been sent down from Oxford—true. He had been a Socialist, in some sense a failure—true. Still the future of civilization lies, he thought, in the hands of young men like that; of young men such as he was, thirty years ago. . . . A patter like the patter of leaves in a wood came from behind, and with it a rustling, regular thudding sound, which as it overtook him drummed in his thoughts, strict in step, up Whitehall, without his doing. Boys in uniform, carrying guns, marched with their eyes ahead of them, marched, their arms stiff. And on their faces an expression like the letters of a legend written round the base of a statue praising duty, gratitude, fidelity, love of England. It is, thought Peter Walsh, beginning to keep step with them, a very fine training. . . . [T]hey wore on them unmixed with sensual pleasure or daily preoccupations the solemnity of the wreath which they had fetched from Finsbury Pavement to the empty tomb . . . . As if one will worked legs and arms uniformly, and life, with its varieties, its irreticences, had been laid under a pavement of monuments and wreaths and drugged into a stiff yet staring corpse by dis-

cipline. One had to respect it; one might laugh; but one had to respect it. (Woolf 55-56)

Walsh's nostalgia for his youthful dreams of changing the world is as obligatory as the marching of soldiers, their love of England, and their well-disciplined deaths. The text relentlessly traces the narrow roads followed by all the characters: "the wild, the daring, the romantic" Sally Seton becomes the wife of the cotton manufacturer, with the big house in Manchester and the "five enormous boys" (Woolf 79, 188); Hugh Whitbread, the "perfect specimen of the public school type" ("No country but England could have produced him"), becomes the food- and power-loving bureaucrat—the "admirable Hugh" (Woolf 80, 5); and so on. The novel's plot development demonstrates how lives fostered by bio-power are rarefied, diminished, aligned along restricted pathways until their owners become normal, ordinary, perfectly understandable and predictable for everyone, and yet strange and incomprehensible to themselves: "But often now this body she wore . . ., this body, with all its capacities, seemed nothing—nothing at all. She had the oddest sense of being herself invisible; unseen; unknown; there being no more marrying, no more having of children now, but only this astonishing and rather solemn progress with the rest of them, up Bond Street, this being Mrs. Dalloway; not even Clarissa any more, this being Mrs. Richard Dalloway" (Woolf 11). She, whose role is now restricted to hosting parties where the richest and most powerful of her class are successfully assembled, thinks of them as "offerings" to life (Woolf 134), but can only cry when identified as the "perfect hostess" (Woolf 8, 67, 132, 133).

The loss of self is accentuated by gender, of course—as wife of a Member of Parliament and mother, Clarissa is exiled out of any individuality. Yet she is the only one who can understand, and literally feel, Septimus's death. It is through her thoughts alone that the event is inscribed in the text:

> He had killed himself—but how? Always her body went through it first, when she was told, suddenly, of an accident; her dress flamed, her body burnt. He had thrown himself from a window. Up had flashed the ground; through him, blundering, bruising, went the rusty spikes. There he lay with a thud, thud, thud in his brain, and then a suffocation of blackness. So she saw it. But why had he done it? And the Bradshaws talked of it at her party! . . . Suppose he had that passion, and had gone to Sir William Bradshaw, a great doctor, yet to her obscurely evil, without sex or lust, extremely polite to women, but capable of some indescribable outrage—forcing your soul, that was it—if this young man had gone to him, and Sir William had impressed him, like that, with his power, might he not then have said (indeed

> she felt it now), Life is made intolerable; they make life intolerable, men like that? (Woolf 202)

Drs. Holmes and Bradshaw had been prescribing liberal doses of the English way-of-life for Smith's mental illness (porridge, soccer, outings), above all insisting that he keep his sense of "proportion, divine proportion" (Woolf 109). But Smith recognizes his current enemies only too well: "human nature, in short, was on him—the repulsive brute, with the blood-red nostrils" (Woolf 101)—and this is what finally kills him. War, for Woolf, is not a temporary aberration, but the *reductio ad absurdum* of her culture's way of life, as fostered by bio-power.[30] Peace is nothing but war waged by other means.[31]

Virginia Woolf's particular materialist feminism leads her to argue, in *Mrs Dalloway* and numerous other texts, that civilization is actually the product, and producer, of war and relations of force; civilization is the acceptable facade of patriarchy. Hence the critique of imperialism (uncommon at the time) which is also expressed in Woolf's writings. One of the most searingly ironic moments in the novel occurs as the body of Septimus Smith is carried away by ambulance:

> One of the triumphs of civilization, Peter Walsh thought. It is one of the triumphs of civilization, as the light high bell of the ambulance sounded. Swiftly, cleanly, the ambulance sped to the hospital, having picked up instantly, humanely, some poor devil. . . . That was civilisation. It struck him coming back from the East—the efficiency, the organisation, the communal spirit of London. (Woolf 165)

The colonizer's tyranny abroad is inextricably connected to the patriarch's tyranny at and in his home. The narrator insists on recognizing what none of the characters understand: that any moment of Western civilization is underwritten by colonial exploitation, and class, gender, and race subjugation.

While her male modernist counterparts were lamenting the loss of essence, of coherence, and separation from an originary state of homogenous cultural grace, Woolf was insisting that origins are fabricated as the after-effects of imperialist, racist, sexist relations of power. These beliefs lead Woolf to define the ethical, conscientious woman, whose patriarchal culture does not admit her at its origins, as a self-fashioned "outsider." As she later explains in *Three Guineas* (1938), an extended essay which reaffirms the necessary connections between feminism and pacifism, the "outsider" must resist any incitements to support war. Instead, she must achieve "an attitude of complete indifference":

> When he says, "I am fighting to protect our country," and thus seeks to rouse her patriotic emotion, she will ask herself, "What does 'our country' mean to me an outsider?". . . . And if he says that he is fighting to protect England from foreign rule, she will reflect that for her

there are no "foreigners," since by law she becomes a foreigner if she marries a foreigner. . . . She will find that she has no good reason to ask her brother to fight on her behalf to protect "our" country. "Our country," she will say, "throughout the greater part of its history has treated me as a slave; it has denied me education or any share in its possessions. 'Our' country still ceases to be mine if I marry a foreigner. . . . Therefore if you insist upon fighting to protect me, or 'our' country, let it be understood, soberly and rationally between us, that you are fighting to gratify a sex instinct which I cannot share; to procure benefits which I have not shared and probably will not share; but not to gratify my instincts, or to protect either myself or my country. 'For,' the outsider will say, 'in fact, as a woman, I have no country. As a woman I want no country. As a woman my country is the whole world'." (*Three Guineas* 123-25)

Not only can she not conceive of fighting, she cannot conceive of fighting for a country which systematically discriminates against women—including the practice of denying every woman's citizenship immediately upon marriage to a foreigner (while recognizing its male subjects regardless of their matrimonial arrangements). Woolf's writings demonstrate that the uniform, homogenous, national identity which states attempted to secure, and male modernists longed for ("Who shall remember my house"), never was—always was the patient, skillful, soul-forcing government by the few.

But governmentality must be understood variously. The special province of Woolf's literary discourse is to display the extent to which individual identity, one's private self-knowledge, is charted by state institutions fostering life (Clarissa Dalloway) onto death (Septimus Smith). To survey public moments of state intervention in individual lives, however, and to map the extensive relations of force wielded by governmental prerogatives, we must now turn to two stories from the archives of American passport administration. The cases of Paul Robeson and Philip Agee graphically illustrate how the State Department's power to issue identity documents

> There exists a world Communist movement which, in its origins, its development, and its present practice, is a world-wide revolutionary movement whose purpose it is, by treachery, deceit, infiltration into other groups (governmental and otherwise), espionage, sabotage, terrorism, and any other means deemed necessary to establish a Communist totalitarian dictatorship in the countries throughout the world. . . . The direction and control of the world Communist movement is vested in and exercised by the Communist dictatorship of a foreign country.
>
> U.S. *Internal Security Act* (also known as *Subversive Activities Control Act*), 1950, §2

at will—and the judiciary's willingness to protect this power—can significantly alter individual lives.

During the 1950s, those Americans who were members, or suspected members, of a Communist organization were not entitled to passports and were therefore imprisoned behind what one commentator called "the paper curtain." Such measures proved to be all too far-reaching and effective, as in the case of Paul Robeson.[32] From 1924 to 1939, he pursued a successful career as actor and best-selling recording artist. But Robeson was suspected of being a Communist sympathizer. During a 1947 House Un-American Activities Committee (HUAC) hearing, Richard Nixon noted that "'the surest criteria for identifying someone as a communist was applauding at a Paul Robeson concert or owning a Paul Robeson recording'" (qtd in Michaels 137). Two years later, while on tour in the Soviet Union, Robeson commented that, "'It is unthinkable that American Negroes could go to war on behalf of those who have oppressed us for generations against the Soviet Union, which in one generation has raised our people to full human dignity'" (Michaels 136). These comments, as they were publicized, were to change his life. Riots erupted at his Peekskill, New York, concerts later that fall. Subsequently, nervous promoters began to cancel engagements. Robeson responded by strengthening his ties with the USSR; the State Department upped the ante by refusing to renew his passport. He sued the government, but his case was dismissed by a district court. The Appeals Court found for the government. In 1957, the Supreme Court refused to hear the appeal of the earlier Appeals Court decision. In his summary of the case, Michaels observes that: "In refusing a passport, the State Department denied Robeson a right to earn a living. In addition to refusing to renew his passport, the State Department also denied Robeson the right to travel to Canada, where a passport was not needed. [The President] gave orders to shoot Robeson if he attempted to cross the US-Canadian border" (138). In 1958, however, Robeson was finally issued a passport, and left immediately for a concert tour of Europe and the USSR. This change of heart, or policy, was forced upon the State Department by a series of Supreme Court rulings (for Rockwell Kent, Walter Briehl, and others) which recognized "the right to travel as a liberty guaranteed in the Due Process Clause of the Fifth Amendment of the American Constitu-

> When he testified before HUAC in July 1956, Robeson was informed by Rep. Walter, Committee chair, that the current passport regulations had been enacted because "we are trying to make it easier to get rid of your kind." When asked why he hadn't simply moved to Russia, Robeson explained: "Because my father was a slave, and my people died to build this country, and I am going to stay here and have a part of it just like you. And no Fascist-minded people will drive me from it. Is that clear?" (Michaels 139, n58)

tion" (*Kent v. Dulles* 357 U.S. 116, 125). The opinion of the Court in *Kent v. Dulles*, delivered by Mr. Justice Douglas, held that,

> We deal with beliefs, with associations, with ideological matters. We must remember that we are dealing here with citizens who have neither been accused of crimes nor found guilty. They are being denied their freedom of movement solely because of their refusal to be subjected to inquiry into their beliefs and associations. They do not seek to escape the law nor to violate it. They may or may not be Communists. But assuming they are, the only law which Congress has passed expressly curtailing the movement of Communists across our borders has not yet become effective. It would therefore be strange to infer that pending the effectiveness of that law, the Secretary has been silently granted by Congress the larger, the more pervasive power to curtail in his discretion the free movement of citizens in order to satisfy himself about their beliefs or associations. (357 U.S. 116, 130)

However, exercising the "liberty" to travel (whatever your beliefs), only lasted until Philip Agee entered the scene in the mid-1970s. Agee, a former CIA agent, was then residing in West Germany. In 1974, he announced "'a new campaign to fight the . . . CIA wherever it is operating. This campaign will have two main functions: first, to expose CIA officers and agents and to take the measures necessary to drive them out of the countries where they are operating; secondly, to seek within the United States to have the CIA abolished'" (qtd in Ansbacher 763). When his passport was revoked in 1979, Agee responded with a suit in Federal Court, hoping that national security interests would be outweighed by the civil liberties involved. He was only partially right. Citing the cases of Kent and Zemel, the District Court and then the Circuit Court of Appeal upheld Agee's right to a passport—but these decisions were overturned by the Supreme Court in 1980. Citing the above quotation from *Kent v. Dulles*, Chief Justice Burger wrote on behalf of the Court that, "The protection accorded beliefs standing alone is very different from the protection accorded conduct. . . . Agee's conduct in foreign countries presents a serious danger to American officials abroad and serious danger to the national security" (*Haig v. Agee* 453 U.S. 280, 305). The Court maintained, moreover, that

> the freedom to travel outside the United States must be distinguished from the right to travel within the United States; the constitutional right of interstate travel is virtually unqualified. By contrast, the right of international travel has been considered to be no more than an aspect of the liberty protected by the due process clause of the Fifth Amendment. As such this 'right,' the Court has held, can be regulated within the bounds of due process. (*Haig v. Agee* 453 U.S. 280, 306)

Only Justices Brennan and Marshall dissented because of what they perceived to be "the Court's *sub silentio* overruling" of the Kent and Zemel cases. In Brennan's words,

> I suspect that this case is a prime example of the adage that "bad facts make bad law." Philip Agee is hardly a model representative of our Nation. And the Executive Branch has attempted to use one of the only means at its disposal, revocation of a passport, to stop respondent's damaging statements. But just as the Constitution protects both popular and unpopular speech, it likewise protects both popular and unpopular travelers. And it is important to remember that this decision applies not only to Philip Agee, whose activities could be perceived as harming the national security, but also to other citizens who may merely disagree with government foreign policy and express their views. (*Haig v. Agee* 453 U.S. 280, 319)

This 1980 decision of the American Supreme Court regarding Philip Agee is based on virtually the same principles as the medieval sovereign privilege of *Ne Exeat Regno* (described above).

Agee and Robeson were high-profile people who had the money, connections, and knowledge necessary to bring the government to court. Their cases call attention to the unknown numbers who, failing to meet governmental identity requirements, remain silenced—and unable to move. Thus passports are the great "out" of democratically elected governments: these powerful little identity documents allow governments to keep their citizens at home, at will; to restrict their movements abroad; and to discipline their conduct when out of the country. They also allow governments to close their borders to pernicious individuals, as well as to masses of people (such as the inhabitants of Hong Kong).³³ And all of this without let or hindrance from the law. Rather than introduce legislation specifically governing the administration of the passport, and thereby give citizens legal rights and judicial remedies, one national government after another has maintained that the issuance of this instrument is the state's prerogative. As Lord Wilmot wryly

> Reflecting on the staggering discretionary powers which the passport extends to the American government, Reginald Parker ironically observes: "[If they] were covered by law, then it would be proper to question whether we had forsaken the democratic way of law and life, for. . . this type of administrative decision is contrary to the very heart of our idea of state which guarantees freedom of association, of fact-finding, of dissenting and non-conforming, of expatriation, and of pursuing one's happiness, which indubitably includes the liberty to take a vacation or attend meetings abroad. Fortunately, the State Department's practice is not grounded in any law." (861)

observed in a House of Lords debate, "the only redress open to a person aggrieved by the withdrawal of his passport is to secure the defeat of the Government in the House of Commons" (Jaconelli 320). In a more somber tone, the British Section of the International Commission of Jurists reports that "as the law stands, there is no legal safeguard against any future descent into arbitrary absolutism by the executive, even were such arbitrariness to exceed anything known by present European society, whether east or west" (Thornberry 19).[34]

ON COMMUNITIES

From its inception, the passport system had been criticized in some quarters for its awkwardness to bearers and its negative impact on economic exchange and prosperity. The League of Nations' Passport Conferences of 1920 and 1926 looked forward to a time when past conditions would be reinstated and passports eliminated.[35] During the May 1926 Conference, delegates were reminded of the resolution adopted by the League's Sixth Assembly: "public opinion, particularly in economic circles, undoubtedly expects [us] to take at least a step towards the abolition, to the widest extent possible, of the passport system, and to mitigate considerably the disadvantages and expense which that system entails for the relations between peoples and for international trade facilities" (*Minutes* 44). Economic and security interests seemed at odds; by the third plenary meeting, measures to be instituted "should the passport regime be maintained" were being refined. All-encompassing governmental interests had prevailed. The fledgling United Nations adopted an entirely different tactic: the 1948 *Universal Declaration of Human Rights* declared mobility to be an inalienable human right, leaving the question of passports to individual national governments.[36] Since the 1950s (from the Treaty of Rome to Maastricht), the European Union has emerged as the most comprehensive governmental response to the problematic of freedom of movement (the flow of goods, capital, and people). Whereas international agreements such as NAFTA and GATT focus solely on economic exchange, leaving questions of national borders and citizenship untouched, the EU implicates issues of individual and national (and transnational) identities, citizenship, and economic integration.[37]

According to the EU Commission's August 1996 *Report on the Operation of the Treaty on European Union,* the project was conceived primarily as a deterrent for future wars on the continent:

> In the 1950s, as the principles which were to lead . . . to the Treaty of Rome [1957] were starting to take shape, the war was still in everyone's mind. The deep psychological scars it left behind helped create a consensus as to the fundamental objectives of European integration: the future would have to be different from the past. . . . It can be said that Europe, the stage for the two greatest conflicts of the century,

has—in creating the Community—invented a new form of government in the service of peace. (*Report*)

Thus, the best way to avoid war is to create economic integration in a new Europe. The Commission's report continues:

> In setting up a community designed to last indefinitely, equipped with its own institutions, *enjoying legal personality, and internationally represented in its own name*, the Member States . . . have pooled their sovereign rights and created a new legal order, involving not just the Member States themselves, but also their citizens in the specific fields concerned. (*Report*; emphasis ours)

> "1. Citizenship of the Union is hereby established. Every person holding the nationality of a Member State shall be a citizen of the Union.
> 2. Citizens of the Union shall enjoy the rights conferred by this Treaty and shall be subject to the duties imposed thereby."
> — Article 8a, Maastricht Treaty

Balibar describes "a state of this type. . . as fundamentally conceived as *the state institution of a market*, a kind of 'liberal' utopia in practice" (17).

The Maastricht Treaty (1992) establishes a new kind of citizenship at the European level. Passports are now issued under the generic rubric of the Union, with the nation state actually granting the identity document taking second billing. European citizens enjoy "the free movement of goods, services, labor, [and] capital" (Abbey 1332), as well as the right of residency in any member state (regardless of economic function[38]). European integration has also meant the multiplication of opportunities for political work across national borders (an Italian national, for example, can run in municipal elections in London or represent a Swedish constituency in the European Parliament, if elected), and of judicial instances of appeal (to the European Ombudsman, Court, or Parliament).

Yet many critics have questioned the practical significance of European citizenship. Article 8a, for example, admits limits to the freedom of movement: member states can, for reasons of public policy, security, or health, restrict movement or residence within their borders. As La Torre summarizes, "The 'heavy' rights attributed through European citizenship either were already granted to member state nationals (as is the case, in great measure, of freedom of movement and residence) or are symbolic rights, that is, devoid of a real impact on the powers which constitute and direct the Union" (121).

More importantly, however, the rights and privileges of this citizenship are reserved exclusively for *nationals* of the member states, and each state retains the right to determine who can become a national and under what cir-

> "Europe finds it hard enough to agree on what it means to be a European. But there seems, in some quarters at least, to be a rapidly developing consensus about who is to be excluded from any access to any definition which might emerge."
>
> Paul Boateng, MP, British House of Commons, in the Preface to *Unequal Migrants* (Joint Council I)

cumstances. The result of this distribution of powers is the exclusion from European citizenship of more than seven million resident aliens—some of whom are second and third generation *Gastarbeiter* (guest workers). As succinctly outlined by Britain's Joint Council for the Welfare of Immigrants:

> Third country nationals settled in the member states have no right to move across intra-community borders for economic purposes. They cannot seek employment or obtain the right to establish themselves in self-employment or move across borders to use or provide a service . . . . A higher proportion of third country nationals have become subject to pre-entry visa requirements which make travel in the Community more difficult even for casual vacation trips. (Joint Council 39)

As Balibar reminds us, "until the middle of the 20th century, the principal meaning of [Europeans] referred to groups of colonizers in each of the colonized regions elsewhere in the world" (7). We would argue that it still does: European citizenship excludes the internal colonies of its ethnicized class division of labor. Once again, the granting and denial of citizenship and passports constitute the acceptable face of institutional racism.[39] The exclusion of more than seven million European residents thus reproduces the well-known process of unequal development fostered by capitalism, both at home and abroad.[40]

But economic relations alone cannot fully account for the historical link between national identities, citizenship, and racism, as the ongoing twentieth-century obsession with alienage confirms. Balibar reminds us that

> there is virtually no historical example of nationalism without a racist supplement. . . . Racism is an elaboration and forward rush of the contradictions of nationalism, driven both by its historical necessity and by its practical impossibility. (I say impossibility because no nationalism can achieve in the real world its ideal of a purified, totally hegemonic community). (12–13)

But then why does nationalism *necessarily* need a purified, homogenous essence? Foucault's analysis of governmentality provides a critical perspective on this problematic. When nation states deploy a series of security mechanisms designed to foster the life of their population (rather than merely to secure a territory), when, in other words, the biological continuum of the *life* of a nation becomes the target of governmental power, there arises a *vital* need to establish and qualify differences. Racism is required by the exercise of power relations geared to secure the quality, the purity, and the strength of a national population, as the best means to enforce distinctions and exclusions, and to wield the ancient right to kill:

> "For me the importance of hybridity is not to be able to trace two original moments from which the third emerges, rather hybridity to me is the 'third space' which enables other positions to emerge. This third space displaces the histories that constitute it, and sets up new structures of authority, new political initiatives, which are inadequately understood through received wisdom."
> Homi Bhabha (Rutherford, "The Third Space" 211)

What permitted the inscription of racism in the mechanisms of the State was precisely the emergence of bio-power. . . . If the power of normalization wishes to exercise the old sovereign right to kill, it must pass through racism . . . . Let it be clear that when I speak of 'killing' I am not thinking simply of direct assassination, but rather of all that can also be indirect death: the fact of exposing to death or of multiplying, for some, the risk of death, or more simply political death, expulsion. (Foucault 1992: 263-266; our trans.)

National governments of the EU, and the European Parliament, like to maintain that economic development, sound immigration policies coupled with pro-active legislative measures, and education will eventually eradicate racism (even as it is gaining ground at both street and political party levels). The EU might prove successful in bypassing war among its member states (though it has been so far unable either to prevent war or broker peace on the European continent at large). Despite its claims to the contrary, however, it shows no signs of altering the racist war relations *necessarily* established in peace time, by the very exercise of governmentality itself, between its citizens and resident aliens.

But what happens when governments are shattered? Could a third space emerge, where alternate relations of power and knowledge, of love and self-fashioning, become possible? Michael Ondaatje's *The English Patient* (also 1992) stages two different attempts at building such novel communities, outside of nations and governments, just before and near the end of World War II. The first is created in the 1930s by a group of men who choose the Libyan desert as their site to learn life and become themselves: "We were German, English, Hungarian, African—all of us insignificant to them [the Bedouin]. Gradually we became nationless. I came to hate nations. We are deformed by nation states. Madox died because of nations"[41] (Ondaatje 138). Unlike many modernist texts, in which the desert serves only as a figure for solitude and the arid sterility which characterizes urbanized Western society, Ondaatje's text celebrates the desert's "rambling feasts and cultures"(139) and their numerous histories. With Herodotus as his guide, Count Ladislaus de Almàsy uncovers the desert's subjected knowledges and ways of life. Through their travels and writings, he and his fellow explorers transform their internal topographies:

> It was as if he had walked under the millimetre of haze just above the inked fibres of a map, that pure zone between land and chart between distances and legend between nature and storyteller. Sandford called it geomorphology. The place they had chosen to come to, to be their best selves, to be unconscious of ancestry. Here, apart from the sun compass and the odometer mileage and the book, he was alone, his own invention. He knew during these times how the mirage worked, the fata morgana, for he was within it. (Ondaatje 246)

The text reiterates that this escape from governmentality was never more than a mirage. Although they wanted to believe that "there is God only in the desert. . . . Outside of this there was just trade and power, money and war. Financial and military despots shaped the world" (Ondaatje 250), these forces were always among them. Their homosocial community is first interrupted by the arrival of Geoffrey Clifton, a British intelligence officer posing as a wealthy dilettante traveling with his new wife, Katherine. With the outbreak of World War II, their expeditions, sponsored all along by the Royal Geographical Society, are suddenly terminated. In other words, these "planetary strangers" (Ondaatje 244) were never elsewhere, were never free to be "outsiders." Moreover, the love between Katherine Clifton and Almàsy reproduces the life-death struggles of the world at large; their passion produces a "list of wounds" (Ondaatje 153).[42] Ultimately, their relationship results in three horrific deaths—love as war by other means, and all of this under the careful scrutiny of government agents.[43]

The community of "desert Europeans" (Ondaatje 135) is reconstructed through the stories and memories of the novel's primary community, which gathers around the English patient from April to August 1945 in the Villa San Girolamo just north of Florence. Functioning as a palimpsest, the text writes the nomadic movement of desert cultures onto a privileged site of emergence for Western modernity, to show the latter's ruination by war. All is "in near ruins": the villa (which might have hosted "Pico and Lorenzo and Poliziano and the young Michelangelo" [Ondaatje 57]), the countryside, and the four main characters, who have been literally or figuratively defaced by war. Governmental power relations are suspended at the villa, and "now there is hardly a world around them and they are forced back on themselves" (Ondaatje 40). Before they forged this unlikely community, all had withdrawn their names and identities: Almàsy, the Hungarian count turned German spy had become "the English patient"; the Canadian nurse, Hana, called herself by the same name she gave all her patients, "Buddy"[44]; the Italian-Canadian thief turned British spy, David Caravaggio, never spoke and "revealed nothing, not even his name, just wrote out his serial number" while a patient in a Rome military hospital (Ondaatje 27); and the Sikh sapper (and future doctor), Kirpal Singh, went by the nickname Kip, given to him by his British military "comrades."[45] Gradually, by learning each other's stories, they reinvent their selves: "But here they were shedding skins. They could imitate nothing but what they were. There was no defense but to look for the truth in others" (Ondaatje 117). This process allows them to invent different kinds of relations, however large the difficulties: a friendship forms between the two spies; the "Englishman" and Kip "'get on so well together'" because "'both [are] international bastards'" (Ondaatje 176-177); Hana and Kip negotiate their desire despite the wounds that have been inflicted because of gender ("'I was sick of the hunger. Of just being lusted at. So I stepped away'" [Ondaatje 85]) and race ("he was accustomed to his invisibility. In England he was ignored in the various barracks. . . . being the anonymous member of another race, a part of the invisible world" [Ondaatje 196]).

For all four, "defenses of character" and behavior (Ondaatje 196) are gradually discarded. But just as they achieve and enjoy their community, when they agree that it finally does not matter who the English patient is ("'He's fine. We can let him be'" [Ondaatje 265]), Kip hears of the bombing of Hiroshima and Nagasaki, and all becomes impossible, intolerable. For Kip, previous national identities reappear, indomitable: "'My brother told me. Never turn your back on Europe. The deal makers. The contract makers. The map drawers. Never trust Europeans, he said'" (Ondaatje 284). As he holds the English Patient in his rifle sights, Kip is told by Caravaggio that the burned man is not English: "'American, French, I don't care. When you start bombing the brown races of the world, you're an Englishman. You had King Leopold of Belgium and now you have fucking Harry Truman of the USA. You all learned it from the English'" (Ondaatje 286). Caravaggio can only agree: "He knows the soldier is right. They would never have dropped such a bomb on a white nation" (Ondaatje 286). The text explodes the mirage of "communal histories, communal books" (Ondaatje 261); when Kip closes his eyes, he "sees the streets of Asia full of fire. It rolls across cities like a burst map, the hurricane of heat withering bodies as it meets them, the shadow of humans suddenly in the air. This tremor of Western wisdom" (Ondaatje 284). This is bio-power at its most extreme, contradictory end: to foster life through mass death. And in the face of this, Hana knows that *"from now on. . . the personal will forever be at war with the public*" (Ondaatje 292). And Kip knows that "his name is Kirpal Singh and he does not know what he is doing here" (Ondaatje 287).

The villa community is suddenly ruined; the narrative provides few subsequent details, as if it can barely speak of an "after." Caravaggio and the English patient disappear from its lines. Both Hana and Kip return to their homes in Britain's dominions. Kip's solution is to take no further "risks": to follow instead Eliot's prescription and return to his own home, by his fire, and have a wife and playing children nearby. Ondaatje, like Eliot, uses the ancient wars between the West and the East as figures for twentieth-century conflagrations[46]; and, just as in Eliot, this rhetorical strategy seems to suggest an essentialist argument. By pasting recent wars onto Herodotus's *Histories*, Ondaatje's novel opens up the possibility of reading a transhistorical human nature, drawn along racial lines, into its own story. Nuclear bombs make Singh realize that he can no longer tolerate the colonizer's racism and violence in exchange for his "civilization"; he reassumes his national and racial identity, and the text barely questions the happiness which ensues: "He is a doctor, has two children and a laughing wife. . . . At this table all of their hands are brown. They move with ease in their customs and habits" (Ondaatje 299, 301). This scene of private happiness takes place in 1958: the text has elided the internecine struggles of India's post-colonial history, especially the public mass slaughters which marked India's partition.[47] Moreover, the text completely ignores the Holocaust—and these two silences suggest a simplified racial argument.

And yet there is Hana, wise and alone, whom the text cannot explain or erase: "She, at even this age, thirty-four, has not found her own company, the ones she wanted. She is a woman of honor and smartness whose wild love leaves out luck, always taking risks, and there is something in her brow now that only she can recognize in a mirror" (Ondaatje 301). Or, in the words of Virginia Woolf, "There she was"—an alien at home, as the passport has been saying all along.

FACING GOVERNMENTS

This multifaceted discursive critique of the problematic of identity has focused on a crucial yet overlooked twentieth-century power-knowledge matrix—the passport—which allows an ever-more invasive exercise of governmental powers through the identification of the One and the Other. Authorizing an *administrative* consolidation of "the national essence," the passport emerges as a key instrument for the concomitant determination of state security and foreign policy. And yet the reverse is also true: it is because this document is constantly positioned as being essential for such vital state concerns that governments have been able to grant themselves extensive discretionary powers in the granting and withholding of passports, against all hegemonic beliefs in freedom of movement. In many respects, the passport acts as a hinge between the nineteenth-century preoccupation with history as organic evolution of the same and the twentieth-century obsession with fractured spaces: it localizes individuals and helps to secure sovereign spaces—all in the name of a nation developing throughout the centuries (or ever since the last international treaty).

The passport and its constellation of concepts (citizenship, allegiance, state protection) also extend governmental powers over the One and the Many. The stories of Shipley, Robeson, Agee, and Lord Haw-Haw make manifest the degree to which individual beliefs and conduct, indeed entire lives, can be determined or terminated with this identity document. Moreover, the ethnic, racial, and class composition of the population as a whole can be calibrated through attendant systems of visas and work permits, and the institution of various immigration policies, nationality and citizenship acts.

Foucault's critique of governmentality demonstrates that this mode of biopower fosters life and administers death through racism: the biological, economic, and political health of the nation must be secured at the expense of specified others. We have shown that this process is writ large in the EU, the greatest governmental project since World War II, for its transnational citizenship (complete with passport) can only confirm state racisms. Yet the latter, ironically, can no longer be "naturalized" so readily: as each country's particular exclusions do not correspond to the others' (the German *Gastarbeiter/Ausländer* is not synonymous with the French *immigrés/étrangers*), the political nature of all forms of inclusion and exclusion becomes glaringly apparent in a Fortress Europe.

The literary fictions concerned with issues of individual and national identities we have analyzed have either confirmed or countered the governmental production of homogeneity and disparity, of the One and the Other. Texts by male modernists such as James and Eliot lament the loss of unadulterated identities and formally reproduce the modern neighborhood as a fractious, threatening, incomprehensible fact. Cultural purity was so intensely valued that it made sense for both authors to reinvent themselves by assuming a prefabricated English identity—just as it did for the British monarchy itself. Alternatively, through the ineradicable presence of such characters as Clarissa Dalloway and Hana, Woolf and Ondaatje (aliens, because of gender and race, to the dominant white masculinist identity) instantiate the possibility of constructing other subject positions and performing identities differently.

But how can power relations that exceed the economic and political to include the fostering of life, of knowledges and desires, be countered and transformed? Perhaps, most immediately, by resisting specific, seemingly commonsensical practices: what should be advocated, for example, is not "an inalienable human right" to mobility, but rather an international legal right to a passport, in order to end its status as a government prerogative. Winning this right would of course mean complying with governmental procedures operating through identification and localization. A similar situation arises when Jean-François Lyotard, at the end of The Postmodern Condition (a report commissioned by the government of Québec and the Council of Québec Universities), calls for universal access to databases in order to protect individual freedoms—a condition which, if realized, would meet the needs of both governments and businesses to have every citizen so inscribed. Much in the same way, the right to a passport means registering everyone in governmental information systems—but only through such a right could legislative recourse become not only possible but effective.

> When I landed in the republic of conscience
> it was so noiseless. . . .
>
> At immigration, the clerk was an old man
> who produced a wallet from his homespun coat
> and showed me a photograph of my grandfather. . . .
>
> No porters. No interpreter. No taxi.
> You carried your own burden and very soon
> your symptoms of creeping privilege disappeared. . . .
>
> At their inauguration, public leaders
> must swear to uphold unwritten law and weep
> to atone for their presumption to hold office—. . . .
>
> I came back from that frugal republic
> with my two arms the one length, the customs woman
> having insisted my allowance was myself.
>
> The old man rose and gazed into my face
> and said that was official recognition
> that I was now a dual citizen.
>
> He therefore desired me when I got home
> to consider myself a representative
> and to speak on their behalf in my own tongue. . . .
>
>   Seamus Heaney, "From the Republic of Conscience"

This problem leads to a more general consideration of the relative effectiveness of identity politics as a mode of resistance to dominant forms of power relations. What does it mean to claim an original identity determined in terms of space, gender, or race, when governments know and direct their populations precisely in those terms? The alternative might be to think of identity not as origin in space, or essence in place, but rather as a series of ongoing negotiations.[48]

Finally, there is the opportunity, and the need, to promote a new kind of conscientiously international citizenship, a transnational literacy. Addressing a 1981 press conference in Geneva to mark the creation of an International Committee Against Piracy (to defend Vietnamese boat people against armed aggression), Foucault described the emergence of such a citizenship, with its rights and obligations, committed "to rise against all abuses of power, regardless of the [identity of] their authors, regardless of their victims. After all, we are all the governed, and thus, solidary" (*Des espaces* 707; our trans.). Thus governmental bio-power, as exercised worldwide, is actually producing the conditions of possibility for new forms of solidarity and common action (Amnesty International, Physicians Without Borders). One duty of this international citizenship is to "bring to the eyes and ears of governments the misery" for which they are responsible: "human misery must never be a mute leftover of politics. It establishes an absolute right to rise and address oneself to those who hold power" (Foucault, *Des espaces* 708; our trans.). In order to elaborate new practices of the self which acknowledge others, international citizens must first refuse governmental procedures that work by fixing identity.[49] Or as Foucault suggests, "Maybe the target nowadays is not to discover what we are, but to refuse what we are.... The conclusion would be that the political, ethical, social, philosophical problem of our days is not to try to liberate the individual from the state, and from the state's institutions, but to liberate us both from the state and from the type of individualization which is linked to the state. We have to promote new forms of subjectivity through the refusal of this kind of individuality which has been imposed on us for several centuries" (*Omnes* 216). But don't refuse until you have the right to have and to hold a passport.

NOTES

[1] As section IV details, Michel Foucault explored governmentality and bio-power in his lectures at the Collège de France in the 1970s and in his *Introduction* to *The History of Sexuality*. See also Burchell, et al., *The Foucault Effect: Studies in Governmentality*.

[2] For such a discussion, see Paul Fussell (*Abroad*), especially "The Passport Nuisance" 24-31.

[3] In a 1977 interview, Lucette Finas asked Foucault to explain his writing technique, which gathered facts and discourses into its own discourse, which seemed to be disordered, flying from one point to another, and yet established abstract and far-reaching relations, achieving a dramatic, fictional form of analysis. Foucault replied, "I realize full well that I have never written anything other than fictions. I do want to say that this is outside of truth. It seems to me that it is possible to make fictions work within truth, to induce truth effects with a fictional discourse and to work in such a way that the discourse of truth elicits, fabricates, something that doesn't yet exist, and therefore 'fictionalizes.' One can 'fictionalize' history starting from a political reality that makes it true; one can fictionalize a politics that doesn't yet exist starting from a historical truth" (our trans.; *Des espaces* 3:236).

[4] See note 29, below.

[5] For pre-World War I studies of U.S. passport policies, see Hackworth 435-52, Hunt, and Moore 855-1022.

⁶ Legal historians point out that, whereas the 1856 statute (ch. 127, §23, 11 Stat. 52, 60) reads that the Secretary of State "shall be authorized to grant and issue passports, "an amendment of 1874 (Rev. Stat. §4075) changed the wording to "may," thereby reinforcing the discretionary character of the Secretary's power (Limoncelli 445).

⁷ Canadian legal scholars are only beginning to address the conflict between the Constitution and the country's passport regulations. The passport, instituted in 1947 when Canadian citizenship was legally established, offers an interesting conflation of sovereign and governmental prerogatives: "The Secretary of State for External Affairs of Canada requests, in the name of Her Majesty the Queen, all those whom it may concern to allow the bearer to pass freely without let or hindrance and to afford the bearer such assistance and protection as may be necessary. THIS PASSPORT IS THE PROPERTY OF THE GOVERNMENT OF CANADA." Yet the Constitution, cited at the beginning of the paper, guarantees its citizens mobility rights, thereby contradicting the state's prerogative to issue passports. See Arkelian, Lansing. The institution of Canadian citizenship, however, did not mean the end of internal colonialism. Thomas King's short story "Borders" vividly presents the experience of a Blackfoot woman who refuses to declare Canadian or American citizenship at the Canada-U.S. border. She eschews any passport or citizenship declaration which has been imposed on her and her people and is left stranded in the no-man's land between the two borders. Customs officers, on both sides, only let her through when the television news reporters arrive (King 129-45).

⁸ See Woolf below, section IV.

⁹ In its 1974 report, the British Section of the International Commission of Jurists commented that "the category of persons qualified to countersign is conceived in such a way as to cause practical problems for many applicants. Some feel, additionally, that the category of qualified countersignatories is expressed in a way *strangely* reminiscent of early twentieth-century middle-class attitudes, omitting as it does teachers, trade union officials, university lecturers, etc" (Thornberry 21; emphasis ours).

¹⁰ The size of the forehead, for example, was believed to indicate level of intelligence, propensity for violent or criminal behavior, and even class. "Hooked" noses, as opposed to "normal" ones, identified Jews negatively. See Gilman, Leps.

¹¹ Baldwin (1867-1947) was British prime minister three separate times: May 1923-January 1924; November 1924-June 1929; and June 1935-1937.

¹² As Balibar suggests,

> In essence, modern racism is never simply a "relationship to the Other" based upon a perversion of cultural or sociological difference; it is a relationship to the Other mediated by the intervention of the

> state. . . . In fact it is the state qua nation-state which actually produces national or pseudo-national "minorities" (ethnic, cultural, occupational). Were it not for its juridical and political intervention, these would remain merely potential. Minorities only exist in actuality from the moment when they are codified and controlled. Similarly, it is the state which, for more than a century, has established the strictest possible correlation . . . between citizenship or nationality rights and individual or collective social rights, thereby becoming itself a "national-social state." (15)

13 As Wier observes, "It was one of the supreme ironies of history that the monarchy which led Britain and the Empire through two wars against Germany should itself be of German origin and its members closely intermarried with high-ranking supporters of Kaiser William II or Adolf Hitler. Queen Victoria herself spoke English with a strong German accent, and German at home with Albert" (317). Victoria was the last Hanoverian monarch; Edward VII was the first from the House of Saxe-Coburg Gotha.

14 From Eliot's 1928 poem, "A Song for Simeon":

Grant us thy peace.
I have walked many years in this city,
Kept faith and fast, provided for the poor,
Have given and taken honor and ease.
There went never any rejected from my door.
Who shall remember my house, where shall live my children's children
When the time of sorrow is come?
They will take to the goat's path and the fox's home,
Fleeing from the foreign faces and the foreign swords.
(*Complete Poems* 105)

15 Foucault contextualizes the notion of "neighborhood" in terms of the larger problematic of space in our century. "The haunting obsession of the nineteenth century," Foucault suggests,

> was, we know, history; themes of development and stoppage, themes of crisis and cycle, themes of the accumulation of the past, the great overburdening of the dead, the menacing cooling down of the world. . . . Perhaps the current epoch would be, rather, the epoch of space. . . . We are in a moment when the world knows itself, I believe, less like a large life which would develop through time, than like a network which connects points and which interlaces its skein. (*Des espaces* 752; our trans.)

The localization of populations is mentioned by Foucault as an instance of the twentieth-century's fixation on space:

In an even more concrete manner, the problem of placement or of position arises for men [sic] in terms of demography; and this problem of human placement is not simply the question of knowing whether or not there is enough place for man in the world—a problem which is after all very important—, it is also the problem of knowing which relations of neighborhood, what type of stockpiling, of circulation, of spotting, of classification of human elements must preferably be retained in such and such a situation to arrive at such and such an end. We are in an epoch when space gives itself to us in the form of relations of place. (*Des espaces* 753-54; our trans.)

16 "The value of universality," Jacques Derrida suggests,

capitalizes all the antinomies, for it must be linked to the value of exemplarity that inscribes the universal in the proper body of a singularity, of an idiom or a culture, whether this singularity be individual, social, national, state, federal, confederal, or not. Whether it takes a national form or not, a refined, hospitable or aggressively xenophobic form or not, the self-affirmation of an identity always claims to be responding to the call or assignation of the universal. There are no exceptions to this law. No cultural identity presents itself as the opaque body of an untranslatable idiom, but always, on the contrary, as the irreplaceable inscription of the universal in the singular, the unique testimony to the human essence and to what is proper to man. Each time, it has to do with the discourse of responsibility: I have, the unique "I" has, the responsibility of testifying for universality. Each time, the exemplarity of the example is unique. That is why it can be put into a series and formalized into a law. (*Des espaces* 72-73)

17 A similar scene is featured in E.L. Doctorow's *Ragtime* (1974), which, like Michael Ondaatje's *In the Skin of a Lion* (1987), revisits and reassesses the era of massive immigration to Canada and the U.S. in the first two decades of the century.

18 Pound persuaded Harriet Monroe, editor of *Poetry* magazine, to publish "Prufrock" in 1915; see Paige 50. At Pound's instigation, Eliot's first volume of poetry, *Prufrock and Other Observations*, was published by the Egoist Press in 1917. To assess the full extent of Pound's editorial role in the production of *The Waste Land*, see Valerie Eliot, "*The Waste Land.*"

19 In June 1927, Eliot was officially received into the Church of England (see Gordon 132-133); in November 1927, he became a British citizen (Ackroyd 165). Both acts were publicly announced in the Preface to his 1928 essay collection *For Lancelot Andrewes*.

20 The history of one's being is figured in terms of the trajectory from young child playing to the "dust" of previous generations.

²¹ The poem is organized into five parts, each of which is titled; the structure mimics that of a well-made play—but there is no climax, no *dénouement*. The mythic subtext—the quest for the Holy Grail—is displaced as rigorously as it is inscribed.

²² Eliot himself suggests as much in the footnote which explains the figure of Tiresias:

> Tiresias, although a mere spectator and not indeed a "character," is yet the most important personage in the poem, uniting all the rest. Just as the one-eyed merchant, seller of currants, melts into the Phoenician Sailor, and the latter is not wholly distinct from Ferdinand Prince of Naples, so all the women are one woman, and the two sexes meet in Tiresias. What Tiresias sees, in fact, is the substance of the whole poem. (*Complete Poems* 78)

²³ At a time when anti-German sentiments remained strong in Britain, Eliot insisted on rehabilitating German culture. The text repeatedly quotes Wagner's operas, some of which deal with Arthurian figures (Parsifal, Tristan and Isolde) but others which reinscribe myths central to the construction of the "German" (as opposed to Austrian or Prussian) identity. Interestingly, Eliot's working title for the poem was "'He Do the Police in Different Voices,'" a quotation from Dickens's *Our Mutual Friend*; Ezra Pound insisted that it be changed to *The Waste Land*.

²⁴ Rather than positing a historical evolution from one mode to another (from a sovereign regime with its juridico-legal mechanisms drawing the boundaries between the permitted and the forbidden, to a disciplinary regime with its mechanisms of surveillance and correction, and finally to a governmental regime with its mechanisms of security), Foucault recognizes a triangular system of correlations between these mechanisms, within which one mode of power relations becomes dominant for a given period of time.

²⁵ *British Nationality Act*, 1948 c.56; *Aliens Order*, 1953; *British Nationality Act*, 1958, c.10; *Commonwealth Immigrants Act*, 1962, c.21; *British Nationality Act*, 1965, c.34; *Commonwealth Immigrants Act*, 1968, c. 9; *Immigration Act*, 1971, c. 77; *British Nationality Act*, 1981, c.61.

²⁶ Miles, who cogently argues that "the ideological notion of 'race' is embedded in the British political process and political culture," also comments on the "simultaneous narrowing and widening of the category of British nationality by a succession of immigration and nationalist Acts from 1962 onwards, which reinforced 'whiteness' as a central symbol of Britishness" (191, 196-197).

²⁷ "Instead of attaining individuals as legal subjects," Foucault observes,

> capable of voluntary actions, as in sovereignty, instead of attaining them as a multiplicity of organisms and bodies susceptible of perfor-

mances and required performances as in discipline, [governmental procedures] will try to attain specifically a population, ... a multiplicity of individuals who exist only as profoundly, essentially, biologically linked to a materiality within which they live. (1989; our trans.)

28 The Soviet passport was perhaps the most extreme instantiation of the principles and security mechanisms of the police, in this century. Every Soviet citizen had to bear a passport which was, as Pipko and Pucciarelli state, "a biographical capsulization of its bearer in booklet form." The document contained, in addition to the usual information as to name (and photograph), place and date of birth, nationality (based on that of the parents), marital status and children, "a record of military service, place of work, notations concerning required alimony payments, if any, where the bearer ha[d] failed to make the required payments, and, most importantly, a *propiska*" (Pipko 34). The latter was a stamp, akin to an internal 'visa' system, granted by the agencies of internal affairs, giving its bearer the legal right to live in an exact location (not just a region in the Soviet Union, but a city, street, building, and apartment). The *propiska* was thus "at the very core of the means by which the ministry controls the Soviet population" (Pipko 34). For a more complete discussion of Russian and Soviet passports, see Matthews.

29 The state (the Prime Minister; various Lords; politicians such as Richard Dalloway, M.P.; bureaucrats like Hugh Whitbread); the judiciary (Sir John Buckhurst); the industrial middle class (Sally Seton, wife of the cotton manufacturer); the army (Septimus Smith, Evans, Mrs. Foxcroft's "nice boy [who] was killed," the soldiers who continue to march in London); the empire (Peter Walsh, the administrator, and Lady Bruton, who believes in enforced emigration to Canada of the unemployed working class); immigration (Rezia Smith, the Italian war bride; the "colonial" who "insulted the House of Windsor"); the church (Miss Kilman); mental and physical health (Drs. Bradshaw and Holmes); and academia (Prof. Brierly).

30 Only when discussing Sir William Bradshaw does the narrative irrupt into personification and didacticism. The narrator does not disguise its censure; instead, it directly specifies the necessary link between Bradshaw's "Proportion" and imperialism's "Conversion":

> But Proportion has a sister, less smiling, more formidable, a Goddess even now engaged—in the heat and sands of India, the mud and swamp of Africa, the purlieus of London, wherever in short the climate or the devil tempts men to fall from the true belief which is her own—even now engaged in dashing down shrines, smashing idols, and setting up in their place her own stern countenance. Conversion is her name and she feasts on the feasts of the weakly, loving to

impress, to impose, adoring her own features stamped on the face of the populace. (Woolf 109)

31 In a series of lectures given at the Collège de France in 1975-76, Foucault proposes that we reverse Clausewitz's famous saying to consider *peace* as war waged through other means. In this hypothesis, "political power. . . perpetually inscribes, through a kind of silent war, relations of force in institutions, in economic inequalities, in language, and onto the bodies of the one and the many." And these effects, we would argue, are mediated through such seemingly benign governmental measures as granting or withholding passports. The lectures are available on audio cassette at the Biblioteque du Saulchoir in Paris; they have been translated into Spanish and published as *Genealogía del racismo* (29; our trans.).

32 For a summary of those cases from the 1940s and early 1950s in which U.S. citizens were refused passports, see "Passport Refusals."

33 On July 1, 1997, three million Hong Kong inhabitants who hold British passports became "British Nationals (Overseas)," bearers of passports "appropriate to their status" (*Hong Kong [British Nationality] Order* 1986) which disallow immigration into the UK.

34 The case of William Joyce is emblematic in this regard. Although an American citizen, Joyce had lived in Britain for more than two decades and obtained a British passport by misrepresentation. During World War II, he broadcast Nazi propaganda from Berlin using the pseudonym of "Lord Haw-Haw." He was arrested in 1945, tried for treason, convicted, and hanged (in 1946). The British government used the fact that he held a British passport, and therefore owed allegiance to the Crown, to argue that it had the right to try him. But as the British Section of the International Commission of Jurists has subsequently noted,

> The judgement has been widely criticized, and it is our view that the case was wrongly decided. . . . Its illogicality bars the way to any clear understanding of the law relating to passports. It is evident that the Crown owed the alien, Joyce, no duty of protection by virtue of his having a passport. (It would have owed him no legal duty of protection even had he been a citizen.) Why, then, should Joyce have owed allegiance while in Germany? A leading authority [de Smith, *Constitutional and Administrative Law*, 438] comments on this case that, "It is impossible to believe that the Crown has any legal duty to afford diplomatic protection to an alien outside H.M. dominions, even if he has obtained a United Kingdom passport by misrepresenting his citizenship." (Thornberry 7-8)

Thus, the British authorities were able to use the instrument of the passport as an expedient means of executing an alien.

35 The *Minutes* of the 1926 Conference record that

> Mr. Sperling (Great Britain) said that, in order to shorten the discussion, it would be well for him to state quite definitely that the only resolution to which his delegation would be able to agree would be one to the effect that the world should be restored to such a state of affairs that passports would be no longer necessary. Such a resolution, however, would have little practical value. (45)

36 Resistance to the elimination of the passport has always been reiterated at the UN level. At a 1963 international conference on passports and other travel policies, Ehrlich notes, a

> group of experts had recommended that the conference propose "replacement of passports by national identity documents. . . ." In part because of American opposition to this proposal, however, the conference members could agree only that national passports requirements should be reduced "to the minimum that is compatible with . . . national interests and security." (U.N. Doc. No. E/ Conf. 47/18, at 6 [1963]; Ehrlich 131)

37 The European Union (EU) is the most recent name given to the association of European states. It was at first often referred to as "the Europe of Rome" (after the Treaty of Rome, 1957), then as the European Economic Community, which was instituted as the European Community with the Maastricht Treaty (signed in 1992, effective 1 November 1993). This series of name changes works to push the driving economic imperatives to the background and to foreground instead the ostensible social and political dimensions of the treaties. Extensive documentation can be obtained at:
   http://www.chemie.fu-berlin.de/adressen/eu.html
   http://www.sdmadeira.pt/html_docs/EU.html

38 The Treaty of Rome (1957) entitled workers to reside in member states only after they had secured employment there.

39 Balibar cogently discusses the racism inherent in EU structures, but conceptualizes it in terms of an absence of state power, "a decomposition or deficiency of the state" (16, 6-7). We are suggesting that Foucault's concept of governmentality effectively reconfigures the problematic in terms of actual state practices.

40 Mandel describes the process of unequal development as does Wallerstein in both *The Capitalist World* and *Geopolitics*. Etienne Balibar concurs: "It is precisely this mode of differential reproduction which the European Community officially ratifies and will probably seek to protect" (13). See also Neil Smith and Balibar and Wallerstein.

41 "'And Madox returned to the village of Marston Magna, Somerset, where he had been born,'" Almásy gradually explains:

"It was July 1939. [Madox and his wife] caught a bus from their village into Yeovil. . . . When the sermon began half an hour later, it was jingoistic and without any doubt in its support of the war. . . . Madox listened as the sermon grew more and more impassioned. He pulled out the desert pistol, bent over and shot himself in the heart. He was dead immediately. A great silence. A desert silence. . . . Yes, Madox was a man who died because of nations." (Ondaatje 260)

[42] "The plate she walked across the room with, flinging its contents aside, and broke across his head, the blood rising up into the straw hair. The fork that entered the back of his shoulder, leaving its bite marks the doctor suspected were caused by a fox" (Ondaatje 153).

[43] As the English patient is later informed by David Caravaggio, to his great surprise, "'I was always a private man. It is difficult to realize I was so *discussed*.' 'You were having an affair with someone connected with Intelligence. There were some people in Intelligence who knew you personally.' 'Bagnold probably.' 'Yes.' 'Very English Englishman.' Yes'" (Ondaatje 255).

[44] Readers of Ondaatje's *In the Skin of the Lion* know her as Hana Gull Lewis, but no family name is given in *The English Patient*. Her biological parents, Alice Gull and Cato, are identified only by pseudonyms; Patrick Lewis and Clara Dickens are her step-parents.

[45] "The name had attached to him curiously," the narrative explains.

In his first bomb disposal report in England some butter had marked his paper, and the officer had exclaimed, "What's this? Kipper grease?" and laughter surrounded him. He had no idea what a kipper was, but the young Sikh had been thereby translated into a salty English fish. Within a week his real name, Kirpal Singh, had been forgotten. He hadn't minded this. (Ondaatje 87)

[46] *The Waste Land* alludes to the First Punic War fought between Rome and the Carthaginians ("'You who were with me in the ships at Mylae!'"[Eliot, *Complete Poems* 62]); *The English Patient* frequently cites Herodotus's *Histories*, which narrates "the struggle between Asia and Greece, substantially from the time of Croesus to that of Xerxes" (Harvey 206).

[47] The only exception to this textual silence is a historical reference by Kip which Hana ironically records "into the flyleaf" of an old copy of Kipling's *Kim*: "*[Kip] says the gun—the Zam-Zammah cannon—is still there outside the museum in Lahore. There were* two *guns, made up of metal cups and bowls taken from every Hindu household in the city—as jizya, or tax. These were melted down and made into the guns. They were used in many battles in the eighteenth and nineteenth centuries against Sikhs*" (Ondaatje 118).

[48] What is at times referred to as "strategic essentialism"—claiming an essential identity because of the pressures of a specific political conjuncture, and only until immediate goals are achieved—is a difficult line to walk. Essentialism has always been strategic, and its history written largely in violence. Kobena Mercer discusses the limits of essentialism in "Welcome to the Jungle: Identity and Diversity in Postmodern Politics."

[49] Bhabha discusses these issues in the interview "The Third Space" (see Rutherford) and at greater length in *The Location of Culture*.

WORKS CITED

Abbey, Michael, and Nicholas Bromfield."A Practitioner's Guide to the Maastricht Treaty. "*Michigan Journal of International Law* 15 (1994): 1329-357.

Ackroyd, Peter. *T.S. Eliot*. London: Hamish Hamilton, 1984.

Ansbacher, Richard. "Passport Revocation: Balancing Constitutional Freedoms with National Security Concerns." *University of Florida Law Review* 33 (1981): 763-76.

Arkelian, A. J. "The Right to a Passport in Canadian Law." *The Canadian Yearbook of International Law* 21 (1983): 284-93.

———. "Freedom of Movement of Persons Between States and Entitlement to Passports." *Saskatchewan Law Review* 49 (1984/1985): 15-35.

Baimbridge, Mark, Brian Burkitt, and Mary Macey. "The Maastricht Treaty: Exacerbating Racism in Europe." *Ethnic and Racial Studies* 17.3 (July 1994): 420-41.

Balibar, Étienne. "Es Gibt Keinen Staat in Europa: Racism and Politics in Europe Today." *New Left* 186 (1991): 5-19.

Balibar, Étienne, and Immanuel Wallerstein. *Race, nation, class: Ambiguous Identities*. Trans. Chris Turner. London: Verso, 1991.

Barone, Dennis, ed. *Beyond the Red Notebook: Essays on Paul Auster*. Philadelphia: U of Pennsylvania P, 1995.

Bernhardt, Rudolf, and John Anthony Jolowicz, eds. *International Enforcement of Human Rights: Reports Submitted to the Colloquium of the International Association of Legal Science, 1985*. Berlin: Springer-Verlag, 1985.

Binavince, Emilio. "The Impact of the Mobility Rights: the Canadian Economic Union—Boom or a Bust?" *Ottawa Law Review* 14 (1980): 340-65.

Bunting, Basil. *Collected Poems*. London: Fulcrum P, 1968.

Burchell, Graham, Colin Gordon, and Peter Miller, eds. *The Foucault Effect: Studies in Governmentality*. Chicago: U of Chicago P, 1991.

———. Preface. Burchell ix-x.

Cameron, Iain, and Maja Kirilova Eriksson. *An Introduction to the European Convention on Human Rights*. Uppsala: Iustus Förlag, 1993.
Capassakis, Evelyn. "Passport Revocations or Denials on the Ground of National Security and Foreign Policy." *Fordham Law Review* 49 (1981): 1178-196.
Dashwood, Alan. "The Limits of European Community Powers." *European Law Review* 21 (1996): 113-28.
Dawson, Frank, and Ivan Head. *International Law, National Tribunals and the Rights of Aliens*. Syracuse: Syracuse UP, 1971.
Derrida, Jacques. *The Other Heading: Reflections on Today's Europe*. Trans. Pascale-Anne Brault and Michael Naas. Bloomington: Indiana UP, 1992.
D'Hartoy, Maurice. *Histoire du Passeport Français, Depuis l'antiquité jusqu'à nos jours*. 5th ed. Paris: Librairie Ancienne Honoré Champion, 1992.
Edel, Leon. *Henry James: 1901-1916, The Master*. Philadelphia: Lippincott, 1972.
Ehrlich, Thomas. "Passports." *Stanford Law Review* 19 (1966-67): 129-49.
Eliot, T.S. *After Strange Gods*. New York: Harcourt, 1934.
———. *The Complete Poems and Plays of T.S. Eliot*. London: Faber, 1969.
———. *For Lancelot Andrewes*. London: Faber, 1970.
———. *Inventions of the March Hare: Poems 1909-1917*. Ed. Christopher Ricks. London, Faber, 1996.
Eliot, Valerie, ed. *The Letters of T.S. Eliot*. Vol. 1: 1898-1922. London: Faber, 1988.
———. *"The Waste Land": A facsimile transcription of the original drafts*. London: Faber, 1971.
European Union: Selected Instruments Taken from the Treaties. Book 1, Vol. 1. Luxembourg: Office for Official Publications of the European Communities, 1993.
Fagen, Leslie Gordon. "The Right to Travel and the Loyalty Oath: *Woodward v. Rogers* (D.D.C. 1972)." *Columbia Journal of Transnational Law* 12 (1973): 387-400.
Farber, Daniel. "National Security, the Right to Travel, and the Court." *The Supreme Court Review* 81 (1981): 263-90.
Finkelstein, Norman. "*In the Realm of the Naked Eye: The Poetry of Paul Auster*."In Barone 44-59.
Foucault, Michel. *"Des espaces autres."Dits et Écrits 1954-1988*. 4 Vols. Eds. Daniel Defert and Francois Ewald. Paris: Gallimard, 1994.
———. *"Face aux gouvernements, les droits de l'homme."Dits et fcrits 1954-1988*. 4 Vols. Eds. Daniel Defert and François Ewald. Paris: Gallimard, 1994.
———. *The Foucault Effect: Studies in Governmentality*. Eds. Graham Burchell, Colin Gordon, and Peter Miller. Chicago: U of Chicago P, 1991.

———. *Genealogia del racismo: de la guerre de las razas al racismo de Estado*. Trans. Alfredo Tzveibely. Madrid: Las Ediciones de la Piqueta, 1992.
———. *Language, Counter-Memory, Practice. Selected Essays and Interviews*. Ed. Donald F. Bouchard. Ithaca: Cornell UP, 1977.
———. *Omnes et Singulatim: Towards a Criticism of 'Political Reason.'* The Tanner Lectures on Human Value. Ed. S. M. McMurrin. 2 vols. Cambridge: Cambridge UP, 1980-81.
———. "*Sécurité, territoire, population*." Introduction to the 1978 course, cassette recording. Paris: Seuil, 1989.
Fussell, Paul. *Abroad: British Traveling Between the Wars*. Oxford: Oxford UP, 1980.
———. *The Great War and Modern Memory*. London: Oxford UP, 1975.
Garcia, Soledad. *Europe's Fragmented Identities and the Frontiers of Citizenship*. London: Royal Institute of International Affairs, 1992.
Giles, Judy and Tim Middleton, eds. *Writing Englishness 1900-1950: An Introductory Sourcebook on National Identity*. London: Routledge, 1995.
Giles, Judy, and Tim Middleton. Introduction. In Giles and Middleton 1-12.
Gilman, Sander. *The Jew's Body*. London: Routledge, 1991.
Going Abroad: A Report on Passports. Justice Educational and Research Trust. London: Barry Rose Publishers, 1974.
Goodwin-Gill, Guy. *International Law and the Movement of Persons Between States*. Oxford: Clarendon P, 1978.
Gordon, Colin. "Governmental rationality: An introduction." In Burchell 1-51.
Gordon, Lyndall. *Eliot's Early Years*. Oxford: Oxford UP, 1977.
Graff, Gerald. "*Keep off the Grass, Drop Dead*, and Other Indeterminacies: A Response to Sanford Levinson." In Levinson 175-80.
Hackworth, G. *Digest of International Law* (1942): 435-52.
Hall, Stephen. "Loss of Union Citizenship in Breach of Fundamental Rights." *European Law Review* 21 (1996): 129-43.
Hinton, Harold. "Guardian of American Passports." *New York Times Magazine* (27 April 1941): 21.
Hurwitz, Leon. "Judicial Control Over Passport Policy." *Cleveland State Law Review* 20 (1971): 271-85.
Hutchinson, E. P. *Legislative History of American Immigration Policy, 1798-1965*. Philadelphia: U of Pennsylvania P, 1981.
Jaconelli, J. "The Justic Report on Passports." *The Modern Law Review* 38 (1975): 314-320.
Joint Council for the Welfare of Immigrants. *Unequal Migrants: The European Community's Unequal Treatment of Migrants and Refugees*. Policy Papers in Ethnic Relations No. 13. Warwick: Centre for Research in Ethnic Relations, 1989.

Jones, Andy, and John MacLeod. *Mathematical Models for Forecasting Passport Demand*. Research and Planning Unit Paper 83. London: The Home Office, 1994.
King, Thomas. *One Good Story, That One*. Toronto: HarperCollins, 1993.
Lane, Jan-Erik, and Svante Ersson. *Politics and Society in Western Europe*. 2nd ed. London: Sage, 1991.
Lansing, Paul. "Freedom to Travel: Is the Issuance of a Passport an Individual Right or a Government Prerogative?" *Denver Journal of International Law and Policy* 11 (1981): 15-35.
Lash, Scott, and Jonathan Friedman, eds. *Modernity and Identity*. Oxford: Blackwell, 1992.
La Torre, Massimo. "Citizenship: A European Wager." *Ratio Juris* 8 (1995): 113-23.
Laursen, Thomas. "Constitutional Protection of Foreign Travel." *Columbia Law Review* 81 (1981): 902-31.
Leps, Marie-Christine. *Apprehending the Criminal: The Production of Deviance in Nineteenth-Century Discourse*. Durham: Duke UP, 1992.
Levinson, Sanford. "Law as Literature." In Levinson 155-73.
Levinson, Sanford, and Steven Mailloux, eds. *Interpreting Law and Literature: A Hermeneutic Reader*. Evanston: Northwestern UP, 1988.
Limoncelli, Gregory. "Clarifying the Authority Delegated to the Secretary of State for the Control of passports: *Haig v. Agee*." *Boston College Law Review* 24 (March 1983): 435-67.
Lyotard, Jean-François. *The Postmodern Condition: A Report on Knowledge*. Manchester: Manchester UP, 1984.
Mandel, Ernest. *Late Capitalism*. Trans. Joris De Bres. London: Verso, 1980.
Marcus, George. "Past, Present, and Emergent Identities: Requirements for Ethnographies of Late Twentieth-Century Modernity Worldwide." In Lash 3039-330.
Matthews, Mervyn. *The Passport Society: Controlling Movement in Russia and the USSR*. Boulder: Westview P, 1993.
Mercer, Kobena. "Welcome to the Jungle: Identity and Diversity in Postmodern Politics." In Rutherford 43-71.
Michaels, Pete Stuart. "Free Speech Denied: 1950's Anti-Communist Passport Laws and Paul Robeson." *Lincoln Law Review* 18 (1988): 127-41.
Miles, Robert. "Explaining Racism in Contemporary Europe." In Rattansi 189-221.
Milne, A.A. *Wurzel-Flummery: A Comedy in Two Acts*. London: Samuel French, 1922.
Moore, J. *Digest of International Law* (1906): 855-1022.
1993: The New Treaties. European Parliament Proposals. Luxembourg: Office for Official Publications of the European Communities, 1991.

Ondaatje, Michael. *The English Patient*. Toronto: Vintage Books, 1992.
Paige, D. D., ed. *Selected Letters of Ezra Pound, 1907-1941*. London: Faber, 1950.
Parker, Reginald. "The Right to Go Abroad: To Have and To Hold a Passport." *Virginia Law Review* 40 (1954): 853-873.
Partsch, Karl. "The Enforcement of Human Rights and Peoples' Rights: Observations on Their Reciprocal Relations." In Bernhardt and Jolowicz 25-29.
"Passport Refusals for Political Reasons: Constitutional Issues and Judicial Review." *Yale Law Journal* 61.2 (1952): 170-203.
Pieterse, Jan Nederveen. *Emancipations, Modern and Postmodern*. London: Sage, 1992.
———. "Unpacking the West: How European is Europe?" In Rattansi and Westwood 129-49.
Pipko, Simona, and Albert J. Pucciarelli, Jr. "Passport to Dictatorship." *Human Rights* 13 (1986): 32-36.
Posner, Richard. *Law and Literature: A Misunderstood Relation*. Cambridge: Harvard UP, 1988.
Rattansi, Ali. "Western Racisms, Ethnicities, and Identities in a 'Postmodern' Frame." In Rattansi and Westwood 15-86.
Rattansi, Ali, and Sallie Westwood. "Modern Racisms, Racialized Identities." In Rattansi and Westwood 1-11.
———, eds. *Racism, Modernity, and Identity on the Western Front*. Cambridge: Polity P, 1994.
Report on the Operation of the Treaty on European Union. Online. Europa. Internet. 17 August 1996.
Richards, Jeff. *Identity, Community, and Nationalism in Europe*. Southampton Institute Social Science Occasional Papers Series No. 6. Southampton: Southampton Institute, 1994.
Rutherford, Jonathan, ed. *Identity, Community, Culture, Difference*. London: Lawrence and Wishart, 1990.
———. "The Third Space: Interview with Homi Bhabha." In Rutherford 207-21.
Shah, Ramnik. "Passport control and mistake." *New Law Journal* (3 April 1992): 450-52.
Sibley, N.W. and Alfred Elias. *The Aliens Act and the Right of Asylum*. London: William Clowes, 1906.
Sigg, Eric. *The American T.S. Eliot*. Cambridge: Cambridge UP, 1989.
Sinderson, Mary. "Executive Restriction on Travel: The Passport Cases." *Houston Law Review* 5 (1967-68): 499-513.
Slater, David. "Exploring Other Zones of the Postmodern: Problems of Ethnocentrism and Difference Across the North-South Divide." In Rattansi and Westwood 87-125.

Smith, Anthony. "The Problem of National Identity: Ancient, Medieval, and Modern?" *Ethnic and Racial Studies* 17.3 (1994): 375-99.
Smith, Neil. *Uneven Development: Nature, Capital, and the Production of Space*. New York: Blackwell, 1984.
Sternhell, Zeev. *La droite revolutionnaire 1885-1914: Les origines francaises du fascisme*. Paris: Seuil, 1978.
Terry, Thomas. "Administrative Law—Passports May Not Be Revoked For National Security and Foreign Policy Reasons Without Congressional Authorization—*Agee v. Muskie*." *The Notre Dame Law Review* 56 (1981): 508-14.
Thornberry, Cedric et al. [British Section of the International Commission of Jurists]. *Going Abroad: A Report on Passports*. Justice Educational and Research Trust. London: Barry Rose, 1974.
Tratner, Michael. *Modernism and Mass Politics: Joyce, Woolf, Eliot, Yeats*. Stanford: Stanford UP, 1995.
Turack, Daniel. *The Passport in International Law*. Lexington: Heath, 1972.
Vogel-Polsky, Eliane. *Social Policy in a United Europe*. Social Policy Series 9. Luxembourg: Office for Official Publications of the European Communities, 1991.
Wallerstein, Immanuel. *Geopolitics and Geoculture: Essays on the Changing World-System*. Cambridge: Cambridge UP, 1991.
———. *The Capitalist World-Economy: Essays*. Cambridge: Cambridge UP, 1979.
Whiteford, Elaine. "Social Policy after Maastricht." *European Law Review* 18 (1993): 202-22.
Wier, Alison. *Britain's Royal Families: The Complete Genealogy*. London: Bodley Head, 1989.
Wieviorka, Michel. "Racism in Europe: Unity and Diversity." In Rattansi and Westwood 173-88.
Wildes, Leon. "Review of Visa Denials: The American Consul as 20th Century Absolute Monarch." *San Diego Law Review* 26 (1989): 887-909.
Williams, David. "Passport: Without Let or Hindrance." *New Law Journal* 123 (1973): 605-07.
———. "British Passports and the Right to Travel." *International and Comparative Law Quarterly* 23 (1974): 642-56.
Woodmansee, Martha, and Peter Jaszi, eds. *The Construction of Authorship: Textual Appropriation in Law and Literature*. Durham: Duke UP, 1994.
Woolf, Virginia. *Mrs Dalloway*. 1925. Harmondsworth: Penguin Books, 1992.
———. *Three Guineas*. 1938. London: Hogarth, 1991.

PERTINENT LEGISLATION, CONVENTIONS, AND TREATIES

Universal Declaration of Human Rights, 1948. Rpt. in Bernhardt and Jolowicz, eds.
International Covenant on Economic, Social, and Cultural Rights, 1976.
International Convenant on Civil and Political Rights, 1976.

CANADA

Canadian Citizenship Act, 1946, c. 15, s.1.
Canadian Passport Order. SOR/81-86. P.C. 1981-1472, 4 June 1981. *Canada Gazette* Part II, Vol. 115, No. 12.
Constitution Act, 1982, being Schedule B to the *Canada Act 1982* (U.K.), c.11.
Criminal Code of Canada, Chap. C-46, 57-58.
Immigration Act, Canada, R.S.C. 1976-775, c. 52, s. 1.

EUROPEAN UNION

European Convention for the Protection of Human Rights and Fundamental Freedoms, 1953.
Treaty Establishing the European Economic Community 1957 (signed in Rome on 25 March 1957).
Single European Act 1987.
Treaty on European Union 1992 (signed in Maastricht on 7 February 1992; implemented November 1993).

UNITED KINGDOM

Treason Act, 1351 (25 Edw. 3, stat. 5, c.2)
Regulation of Aliens Act, 1793 (Stat. 33 Geo. III, c.4)
Aliens Act, 1905 (5 Edw. 7, c.13)
Aliens Restriction Act, 1914 (4 & 5 Geo. 5 c.12)
Defense of the Realm Acts, 1914-1915
Aliens Restriction (Amendment) Act, 1919, c.92
Aliens Order, 1920. S.R.O. 1920/138
British Nationality Act, 1948 c.56
Aliens Order, 1953
British Nationality Act, 1958, c.10
Commonwealth Immigrants Act, 1962, c.21
British Nationality Act, 1965, c.34
Commonwealth Immigrants Act, 1968, c. 9
Immigration Act, 1971, c. 77
British Nationality Act, 1981, c.61
Prevention of Terrorism (Temporary Provisions) Act, 1989, c.4

UNITED STATES OF AMERICA

Joint Order Requiring Passports and Certain Information from Aliens Who Desire to Enter the United States During the War. 1917. Rpt. *Laws Applicable to Immigration and Nationality.* E. Avery, ed. US Government Printing Office, 1953. 1042-1045.

Passport Act, 1926, 772 U.S.C.

Title 22: Foreign Relations and Intercourse, Chapter 4 (1926), S.211-227, Stat. 657

Nationality Act, 1940, 54 Stat. 1141, 8 U.S.C. 705

Internal Security Act, 1950, c. 1024, 64 Stat. 987 [also known as the *Subversive Activities Control Act,* 1950]

Immigration and Nationality Act, 1952, Pub. L. 414, 66 Stat. 163 (subsequently amended by *U.S.C. '1185 (b) 1976* and *Act of October 7, 1978, '124, 92 Stat. 971, 22 U.S.C. '211a*)

Public Law No. 90-428, An Act to make several changes in the passport laws presently in force. S.2, 82, Stat. 44.

CHAPTER SEVEN

Narrative Pragmatics and the Genius of the Law
in Lyotard's *Just Gaming*
by Theron Britt

In his "Defense of Poetry" Percy Bysshe Shelley famously put forward the notion that "poets are the unacknowledged legislators of the world," and though few would interpret this claim to mean that a work of literature can inaugurate a new law in the sense that such a law would lay claim to universality or to the requirement that everyone must obey it, his assertion has come to resonate with relatively recent developments in literary and legal theory. Both literary and legal scholars have begun to focus attention on the relationship of law and literature, and for the most part this meeting of these two disciplines has been articulated in the direction suggested by Shelley in which literature, paradoxically enough, takes a certain precedence over law.[1] In other words, many literary and some legal scholars have for at least a decade or more been turning to literary theory for analytical tools that, in sum, bring to the surface of legal argumentation the inherently "literary" moment of the law and expose the various rhetorical strategies by which the law represses its figural fluidity in its attempt to appear objectively fixed.[2] From the literary side of things, J. Hillis Miller gives one of the best formulations of this impulse to reveal the law's figurality in his essay "Laying Down the Law: The Example of Kleist" in which he finds that Heinrich von Kleist's narrative "Michael Kohlhaas" ultimately "establishes the law of the absence, unavailability, or failure of the law" and finally "enunciates the law of the unreadability of that law in the name of which all particular laws are promulgated and justified" (324). Appearing as it does in a recent collection devoted to the connection between deconstruction and justice, no one should be surprised to find Miller's exposure of the law's irreducibly figural nature as based in a literary "law" of unreadability, for the enabling assumption of his position is that both law and literature must share in the indeterminacy of language.[3] Nor should one be surprised, then, to find that Miller's notion of justice is linked to the on-going task of reading that is inevitably put in motion by linguistic figurality; for Miller, we are all "arraigned before the bar of justice each reader carries in his or her own breast," and facing the absence of authority, we all must fill in our meanings ourselves and, by implication, take responsibility for our readings (324). This is to say that Miller's justice is not to be found in absolute rules but in the openness to alternatives, to readings, enabled by a literary understanding. Based, as is literature, in the endless process of reading, the world of courts and legal argument, Miller and others argue, is a more or less coherent series of narratives endlessly open to interpretation and redefinition. But the world of courts is ultimately subject to the rule of literary language.[4] Literature, in other words, ultimately gives the law, and the iron law literature gives is always the same one—the law of reading.

This notion of the law of literature which Miller puts forward is not the only way of thinking about how literature and law interact, however. Indeed, his assumption of endless figurality itself needs to be examined, for even if we accept the plausible premise of linguistic indeterminacy, his assertion of language's indeterminate figurality can be read as a moment of saying what is *in fact* the nature of language; that is, the assumption of indeterminacy paradoxically acts as the unmoved mover—the "law"—that enables a particular mode of discourse, in this case the academic debate surrounding the crossing of the two disciplines of law and literature. The sort of question one asks of this crossing is of course crucial, and rather than ask the question as Miller does of whether or not a piece of literature lays down the law of reading, I would rather ask the question of whether or not a competing notion of law is already given in the literary moment, that is, within the very activity of the figural. If it is, then in what way does it inhabit, motivate, or constitute the literary work? Contra Miller, I will argue that the exposure of language's indeterminate figurality acknowledges only one side of an oscillation that includes an unmoved mover, a grounding moment; the argument of law's figurality attends to only one side of the oscillation between a moment of grounding and its undoing, and to forget the moment of grounding is a repression as totalitarian as any other.[5] In the relation of law and literature, I contend that we should pay attention to a bond that is not only one of shared figurality.

As an illustration of literature's moment of law, I would like to turn to an example of this bonding that is present even in the most antiauthoritarian and pluralistic of texts. Jean-François Lyotard's *Just Gaming* (1985) (originally published as *Au Juste* [1979]) is such a text, for in this text, and indeed throughout later works including *The Differend* (1988), Lyotard takes up this problem of what is now labeled the postmodern, focusing on the question of injustice.

Explicitly against all forms of totalitarian thinking, in *Just Gaming* he enacts through the format of the dialogue between himself and his interlocutor, Jean-Loup Thébaud, both the problem and a sort of answer to the question(s) of the relationship between law, justice, and narrative. Here in this text is an early example of Lyotard's postmodern approach that he has consistently continued to articulate in further work. Here he outlines an alternative to what in *The Postmodern Condition* he calls the failure of metanarratives, and it is here that he elaborates a model of narrative pragmatics that he returns to many times elsewhere. For Lyotard, we currently live within the horizon of failed metanarratives. They are "narrations with a [previously] legitimating function" that "have marked modernity: the progressive emancipation of reason and freedom, the progressive or catastrophic emancipation of labor (source of alienated value in capitalism), the enrichment of all humanity through the progress of capitalist technoscience" (*PE* 17, 19). In response to these failed past "grand narratives," Lyotard suggests an alternative strategy of narrative pragmatics, but his strategy serves in my analysis not so much to show an alternative to the failure of metanarratives as it serves to elucidate the structural necessity of the very things Lyotard seems inclined to dispel. Contrary to his argument, his strategy specifically shows the way in which law necessarily inhabits literature and that justice and ethics are not restricted merely to the horizon of legal argument but are constitutive of the literary moment as well in a way other than that articulated by Miller. Since Lyotard is widely recognized as "the champion of difference and plurality in all theoretical realms and discourses" (Best and Kellner 146), his work offers perhaps the best space for examining a possible alternative articulation of the law in literature, an example, in other words, of my contention that the literary moment is itself constituted by a moment of law, not as the law of textuality but as a structurally necessary moment of grounding entailed within narrative expression.[6]

In the first of seven "Days" of conversation structuring *Just Gaming*, Lyotard confronts the problem of judgment and justice within the horizon of modernity, though he does not here take up the debate with Habermas as to whether or not modernity is an incomplete project—i.e., that there may remain untapped resources and/or options to the narratives of emancipation; rather, he assumes more or less the failure of that project.[7] When quizzed in the dialogue of *Just Gaming* as to how one makes a judgment, he seems confident that,

> If I am asked by what criteria do I judge, I will have no answer to give. Because if I did have criteria, if I had a possible answer to your question, it would mean that there is actually a possible consensus on these criteria between the readers and me; we would then not be in a situation of modernity, but in classicism. What I mean is that anytime that we lack criteria, we are in modernity, wherever we may be,

whether it be at the time of Augustine, Aristotle or Pascal. The date does not matter. (JG 15)

In general he critiques modern epistemology and postmodern knowledge rather than an historical epoch or artistic movement. "Modernity," then, though it often is thought of as an historical period, is here a more global conception for which "the date does not matter." In other words, for Lyotard the lack of criteria for judgment is an epistemological transhistorical given, though of course the *recognition* of this condition of knowledge is constitutive of the historical moment of postmodernity. This is why he has "no answer to give" to the call for criteria for judgment.

Yet of course Lyotard does have an answer of sorts to the problem of judgment, one relevant to the crossing of law and literature since it depends on narrative. Seeking a way to judge but lacking criteria for judgment (and indeed, indicting such previous certainties presumably associated with "classicism" as totalitarian), Lyotard turns toward narrative pragmatics for a model of justice. This narrative model offers an alternative for him because it seems to offer prescriptives without either the recourse to an ersatz Platonic essence of justice or even a "will-to-power" or Subject as transcendental origin to do the prescribing. Language games such as those practiced by the Cashinahua Indians of the upper Amazon become valorized in *Just Gaming* and elsewhere for Lyotard essentially because they allow for the "next move" in their tribal language game by placing the listener under an obligation to retell or respond; for Lyotard, the locus "from which the prescription to pass on narratives comes is immanent to the narrative pragmatics itself" (*JG* 36). Utilizing Levinas's "other," Lyotard concentrates on an alternative "pagan" conception of time contained in narrative pragmatics epitomized by the storytelling of the Cashinahua Indians.[8] Rather than attempting to hoard or store up the narrative content and preserve it as the West since the Greeks has done (so it can be sold or traded on the market), Lyotard finds that "in the case of popular traditions, and I think that this is universal and not something limited to the Cashinahua, nothing gets accumulated, that is, the narratives must be repeated all the time because they are forgotten all the time. But what does not get forgotten is the temporal beat that does not stop sending the narratives to oblivion" (*JG* 34). In this view, narratives work apart from the subjects who narrate them to subvert capitalist accumulation. No narrative is ever an exact replica of the one that came before it, if only for the fact that it is contextualized or temporally marked by being in relation to the preceding narrative. No narrative can be stored up but must enter into the process of permutation entailed in repetition. No narrative has a single author, definite origin, or final form.

Lyotard's narrative pragmatics model thus unhinges communication from a model of accumulation and links it instead to a perpetual movement ("temporal beat"). He thereby gains a system of continual renewal, a strategy that allows for continual change and permutation—i.e., that allows for the "next move" in a language game whose only prescriptive is to allow for another move. This strategy of continual renewal is Lyotard's vision of justice.

Though his notion of narrative pragmatics offers us some very useful notions of justice, there are at least two related problems with Lyotard's position. The first and lesser problem with his vision of justice is that he has little to say to the (most often Marxist) charge that his thinking cannot offer much in response to the questions of what is to be done—that is, it cannot animate a progressive politics since it has no idea what "progressive" might mean (nor for that matter any suggestion of what might be "wrong" with a particular story) within this "timeless beat" of narrative; or, in simpler terms, one story is as good as another for Lyotard as the timeless beat of narrative sends them to oblivion. In his defense, narrative pragmatics frees him to deal with the social real on a case-by-case basis, a situation that he asserts occurs in the case of a real judgment, rather than merely in the application of pre-given rules. Given this emphasis on the on-going present, it is not surprising that Lyotard's notion of judgment finally rests on a "feeling" that one is judging correctly (in the absence of preset criteria for judgment). On this point he is explicit: "We are in the position of Aristotle's prudent individual, who makes judgments about the just and the unjust without the least criterion," and therefore when judging one has "a feeling, that is all. It is a matter of feelings, however, in the sense that one can judge without concepts" (*JG* 14, 15). This reliance on "feeling" is, of course, reactive, limiting his form of analysis to cases as they arise—a strength in his view. He offers no criteria for steering the ship of state into the future, nor for creating rules or laws: should one vote for apartheid or against; restrict immigration or not; support the death penalty, or not? Which narratives should take precedence? Lyotard would offer a judgment in each case, perhaps, but not in advance of the particulars since for him the most totalitarian gesture is the one that forecloses the options of judgment; in such a situation of foreclosed options, there is no judgment, only rules, because judgment always occurs in the present tense, and "what is to be done" is always a contingent act embedded in a place and time—e.g., a spatio-temporal given.

To forsake feeling for a direct "answer" to the question of criteria for judgment, Lyotard would undermine the system he has constructed upon the rock of indeterminacy. A direct "answer" or prescriptive would reinscribe Lyotard's narrative pragmatist within the horizon of a problematic that he explicitly repudiates as founded precisely on the totalitarian systems that foreclose the gaming he finds in narrative pragmatics. Even so, narrative pragmatics as a model contains at least one such totalitarian gesture telling us what is to be done: the prescription to allow for another move in the language game.

This objection is fairly obvious to Lyotard, and knowing, then, that he cannot continue to think or write or act without prescriptives of some kind implied or explicit in his work, Lyotard allows for the local, provisional, and contingent application of prescriptives. This is his "indirect" answer to the question of criteria for judgment, but it brings up a second and more troubling problem. This second, related problem is precisely that of instituting provisional prescriptions. A provisional prescription is itself an oxymoron because of the nature of prescription; if a prescription is "provisional" or contingent, then it is determined by something outside of itself, in this case Lyotard's "feeling" of appropriate judgment, and therefore loses its sense as a guide or determining instance. It is only as a paradox, then, that a prescription can be "provisional."

Moreover, the gains which Lyotard gets by insisting on the "provisional" status of prescriptions are offset by another kink in the logic of prescriptions. In his system of narrative pragmatics, the key thing he tries to assert is that in the movement of language games the only thing that one can insist on is the possibility of another move in the game; no move should be allowed to foreclose another player's move. But when confronted with a player whose "move" is to foreclose the ability of response by the responder or opponent, Lyotard's narrative pragmatist is caught in a dilemma, what I call the Hitler/Gandhi situation: either he allows himself to be dominated and perhaps eliminated or at the very least silenced (e.g., Hitler's "move" against his enemies and against which Gandhi's passive resistance would not stand), or he himself institutes what he has denied as a possibility by disallowing the totalitarian's move, thereby instituting a type of totalitarianism of his own, the foreclosure of an opponent/responder's move in the game. Quite simply, the "totalitarian" nature of even his own conception of justice cannot in this instance be avoided. He must lay down the law, or lie down.

Lyotard's argument for narrative pragmatics seems to reside in this irreducible play between totalitarian assertion and pluralistic denial. Indeed, the play between these two moments constitutes his framework for justice. As for Derrida, for Lyotard both justice and law appear to be always part of a language game whose origin and legitimacy are self-generated narratives, based for Lyotard on "feeling" rather than concepts or prescriptions. And though he seems to resist it vigorously, there is nevertheless a nonprovisional prescription in his language game. In the Afterword to *Just Gaming*, Samuel Weber notes this problem: "by prescribing that no game, especially not that of prescription, should dominate the others, one is doing exactly what it is simultaneously claimed is being avoided: one is dominating the other games in order to protect them from domination" (*JG* 105). However, Lyotard is well aware of this self-referential difficulty, and when pressed by Jean-Loup Thébaud confronts it by acknowledging that

> one does risk falling back into a sort of indifferentism that is the bad side of the pagan line I am trying to trace. I think that the difficulty comes from this: when one thinks of justice according to a nonunitary

teleology, one tends to merely reverse what was implied in Kant's doctrine, whereas one should be on one's guard, I think, against the totalitarian character of an idea of justice, even a pluralistic one. (JG 96)

At a key moment of his argument, Lyotard warns his interlocutor and the reader to "be on one's guard" against the totalitarian idea of even a pluralistic idea of justice based in a nonunitary teleology; by this he means finally to "listen" to what he has made explicit as what one "feels" is right or just, rather than to rely on prescriptives. In other words, Lyotard's pluralistic model of justice found within narrative pragmatics is founded on "one's guard" that is, finally, a reinscription of "feeling."

A feeling, of course, is notoriously difficult to describe, residing as it does somewhere in the intersection between mind and body. Nevertheless, within Lyotard's argument at least, this prescriptive guard of "feeling" seems to be something very concrete—the body and its desires as resistant counterforce to domination, but ultimately the body as the horizon of prescription as well (needs, wants, the physical). Moreover, this guard of feeling in Lyotard's narrative engine seems to be his own return of the repressed (in the form of a "feeling" that one is judging well) from his earlier work in which he blended Marx and Freud to create a philosophy of forces, intensities, and desires.[9]

By using narrative pragmatics, Lyotard, like the explicitly invoked figure of Kant, seems to want to give judgment without prescription. Yet Lyotard's attempt to do so falls into itself, into at least one ongoing prescription, and into, by implication, a familiar source of grounding, the "feelings" of the subject who feels, the physicality of a subject's body, ultimately to the body as universal nature, as source and origin reinscribed in a double sense, once from the world of prescriptions and once from his own previous work. To remain at this level of insight, however, is merely to criticize Lyotard's position and ignore the next move implicit in his argument.

That next move perhaps can be seen most clearly by looking at the genealogy of Lyotard's "feelings." Lyotard's interlocutor in *Just Gaming*, Jean-Loup Thebaud, gives us a clue for this task when he asks Lyotard, "Don't you have the feeling that you are writing, book after book, a new *Critique of Judgment?*" (15). Thebaud's hunch is very suggestive, for Kant's third *Critique* does indeed have a rule-giving figure caught in the same self-reflexive function that Lyotard ascribes to narrative pragmatics, a figure of "genius" that is apparently free yet also the source of prescription or rule. As well, a source in Kant is not unmotivated by Lyotard's texts, for when he is asked "where does this ability to judge come from?" Lyotard explicitly alludes to Kant's *Critique of Judgment* and makes clear much of what will follow in his own text: "It is obvious that for someone like Kant . . . the ability to judge does not hang upon the observance of criteria. The form that it will take in the last *Critique* is that of the imagination. An imagination that is constitutive. It is not only an ability to judge; it is a power to invent criteria" (*JG* 17). This constitutive power of the imagination to invent criteria in Kant's third *Critique* functions in much the same way as "feelings" do in Lyotard's pagan alternative of narrative pragmatics. Shifting the terms from "imagination" to "feeling," Lyotard's narrative pragmatics model repeats a problem of the aesthetical situated within Kant's conduit of imagination, the figure of genius, a figure key to Kant's attempt to bridge the gap between the world of phenomena—mere appearance—and the world of noumena—ideas.

Genius is key in Kant's thought because it is the origin of art and the figure by which Kant can unify the two worlds of appearance and ideas.[10] For Kant, "*Genius* is the innate mental aptitude (*ingenium*) *through which* nature gives the rule to art" (*CJ* 2. 46. 168), and so in Kant's system the genius allows us to pass—as the imagination becomes subject to the understanding—beyond the particular to something more general and universal, as it were to raise man up from nature, but at the same time to naturalize man and bridge the two separate realms of appearance and ideas. For Kant, the genius is the conduit by which the noumenal spark in nature gives the rule to art, the agent which puts free will to work in service of nature. While the genius gives rules or at least examples for others to follow, she carries freedom of play and the pure productivity of the imagination to its highest point. Beyond law, the genius's gift passes to the understanding (though it derives from the figural) and thus serves as an origin of standard or rule—of the law (e.g., 46. 169). Genius is thus inside and outside at the same time; she is beyond or outside of rule and law, but at the same time the source of rule and law in the arts.

This figure of genius in Kant gives rules in the same way as Lyotard's idea of narrative pragmatics: genius works through a timeless repetition that is always original, never the same, unavailable to be stored up and traded in the market place. Like Kant's use of genius, Lyotard's use of narrative pragmatics, too, is both inside and outside at the same time; it both attempts to *deny* prescriptions and at the same time to *give* us an overarching prescription which serves as our standard for judgment. Genius' rules require the ineffable quality of "imagination," the prescriptives of Lyotard's narrative pragmatics, the mystery of "feeling."

In the same way that Kant tied together his system of noumena and phenomena through the figure of genius and the aesthetic concept of "imagination," Lyotard must turn to the naturalizing function of "feeling" to ground his system of judgment using narrative pragmatics. Like the figure of genius, narrative pragmatics gives us the law immanent to itself, perhaps, but it is not the law of infinite textuality of Miller, nor the "law" of the "other" and the necessity to pass on a story. Rather, it is an apparently unwitting law of the literary moment itself inhabited by a necessity of prescription, of grounding, of totalizing discourse, even in the name of the most extreme and thorough democratic pluralism.

This apparent drawback, however, may also be an opportunity, for without explicitly anticipating it, Lyotard has opened an avenue for our "next move" in the pagan line he has traced in attempting to relate the power and function of narratives to justice. Just narratives for him must be flexible, pluralistic, and open to permutation and change, but it should be clear from my argument that these qualities are not simply the qualities immanent to narrative pragmatics but values justly chosen out of the complexity of "feelings" and instituted in a type of "totalitarian" moment.

In the meeting of law and literature, many scholars have shown that legislators become in a sense poets because they depend on literary narratives as they create the evolving discourse of the law. But poets, too, are legislators, as Shelley might have it, for the narrative element that inhabits the discourse of law contains its own moment of grounding, marking the literary moment with the force of law's aggressive, "totalitarian" violence. If this is so, given that we retain an interest in a concept of justice, the next gesture implied in Lyotard's argument is not to seek once again for the impossible dream of the truth of an abstract justice, nor to depend on the ebb and flow of narrative pragmatics, but to debate the relative merits of the values implied in the stories we tell. Ghandi's story may well be more worth telling than Hitler's, not because of some inscription of the regime of truth but because of pragmatic collective democratic agreement (this latter itself but a totalitarian prescription). The next gesture implied in Lyotard's narrative pragmatics argument is a turn to a values debate because, even in narratives of greatest freedom such as Lyotard's, there is a moment that requires some form of prescription, repression, or "totalitarian" assertion that can itself only be a value.

NOTES

[1] Shelley's notion that poets are the unacknowledged legislators of the world is based in the idea that acts of the imagination, which poets provide, are both necessary to human society and open to rational contemplation.

[2] Scholars in the Critical Legal Studies movement have done much of this work. One of the most recent articulate voices extending this critique is Cornell; see also Cornell, Rosenfeld, and Carlson. Another good example of this line of argument is Douzinas, Warrington, and McVeigh.

[3] See, for example, Levinson and Mailloux. This excellent collection of essays on the whole brings together literary and legal scholars under the aegis of law *as* literature, privileging the literary over the legal.

[4] Miller presents himself as neither looking at how legal conditions in a particular time or place affect literature, nor at how the particulars of literary theory have interacted with legal theory. He does note a problem raised by the

application of literary theory to legal argument: "as legal scholars well know, there are disquieting implications for the law in recent work suggesting some fundamental unreadability in narratives generally" (306). Rather than addressing these "disquieting implications," he situates himself as asking the question of "whether a work of literature can in any sense be conceived to be law-making" (307).

[5] Even, and perhaps especially, Jacques Derrida reminds us of the moment of literature's grounding or law-giving gesture, of its obligations. When he writes in his essay "Force of Law," for instance, that "deconstruction is justice," he is reminding us not only that real decisions always contain an ungrounded "literary" moment, but also that out of this moment a decision comes that obligates, grounds, or institutes: for Derrida "the undecidable is not merely the oscillation of the tension between two decisions; it is the experience of that which, though heterogeneous, foreign to the order of the calculable and the rule, is still obliged—it is of obligation that we must speak—to give itself up to the impossible decision, while taking account of law and rules" (24).

[6] Lyotard is especially suited to this analysis since his work on postmodernism situates him at the nexus point of law, narrative, and justice. Best and Kellner lucidly argue in their book, for instance, that Lyotard's postmodern theory affirms itself "as the very principle of justice whereby all are allowed to speak and enter the terrain of social agonistics," and further that *Just Gaming* marks a key point in Lyotard's thinking (170).

[7] Lyotard's debate with Habermas on this issue is succinctly summarized by Wlad Godzich in the Afterword to Lyotard's *The Postmodern Explained*. Another very useful source for following this debate, but from a different perspective, is chapter 7 of Best and Kellner.

[8] Lyotard has returned to the Cashinahua Indians' form of narrative pragmatics as a favorite example in several works, most notably in *Just Gaming* (32-35), *The Postmodern Condition* (20-21), and *The Postmodern Explained* (31-33, 43-46, 49). Lyotard fastens upon the Cashinahua storyteller not as the autonomous individual author but as a heteronomous link in the narrative chain who "presents himself as having first been the addressee of a story of which he is now the teller" (*JG* 32).

[9] The earlier work I am alluding to here includes *Discours, figure* (1971) up to *Economie libidinale* (1974) in which he valorizes desire. But it is precisely the limits to this analysis, specifically the question of injustice, that motivated Lyotard's analysis toward postmodernism.

[10] In what follows, I must acknowledge a debt to Derrida's excellent reading of Kant from his essay "Economimesis."

WORKS CITED

Best, Steven, and Douglas Kellner. *Postmodern Theory: Critical Interrogations.* New York: The Guilford P, 1991.

Cornell, Drucilla. *The Philosophy of the Limit.* New York: Routledge, 1992.

Cornell, Drucilla, Michel Rosenfeld, and David Gray Carlson, Ed. *Deconstruction and the Possibility of Justice.* New York: Routledge, 1992.

Derrida, Jacques. "Economimesis." *Diacritics* 11.2 (1981): 3-25.

———. "Force of Law: The 'Mystical Foundation of Authority'." Trans. Mary Quaintance. In Cornell, Rosenfeld, Carlson.

Douzinas, Costas, Ronnie Warrington, and Shaun McVeigh. *Postmodern Jurisprudence: The Law of Text in the Texts of Law.* New York: Routledge, 1991.

Kant, Immanuel. *The Critique of Judgment.* Trans. James Creed Meredith. New York: Oxford UP, 1982.

Levinson, Sanford, and Steven Mailloux. *Interpreting Law and Literature: A Hermeneutic Reader.* Evanston: Northwestern UP, 1988.

Lyotard, Jean-François. *The Differend: Phrases in Dispute.* Trans. Georges Van Den Abbeele. Theory and History of Literature. 46. Minneapolis: U of Minnesota P, 1988.

———. *Discours, figure.* Paris: Klincksreck, 1971.

———. *Economie libidinale.* Paris: Minuit, 1974.

———. *The Postmodern Condition: A Report on Knowledge.* Trans. Geoff Bennington and Brian Massumi. Minneapolis: U of Minnesota P, 1984.

———. *The Postmodern Explained: Correspondence 1982-1985.* Trans. Julian Pefanis, et al. Minneapolis: U of Minnesota P, 1992.

Lyotard, Jean-François and Jean-Loup Thébaud. *Just Gaming.* Trans. Wlad Godzich. Theory and History of Literature 20. Minneapolis: U of Minnesota P, 1985.

Miller, J. Hillis. "Laying Down the Law: The Example of Kleist." *Deconstruction and the Possibility of Justice.* Ed. Drucilla Cornell, Michel Rosenfeld, and David Gray Carlson. New York: Routledge, 1992.

CHAPTER EIGHT

Antonio's Legalistic Cruelty:
Interdisciplinarity and *The Merchant of Venice*[1]
by Richard H. Weisberg

INTRODUCTION

The law and literature movement now involves hundreds of scholars across the disciplines. Among the movement's contributions to scholarship and teaching in literature has been its attention to several well-worked "legalistic" stories. Particular success has been achieved in the debates about Melville's *Billy Budd, Sailor*, where an established critical perspective on Captain Vere has been challenged by recourse to legal materials and closer readings of the story's legalistic passages.[2]

In recent years, a similar methodology has been applied to *The Merchant of Venice*.[3] Abjuring the mainstream critical insistence on "non-ironic" readings of what is clearly one of Shakespeare's most complex and ironic plays, law and literature scholars have again simply noticed what the text affords in rich abundance: passages of legalistic complexity that—once engaged—reverse traditional patterns of understanding.

So, in *Poethics and Other Strategies of Law and Literature* (94-104), I endeavored to show that Act V's legalistic language—epitomized by Portia's rejection of Antonio's persistent intermeddling in her relationship with Bassanio—evokes Shylock and leaves the audience wondering at Belmont's new usages: "surety"; "deed of gift"; "inter'gatories." The Jew, with his insistence on oathkeeping, bonds, and the law, must be defeated at trial, for his verbal directness contradicts Christian linguistic maneuvering as much as his excessive legality offends their notion of "mercy"; yet he seems in the final act quite to have overpowered (on the level of language) the Christian characters and their earlier rejection of him. Portia will not tolerate yet another episode of Antonio's "suretyship" for his young friend, her new husband. She prefers, and will probably enforce on Belmont as best she can, the more directly committed system of the old Jewish moneylender, who has never been able to stomach "Christian intercessors" and their flouting of the law.

On this reading, however appropriate it is to the play's comic medium, which mandates the defeat of Shylock's bond, Portia is at trial always alert to the Jew's constancy and ethics in the domain of human relations. Although she briefly becomes a fellow traveler herself along the path of Christian distortions of law—where ostensible "mercy" quickly is debased to forms of legalized cruelty unimaginable in Jewish communities—she does so merely to solve the comedy's central problem and then to move ahead as ethically as she can toward her marriage to a typical Christian whom she happens to adore. But to do this, she must reject on the island of Belmont the nagging presence of Antonio, whose main aim is, precisely, to keep Bassanio from direct commitments to others.

Debate on many of these issues ensued in a spirited exercise of interdisciplinary wit, where the likes of Lawrence Danson and Jay Halio took on some lawyers at the Association of the Bar of the City of New York in late 1992 (*Proceedings*). And it has spilled over into a series of readings by professional actors in which a proper emphasis has been placed on the relationship of Act IV to Act V, with their legalistic origins of course in the "contract formation" scene, I,iii.[4]

CHRISTIAN LEGALISM IN THE TRIAL SCENE

What I like to call "the turn to legalism" among Christian characters in *The Merchant of Venice* begins midway through the trial scene itself. Looked at this way, the prevalent critical dichotomy between some rigid Jewish "law" and some more humane Christian "mercy" breaks down on the most obvious textual level.

Portia, perhaps fascinated by Shylock's excessive yet somehow solid insistence on his bond, is committed to undoing the moneylender's extreme application of what might otherwise be a righteous and ethical reliance on written law. But she is equally repulsed by the overly flexible oathbreaking of the Christian characters, which she sees in open court before her eyes when Bassanio and Gratiano assert their willingness to sacrifice their new wives to save the beleaguered Antonio. Like the old Jew, who remarks in a striking aside (as he is supposedly hell-bent at the time for vengeance), "These be the Christian husbands," Portia notes their willingness to compromise not only the marriage vows but tons of her own ducats, which Bassanio constantly offers the obdurate plaintiff. Later in this same Act, she will deduce that Antonio's baleful influence on Bassanio has moved the latter to give her the ring that symbolized those vows; the audience to the play will also compare that easy traducement to Shylock's ethical unwillingness to give his wife's ring away "for a wilderness of monkeys."[5] So Portia watches all these men in open court, and it cannot be that she wishes to adopt the easy oathbreaking of her spendthrift husband and his flighty circle of friends, nor that she comes to detest everything that Shylock represents in the domain of ethics and law.

Portia begins in court a process that carries her through to the Belmont of Act V: the emulation of Shylock's ethical system once—through her efforts—it has been drained of its excesses, which she perceives to be less legalistic than situational. She comes quickly to learn that Shylock's villainy consists in a Christian-imposed condition of ostracized resentment. Neither she nor any even-handed observer of the play as a whole needs find any *necessary* linkage of "legalism" to vengeance. On the contrary, she perceives the very opposite: the source of the deepest resentment and the most violent hatred derives from Christian applications to moral outsiders of a superficial and self-serving "mercy." Although personally unaware of Antonio's cruelty to Shylock on the Rialto, Portia will have sufficiently good reason to associate with the merchant this degradation of Christian love. Once the trial and its immediate aftermath reveal his threat to her values, she moves as graciously as possible to remove Antonio from her husband's circle. But this must await the "happy resolution" of Shylock's vengeful lawsuit.

It is clear to most analysts that Portia follows Shylock's legalistic method in open court, where she reads his bond so narrowly, so literally, that it cannot be enforced on its terms. Then, reveling perhaps in her mastery of a complex situation irresolvable by men, she hauls out a statute and continues, with an excess of zeal that parallels Shylock's in a way, to defeat his cause. This "Alien Statute" gives the state the right to take the Jew's life and half his property—but the Duke instantly forgives the former and virtually returns to Shylock all but a small "fine" for the latter. Touched perhaps by the state's graciousness, she turns to the merchant, who is entitled to the other half. Portia explicitly begs Antonio to make the theoretical Christian move beyond law for which she is better known to audiences than for her contractual legalisms. She asks him to undo the legalistic persecution of the Alien Statute by reducing its effect on his enemy: "What mercy can you render him, Antonio?" (IV. i. 394)

It is here that Antonio, ostensibly the model of Christian courtesy and otherwise the voice of what I have called Christian "mediation" (*Poethics*) throughout the play, might be fully expected to outdo the Duke's generosity.

Instead, Antonio proceeds to fail every test of moderation, mercy, and forgiveness that Portia has imposed upon him. (She was not, of course, privy to his earlier similar failure in rejecting Shylock's offer of friendship in I. iii.) She fathoms what happens when Christian intercessors are given sway over earthly law.

She hears, feelingly, the following amazing cruelties, which—in the absence of legal understanding—critics have taken as signs of Christian generosity:

> So please my lord the Duke and all the court
> To quit the fine for one half of his goods,
> I am content, so he will let me have
> The other half in use, to render it
> Upon his death unto the gentleman
> That lately stole his daughter,
> Two things provided more: that for this favor
> He presently become a Christian;
> The other, that he do record a gift,
> Here in the court, of all he dies possessed
> Unto his son Lorenzo and his daughter. (IV. i. 396–406)

The chief hurdle to understanding this bizarre show of "mercy" is its opening two and one-half lines, which are "precatory"—they mean nothing at all to the law. Antonio merely reiterates the Duke's disposition of the half of Shylock's goods that are to go *to the state*! Antonio has no power over, nor any interest in, that half. Thus *he is in fact forgiving the "fine" that only the state has a right to get*. So Antonio begins his speech by winning the hearts of his listeners through a gracious disposition of that which he does not own.

The legally irrelevant opening rhetorical gambit might be understandable in one untrained in the law. But Antonio turns out to be no *ingenu*: his false generosity is but the preface to a highly legalistic maneuver that will totally destroy Shylock. Furthermore, the first two and one-half lines deliberately evoke earlier examples of Christian rhetoric masking self-interest, greed and theft. To take three such cases only: in Act I, Bassanio succeeds in getting Antonio's support for the loan of 3000 ducats not by using direct speech, such as "Lend me this; I'll pretty myself up, head over to Belmont, win the hand of the rich heiress and return to you not only this loan but the previous ones I have welched on." Instead, he uses the graceful image of the bow and arrow, a lovely figure that couches in ethereal language what is in fact a grimy purpose. In the same act, Shylock's usury is seen as evil, but the plundering of colonials engaged in by Antonio's ventures is masked by the romantic imagery of "ships at sea." As Judith Koffler has masterfully shown in a leading law and literature piece on the play, the Christian contribution is one of elevated rhetoric, not improved human relations (116–34). And, finally, Lorenzo spirits away Jessica and much of Shylock's wealth, robing with some of the play's loveliest lines the breach of at least two Commandments.

So Antonio uses the opening moment of his response to Portia to do what he—and the Christians generally—are best at: rhetorical but not actual generosity. (Shylock's method, unfortunately for him, is that of the comedic villain but not always the earthly wrongdoer: he speaks what is on his mind, often in a more literal language than would please the Christians.) He merely mimics Bassanio, who throughout this same scene has managed to hide through rhetorical flourishes that the ducats he constantly offers Shylock are, of course, Portia's (and her avoiding the loss of this wealth goes a long way to explain why she instead brings Shylock down). How sweet of Antonio to forgive even the meager "fine" that the Duke fashioned for Venice ("Ay for the state," says Portia, "not for Antonio") as a way of reducing Shylock's penalty in the face of an already humiliating and procedurally questionable reversal of fortune. Generations of critics, if not necessarily the play's audiences, have been hoodwinked by the opening rhetorical move. The rest of the speech, replete with legalistic exactitude, usually goes unexamined.

Let us pay Shakespeare the compliment of understanding the substance of his merchant's "mercy" to Shylock. Antonio fleshes out the Alien Statute—and I've chosen my verb carefully—as follows:

1. Shylock must place half of his *present* wealth into a trust, with Lorenzo and Jessica receiving the principal at Shylock's death;

2. Shylock must convert to Christianity;

3. Shylock must pledge to will *all of his after-acquired* wealth to Lorenzo and Jessica.

To make this Draconian "mercy" more comprehensible—and putting aside for the moment Shylock's forced conversion—we'll assume that Shylock currently is worth 1,000,000 ducats. Recall that, under the Alien Statute, half of that was to go to the state, but that the Duke reduced the penalty to a fine of undetermined amount. We can assume further, then, that Shylock has been permitted by the state to keep 400,000 ducats and required by Venice to pay 100,000 as his fine.

Compared to that scenario, as we shall see, Antonio's disposition of Shylock's present wealth is by no means generous.

THE "SHYLOCK TRUST"

The merchant, apparently knowledgeable in the intricacies of property law, seizes the half of the moneylender's present wealth under his dominion and places it in "use"—the Elizabethan and indeed the present synonym for a "trust." We will call this the *"Shylock Trust."* Shylock's wealth provides the *res*, or subject matter of the Trust (namely 500,000 ducats). Antonio will be the administrator of the trust (the "trustee"). Under his direction alone, subject only to a use of the wealth that will be deemed responsible by some eventual court of equity, the 500,000 ducats will be invested, and they will provide both income and preservation or growth of the principal itself. The Trust provides for two categories of "beneficiaries," the income beneficiary and the remaindermen, that is, those who will get the principal upon the death of Shylock.

Who gets the income from the Shylock Trust? Antonio's failure to name the income beneficiary is not fatal to the formation of the trust. In fact, he seems either to be giving Shylock the income benefit or else himself. This can be clarified later. What Antonio makes clear is that he is vesting the remainder interest, i.e., the right to take the principal upon Shylock's death, in Lorenzo and Jessica.

So—since this is the fairer reading of his words—if we assume that Antonio is keeping the income interest for himself, the Shylock Trust would be enforceable as follows:

1. 500,000 ducats, yielding approximately 5% a year, provides an annual income of some 25,000 ducats to Antonio for as long as Shylock lives. Antonio would thus be the income beneficiary *pur autre vie* (bad lawfrench for "for the life of another," i.e., for as long as Shylock lives).

2. Meanwhile, through careful investment, the 500,000 ducat principal is preserved. At Shylock's death, Jessica and Lorenzo get these monies. The Shylock Trust is terminated.

THE "SHYLOCK WILL"

Antonio goes much further, however. Exceeding the terms of the Alien Statute, he insists that even Shylock's after-acquired wealth be subject to his command. Recall that Shylock, although elderly, is still active and successful on the Rialto. He may be stripped of 60% of his present wealth, but he may well go on to earn millions more. Furthermore, he may receive gifts from others or in some different manner acquire new property. The Alien Statute gives neither the state nor Antonio the right to control these future earnings or possessions. Antonio, drunk with legalistic power, grabs them anyway, imposing the following scheme: Shylock must pledge immediately that he will bequeath to Jessica and Lorenzo all of his after-acquired wealth. Of course, this permits him to continue to earn and to live from those earnings. (If he finally gets himself good legal counsel, which he now knows he should have done before going into court, Shylock may also be able to plan his estate so that there's nothing left when he dies. Or he may covertly amend his will, which lawfully may be done until the moment of his death, to leave his wealth to someone who has truly loved him.) On the other hand, if really forced to convert to Christianity, he may not be able to pursue his work as a moneylender. In any event, what is left in Shylock's estate at his death must presently be pledged to Lorenzo and Jessica.

Few late-twentieth-century audiences applaud Antonio's insistence upon Shylock's conversion to Christianity. Once heeded and understood, these property arrangements seem almost as odious. Shylock, whose acuity with language surpasses most of the Christian characters—but who errs, as we have seen, by refusing to adjust his own direct speech to their hypocritical patterns—knows that "You take my life/ When you take the means whereby I live." Although the conversion must strike him as disgusting, its enforced effect plays equally upon his profession. Antonio, of course, also understands that Christians do not take money for interest; they leave this to the Jews, having monopolized other and more covert forms of plunder. Shylock is left only with what the Duke has provided him. And he must face the additional torment of being the enforced benefactor of a young couple he has every good reason to despise.

"These be the Christian mercies."

THE COMEDIC CIRCLE SQUARED: MERCY TO LEGALISM TO LAW

Yet the play remains a comedy. As I have elsewhere argued, Shylock must be brought down; his comedic villainy consists in equal parts of vengeful excess, linguistic directness, and ethical precision. Oathkeepers and direct talkers, as everyone from Shakespeare and Molière to Stoppard and Ionesco know, do not fare well in a comic arena. Nor do monomaniacs, although that term is too strong for Shylock, whose obsession about the pound of flesh commences only as his daughter elopes and is mediated even at the trial by accurate reflections upon the Christians that are as keen as his sharpened knife. Shylock must fall because ethical behavior, which can often seem compulsive to an observer, sits poorly on a religious outsider trying to exert himself lawfully in a comedic environment.

The audience to a comedy wants and deserves the defeat of such a character. Having received that in the trial scene, in Act V it expects nothing but music, poetry, and conjugal bliss. Shakespeare provides, instead, discords, arguments, and still unconsummated marriages. These peculiar elements alone make the play "ironic" despite the flawed and even transparent attempts of mainstream critics to find harmonies, dances, and resolutions.[6]

As we have seen, the disharmonies of Act V conjoin with a strange move, led by Portia, to the language of law otherwise embodied in the play largely by the comedic villain himself. It is as though her dealings with the Christians during the trial have left her at least as exasperated with their cruelties as with the single excess she disguised herself to remedy. Now speaking in her own voice, she adopts for Belmont neither the "mercy" of her own most famous speech nor the legalisms of her (and Antonio's) victory over Shylock. Instead, she leads her world of Venice to *law*—to an insistence on the primacy of language used directly to promise and to commit one individual to another.

To do this, Portia must, of course, accomplish more than the mere imparting of legal language she has learned from Shylock. But even this is far from trivial. When the curtain virtually falls with Gratiano calling for an "inter'gatory"—formal legalized questioning under oath—as to whether he and Nerissa should finally bed down, the most extreme anti-Semitic Christian in the play has adopted Shylock's legalistic turn of phrase.

Portia must also, however, reject Antonio. There is little doubt, now that we have read carefully the trial scene and its aftermath in the giving away of the rings, that Portia sees Antonio as a direct threat to her still unconsummated relationship with Bassanio. When the merchant absurdly thrusts himself again between them, she is much too intelligent not to see the grotesque repetition of Antonio's earlier commercial mediation. She remains polite, but the following dialogue should be read as her ironic rejection of the mediated "surety" relationship that permits one party to stand in the place of another:

> *Antonio*: I once did lend my body for his wealth,
> Which but for him that had your husband's ring
> Had quite miscarried. I dare be bound again,
> My soul upon the forfeit, that your lord
> Will never break faith advisedly.
>
> *Portia*: Then you shall be his surety. (V. i. 268-73)

A surety is, somewhat like a guarantor, a "middleman" who can be sued in the place of the actual debtor. The implications of Antonio's excessive, repetitive impulse to "stand in" for Bassanio are all too clear to Portia. She sees that the merchant's urge to mediate is as compulsive as the Jew's impulse to "stand on the law."

Which is better? For Portia, as for the thoughtful member of this play's audience, there is no easy answer. But she now feels empowered, in her own domain and voice, to try out the regime of law and to see if—stripped of an excess forced upon it by the mainstream culture—Jewish ethical modes might be less formalistic and less cruel than Christian "mercy" of the Antonio variety.

CONCLUSION

Law and literature crosses disciplinary borders to seek enlightenment where important sections of stories have remained mere inkblots to decades and even centuries of otherwise sentient readers. In the case of the text we have just been examining, law—as Shakespeare's precision in these matters makes clear—is meant to help identify character. We cannot emerge from Antonio's legalisms without wondering about his cruelty. If, instead, we stop reading the end of the trial scene before embracing the language of property law as it is given to us, we are likely to mistake Shylock's fidelity for intractability, Antonio's technical manipulation for graciousness, and Portia's increasing dislike of the merchant of Venice for a loving friendship or even a three-way "dance" of comedic alliance. The stakes are, at the least, the meaning and staging of Act V and, at the most, the comprehension of the play's values as attuned to those of the defeated litigant.

NOTES

[1] The author gratefully acknowledges the suggestions of Peter Alscher, Lawrence Danson, and Jay Halio, none of whom, however, is responsible for any of the opinions expressed in what follows.

[2] See, for example, the *Symposium Issue* with articles on the story by Judith Koffler, Robin West, James Warren, Brook Thomas, Steven Mailloux, Richard Posner, Michael Hancher, and the present author, whose work on the story in the earlier *The Failure of the Word* has been discussed in Sealts 39-61 and Appendix 3: "With regard to Vere's conduct of Billy's trial and execution [our 1962 'generic text'] concluded—perhaps somewhat hastily—that Melville 'simply had not familiarized himself with [naval] statutes of the period'" (51). In a similar vein, see Milder 77-79.

[3] See *Proceedings* with articles on the play by Peter Alscher, Jay Halio, Charles Spinosa, Susan Oldrieve, Clayton Koelb, Judge David B. Saxe, Marci Hamilton, and Daniel Kornstein. All these sources point to the origins of legal analysis of the play dating to the natural lawyer Von Ihering (who took Shylock's side in the late 19th century) and various English and American explanations of the *contract formation* scene (I. iii). My analysis below focuses on Antonio's disposition of Shylock's wealth in IV. i.

[4] Productions influenced by lawyerly readings of the play include those of the Peter Royston Players (New York, 1992-93) and of the Hofstra Theater Department (1996).

[5] The famous "ring plot" has been much discussed by critics and with recent excellence by Kahn 107-111. Kahn's view that Portia deems Antonio an unworthy rival for Bassanio's affections parallels mine here. But it is significant to me that Kahn barely touches on Shylock as a player in this plot, despite the text's obvious association of the Jew with values connecting ethical marital behavior to the ring, values everywhere betrayed by the Christians (led by Antonio) until Portia formally espouses them in Act V. Yet there, Kahn—allowing that "ironic similarities between Jew and Christian abound"—places these less in the realm of a positive morality in fact espoused by Portia than in the negative vengeance Portia displays toward her transgressing husband (110).

[6] See Danson.

WORKS CITED

Danson, Lawrence. *The Harmonies of "The Merchant of Venice."* New Haven: Yale UP, 1978.

Kahn, Coppelia. "The Cuckoo's Note." In *Shakespeare's "Rough Magic."* Ed. Peter Erickson and Coppelia Kahn. Newark: Delaware UP, 1985.

Koffler, Judith. "Terror and Mutilation in the Golden Age." *Human Rights Quarterly* 5 (1983): 116-34.

Milder, Robert. "ARTICLE?" *American Literary Scholarship* (1982): 77-79.
"Proceedings of the Association of the Bar of the City of New York." *Cardozo Studies in Law and Literature* 5.1 (1993).
Sealts, Merton. *Beyond the Classroom: Essays on American Authors*. Columbia: U of Missouri P, 1996.
"Symposium Issue." *Cardozo Studies in Law and Literature* 1.1 (1989).
Weisberg, Richard H. *Poethics and Other Strategies of Law and Literature*. New York: Columbia UP, 1992.
———. *The Failure of the Word*. New Haven: Yale UP, 1984.

CHAPTER NINE

Shakespeare's *Richard II*
as Landlord and Wasting Tenant
by Dennis R. Klinck

> If waste be made by a tenant for a term of life of houses or
> of gardens . . ., although it be of one house or twenty
> apple-trees in a garden, the tenant will lose the whole
> messuage; and so he will lose the whole garden.
> (Bereford 274)

That the law of real property occupies a prominent place in Shakespeare's *Richard II* has been frequently remarked.[1] For example, Bolton argues that the play "makes central use of property law as it stood in the late fourteenth century" (55) and Gohn observes that, among other things, Richard "set[s] aside the law of property, perhaps the most sacred form of law to Medieval and Renaissance Englishmen" (959).[2]

One aspect of this preoccupation with property law in the play—the one I shall address in this essay—is the paradoxical depiction of Richard as, on the one hand, "landlord," and, on the other, perpetrator of "waste"—something which, conventionally, only a "tenant" can be. Facets of this paradox have been remarked previously. Donna Hamilton addresses some implications of Gaunt's accusation that Richard is "Landlord of England . . . not king" (II. i. 113),[3] and both Bolton and Gohn take note of the doctrine of "waste," alluded to at various points in the play. Bolton considers the "connection between the reversion of an estate and a tenant's waste on it" that "surfaces" in the play (61), and Gohn, in a lengthy footnote, discusses "legal real estate imagery" in Gaunt's speeches in II. i, including "The waste is no whit lesser than thy land" (II. i. 103).[4]

Some of Bolton's insights are particularly germane to my concerns here. He says that "Richard, though he is in reality lord paramount, has abused the country as though it were land 'holden' and he were its wasteful tenant" (62): this is, essentially, the thesis that I want to develop. I believe, however, that there is considerably more to be said about it than Bolton says. For one thing, it is not his central thesis: he is concerned to demonstrate how several different legal references in the play might be illuminated by looking at cases reported in the Year Books of the historical Richard's reign. Thus, he does not fully explore the ramifications of his insight. Further, he does not really give a coherent picture of the law regarding waste: the cases he relies on offer a rather fragmentary account of the doctrine. Moreover, some of his comments seem rather strange or imprecise, at least from a legal perspective, for example, "Richard is wasting his tenement, so Bolingbroke seizes him"[5] and "now time is 'wasting,' or suing for waste, its injurious tenant [namely, Richard]" (63).[6]

My project, then, is to consider Shakespeare's portrayal of Richard as, at once, "landlord" of England—in more than one sense, as we shall see—and as a tenant who "wastes" what he holds, both the "land" itself and what can be termed the "Dignity royal." In other words, I shall attempt to elaborate upon and give greater precision to Bolton's insight. As I have already noted, such a thesis involves a paradox. In Blackstone's words,

> [t]he grand and fundamental maxim of all feudal tenure is this; that all lands were originally granted out by the sovereign, and are therefore holden, either mediately or immediately, of the crown . . . and the grantee, who had the use and possession, according to the terms of the grant, was stiled the feudatory or *vasal*, which was only another name for the tenant or holder of the lands." (Blackstone 2. 53)

Waste—at least actionable waste—can, as we shall see, be committed only by a tenant and, indeed, only by certain classes of tenant.[7] So, Bolton is correct when he observes that "Richard as lord paramount is the one person in the kingdom who cannot be a tenant, so no literal writ of waste can lie against him" (63).

How to resolve the paradox? One way is that advanced by Bolton: eschew "literalness" and see Shakespeare as simply likening Richard's conduct to that of an actual tenant who commits waste. In other words, understand Shakespeare merely to be invoking a suggestive analogy, which cannot be taken very far without collapsing in internal contradiction.

A more searching account of the paradox is possible if one recalls Ernst Kantorowicz's discussion of the doctrine of "the king's two bodies." In the first chapter of his book, Kantorowicz cites a number of cases from the sixteenth-century law reports of Edmund Plowden as illustrating the understanding of this notion in Shakespeare's time. Thus, in the *Case of the Duchy of*

Lancaster, we learn that "the King has in him two Bodies, *viz* a Body natural, and a Body politic," the former mortal, the latter "a Body that cannot be seen or handled, consisting of Policy and Government, and constituted for the Direction of the People, and the Management of the public-weal" (4 Eliz. I 1 *Plowden* 212 at 213, 75 *English Reports* 325 at 326).

One implication of this, as we are told in the case of *Willion v. Berkley*, is that "the King has two Capacities, and he comes to some things meerly as King . . . and to some other Things he comes not as King, as if Lands descend to him from any of his Ancestors" (4 Eliz. I 1 *Plowden* 222a at 242, 75 *English Reports* 339 at 370). Although the case does go on to intimate that land which comes to the king in his body natural is, because of the unity of the two bodies, appropriated to the King in his body politic, the ambiguity of the monarch remains (*Sir Thomas Wroth's Case* 14 Eliz. I 2 *Plowden* 452 at 456, 75 *English Reports* 678 at 683-84)—an ambiguity which offers potential for internal disjunction.[8]

Another implication of the doctrine of the king's two bodies is that, as to the body politic, "the King never dies, and his natural Death is not called in our law . . . the Death of the King, but the Demise of the King, not signifying by the Word (*Demise*) that the Body politic of the King is dead, but that there is a separation of the two Bodies, and that the Body politic is transferred and conveyed over from the Body natural now dead, or now removed from the Dignity royal to another Body natural" (*Willion* 234).[9] One thing worth remarking about the language here is that it treats what happens to the "Body politic" in terms of property law: it is "demised," "transferred," "conveyed."[10] Indeed, Blackstone tells us that the king's "natural dissolution" is called "his *demise*; *demissio regis, vel coronae*: an expression which signifies merely a transfer of property" (1. 242). Although the cases do not say this in so many words, the "Body politic" or "Dignity royal" is occupied or held first by one "body natural," then by another, each being a kind of "tenant" for a time, or for life.

In his second chapter, Kantorowicz goes on to consider *Richard II* in terms of the doctrine of the king's two bodies; indeed, he argues that the play is "the tragedy of the King's Two Bodies" (26). Essentially, his thesis is that the play depicts the separation of the body natural from the body politic, finally revealing the "feeble human nature of [the] king" (30). He says nothing, however, about the particular point I am addressing here. If Kantorowicz is correct in identifying the doctrine (which he conjectures must have been part of the "ordinary and conventional" discourse of "English jurists of that period" 20) as central to the play, it is not implausible that it should apply to this point as well. In short, the paradox might be explained by saying that Richard, who in his "Body politic" is lord paramount, is in his body natural a tenant who holds or occupies the "Dignity royal" and its appurtenances; as tenant, he commits waste upon that which he holds, the consequence being that he is deprived prematurely of that holding.

Having thus set the stage, so to speak, I want to consider in more detail how Richard, though "landlord," might nevertheless be as well a wasting tenant. In order to do this, I must first say something more about the doctrine of waste.

Bolton is at pains to distinguish the law as it stood in Richard's time from the law as it stood in Shakespeare's time—hence, his reliance on the Ricardian Year Books. However significant this distinction may be in some areas,[11] one might question its importance in relation to waste, the law of which, though it no doubt developed between the two periods, remained in its fundamentals fairly constant. Thus, Sir Edward Coke, in his authoritative discussions of the law of waste—discussions which are "spacious" "for that [this learning of waste] is most necessary to be knowne of all men" (I. 54b)—takes as points of reference the *Statute of Marlbridge* (1267; 52 Hen. III c. 23) and the *Statute of Gloucester* (1278; 6 Edw. I c. 5), which long predate Richard's reign.[12] And Blackstone, writing in the late eighteenth century, suggests that, in its basic aspects, the law of waste had remained unchanged "for above five hundred years past" (Blackstone 2. 283)—the touchstones being, again, these two statutes.

The crucial effect of the *Statute of Marlbridge* was to enlarge the categories of persons who were liable for waste. Under the old common law, these categories were limited to tenants by the curtesy, tenants in dower, and guardians in chivalry (Blackstone 282ff).[13] The statute provided: "Also fermors, during their terms, shall not make waste, sale, nor exile of house, woods, and men, nor of any thing belonging to the tenements that they have to ferm."[14] Coke explains that the word *firmarii* ("fermors," or farmers) comprehends "all such, as hold by lease for life, or lives, or for years" (II. 145). He observes that the reason for this extension of the application of the doctrine was that "waste and destruction is hurtful to the common-wealth" (II. 145)—a point that has some resonance with regard to *Richard II*.

The effect of the *Statute of Gloucester* was to create new remedies in cases of waste:

> a Man from henceforth shall have a Writ of Waste[15] in the Chancery against him that holdeth by Law of England, or otherwise for Term of Life, or for Term of Years, or a Woman in Dower; and he which shall be attained of Waste, shall leese the Thing that he hath wasted, and moreover shall recompense thrice so much as the Waste shall be taxed at.[16]

What is most noteworthy here for our purposes is that the wasting tenant is liable to lose the thing that he has wasted.[17] And, again, in his commentary on this statute, Coke emphasizes that waste is not simply a private wrong, but is "hurtful to the common-wealth": "this excellent law" was "enacted *pro bono publico*, for preservation of buildings for the habitation of mankinde, and of woods and timber, sometime one of the beautiful, and profitable ornaments of England" (II. 306).

Coke tells us as well that neither the *Statute of Marlbridge* nor the *Statute of Gloucester* created new kinds of waste; rather they provided "new remedies for old wastes." To discern what is waste and what is not, one must resort to the common law (II. 300). In the *First Part of the Institutes*, he gives a number of instances of what constitutes waste, of which Blackstone's definition is a fairly adequate summary:

> waste is a spoil and destruction of the estate, either in houses, woods, or lands; by demolishing not the temporary profits only, but the very substance of the thing; thereby rendering it wild and desolate; which the common law expresses very significantly by the word *vastum*: and that this *vastum*, or waste, is either voluntary or permissive; the one by actual and designed demolition of the lands, woods, and houses; the other arising from mere negligence, and want of sufficient care in reparations, fences, and the like. (3. 223)

Particularly noteworthy here are the facts that waste affects the integrity of the thing itself, not simply its product, and that waste can occur as a result of either positive acts or neglect.[18]

Although Blackstone notes that several categories of persons may bring an action for waste, "the most usual and important interest, that is hurt by this commission of waste, is that of him who hath the remainder or reversion of the inheritance, after a particular estate for life or years" (3. 224)[19]; the effect of waste on the inheritance is that "it tends to mangle and dismember it of it's [*sic*] most desirable incidents and ornaments" (3. 225). In Coke's words, the action is available to "him that hath the immediate estate of inheritance, for waste or destruction in houses, gardens, woods, trees, or in lands, meadows, &c. or in exile of men to the disherison of him in the reversion or remainder" (I. 53a).

With this context in mind, we can now look more closely at how "waste" figures in *Richard II*. Recall that Richard, in his body natural, is a kind of "tenant"; what he holds is the Kingship, which entails being lord of the land, literally, but also occupying the "Dignity royal." The "waste" he commits can be seen to affect not only the land as a physical inheritance, but also the substance of the Kingship itself.

Bolton suggests that one aspect of the "waste" in the play is Richard's seizure and disposal of Bolingbroke's lands. Indeed, some of the language associated with this process is suggestive of waste; Bolingbroke tells Bushy and Green, "you have fed upon my signories, / Dispark'd my parks and fell'd my forest woods, / From my own windows torn my household coat, / Ras'd out my imprese, leaving me no sign" (III. i. 22-25). As we have seen, waste typically (or, to use Coke's word, "properly") "is in houses, gardens, . . . in timber trees" (Coke I. 53a). Certainly, we have the cutting of trees, or destruction of woods, here.[20] Further, if the editor of the play in *The Riverside Shakespeare* is right in saying that "Dispark'd" means "put to uses unrelated to forestry and hunting," this too could constitute waste—analogous to a change in the course of husbandry (Coke I. 53b). Thus, in the case of *Lord Darcy v. Askwith*, we are told that "it is generally true, that the lessee hath no power to change the nature of the thing demised; he cannot turn meadow into arable, nor stub a wood to make it pasture . . . ; nor suffer ground to be surrounded, or decay the pale of a park: for then it ceaseth to be a park" (1618; *Hobart* 234, 80 *English Reports* 380).

The "rasing" out of the imprese is more doubtful; the common law, materialistic as it was in at least some of its aspects, did not incorporate within the concept of waste the mere erasure of a sign. However, such an erasure certainly can be taken as a representational dismemberment of Bolingbroke's inheritance.

While this conduct, or some of it, could constitute the substance of waste, satisfying other criteria of the legal doctrine is more problematic. As we have seen, the typical players in an action for waste are a tenant for life (or some other limited period of time) and the person entitled to the reversion or remainder, that is, the residual interest after the "particular" estate comes to an end. Here, Richard is not a tenant for life of Bolingbroke's inheritance; nor is Bolingbroke, strictly speaking, a reversioner or remainderman: he is, more simply, an heir whose inheritance has been "intercepted" by the king.[21] Other relationships that could give rise to an action in waste are suggestive of, if not exactly congruent with, the situation in *Richard II*. By the statutes 28 Edward I ch. 18 (1300) and 14 Edward III ch. 13 (1340), for example, provision is made against waste of wards' lands by those having care of them. The preamble to the latter reads:

> whereas in the Great Charter it is contained, that after the Death of the Ancestors, which hold of the King in chief, and whose Heirs be within Age, that the King shall keep the Lands without Waste and Destruction, and restore them wholly to the Heirs when they come to their full Age. And against God and Right, and the said Establishments, [those] to whom the Lands of Such Heirs have been committed, have done Waste and Destruction, to the great Mischief . . . of the Heirs of Earls, Barons, and other great Men . . ., and nevertheless [such persons] have had no Conscience to do such Destructions.

This sounds roughly analogous to the situation in *Richard II*: Bolingbroke's lands have come into the possession of persons who have "done Waste and Destruction," and who are portrayed as having "no Conscience to do such

Destructions." However, these lands did not come into the hands of the wasters because of Bolingbroke's nonage, but by a rather different process.

Thus, there may be technical obstacles to bringing what happens to Bolingbroke's lands within the strict doctrine of waste. But if we are to believe Coke about the importance of the doctrine and the values that it incorporates, it is likely that the enormity of Richard's seizure of Bolingbroke's inheritance would have been aggravated, in the minds of an Elizabethan audience, by the physical insults committed against it—irrespective of whether that audience thought that Bolingbroke might actually be able to bring an action in waste against anybody. Arguably, waste is waste, regardless of whether it is technically actionable.[22]

Another way of assimilating what happens to Bolingbroke's inheritance to the waste perpetrated by Richard is to see it as part of Richard's maladministration of the kingdom—his wasteful conduct as tenant or occupant of the "Body politic" of King—to which I now turn.

Unlike Bushy and Green, whose conduct appears, at least in some of its aspects, to amount literally, or physically, to waste, Richard is portrayed as having committed waste essentially in a figurative sense. To be sure, we are constantly reminded of the *land* of England, in a physical sense, in the play, and, as Gohn points out, we are frequently told that it is *Richard's* land, specifically. Thus, Richard speaks of "our kingdom's earth" (I. iii. 125), "our territories" (I. iii. 139), "our fields" (I. iii. 141), "Dear earth" (III. ii. 6), "my earth" (III. ii. 10), "my gentle earth" (III. ii. 12); Bolingbroke refers to "England's ground," "sweet soil" (I. iii. 36), and "fair King Richard's land" (III. iii. 47); Gaunt calls England "this blessed plot, this earth" (II. i. 50). Indeed, Gaunt likens England to a dwelling ("the silver sea, / Which serves it in the office of a wall, / Or as [a] moat defensive to a house"—II. i. 46-48), an image which is picked up later in the garden scene, where England ("the whole land") is "a sea-walled garden" (III. iv. 43). While we are not allowed to forget this physical aspect of Richard's kingdom and its degradation, the "waste" that he commits is primarily in the form of affronts to the political order.

The word "waste," with reference to the political order, is explicitly associated with Richard at two points in the play. The first of these I have already quoted: Gaunt, upbraiding Richard, says:

> A thousand flatterers sit within thy crown,
> Whose compass is no bigger than thy head,
> And yet, [incaged] in so small a verge,
> The waste is no whit lesser than thy land. (II. i. 100-03)

This is an intriguing passage; suffice it to say for our purposes that the effect of Richard's attending to "flatterers" is the wasting of his land—no doubt with a complex of connotations of "waste." What he is doing is "wasting" his land, in the sense I have been discussing; at the same time, "waste" could suggest "loss"—as, indeed, is indicated shortly after: You, Richard, "Which art possess'd now to depose thyself" (II. i. 108). As we have already noticed, there is a connection between these two senses: according to the *Statute of Gloucester*, the penalty for waste is the loss of the thing wasted.

It is in this same speech that Gaunt tells Richard, "Landlord of England art thou now, not king" (II. i. 113)—an accusation to which I have already alluded. I have, as well, signaled the ambiguity inherent in this word. From one perspective, the King is the universal "landlord"—as we have seen, all land is held from him, directly or indirectly. Yet, in this line, "landlord" is a pejorative term, contrasted with "king."

The pejorative sense of "landlord" is associated with Richard's having "let this land by lease" (II. i. 110), with his having leased it out "Like to a tenement or a pelting farm" (II. i. 60). Again, it is not immediately obvious what is objectionable about "tenements" or "farms." In a broad sense, a "tenement" is that which is held, and any grant of land (originally from the Crown) creates a tenement; any land which anyone holds is a tenement. Gohn, again relying on the OED, notes that "as early as 1593" the word meant "a rented suite of rooms and apartments" and argues that this must have been the meaning that Shakespeare intended (957n.). Frankly, I do not find this argument entirely satisfying, partly because (whatever the OED says) I doubt that the word tenement would have struck the Elizabethan ear as referring to low-rental urban housing in the way that it tends to strike the contemporary ear. My sense is that Shakespeare's message depends not on his audience's thinking that a tenement was a rented suite of rooms, but on their knowing that what he was referring to was a leasehold tenement in the ordinary broad sense.[23]

Similarly, the word "farm," in itself, is not obviously a term of vilification—although Shakespeare clearly intends it to carry a negative connotation, reinforced by the adjective "pelting." But, as we have already seen, "farm" was a recognized legal term—used, for example, in the *Statute of Marlbridge* (where, incidentally, what the farmer has to farm is a "tenement"), apparently without any suggestion of opprobrium. Coke tells us that "farmers" simply "doe comprehend all such as hold by lease for life, or lives, or for years" (II. 145). That a "farm" was something specifically *leased* is made clear in the Elizabethan case of *Wrotesley* v. *Adams* (1 Eliz. I 1 *Plowden* 187, 75 *English Reports* 287), in which the question "what is a *Farm*" is explicitly considered. A farm, we are told, at least in one of its significations "is a collective Word, consisting of divers Things collected together, whereof one is a Messuage, and the others are the Lands, Meadows, Pastures, Woods, Commons, and other Things lying or appertaining thereto." However, "all this does not make it to be called a Farm, if it has not another Thing also; and that is, that it has been let or demised to another for Life, for Years, or at Will" (*Wrotesley* 195). That is, it is not so much the physical components that make a farm, but the fact that they are held temporarily, usually by lease. Citing the *Statute of Marlbridge*, the case continues: "But a Farm is oftentimes used in other Senses, for as to the Lessee only he may be said to be a Farmer of whatever Thing he has in Lease; and that which he holds may, as to him, be called his Farm" (195). Indeed, the case goes on to suggest that, in the statute, "farm" is virtually synonymous with "lease" (195). This sense of "farm" (in the verb form) is fairly evident in Richard's "We are enforc'd to farm our royal realm" (I. iv. 45); an essentially equivalent expression is Gaunt's "let by lease" (II. i. 110).

But what is so bad about Richard's "farming" the land, and how does this relate to the question of waste?

The connection at one level is suggested by Nathaniel Bacon's comment on the historical (as opposed to the dramatic) Richard that "the King . . . leaves the noble Crown of *England* in the base condition of a Farme, subject to strip and waste by mean men" (*Continuation* 12-13). That is, by leasing the kingdom, Richard exposes the realm to the wasting conduct of the lessees, or farmers. But this does not suggest that there is anything inherent in the act of leasing itself that is objectionable: presumably, if the "farmers" were good husbandmen, there would be no waste in this sense.

More radically, however, any change in "the nature of the thing demised" can amount to waste: thus, it would be waste to convert a "royal realm" into a "pelting farm." But we should recall that Richard is not tenant of the land, so much as he is tenant of the Kingship: thus, for example, in the passage quoted above, Bacon complains not that the land has been made into a farm, but that the *Crown* has. Two aspects of this process are worth remarking.

The first is that Richard subverts the Kingship by acting as landlord in the sense of "lessor" rather than of "lord paramount." Simpson tells us that early leases were essentially mechanisms of investment, frequently "designed to evade the ecclesiastical prohibition of usury," and that in the early literature the "termor" (farmer, or lessee) is "treated as a thoroughly undesirable person" (72).[24] Be that as it may, Simpson points out that, in the lease situation, "whereby an individual hired land in order to exploit it economically, no feudal relationship of subservience and protection, sealed by homage, was included: the social significance of the transaction was quite different" (73). For the King, then, to become a landlord in this sense would be ostensibly to compromise his Kingship.

The second point is that in "farming" specifically his *Crown*, Richard further degrades his Kingship. Some of the implications of this are made crudely explicit in the anonymous *Thomas of Woodstock*,[25] in which, for example, Green tells Richard that when he farms out "the kingdome to us four," he will not have to "trouble" himself "[w]ith any business"; moreover, "wele governe the land moste rarely" (ll. 1876-78). In other words, Richard is not simply leasing land, or granting tenements, but he is giving over what appertains to him as *King*, abdicating his stewardship and permitting others effectively to occupy his office. That the word "farm" could be used in the sense of leasing an office is evidenced by a statute of 1402 providing that "the searchers in every port of *England* shall be charged and sworn, that they shall not let to ferm their offices of searching, nor occupy the same by a deputy" (4 Henry IV, ch. 21)[26]—on pain of being put out of office forever.

To recur to the framework suggested by Kantorowicz, Richard, who in his body natural is the occupant or tenant of the King's body politic, by farming out his "royalties," his prerogatives and responsibilities, effectively changes the relationship of King to subject and relinquishes incidents of the "Dignity royal" to base men. By subverting the essential nature of the King's body politic, he debases it or commits waste upon it.

The second point at which the word "waste" occurs in connection with Richard's administration of the realm is in the garden scene, which, as we have already noticed, resonates with some of Gaunt's speeches in II. i. One of the gardener's men has just complained that while they, "in the compass of a pale / Keep law and form and due proportion, / Showing as in a model our firm estate," the "sea-walled garden, the whole land,"

Is full of weeds, her fairest flowers chok'd up,
Her fruit-trees all unprun'd, her hedges ruin'd,
Her knots disordered, and her wholesome herbs
Swarming with caterpillars (III. iv. 40-47).

The gardener observes, however, that the expected consequences of this situation have now materialized: Bolingbroke has "seiz'd the wasteful King" (III. iv. 55), "[h]e that hath suffered this disordered spring" (III. iv. 48). At the end of the same speech, the gardener says that if Richard had lopped away some of the "superfluous branches" in the kingdom, "himself had borne the crown, / Which waste of idle hours hath quite thrown down" (III. iv. 63-66).

To be sure, the words "waste" and "wasteful" here are capable of bearing connotations other than the one I am foregrounding. However, I believe that the salience of this one is unmistakable, given the context of description of a fairly typical example of waste in the legal sense. We will recall from Coke that "[w]ast properly is in houses, *gardens*, . . . timber trees" (my emphasis), so that "[i]f the tenant cut downe or destroy any fruit trees growing in the garden or orchard, it is waste" (I. 53a). In this scene, there is no mention of the active cutting down of "fruit trees"—or their human analogues, but, as we will recall as well from Coke, waste may be voluntary or *permissive*. Coke gives no example of permissive waste specifically in a garden, but he does provide a number of other illustrations: "to suffer the pale to decay, whereby the deere is dispersed, is waste" (I. 53a), "[i]f the tenant suffer the houses to be wasted," and "[i]t is waste to suffer a wall of the sea to be in decay" or not to repair "the bankes or walls against rivers, or other waters, whereby the meadows or marshes be surrounded, and become rushy and unprofitable" (I. 53b). Certainly, Richard seems to have permitted the realm to become "unprofitable" through his neglect.

Arguably, in terms of this extended garden metaphor, Richard has been guilty of more than just permissive waste. For example, the Duke of Gloucester, "One flourishing branch of [Edward III's] most royal root . . . Is hack'd down, and his summer leaves all faded" (I. ii. 18-20)—apparently with Richard's connivance; Gaunt accuses Richard (Edward's "son's son") of "destroying" Edward's sons. It is perhaps worth recalling here Blackstone's images of waste as involving the "mangling" and "dismembering" of the inheritance. Not only has Gloucester been "hack'd down," but Bolingbroke has been "gelded of his patrimony" (II. i. 237). That which was flourishing has been destroyed, that which was fecund has been rendered unfruitful. We know from the law that "If a man *cuts trees, and after suffers the germans to be destroyed* this is a double waste" (Viner 444).[27] This seems to be what Richard, figuratively, has done. Ironically, of course, he himself is "gelded" of his patrimony: he loses his Crown, and all his Queen is able to give birth to is "woe" (II. ii. 62-66); what she has "in reversion" is only grief or woe (II. ii. 38-40). Indeed, it might be argued that the banishment of Bolingbroke is itself a kind of "voluntary" waste, for, as Coke says, "exile or destruction of villaines, or tenants at will, or making them poore, where they were rich when the tenant came in, whereby they depart from their tenures, is wast. And yet the statute of *Gloucester* speaketh not of exile, but it is comprehended under the general word of wast" (I. 53b). Bolingbroke is obviously not a "villaine" or a "tenant at will," but his exile and impoverishment by Richard may suggest another dimension of the king's "wastefulness."

Richard, thus, can be seen as one who commits "waste" in the legal sense. The word is associated with him at several points in the play, and his conduct corresponds, either literally or figuratively, to the kind of conduct the law identified with waste.

I turn now to the consequences of the commission of waste.

As we have seen, recourse against the wasting tenant typically lies in "him who hath the remainder or reversion of the inheritance, after a particular estate for life or years in being," or, in other words, "him to whom the *inheritance* appertains in expectancy" (Blackstone 3. 224-25).[28] We know that Richard himself describes Bolingbroke in these terms, when he complains of the latter's courting of the common people, "As were our England in reversion his / And he our subjects' next degree in hope" (I. iv. 35-36).[29] And we know that, as a result of the *Statute of Gloucester*, one consequence of the commission of waste is the forfeiture of the thing wasted. In general terms, this is the situation that Shakespeare depicts: Richard, the wasting tenant for life, is forced by "him who hath . . . the reversion" to lose the thing he has wasted.

There are, again, difficulties of congruence with a strict analysis of the legal doctrine of waste—difficulties that can at best be tentatively met. For one thing, although the word "reversion" is suggestively applied to Bolingbroke, it is hardly appropriate to describe the heir to the throne as a "reversioner." Indeed, it is doubtful that Bolingbroke is Richard's heir in the relevant sense, for "no one is the heir of a living person."[30] Further, if Richard is only a tenant for life of the Crown, Bolingbroke can be no more than this himself, in expectancy. Blackstone tells us that "he, who hath the remainder *for life* only, is not entitled to sue for waste; since his interest may never perhaps come into possession, and then he hath suffered no injury" (3. 225). A possible response to this objection is suggested by what follows immediately in Blackstone: ecclesiastics "who are seised in right of their churches of any remainder or reversion, may have an action of waste"—in which case the writ reads not *ad exhaeredationem ipsius*, but *ad exhaeredationem ecclesiae*" (3. 225). By analogy,[31] and recalling Kantorowicz, one might say that the reversion is in the King, that, if Bolingbroke has this reversion, it can only be in right of the King, and if he can act against the king-tenant, it is only in this representative capacity.

Another problem is that the "reversioner" here does not exactly bring a writ of waste against Richard. Coke tells us that "he in the reversion" had authority "either by himself, or by another to enter into the houses or lands so letten for life or years, to see if any waste be done" (II. 306); however, this was only to ascertain whether waste was being committed. Self-help was not permitted: "the place cannot be recovered without a plea" (I. 53b). Again, one might make the (probably tenuous) argument that the circumstances here are unusual: here it is the king himself, in some ways the embodiment of the law, who is the wasting tenant. Moreover, one form of the waste that he has committed is a kind of lawlessness; he has not kept "law and form and due proportion" in the realm. Therefore, the ordinary law is not available to Bolingbroke in this case.

Again, such analysis points to the limits of what might be called "legal literalism." However we stretch the doctrine of waste, we cannot make the situation in the play strictly congruent with it: the doctrine has never applied, literally, to a monarch's abuse of the "Dignity royal." The notion of Richard as wasting tenant is ultimately figurative. Nevertheless, the allusions to his "waste" and to Bolingbroke's "reversion" are laden with implication, and in all likelihood would have resonated with Shakespeare's original audience. They point to a dimension of meaning in the play that has not hitherto been as fully foregrounded as I have endeavored to foreground it.

NOTES

[1] See White 233ff; Clarkson and Warren; Hexter; Bolton; Gohn.

[2] Hexter makes a similar point in explaining why Shakespeare has Bolingbroke "justify *all* his actions . . . on the ignoble grounds that he has suffered wrongful loss of property at the king's hands" (11-12).

[3] She does not, however, make the connection with "waste."

[4] His concern with this point is incidental to his central theme—as his relegation of it to a footnote suggests.

[5] The strangeness here lies in the suggestion that seizing a *person* might be a remedy for waste.

[6] What is strange here is the suggestion that wasting and suing for waste might be equivalent notions. At the same time, Bolton is, I believe, correct to make the connection between Richard's "I wasted time, and now doth time waste me" (V. v. 49) and other instances of "waste" in the play. Indeed, aspects of Richard's waste of time are directly implicated in his "waste" of the Kingship. York tells him: "Take Herford's rights away, and take from Time / His charters and his customary rights; / Let not tomorrow then ensue today" (II. i. 195-97). Richard is portrayed as subverting the incidents of time itself. However, the question of Richard's "waste of time" is beyond the scope of the present essay.

[7] Thus, Blackstone tells us that the "absolute tenant in fee simple" "may commit whatever waste his own indiscretion may prompt him to, without being impeachable or accountable for it to any one" (3. 223-24).

[8] Thus this case distinguishes service which touches only the natural body of the king (as, for example, medical attendance or instruction in grammar and music) from that which touches "the Majesty of the body politic."

[9] Compare *Wroth* 456, making essentially the same point. Blackstone notes that the death of the king was not the only form that such demises might take—so, when Edward IV was briefly "driven from his throne" by the Lancastrians, "this temporary transfer of his dignity was denominated his *demise*." (1. 242).

[10] In *Hill v. Grange*, 3 & 4 Philip and Mary 1 *Plowden* 164 at 177, 75 *English Reports* 253 at 273, we are told that the king who dies "thereby demises the Kingdom to another."

[11] Bolton refers, for example, to the quite fundamental change in the law wrought by the *Statute of Wills* (1540).

[12] A number of other medieval statutes dealt with the issue of waste: 9 Henry III ch. 4 (1225) (waste by guardian in ward's lands); 13 Edward I ch. 14 (1285) (procedure in an action of waste); 13 Edward I ch. 22 (1285) (action for waste by tenant in common); 20 Edward I stat. 2 (1292) (heir of reversioner bringing action for waste); 28 Edward I ch. 18 (1300) (escheators committing waste in wards' lands); 14 Edward III (1340) (waste in wards' lands);

11 Henry VI ch. 5 (1433) (tenant granting his estate, taking profits, and committing waste).

13 See also Coke 2. 299. For an early discussion of the law regarding waste committed by a woman holding land in dower, see Henry of Bracton 4:595ff.

14 The original read: "Item firmarii tempore firmarum suarum vastum, venditionem, vel exilium non facient de domibus, boscis, vel hominibus, nec de aliquibus ad tenementa quae ad firmam habent spectantibus."

15 Gohn, relying on the OED, says that the word "waste" in the legal sense had been current since at least 1414 (957n.). Clearly the word was appearing in primary legal materials (albeit in "law French") long before that.

16 The original reads: "Ien eit desoremes bref de Wast en la Chauncelrie, [fet de ceo sur] home qi tient par la lei de Engleterre, ou en autre manere a terme de vie, ou a term de annz, ou femme en doweire, e celui qi serra ateint de Wast perde la chose [qil ad] wastee e estre ceo face gre del trebble de ceo qe le Wast serra taxe."

17 See Coke 2. 303 ("the purview of this act is, that he shall lose the thing that he hath wasted"), and Blackstone 2. 283 (wasting tenants "shall lose and forfeit the place wherein the waste is committed").

18 Compare Coke 1. 53a.

19 The distinction between a reversion and a remainder is that the former reverts or goes back to the original grantor when the "particular" or temporary estate ends, while the latter goes to a third party, specified in the original grant.

20 See Coke 2. 303.

21 More technically, upon the death of a tenant-in-chief (Gaunt), the King was entitled to *primer seisin* of the tenant's lands, until the tenant's heir "recovered" them, upon payment of a money amount ("relief") or the fulfillment of other requirements ("suing for livery"). See Simpson 16-17. Richard will not permit Bolingbroke to "recover" his inheritance.

22 Recall that Blackstone says that the acts of waste committed by an absolute tenant in fee simple are "undoubtedly *damnum*, [but] *damnum absque injuria*" (3. 224).

23 Bolton argues for this broad meaning as well—on the basis that the only meaning of "tenement" in Richard II's time was "a holding" (62). As I have already intimated, I doubt that such precision is necessary: Did Shakespeare, or his audience, really say: "Now, let's remember that what is at issue here is property law as it stood at the end of the fourteenth century"?

24 Citing des Longrais.

25 Reproduced in Bullough.

26 The original is: "les sercheours en chescun port d'Engleterre soient chargiez & jurrez qils ne lessent a ferme leur office de sercherie ne les occupient par deputee."

[27] Citing a case from the ninth year of Henry VI's reign.

[28] Coke says that "No person shall have an action of wast, unlesse he hath the immediate state of inheritance." (1. 53b.)

[29] Earlier, Richard had ironically, in what he regarded as a counterfactual conditional, referred to Bolingbroke as "my kingdom's heir" (I. i. 116).

[30] The maxim is *nemo est haeres viventis*. See Blackstone 3. 225.

[31] The analogy between the King and ecclesiastics is made explicit by finch: "the king hath two capacities, a bodie naturall . . . and a bodie politique. . . . So a Parson is a corporation by the Common Law, and hath two capacities" (87-88).

WORKS CITED

Bacon, Nathaniel. *The Continuation of an Historical Discourse of the Government of England*. London: n.p., 1651.

Bereford, C. J. "Anonymous case." *The Year Books of Edward II*, 10 (5 Edward II 1311). Ed. G. J. Turner. London: Quaritch, 1947.

Blackstone, William. *Commentaries on the Laws of England*. 4 vols. 1765-69. Chicago: U of Chicago P, 1979.

Bolton, W. F. "Ricardian Law Reports and Richard II." *Shakespeare Studies* 20 (1988): 53-65.

Bullough, Geoffrey. *Narrative and Dramatic Sources of Shakespeare*. Vol. 3. New York: Columbia UP, 1960.

Clarkson, Paul S., and Clyde T. Warren. *The Law of Property in Shakespeare and the Elizabethan Drama*. Baltimore: The Johns Hopkins UP, 1942.

Coke, Sir Edward. *The First Part of the Institutes of the Laws of England, or, a Commentary upon Littleton*, 15th ed. Ed. Francis Hargrave and Charles Butler. London: E. and R. Brooke, 1794.

———. *The Second Part of the Institutes of the Laws of England*. 15th ed. Ed. Francis Hargrave and Charles Butler. London: E. and R. Brooke., 1797.

des Longrais, J. *La Conception Anglaise de la Saisine, du XIIe au XIVe Siècle*. Paris: n.p., 1924.

Finch, Henry. *Law, or a Discourse Thereof*. London: Society of Stationers, 1627.

Gohn, Jack B. "Richard II: Shakespeare's Legal Brief on the Royal Prerogative and the Succession to the Throne." *Georgetown Law Journal* 70 (1982): 943-73.

Hamilton, Donna. "The State of Law in Richard II." *Shakespeare Quarterly* 34 (1983): 5-17.

Henry of Bracton. *De Legibus et Consuetudinibus Angliae*. Ed. Travers Twiss. Vol. 4. London: Longman, 1881.

Hexter, J. H. "Property, Monopoly, and Shakespeare's Richard III." In *Culture and Politics From Puritanism to the Enlightment*. Ed. Perez Zagorin. Berkeley: U of California P, 1980.

Kantorowicz, Ernst. *The King's Two Bodies: A Study in Mediaeval Political Theology*. Princeton: Princeton UP, 1957.

Shakespeare, William. *The Tragedy of King Richard the Second. The Riverside Shakespeare*. Ed. G. B. Evans. Boston: Houghton Mifflin, 1974.

Simpson, A.W.B. *A History of the Land Law*. 2nd ed. Oxford: Clarendon, 1986.

Viner, Charles. *A General Abridgement of Law and Equity*. 2nd ed., 1794.

White, Edward J. *Commentaries on the Law in Shakespeare*. 1911. Buffalo: William S. Hein, 1987.

CHAPTER TEN

The Trial in *A Passage to India*:
"Justice" Under Colonial Conditions
by Richard Clarke Sterne

A Passage to India, according to George Orwell who admired it, was broadcast during World War II by Nazi Germany in a series of "shortened versions of books that they considered damaging to British prestige." Orwell adds that as far as he knows, "they didn't even have to resort to dishonest quotation. Just because the book was essentially truthful, it could be made to serve the purposes of Nazi propaganda" (Orwell 35). Even from the viewpoint of Nirad C. Chaudhuri, an Indian critic of *A Passage to India* who faults Forster for not depicting any Indians openly committed to independence, and for merely "pitting humane feelings" against the "political phenomenon" of British colonial rule, the novel had "possibly been an even greater influence in British imperial politics than in English literature." *A Passage to India*, Chaudhuri believed, "helped the growth of that mood which enabled the British people to leave India with an almost Pilate-like gesture of washing their hands of a disagreeable affair" (70, 68, 68–69).

The book's central episode, the trial of the Moslem Doctor Aziz, must especially have helped that mood to grow. For Forster's depiction of the administration of colonial justice—whatever the limitations of his knowledge of Anglo-Indian legal procedure[1]—was bound to disconcert British readers. Readers who tried to imagine a postcolonial India might also have been troubled, however, by Forster's evocation of ethnic/religious and caste antagonisms among the native population. Such antagonisms, to some extent thrown into relief by the accusation against Aziz, would in actual history lead to warfare and massacres after the 1947 division of the British raj into independent India and Pakistan. Although *A Passage to India* presents a fortuitous courtroom victory for real justice over colonial power, followed by a local rapprochement between Hindus and Moslems, the trial episode of this 1924 novel points to the human costs of colonialism, and some of the wrenching problems of present-day India.

As soon as the news spreads at Chandrapore that Adela Quested, "an English girl fresh from England" (Forster 142)[2] (in the self-righteous words of one British official) has accused Aziz of making "insulting advances" (144) to her in a Marabar cave, the machinery of fear and loathing of dark-skinned natives is set in motion among the Anglo-Indians. It's true that the District Superintendent of Police, McBryde, "the most reflective and best educated of the Chandrapore officials," wears his prejudice with a "scientific" difference. To him, "All unfortunate natives are criminals at heart [because] they live south of latitude 30. They are not to blame, they have not a dog's chance—we should be like them if we settled here" (143-44). Nevertheless, discussing the case with Cyril Fielding, the iconoclastic school principal and teacher who astonishes him by suggesting that Miss Quested is deluded and Aziz innocent, McBryde cites as evidence of the doctor's bad character a letter to Aziz "'from a friend who apparently keeps a brothel.'" Fielding retorts that he himself did "'the same at his age,'" and the omniscient narrator remarks, "So had the Superintendent of Police" (146). But McBryde feels that Fielding has given the conversation an undesirable turn. Racism of a more mindless sort than McBryde's pervades the "siege" atmosphere of the British club, where one young mother with her baby in her arms, is afraid to return to her bungalow lest the "'niggers attacked'" (Forster 156). Although some men tell her that the drums she hears are only those of Mohurram, a Moslem holiday, many of the men have begun speaking of "women and children—that phrase that exempts the male from sanity when it has been repeated a few times" (158). Aziz, unfortunately, after losing sight of Miss Quested at the Marabar caves, lost his poise as well, and did things that subsequently gave rise to reasonable suspicions in the minds of the police. Angry at the native guide who had accompanied him and Miss Quested for not knowing where she was or which cave she had entered, the doctor struck him in the face, whereupon the guide ran away, then disappeared. A few moments later he made a well-meaning mistake after glimpsing, to his relief, Miss Quested in the distance, talking with another lady. He put into his pocket her field glasses, with the leather strap broken, which he'd just found inside the entrance to a cave. Then, when Fielding arrived at the Marabar, very late after missing the early morning train from Chandrapore, Aziz's delight at seeing his friend led him to pretend to know that Miss Quested had simply left to see Miss Derek, with whom she'd subsequently "'gone for a spin'" (Forster 135). Finally, and almost disastrously, upon his and Fielding's return by train, his reaction to being told at Chandrapore that he was under arrest was to try to escape. He had to be pulled back by the teacher "before a scandal started" (139).

Although Fielding is especially troubled when he learns from McBryde about the discovery in Aziz's pocket of Miss Quested's field glasses, with their newly broken strap, and about the absence of the guide after the alleged attempted rape, he is convinced of Aziz's innocence. What worries him more, as he turns definitively against the Anglo-Indian "herd," is the occasional tendency of Indians to "jib" (Forster 149) out of fear of their British rulers. Thus Chandrapore's leading barrister, Hamidullah, who knows his close friend Aziz has been calumniated, saddens Fielding by talking only in strategic legal terms of the coming trial. Fielding's optimism about the case, however—and his being, as Hamidullah says in respectful surprise, "'actually . . . on our side against your own people?'" (151)—soon inspires the lawyer to think boldly. He tells Fielding of his intention, in order to "'hit with all our strength'" (150), to ask Amritrao, a highly capable Hindu barrister but so notoriously anti-British that he is loathed at the club, to take charge of the case. Fielding knows from this moment that he himself will be labeled "seditious," through association with Amritrao, by his compatriots; however, born "in freedom" (151), he's better prepared for that unpleasantness than for the *sub specie aeternitatis* attitude of Professor Godbole, his Brahman assistant, toward Aziz's calamity. Godbole, once Fielding can induce him to express an opinion about the doctor's innocence or guilt, says, "'according to our philosophy,'" no action can be performed in isolation. "'All perform a good action, when one is performed, and when an evil action is performed, all perform it.'" Thus, he continues, when told that an evil action has been performed in the Marabar Hills, he concludes that it was performed by Dr. Aziz—but also by the guide, by Fielding, and by me. And by my students. It was even performed by the lady herself. When evil occurs it expresses the whole of the universe. Similarly when good occurs. "Fielding's irritated retort—"'everything is anything and nothing something,'" (153)—elicits Godbole's polite correction that although good and evil certainly do differ, he believes both of them to be aspects of his Lord. "He is present in the one, absent in the other. . . . Yet absence implies presence, absence is not non-existence, and we are therefore entitled to repeat, 'Come, come, come, come'" (154).

Godbole's perspective seems to me important for two reasons: the first is that it points to a significant disagreement between whatever portion of the Hindu population shares it (Amritrao, the barrister chosen by Hamidullah for Aziz obviously does not) and the British and probably most of the Moslems, concerning the validity of a criminal trial. For at the heart of any criminal trial is the assumption of individual moral accountability—the defendant or defendants must be found innocent or guilty—as opposed to the widely *participatory* accountability in which Godbole believes. The second reason is that it helps us a little to understand both Aziz's dismissive comment at one point on "'slack Hindus'" with "'no idea of society'" (Forster 56), and the similarly biased thought of the Hindu judge Das (during a friendly conversation with Aziz after Aziz's trial, over which Das has presided) that "'some Moslems are very violent'" (232).

The Moghuls revered by Aziz certainly had been violent, and the narrator has described Aziz as "tender to every one except a few family enemies whom he did not consider human: on these he desired revenge" (Forster 58), but the doctor never gives way to this violent inclination in the novel. And Das's tactful behavior toward Aziz does not accord at all with the latter's stereotype of the "slack" Hindu. The Brahman Godbole, however—toward whom Aziz happens to be well disposed—appears completely uninterested in social conventions and might be said to have "no idea of society."[3]

The ever-present tension between Chandrapore's Moslems and Hindus turns to hostility as the former prepare for the Mohurram holiday. A large paper tower they have built gets stuck in a branch of a pepul tree; a Mohammedan climbs up the tree and severs the branch; the Hindus protest, a religious riot ensues; and "all the normal work of Chandrapore had been hung up" (Forster 80).

Forster also points to a mixture of intra-caste and anticolonial conflicts in the heterogeneous society over which the British rule. Half of the Sweepers have just gone on strike as the trial begins, "and half the commodes of Chandrapore remained desolate in consequence—only half, and Sweepers from the District, who felt less strongly about the innocence of Dr. Aziz, would arrive in the afternoon, and break the strike . . . (185-86)." In what sounds more like a querulous Anglo-Indian tone than his own even-tempered one, the narrator asks, "why should the grotesque incident occur" (186)? There is a reasonable answer. At the hospital, Major Callendar, the Civil Surgeon, has brutalized a Moslem, Nureddin, whose face had been lacerated when a car in which he'd been driving Aziz (let out of jail until Mohurram) had gone into a ditch. And Aziz had been imprisoned again, "with an additional charge against him" (ironically) of "disturbing the peace" (176). News of all this may well have spread among the Sweepers—Untouchables who do the latrine-cleaning that less lowly Hindu castes avoid. And those Sweepers already sympathetic to Aziz would probably be incensed by his being victimized again, as well as by the Civil Surgeon's mistreatment of Nureddin.[4]

Another sort of occurrence, also inexplicable to the Anglo-Indians, is the vow of some Mohammedan ladies to fast until the prisoner is acquitted. The narrator's comment here clearly parodies the arrogant, dismissive colonial voice: "their death would make no difference, indeed, being invisible, they seemed dead already, nevertheless it was disquieting." And the Anglo-Indians tend to see Fielding, "who received letters with foreign stamps on them, and was probably a Japanese spy," as back of a "new spirit" in Chandrapore that none of the whites can explain (Forster 186).

In this disturbed atmosphere, the British are vengefully eager to hear Adela Quested's testimony, which in earlier colonial times she would simply have given in a deposition. Now, not only must she go through a public ordeal, but as Ronny, the City Magistrate and Adela's fiance, explains to her in pain, the case will not come before him—"'they've objected to me on personal grounds'" (169). And McBryde, who is to prosecute, sadly tells her that Das, Ronny's assistant, will be the presiding judge.

Presiding invisibly, however, over the trial will be the spirit of Mrs. Moore, Ronny's mother, who had brought Adela to India and who has just left for England in the wake of Adela's engagement to her son. Shortly after the women's arrival in Chandrapore, a warm friendship had sprung up between Mrs. Moore and Aziz who had met by chance while visiting a mosque. Touched by her sympathetic nature, he had called her an "Oriental." The Marabar expedition, during which Adela had had her awful experience, had also been shattering for Mrs. Moore. She had heard an echo in a cave that overwhelmed her with a sense of the equivalence of all values and the meaninglessness of life. But even though she had subsequently fallen into a cynical lethargy, she almost offhandedly remarked to Ronny and Adela on the eve of the trial that "[o]f course" Aziz was innocent (Forster 177). Despite the City Magistrate's irritated suggestion, however, that if she had any evidence to give in the prisoner's favor, it was her duty to testify for him, she would not reverse her earlier refusal to have anything "to do with your ludicrous law courts" (173).

Mrs. Moore's rejection of law courts as ludicrous recalls Godbole's implicit rejection of them as irrelevant. But her attitude toward them differs strikingly from his. Godbole believes that God's absence from an evil act paradoxically implies his presence there and that any person connected, however remotely, with such an act, has in some sense committed it. Hence, the very raison d'etre of a criminal trial disappears. Mrs. Moore, on the other hand, has ceased since her Marabar experience to believe in God, or in any difference between "good" and "evil" except the sounds of these words. Because she now thinks of the act of "love" and the act of "rape" (which Aziz is accused of having attempted) as equivalent, she is bound to find ludicrous any law court proceeding against him.

The most important immediate effect of her exonerating Aziz—she says she "'felt it wasn't the sort of thing he would do'" (Forster 178)—is to make Adela, who has already begun to doubt the accuracy of her own accusation, extremely uneasy about pressing it. She longs now to withdraw the case, but as Mrs. Moore says, sourly echoing Ronny's assertion that the machinery has already started, "'She has started the machinery; it will work to its end'" (179). This observation impels the City Magistrate to arrange an immediate departure from India for his mother. And the apparent suddenness of her leaving the country will evoke Indian suspicions of Ronny, and the virtual deification of Mrs. Moore in Chandrapore.

In the courtroom just before the trial begins, Ronny's *sotto voce* comment to two other Anglo-Indian officials, "'My old Das is all right,'" leads one of them to reply, "'You mean he's more frightened of acquitting than convicting, because if he acquits he'll lose his job.'" The narrator observes, "Ronny did mean that, but he cherished 'illusions' about his own subordinates (following the finer traditions of his service here); and he liked to maintain that his old Das really did possess courage of the Public School brand" (Forster 186).

Das proves to be cultivated, conscientious—and obviously uncomfortable in presiding over a trial pitting the colonial power that employs him against a defendant and defense lawyers who are his own countrymen, in a courtroom overwhelmingly sympathetic to Aziz. He does handle decisively the first problem he faces after the trial begins. McBryde, having opened for the prosecution by observing that "the darker races are physically attracted by the fairer, but not vice versa," is interrupted by a voice from somewhere: "'Even when the lady is so uglier than the gentleman?'" (Forster 189). Das's immediate order, "'Turn that man out,'" results in a native policeman's expulsion of a person "who had said nothing"—a mistake that can hardly be held against the judge.

A moment later, however, Das's authority as magistrate is dramatically challenged. Callendar, who's been caring for Adela Quested (this medical solicitude contrasts with his private boast, a few minutes earlier, about "'cutting up'" Nureddin, one of "'these buck niggers'") (Forster 187), demands that his patient—faint and trembling after being called ugly—be given a seat on the platform. Das responds by providng a chair at his own level for her. But this causes a procession to the one-foot high platform by the whole Anglo-Indian contingent, except Fielding. Callendar's remark, "'Thoroughly desirable change for several reasons,'" is one that Das "knew that he ought to censure . . . but did not dare to." And the judge appears, in effect, to have lost control of the trial when a British official calls out patronizingly, "'Go on, Mr Das, we are not here to disturb you'" (190). Only Amritrao's comment, in his Oxford voice, that the defense does not object to Miss Quested's sitting on the platform, since she is unwell, but does object, because of the intimidating effect on "'our witnesses'" (191), to so many European persons enables Das to reassert his authority by asking all of Adela's "'friends'" to "'be so excessively kind as to climb down.'" (In a fine stroke of characterization at this point, Forster has Ronny say "with devastating honesty," "'Well done, Das, quite sound'" [192].)

Resuming at last his opening speech, McBryde soon launches into an attack on Aziz's "double life," then accuses him, in a bizarre distortion of what had happened at the Marabar, of behaving "most cruelly, most brutally, to another of his guests, another English lady. In order to get rid of her, and leave him free for his crime, he crushed her into a cave among his servants." This reference to Mrs. Moore precipitates a courtroom storm as Mahmoud Ali, the Muslim lawyer associated with Amritrao in Aziz's defense, asks with a shriek whether his client "was charged with murder as well as rape." He proceeds to accuse McBryde of not calling Mrs. Moore as a witness because "'you have smuggled her out of the country . . . she would have proved his innocence, she was on our side . . .'" (Forster 192).

The way in which both the prosecution and the defense are now referring to Mrs. Moore seems emblematic of the difficulty of establishing, in a criminal trial under colonial conditions, either what is true or what is just. McBryde has charged the dark-skinned native defendant with attempting to "'get rid of'" her in order to be free to attack—in the earlier words of a British official—"'an English girl fresh from England.'" Mahmoud Ali, almost as inaccurately, though with an apparent factual basis in the haste of Mrs. Moore's departure, has accused British officials of getting her out of the country to prevent her from exculpating a maligned Indian. Unrevealed in these bitter vituperations is the truth that Mrs. Moore had been both convinced of Aziz's innocence and absolutely unwilling to testify at his trial.

Nevertheless, McBryde's allusion to her has provoked a storm, which attains hurricane strength after Mahmoud Ali, defying Das's warning "'This is no way to defend your case,'" replies, "'I am not defending a case, nor are you trying one. We are both of us slaves'"; he then histrionically quits as Aziz's lawyer. Mrs. Moore, transformed into "a Hindu goddess" as "'Esmiss Esmoor/Esmiss Esmoor. . .,'" is now being invoked both inside the courtroom and in the street. In striking contrast to this tumult is the tense silence once the courtroom chant, though not the one outside, stops and Miss Quested is called to give her testimony. Her state of mind is inimical to the case that the pressure of the Anglo-Indian community and the legal "machinery" have made her continue despite her misgivings. She is thinking now of her preoccupation with love just before her entrance into the fatal Marabar cave. Suddenly, definitively, and shamefully to her at that moment, she had realized she didn't love Ronny. Still, she was not inclined to break off her engagement—for if love "is everything," she had thought, "few marriages would survive the honeymoon." She asked Aziz, with a frown, whether he was married. The doctor, although a widower, "felt it more artistic to have his wife alive for a moment," so he spoke of her in the present tense. And Adela, after learning that he has children, and admiring him almost impersonally as "a handsome little oriental," asked, "'Have you one wife or more than one?'" (Forster 131). His flustered response, "'One, one in my own particular case,'" reflected what the narrator has explained was the shock of an educated, modern Moslem at such a question. Adela, however, was apparently as unaware of this reaction as of his plunging into one of the caves "to recover his balance." As she now prepares to testify, she is thinking that "she had innocently asked Aziz what marriage was like," but that "her question had roused evil in him (197)."

This conclusion, however, she corrects almost as soon as she hears her own voice replying to McBryde. Actually returning in her mind's eye, rather than remembering, the Marabar Hills, she sees everything there with complete clarity when he asks her a series of questions. Yes, the prisoner and the guide had taken her to one of the hills. Yes, she had "'gone alone into one of those caves.'" But upon McBryde's suggesting, "'And the prisoner followed you,'" she says nothing, because she is "watching [the cave's] entrance, for Aziz to pass in," and failing to see him. Her "'I cannot be sure'" (Forster 198) frightens the prosecutor, whose suggestion, repeated, she finally rejects with "'No'" (199). Then, the magistrate urgently having asked her to speak up again, she says she's afraid she'd made a mistake: Dr. Aziz never followed her into the cave. This courageous honesty impels a desperate McBryde to attempt to read aloud the deposition Adela had signed after the Marabar incident. He is stopped, however, by Das, who then ignores Callendar's effort to end the proceedings on medical grounds and elicits from Miss Quested a withdrawal of her charge. With a kind of absurd appropriateness, in view of the expectations the Anglo-Indians have had of her testimony, McBryde asks the witness if she is mad, and the wife of another official screams insults at her.

Indeed, except for Fielding—against whom, after the trial's end, she's flung by shouting, exulting Indians, and who insists she get into his own carriage—nobody has a kind word for Adela. The judge has ended the trial with the declaration, "'The prisoner is released without one stain on his character; the question of costs will be decided elsewhere'" (Forster 200). But when Fielding asks Aziz that evening not to plunge Miss Quested into financial ruin by charging her the amounts that have been mentioned at a Victory Dinner, Aziz, says, "'No, no. It will be put down to weakness and the attempt to gain promotion officially'" (219). In time, because Fielding persuades him it's the wish of Mrs. Moore—still vividly present to him, although she has died at sea—Aziz renounces "with a passionate and beautiful outburst the whole of the compensation money, claiming only costs." His dour prediction, however, proves accurate. Despite Das's declaration at the end of the trial, the English still believed he was guilty. They believed it to the end of their careers, and retired Anglo-Indians in Tunbridge Wells or Cheltenham still murmur to each other, "'That Marabar case which broke down because the poor girl couldn't face giving her evidence—that was another bad case'" (227).

A positive result of the trial on the Indian side is a rapprochement at Chandrapore between Hindus and Moslems, who had been so bitterly at odds at Mohurram. A Hindu associate of Aziz's, and like him a subordinate of Callendar's, Dr. Panna Lal, had "offered to give evidence for the prosecution in the hope of pleasing the English, also because he hated Aziz." Now, when an angry mob that has learned of Callendar's boasts about torturing Nureddin approaches the hospital, looking for the injured man, Panna Lal first apologizes fulsomely to Aziz for his

> "wicked lies," then rushes to do the Indians' bidding. Of ignoble origin, Dr. Panna Lal possessed nothing that could be disgraced, and he wisely decided to make the other Indians feel like kings, because it would put them into better tempers. . . . When Nureddin emerged, his face all bandaged, there was a roar of relief as though the Bastille had fallen. (Forster 205-06)

Aziz's defense has been financed by the Nawab Bahadur, a wealthy Moslem landowner (and grandfather of Nureddin). Preparing to give his Victory Banquet, the Nawab asks Hamidullah "'to bring out our friends Fielding and Amritrao, and to discover whether the latter will require special food'" (Forster 206). Some days later the trial magistrate, Das, showing in his own gracious way the "genuine desire for a good understanding" that animates so many citizens, calls on Aziz to ask two favors—which Aziz accords: a remedy for shingles and a poem for his brother-in-law's monthly magazine. Das makes it clear that the magazine, which Aziz has thought was for Hindus only, "'is not for Hindus, but Indians generally'" (131), and he adds, "'You are our hero; the whole city is behind you, irrespective of creed'" (232). Despite biased ethnic generalizations that flit through the minds of the Hindu and the Moslem as they talk, we don't doubt the friendliness of these two men toward each other.[5]

The chief effect of the trial on Aziz is to intensify his fear and hatred of the British. He almost lets himself be persuaded by some of his "old lawyer friends" (Forster 255) to help in anticolonial agitation. Instead, however, he goes to the princely state of Mau, with the aid of Godbole (now Minister of Education there), to serve as "chief medicine man" (255) at the court of the Hindu Rajah. This has happened despite Aziz's being a marked man in the eyes of the British colonial administration: the Political Agent for the Mau "neighborhood" (257), having learned that the "suspect" Aziz was to be employed at court, had "rallied the old Rajah about permitting a Moslem doctor to approach his sacred person." In superbly ironic terms, however, the Rajah, refusing to take the Briton's hint, "replied that Hindus were less exclusive than formerly, thanks to the enlightened commands of the Viceroy, and he felt it his duty to move with the times" (257).

Aziz, offended by Fielding's not having joined in his victory procession following the trial (the teacher was fully occupied in protecting Adela from the crowd), and convinced that subsequently, in a letter from England of which he has read only the opening lines, Fielding had announced his forthcoming marriage to Miss Quested, he has not even opened later mail from his only active British defender. He regrets his "foolish experiment" in friendship with an Englishman, and thinks, "I am an Indian at last" (Forster 256). Aziz's disenchantment with Fielding, however, is largely based on a completely mistaken interpretation of the latter's friendship with Miss Quested, especially after the Civil Magistrate has broken off his engagement to her. Fielding's wife turns out to be Stella Moore, Mrs. Moore's daughter by the man she'd married after Ronny's father had died. When Fielding visits Mau with Stella and her brother, Ralph, Aziz is secretly happy to discover his error; soon finds Ralph reminding him, almost uncannily, of Mrs. Moore. It is significant, however, that the doctor puts on an act of rejecting Fielding, "Speaking in Urdu, that [his] children might understand, he said: 'Please do not follow us, whomever you marry. I wish no Englishman or Englishwoman to be my friend'" (Forster 264).

Although the two men do reconcile—Aziz even shows Fielding a letter he wants to send to Miss Quested, thanking her "for her fine behavior two years back" (Forster 277)—they have no social meeting-place. The bachelor teacher, who had taken pride in "traveling light," has become an educational inspector, a husband, and a father. He "had thrown in his lot with Anglo-India by marrying a countrywoman, and he was acquiring some of its limitations, and already felt surprise at his own past heroism" (279).

Aziz, for his part, wants the English out of India. During a last horseback ride with Fielding, he says to him, "'Why are we put to so much suffering? We used to blame you, now we blame ourselves. . . . Until England is in difficulties in the next European war—aha, aha! Then is our time.'" Jeeringly, though ominously in the light of the World War that is part of present readers' historical memory, Fielding asks him whether he wants the Japanese instead of the English. Aziz's shouted reaction, "'India shall become a nation! No foreigners of any sort! Hindu and Moslem and Sikh and all shall be one! . .'" (Forster 281), probably expresses less what he believes than what he'd like to believe.

The rapprochement at Chandrapore between Hindus and Moslems does indicate the possibility of a deeper and more extensive reconciliation, but no more than a possibility in view of mutual suspicions and antagonisms. Such grim historic episodes as the inter-ethnic massacres of Hindus, Moslems, and Sikhs that immediately preceded and followed the birth of independent India and Pakistan; and the killings of Moslems in many parts of India after ultranationalist Hindus had destroyed in December 1992 an ancient mosque in Uttar Pradesh, induce doubts that what both Mahatma Gandhi and Jawaharlal Nehru aspired toward—a country tolerant and united—can eventually arise. And Forster's reference to a strike by those Sweepers who perceive the prosecution of Aziz as unfair, points both to the particular situation of Untouchables as a minority and the deep-rooted Hindu, hence Indian, problem of caste. According to the authors of a book based on a BBC Radio 4 series on India, it is "one of the many paradoxes of modern India that although discrimination by caste has been outlawed, most politicians admit that caste, not ideology, continues to dominate Indian politics (Tully and Masani 77).

NOTES

[1] Forster "had much trouble with the trial scenes in the novel, not being sure of his legal detail and doubting—with reason, as it turned out—whether a case as important as that of Aziz would have been tried in a subordinate court." Forster's Indian friend Masood offered at the author's request to check such details "throughout the novel," but his only reply on the typescript sent him by Forster was, "It is magnificent. Do not alter a word" (Furbank 119).

[2] This Everyman edition is notable for its inclusion of a foreword by Forster, an introduction by Peter Burra, who according to Forster, "saw exactly what I was trying to do," and some author's notes.

[3] Edward W. Said, though an able critic, makes misleading comments on Forster's treatment of Hindus and Mohammedans in *A Passage to India*:

> Hindus, according to the novel, believe that all is muddle, all connected, God is one, is not, was not, was. By contrast, Islam as represented by Aziz, apprehends order and a specific God. "The comparatively simple mind of the Mohammedan," says Forster ambiguously, as if both to imply that Aziz has a comparatively simple mind, and that "the Mohammedan," generally speaking, does also. (Said 202)

Particular Hindus in the novel are not all like Professor Godbole, whom Said particularly alludes to. Godbole does believe that all is "connected," and that whatever evil act was performed in a Marabar cave was performed by Aziz, the guide, Fielding, Godbole himself, his students, and even Adela Quested. But this belief is obviously not shared by Das, since he presides over a trial whose rationalist aim it is to find one person, Aziz, either innocent or guilty. Nor could Godbole's perspective be that of the urbane Hindu barrister Amritrao, to whom all is not muddle. While objecting quite sensibly to the whole Anglo-Indian contingent's sitting on the platform, he tactfully makes a point of the appropriateness of Miss Quested's sitting there, "since she has been unwell."

It's true that Forster describes the Krishna celebration in Part III of the novel as a muddle, but Forster exhibits more subtlety in his treatment of Hindus both in that Part (the Rajah of Mau, for example) and in the novel as a whole than Said is willing to perceive (note the characterization of Dr. Panna Lal, and the narrator's comments on the Sweepers).

As for Forster's reference to the "comparatively simple mind of the Mohammedan," Said fails to examine the context in which it occurs—Part I, Chapter VII, where during the social gathering at Fielding's house, Aziz has asked Godbole to describe the Marabar Caves to Adela Quested. Godbole, having replied, "It will be a great pleasure," forgoes the pleasure, "and Aziz realized that he was keeping back something about the caves. He realized because he often suffered from similar inhibitions himself. . . . " The narrator, continuing to observe Godbole from Aziz's perspective, goes on to say, "Handled subtly, [Godbole] might regain control and announce that the Marabar Caves were—full of stalactites, perhaps; Aziz led up to this, but they weren't." It is after noting that Adela had "no conception" of the "underdrift" of the light and friendly dialogue between Aziz and Godbole that the narrator characterizes the dialogue as an encounter between "the comparatively simple mind of the Mohammedan" and "Ancient Night" (Forster 62). This strikes me as a witty rather than an ambiguous comment (note in comparison to *what* Aziz's "Mohammedan" mind is "comparatively" simple!) and certainly not as a derogatory reference to "the Mohammedan" mind in general.

4 Forster was more politically acute in *A Passage to India* than some critics realize. Frank Moraes's *DNB* article on Bhimrao Kamji Ambedkar (1891-1956), an Untouchable himself who became a notable leader of the Untouchables, a distinguished constitutional lawyer, and "one of the principal architects of independent India's constitution," makes a point of Ambedkar's drawing "politically nearer to M. A. Jinnah and the Muslim League" in 1939 "in their opposition to what both characterized as Hindu chauvinism." There's an historical echo here of the sympathetic attitude in *A Passage to India* of many members of one Indian minority, the Untouchable "Sweepers," for two members of another, the Moslems Aziz and Nureddin. It also seems significant that toward the end of his life, Ambedkar became a convert to a minority religion in India, Buddhism (Moraes 15-16).

5 Trilling (154) seems to me to put disproportionate emphasis on the chasm in the novel between Hindus and Moslems, who "can not really approach each other." He continues, "Aziz, speaking in all friendliness to Mr. Das the Magistrate, wishes that Hindus did not remind him of cow-dung, and the Hindu Mr. Das thinks, "Some Moslems are very violent. . . ."

This Moslem and this Hindu clearly do "approach each other"; and despite the gap between them, good will is mutual in their conversation, which is reported by the omniscient narrator immediately after the paragraph containing his chapter-opening remark, "Another local consequence of the trial was a Hindu-Moslem entente" (Trilling 231).

WORKS CITED

Chaudhuri, Nirad C. "Passage To and From India." *Encounter* (June 1954): 19-24. 1970. (Reprint from *Twentieth Century Interpretations of "A Passage* to India": A Collection of Critical Essays. Ed. Andrew Rutherford. Englewood Cliffs, NJ: Prentice, 1970.)

Forster, E.M. *A Passage to India.* 1924. London: J. M. Dent, 1957.

Furbank, P.N. *E. M. Forster: A Life.* Vol. 2. New York: Harcourt, 1977.

Moraes, Frank. "Ambedkar, Bhimrao Kamji (1891-1956)." *Dictionary of National Biography*, 1977.

Orwell, George. *The Collected Essays, Journalism and Letters of George Orwell.* Ed. Sonia Orwell and Ian Angus. 4 vols. New York: Harcourt, 1968.

Said, Edward W. *Culture and Imperialism.* New York: Knopf, 1993.

Trilling, Lionel. *E. M. Forster.* 1943. New York: New Directions, 1964.

Tully, Mark, and Zareer Masani. *India: Forty Years of Independence.* New York: Braziller, 1988.

CHAPTER ELEVEN

Law, Medicine, and the Sex Slave
in Margaret Atwood's *The Handmaid's Tale*
by Linda Myrsiades

This paper will chart the course of our understanding of Margaret Atwood's *The Handmaid's Tale* (HMT) by viewing it in the context of four tales ("The Tale of Separability," "The Judge's Tale," "The Economic Tale," and "The Tale of Property") to yield a fifth tale, which I shall call "Composing Her 'Tail.'" The objective is to discover reproductive woman as triangulated by literature, medicine, and law and to locate the switchpoints at which representations of her through these discourses diverge and converge to construct her. I contend that the central intersection is one at which woman and child collide and at whose crash site the debris of such issues as interests and rights (women's, fetal, and state), woman as property, and the separability of mother and child lie scattered about for society to traffic in and to police.

In "The Tale of Separability," I examine medical representation of women's bodies as containers, a medical construction for reproduction that absents women from a central place in the pregnancy process. Applied to Atwood's novel, woman is only validated insofar as she is capable of being identified with the product she "delivers" and the "labor" from which she is alienated. "The Judge's Tale" unpacks the role of Solomon as a figure of "violence" whose narrative establishes a superordinate male authority that, in the world of Atwood's Gilead, becomes the EYE from behind which divinity presumably rules. The handmaid herself, Offred, is figured both as the true "mother," who is in a larger sense a "false" mother and as the body of the baby "pulled apart by force" (344). The handmaid, marked as a designated breeder, becomes in "The Economic Tale" one of a class of fertile women whose bodies are assigned to "labor" for the state. A commodity of exchange and a home for the "seeds" of state, the handmaid is traded by the commanders of Gilead, passed from house to house in a form of contract pregnancy that determines her role as a "good" mother, one who gives up her child and subserves her gestational rights to the male genetic claim to his property. "The Tale of Property" continues the image of the reproductive woman as an economic commodity, extending the discussion to consider how, as home to the fetus, her body is effectively "inhabited" by the body politic. Here, the metaphor of the house enables us to view reproductive woman as having lost the right to represent herself, being "inhabited" by the judge and the doctor through whose agency alone the pregnant woman can claim her right to her own body. Finally, in "Composing Her 'Tail,'" I introduce the handmaid's effort to reclaim her property by "composing" herself. The handmaid writes herself (the female 'tail') into existence by telling her own tale and thereby taking possession of it. It is, nevertheless, an amorphous shared space that refuses to be overdetermined by medicine and law at the same time that it expresses its relatedness to both that which reproductive woman "houses" (the fetus which recapitulates her) and that in which she is herself housed (the social world she reiterates).

THE TALE OF SEPARABILITY

The representation of woman's reproductive body as a mere container, isolated from the rest of her self and serving merely as walls for the central presence of the embryo, is present as early as William Hunter's 18th century *Gravid Uterus* and William Smellie's 1754 anatomical atlas (Jordanova). Peeling back layers of the truncated body of a pregnant female to penetrate her reproductive organs, the plates of *Gravid Uterus* have "the effect of drawing the eye into the vagina, the cut-off thighs, the sectioned clitoris may all be seen as implicitly violent" (62). The medical literature of the nineteenth century reflects a comparable identification of a woman with her sexual organs, "as if the Almighty, in creating the female sex, had taken the uterus and built up a woman around it" (Holbrook 14-15, as quoted in Smith-Rosenberg and Rosenberg 284). Woman as "product and prisoner or her reproductive system" (283) was considered unique; there was no comparable control over men by their reproductive system. And this was understood to be nature's way of identifying woman as designed for motherhood, her "natural" destiny. Because her organs were secret and internal, so must her emotions be "more interior than man" (Holcombe 201, as quoted in Smith-Rosenberg and Rosenberg 286). Because her reproductive organs formed the center of her being, woman was to be constrained from using her brain, a negative drain of energy that would exhaust "a limited amount of vital force" critical to keeping her from delivering "sickly and neurotic children. . . . The brain and ovary could not develop at the same time" (Smith-Rosenberg and Rosenberg 288). By contrast, to ensure their proper functioning, the sexual organs had to be exercised, allowing the discharge of accumulated male energies and "the soothing presence of the male semen 'bathing the female reproductive organs'"(296). Unnatural and deleterious controls over birth would lead to nymphomania, gynecological lesions, insanity, and heart disease. Little consideration was given to the contribution syphilis (brought into the home by errant husbands) would make to a woman's condition (Savage).

By the end of the twentieth century, images had shifted to focus on the fetus, with the pregnant woman represented as the outer space in which the embryo as spaceship floats. Even the uterine walls have disappeared as the solitary fetus becomes "primary and autonomous" (Petchesky 268). Where the fetus dangles in space, unhoused, unsupported, woman has become empty space. The cyborg notion of fertility dominates "in which man replicates himself without the aid of woman" (Sofia, as quoted in Petchesky 270). Indeed, when the reproductive technology becomes routinized and more clearly tied to the fetus than the pregnant woman (amniocentesis, ultrasound monitoring, cesareans), the pregnant woman is put in the position of being an adversary, hostile to fetal development.[1] Thus, it becomes clear, the imagery of "housing" and the shift to an "unhoused" discourse is critical to understanding the role of the pregnant woman in relation to her fetus, for the fetus encased in an opaque womb is itself removed from our gaze. Only stripping, unpeeling the layers to reveal the inner sanctum will remove "the veil of mystery" (Harrison 774, as quoted in Petchesky 276) and expose "the womb as a space to be conquered . . . by one who stands outside it looking in" (Petchesky 276).

In a postmodern sense, we have arrived at a new construction for reproduction: the extrauterine fetus and the surrogate mother.[2] As Squier makes clear, once we introduce the prospect of actual or hypothetical reproductive technology ("AID, IVF, Gamette Intrafallopian Transfer, Zygote Intrafallopian Transfer, Zona drilling, abdominal pregnancy, cloning, and so on,"115), we expand the prospects for representation of the reproductive body. Indeed, figurations (the mother as a nurturing environment, the pregnant woman as host, or the womb as a container, for example) are, in her view, related to the production of power, including the ideological oppositionality of mother and fetus and the use of a woman's body to enhance male power. The more prevalent the idea that the fetus was pre-formed and whole from the moment of conception, the less consequential is the function of the uterine environment. The mechanics of reproduction become more critical and the pregnant woman less as the fetus is privileged in any balancing of its rights with those of the woman. The machine-like mother becomes a function of rationalizing labor as a means of producing a product. Indeed, "The language of the reproductive technocrats—in which eggs are 'harvested' and so on—presumes the absence of the mother as a speaking, involved subject" (Daly and Reddy 4). In the HMT, Serena Joy's surrogacy arrangement with the handmaid Offred is constructed in comparable terms: "As far as I'm concerned, this is like a business transaction" (21). The concept of an ectogenetic fetus takes the process a step further, replacing "mother" entirely with the "machine"—a test-tube or artificial uterus, as suggested by Huxley's *Brave New World* or Shelley's *Frankenstein* (Squier 117). If woman is not regarded as machine-like, she is, in these terms, replaceable by a machine; even her surrogacy function is thereby threatened, even if only imaginatively. By this analysis, we have now entered the realm of the "posthuman," a new image and context for reproduction.

Robert Goldstein takes up the political-legal implications of this construction, contending that the replacement of individual responsibilities by a concept of "a web of communal obligations" (32) is to "recast the language of rights into the language of duties" (32). The risk to woman is of excluding her from the autonomy that rights language affords. Moreover, the complimentary assertion that fetuses themselves are rights-holders disobligates the pregnant woman insofar as it diminishes our sense of the fetus' dependence. But Goldstein's future poses its own bleak vision of "an exclusively rights-based analysis [that] could logically lead to a regime of separation in which abandoned fetuses are raised in state hatcheries" (34) (a prospect not altogether unlike the Gileadean assignment of handmaids as ambulatory hatcheries for the commander's seed). Indeed, one vision describes the compelling theoretics of such a model: "the neonatal unit filled with orphan fetuses bound to artificial placentas appears as the caricatured and embodied approximation of the Rawlsian original position" (Sandel, as paraphrased in Goldstein 35).[3]

Ashe ("Law-Language") delineates the dilemma in a more direct legal light, citing "the medical model's emphasis on the separability of the pregnant woman and the fetus and its definition of the female reproduction process in terms of discontinuity rather than continuity. Both emphases inform legal discourse as well as medical theory and practice" (539). The infiltration of medical metaphors of separability into the law has the effect of obscuring the role of the pregnant woman, emptying her of those features of reproduction that most clearly distinguish her from the male parent's role. Moreover, while it enhances medical control over the fetus, it also diminishes the gestational role of the woman, an effect of which we find in surrogacy rulings which distinguish genetic (biological) and gestational (contractual) mothers and where the gestational mother's rights are largely disavowed (Tobin; Ashe "Law-Language").

It is clear in the HMT, by contrast, that as long as a woman is identified with her fetus, she achieves a social role that validates her. One of the handmaids, for example, is described as "vastly pregnant; her belly, under her loose garment, swells triumphantly. . . . She is a magic presence to us, an object of envy and desire, we covet her. She's a flag on a hilltop, showing us what can still be done: we too can be saved" (35). Indeed, nurtured within the pregnant woman's body is not merely the fetus but "an interest of the community whose 'growth' progressively consumes her claim on privacy and bodily autonomy" (Siegel 275). Infiltrating her body, "The Republic of Gilead, said Aunt Lydia, knows no bounds. Gilead is within you" (31). Representationally, this interest protects the unborn but through the woman as an absented figure who, unrepresented, is thereby implicitly compelled to bear children. The absented handmaid is, in any case, aware of her erasure: "I avoid looking down at my body, not so much because it's shameful or immodest but because I don't want to see it. I don't want to look at something that determines me so completely" (82).

The model of separability retains a lethal implication for the mother-child relation, allowing for the legal theory that would construct woman and fetus as adversaries,[4] thereby permitting violent intrusions into the woman's body (Ashe, "Abortion" 542)[5] and Solomonic judgments (presumptively objective, external judgments but none the less violent) that permit "taking" the child. Emptying the woman's house may be a figure for her autonomy and liberation,[6] but it is an ambiguous figure and it comes at a significant cost. It separates her irredeemably from her offspring and casts her into a set of communal duties and obligations that are no less likely to "house" her by virtue of her reproductive biology. Mary Poovey puts the question in terms of the definition of personhood; by this argument, reproductive women would be conceptualized not in terms of their individuality or individual rights but in terms of their heterogeneity as part of a social network. Here, the social unit rather than the unitary body is the touchstone for personhood. Reproduction is figured as a social rather than a personal experience. On the one hand, we are looking at the emancipation of reproductive woman (from biological determinism); on the other, at her decentering in the cultural scene. What woman has traded for her communal network is her right of intimate association, which includes her abortion right. What she has gained is a compelled identification with a network that forces on her a social definition of her role as a parent. Such imagery opens the womb to the judge and the doctor,[7] removes the woman from the role of "householder" and puts the "tenant" centerstage as a privileged guest. Feeling (of the woman) is trumped by seeing (of the physician); as one dissenting judge was to declare, a woman has become "a bystander to medical procedures performed upon her own body" (Margolick 26, as quoted in Petchesky 284).

THE JUDGE'S TALE

The question of the woman as "bystander" leads us to the tale of Solomon which provides an illuminating device for framing our understanding of the

HMT as a societal decision disposing of the question of mother-child separability as well as legal representation of the reproductive woman. This tale provides us with a situation in which two women are pitted against one another in a dilemma incapable of resolution from within. Resolution requires the external intervention of male power to "cut through" their entangled claims. Unnamed and identified merely as harlots, the women are not only treated like children, but appear to be regarded as irrational. One moves, by acceding to the threat of violence, from her designation as a harlot to earn a name which is not a real name—"mother"—but a biologically determined and socially useful function. The other asks only for what is, in her view, "fair," a fifty-fifty split. Their own behavior appears to have "judged" both women, but it is the imposed sword and he who wields it that renders judgment, a judgment presumably neutral but permeated by false objectivity. Whereas Solomon's sword appears to express a devotion to a "rule of law," it is clear that there is no code of law operating here but, rather, an instinctive form of judging that responds either to the plea of one of the harlots before him (Allegretti 1132) or to the "unknowable" wisdom of God within him (Schneider 242-43).[8] In Solomon, we are faced with a king whose authority is under challenge in his effort to unify a people. The greatest threat is represented as coming from woman, in this instance a prior matriarchal culture "not-yet-fully-overcome"(Ashe, "Abortion" 84). The patriarchal power of the state had yet to establish itself as more powerful than the cultural force of motherhood and thereby gives rise to that show of power with which we shall be concerned: the judgment of the "true" mother whereby naturalized law is created out of an unnatural act. The violence of the sword of power restores us to nature which, alone, is taken to be determinate and unambiguous.

The contest is thus not merely between the objects of justice and the subjective agent, not merely between matriarchal and patriarchal systems, but also between natural and officialized law. The critical question to be resolved is who is to lead and who to follow. Solomon is under threat of de-legitimization, not knowing "how to go out or come in" (I Kings 3. 7). God alone, he is convinced, can grant him the ability to judge "so great a people" "with an understanding heart . . . [to] discern between good and bad" (3. 9). Solomon, in sum, acts through the external authority of a transcendent power, relying not upon reason but upon a gift whose power allows him to rule through the imposition of an act of violence. Moreover, the gift of judging must be taken at face value; its presumed wisdom must go unchallenged. She who would deny it is denied its rewards. She who accedes is judged worthy. It is resistance to judgment that will be punished, not fitness to mother (Althouse). Solomon thus slices his Gordian knot as a bypass to addressing the legal complexities in which justice must inevitably become entangled. His justice is one of fear rather than wonder, but a fear that rescues uncertainty from the jaws of ambiguity. Without fairness or perceived fairness, Solomon reduces judging to an act of arbitrary authority. Just as the mother who accedes to his power is judged the best custodian of the child, so is Solomon the best custodian of justice, because both reflect an unyielding assertion of power. Both play designated roles in a relation of power that confirms the unassailability of clarity, decisiveness, and order. It is not right but resolution that prevails. No confusion here, no collapse of anything other than justice understood as goodness and reason. The appearance of reason is betrayed by the reality of the sword.

Solomon stands in relation to those he judges as a king before harlots, the superordinate male authority. Centered as king, Solomon is regarded as equal to his task insofar as his "wisdom" is held to emanate from a divine source. He is the EYE of Gilead in the HMT from behind which God presumably rules. His authority inspires an awe bordering on fear, the proper object of a justice enforced by the sword that threatens to bisect the disputed child. What is discovered by means of such "fear" is not who is the true mother; rather, the question shifts, as in the HMT, to who will acquiesce, who will release her claim (Althouse). It is of greater consequence to Gilead that a handmaid give up her child to the state than that she claim true motherhood. The fierce or resistant mother is more likely to end up in the colonies or in the "exile" to which the children of Ham and the Jews have been assigned in the HMT. What must, in the end, be created by Solomon's judgment is clarity regarding one's place in relation to authority. It is this clarity that grants legitimacy to those who rule Gilead. Law that is determinate is preferred, in sum, to one that is merely "just." As with the Jews, this postnuclear holocaust depends upon those who, as Weisberg puts it, question not the validity of inhuman laws, but only the "humanity" of how best to apply them. Law in this sense becomes a means of constructing a "narrative terror" (129) that permits a society to avoid or deny central realities. The focus shifts to a Foucauldian regimen of surveilling and punishing, a "technology of power" (Hammer 45) culminating in the HMT in highly ritualized Salvagings, Prayvaganzas, and Particicutions. By such means, Gilead is a society like Vichy, one which enables itself to "think the unthinkable" (Weisberg 157) and to enact it both by the institutionalization of a network of surveillance and counter surveillance and by the internalization of surveillance such that the handmaids monitor and censor themselves even as they unconsciously adopt and measure themselves against prevalent social norms and values (McCombs; Bouson; Hammer).

In a society in which acquiescence is a true norm, resistance to power is the true crime. Indeed, the second (the presumed "false" mother) harlot's refusal to accept the child when the first (the presumed "true" mother) accedes to the power of the sword is itself a form of acquiescence to violence, belief in its seductive brutality. In either case, the sword wins, but with the first harlot we have a failure of faith, a moment of hesitation that makes her an unworthy mother in the eyes of an absolute ruler like an Abraham, a mother unwilling to make the ultimate "sacrifice" that will give birth to divinely absolute authority. The handmaid Offred is such a mother, one who vacillates, believing neither in the authority, legitimacy, or ultimate beneficence of the state. She does not resist to save her child from Gilead. She wants to run to her paramour Nick to be rescued herself; she waits and considers her alternatives, at length. She could prostrate herself before the commander, a proposal with all the earmarks of a failed strategy. She could suicide, but what value is there to extinguishing that which has already been essentially erased. She could escape, strike out on her own, idle considerations (374-75). In the end, in an act deserving only of pathos, she snatches at Nick's ambiguous offer of rescue with the arrival of the Black Van, giving herself "over into the hands of strangers, because it can't be helped" 378). Hers is a failure of belief, a moment not of choice but of default; she is prepared to accede to authority, or rescue, whichever comes first. The handmaid is like the prototypical rape victim who fails to resist, who cannot beat a law whose justice will punish her assailant only if she risks his violence (Estrich); the rape victim reinforces Solomonic rule—the hierarchical force of power—by failing to call its bluff. She takes a chance on the judge's instincts, a high-risk, low-payback position. As for the first harlot, even if she gets the baby, she loses; because the real winner is the threat of arbitrary violence.[9] The harlot, the handmaid, the rape victim have been trumped by a system that, like the Wizard of Oz, depends on no one pulling back the curtain. This, after all, is the Solomon of Kings I who "know[s] not how to go out or come in" (3. 2).

What, in the end, is the underlying expression of a house-of-cards law founded on an attachment to structures identified with a "valorized motherhood" (Ashe, "Abortion" 84). As Ashe addresses the question, the universal issue is one of transforming "ambiguity and indeterminacy into decidability" (87). Complexity is reduced to binary opposition, simplifying judgment. But such reduction threatens to rupture the fabric of law as suppressed questions break through. The handmaid's testimony, her oral narrative, as we shall later see, unrepresses such questions, requiring that they be thought through even as she herself resists giving them life: "it hurts me to tell it over, over again. Once was enough. . . . But I keep on going with this sad and hungry and sordid, this limping and mutilated story" (344). Her story in fragments, the handmaid is "like a body caught in crossfire or pulled apart by force" (343-44). Split from her own mother, split from authority over decisions that control her own life, the handmaid is herself the judged, the disposed of babe she yearns to find; it is she whom Solomon threatens to slice into parts, she who is designated the ward of the acceding mother (the Aunts). And it is her "true" mother, the resistant "harlot," who is cast into the wastelands and, outlawed, called a false mother for her refusal to accept the violence of Gilead against women.

THE ECONOMIC TALE

In an epigraph to the HMT from the biblical tale of Rachel, Leah, and Bilbah, Atwood refers us to a tale of women as property, both as wives and slaves, used and using (Bilbah as handmaid and surrogate; Rachel as a commander's wife). Here, women's cultural value, like that of the handmaids in the novel, lies in being filled and their shame in being uninhabited: "What we prayed for was emptiness, so we would be worthy to be filled: with grace, with love, with self-denial, semen and babies" (251). Male value, by contrast, lay in serving "in God's stead" to plant the seed in her womb, to fill that which would go unfilled save for the presence of "Man," to inhabit the otherwise uninhabitable. This was the ultimate act of hegemony, domination from within. Human relations are all but eclipsed by images of emptiness and being filled. The only moment the handmaid feels she has value in the Commander's eye is when she considers that "to him I'm no longer merely a usable body. To him I'm not just a boat with no cargo, a chalice with no wine in it, an oven—to be crude—minus the bun. To him I am not merely empty" (211).

Offred is one of a class of fertile women acting as designated breeders for the state of Gilead. She is characterized as having a vague yearning, a "talent for insatiability" (4), ostensibly for the future, an expectation for what is to happen but also a nostalgia for a past that reeked of old sex (3). It is as if having something "inside" was a privilege to be withheld, a privilege granted only in ritual; this denial of access to one's own "room" was ultimately to define a woman's understanding of freedom. Their bodies were patrolled by the Aunts; no guards were allowed inside (the old gymnasium): "to be seen—is to be—penetrated. What you must be, girls, is impenetrable," says Aunt Lydia (38). Their "houses," in effect, were sealed off, policed as an anticipated scene of a crime. Their bodies were not to be traded on, rummaged through, or otherwise sold on the cheap; their "house" was either a property to be condemned by the state or one withheld from the market as a "special purchase" reserved for the target market of the Gileadean elite. Handmaids are thus identified with the biological function that essentializes them as women. Unlike the Aunts (a class of women assigned to educate the handmaids to their roles as surrogates) who pass news from house to house, the handmaid is identified with the "house" to which "news" is brought. The commander visits the handmaids serially assigned to him to transform them into functional homes for his seed. Encased by a cloak of red, the handmaid is a "Sister dipped in blood" (11), a virgin bride of an anointed elite who drips the menstrual fluid that certifies her fertility. A visible sign of her function, the color of blood defines the handmaid even as she herself denies the association: "I never looked good in red, it's not my color" (11). She has been inverted and engulfed in the dissipating egg her womb expels, provoking an image of an incubator housed in that which it incubates and has rejected.

The HMT reveals with clarity what is not always open to view in the present-day dehumanizing uses to which women's bodies are put.[10] Present-day "contract motherhood," for one example, provides a connection with state ownership of women in the HMT by way of making public that which is private. That is, the state, represented by Gilead, injects public ideology into the realm of the private to destroy the dichotomy between the presumably "free" private (domestic uses) and the regulated public (slave trade) domains. Present-day state restraint is thereby "unmasked," that is, its reluctance, positively, to intervene in affairs of the personal/private (in cases of marital rape, sex and child abuse, and incest) to maintain the illusion of what is in reality a permeable boundary between the public and private realms. Regulation by the state in both spheres in the HMT could be regarded as no more dystopic than present-day usage which preserves dominant gender relations in the private sphere, a space where it refuses protection and thereby reinforces subtle state coercion (MacKinnon; Ehrenreich, "Surrogacy").[11]

Surrogacy, for a second example, is disguised in contemporary terms as a reflection of woman's agency when it is a condition arising in effect out of society buying and selling the human products of their reproductive labor.[12] In the HMT, by contrast, women are defined economically by their useful "labor" so that those who are fruitful are "good" mothers (and are therefore "farmed" out to the homes of the powerful) and those who are barren are "bad" (and are therefore banished to the nuclear wastefields or the sex club) (Ikemoto). As in a slavery model, women, considered responsible to "produce" the community, are "good" insofar as they birth its future citizens and maintain the species or race. (Tobin; Ehrenreich, "Surrogacy"; Ikemoto; Siegel; Ashe, "Theoretics").[13] Construction of the pregnant woman herself as slave depicts a woman as compelled to carry a child and thereby condemned herself without cause to involuntary servitude (Koppelman).[14] Compelling a woman to serve involuntarily for the benefit of the fetus creates "that control by which the personal service of one man [sic] is disposed of or coerced for another's benefit which is the essence of involuntary servitude" (as defined in *Bailey v. Alabama*, 219 U.S. 219, 241 [1911]). By this argument, a pregnant woman is regarded as a reproductive slave forced by the state to bear children and not entitled to full human status.[15] The good mother accedes to such a construction, accepting and even contributing to her role of delivering and nurturing the social product that has been assigned to her in this biologically determined division of labor. The good mother/handmaid performs the role of surrogate, carrying on society's genes as the vessel through which they pass. She is alienated from her own "labor" insofar as her own child is really designed for a state intent upon restocking its labor pool and ensuring its viability as a form of government. Challenged by a woman's desire to abort a fetus, the state has construed her non-wage-earning and "uncontracted" labor as somehow owed (as if the woman herself was working off a debt) to the survival and health of some abstracted Family. The good mother, as incubator, will give over her gestational rights to contract rights[16] or to the male genetic claim to his property.[17] By so doing, she gains the additional status of a buffer against social disorder, the preserver of core public values that reside in the private domain.[18] The good mother in the HMT does not, in sum, refuse the construction of herself as one who is productive by virtue of being reproductive.[19]

The bad mother, by contrast, is relegated to the status of an outsider who requires overt coercive control (Ehrenreich), one who is not to be trusted, having rejected the good mother construction that society and its laws have proposed as her model. Operating on the outside of society's preferred construction, the bad mother in present law is the one likely to be surveilled, prosecuted, and punished, pressed into involuntary sterilization, forced pregnancy, coerced cesareans, or forcibly implanted birth control devices (Ehrenreich, Ashe "Theoretics," Tobin). The bad mother—like the resistant Moira, who escapes the Aunts, Offred's mother, a protester relegated to the Colonies, and the handmaid Ofglen, a member of the political underground—is most likely to refuse social constructions of her role and is least mystified about the use to which the state wishes to put her body. It is her class, race, or ethnic group that has traditionally been received into this country as an indentured servant or slave class; it is she who most appreciates what it means to be a "designated breeder." It is she who is most likely to express the material value to herself of her own body through surrogacy contracts or prostitution; she who instinctively understands and most directly experiences her sexual and reproductive capacities as commodities. These are the "bad whores [who] make good virgins possible" (Ehrenreich, "Colonization").

The irony of the story of "good" motherhood in the HMT is its identification with feminist difference theory which asserts a nurturing definition of women, one line of which supports a return to "natural" traditional mothering. A means of liberating women, it nevertheless reduces them to biological determination and to a construction that allows Gilead to enslave them reproductively. Moreover, it requires the oppositionality of "bad" mothers (thereby abjecting an alternative feminist construction based on equality theory) to reinforce the complicity of "good" mothers, under the rubric that bad whores (Moira and the women at the Club) make good virgins (ready flesh for social population planning) possible. The HMT has already erased its minority women, having exiled its undesirables in mass exoduses. It is the privileged white woman and a privileged nurturing feminism (operationalized by the Aunts) that is valued and incorporated in Gilead's homogenized construction of race (white) and class (elite) survival.

In every sense, then, law in the HMT is used as an instrument of control and regulation, focused here on the centrality of female reproduction to survival, the use of the female body standing synecdochically for the social and economic relations of Gilead as a whole (just as the womb is used as a synecdoche for the woman herself as a whole). Here, human bodies are regarded in terms of their use value to the state (tattooed with numbers and an EYE, the handmaid declares, "I will never be able to fade, finally, into another landscape. I am too important, too scarce, for that. I am a national resource" [84–85]), not a far cry from nineteenth- and early twentieth-century treatment of women in law whereby indentured servitude served as a model for women in the workplace as well as the domestic household.[20] At the same time, the handmaid is vaguely aware that society, in the person of the Commander, does not fully understand the use value of women; he takes inventory of those participating in the reproduction ceremony in which he must "perform" "As if we are something he inherited, like a Victorian pump organ, and he hasn't figured out what to do with us. What we are worth" (112).

Pregnancy in the HMT becomes a magic "presence" that ensures being saved (from the Colonies and the Club). It isolates the pregnant woman as one envied and an object endangered by jealousy. She who is life-giving does so by means of that which is itself death-threatening (pregnancy itself puts her life at risk), an embodiment of the very contradiction of her role. Woman is directed to "waste not, want not" and is defined negatively in relation to those who fail to follow the prescription: colonized women (caretakers of the wastelands), the exiled (the "Jews" of the nuclear holocaust), and those designated as sex toys for the powerful (in showcase clubs for visitors and the henchmen of the Gilead-Reich). Reduced to her body, the handmaid is plagued by how painful it is to use her mind and how unreliable and discouraged her instincts and feelings are: "I am not being wasted," she queries, "Why do I want?" Deprived of the "room" that was her own, she must create a space she can claim as hers, a storied space that allows her to possess her whole self and that neither leads to an escape into nostalgia nor inspires the vain hope of an invented future. The irony of such a desire is that it is the very condition of pregnancy that ensures she will occupy space even as her own space itself becomes "occupied." She is no longer emptied, no longer "a boat with no cargo" (211).

In economic terms, the handmaid learns to regard her function as a business transaction, the delivery of a service from which she is alienated, much like the sex work of a prostitute. The exchange value of her service is such that she comes to enjoy her role as a prized commodity, maximizing her value in the swish of a hip which displays her power over men, even if only as a "dog bone" thrown to those (the guardians) who have themselves been cut off from the sexual use of their own bodies. Society tells her that, having lost the "freedom to" (provided by pre-Gilead high capitalism, a society that died of too much choice), she has gained "freedom from" (protection from the abuses of private freedom in a world of public regulation). In this ultimate patriarchy, the handmaid is provided her daily bread by "Him," a meal she must choke to keep down. Passive in the face of such totalizing authority, she needs His forgiveness but cannot ask it from an unresponsive figure she cannot know ("I feel unreal talking to you. I feel as if I'm talking to a wall") and to whom she reluctantly attributes all that has happened. Men themselves act as His agents (guardians, angels, and commanders) under the sign of the omniscient winged white "Eye" printed on the vans of the powerful and represented in gold at the center of a field of red in the physician's office where the handmaids' bodies are examined, upkept, and where their pregnancies are certified. The emblematic folding screen at her physical examination reiterates the ideological centrality of the fetus in the sea of her blood (the fetus identified with the survival of the patriarchal state). The violence of the anachronistic snake-entwined sword beneath the Eye on the screen ("broken symbolism left over from the time before," 78) is displaced, now that patriarchy rules, by the surveillance of the EYE (the handmaid's farewell, "under the Eye," 59, recalls its priority), just as the sword wielded by Solomon the judge becomes irrelevant once he has demonstrated the authority of his rule. That authority and its rule in Gilead is founded on the rationality of "ritual" rape (the commentator Piexoto, as fascinated with Commander's "view" of Gilead as he is suspicious of the handmaid's, himself employs the "reasonable man" standard characteristic of rape law)[21] upon whose "coercive consent" the whole Handmaid system depends. Indeed, under an economic theory that requires efficiency in the use of social resources (so that the sexual commodity is used in maximizing ways), Gilead's system is a fundamentally sound reproductive strategy/policy/law (from the male point of view) in that it reduces opportunity costs for re-population given a commodity (the female reproductive body) for which there is high demand and short supply.

THE TALE OF PROPERTY

Seen through the prism of property law, the handmaid has some responsibility for maintaining her reproductive body prior to its actual use or exercise, for the economic and social life of Gilead depends on her ability to control (or perform) her reproductive function. Indeed, the pregnant woman must maintain two bodies, or property, so that, if there is "waste" to or of that property, she, being landlord, can be held doubly liable. But beyond her two physical bodies, she is also the householder/keeper of her political/social and emotional/spiritual bodies, bodies which are less "natural" and less visible to the eye. She is thus bound to her body in more than one way and bound to more than one body, even if the power to represent them has been coopted by medical and legal authority.

The critical issue is which sense of her body should have priority, if in fact one aspect can exist in isolation from another, and to what use it should be put. The body politic, for example, can be said to precede in importance, or to guide in some significant way, the natural body. Is this no more than to say that woman comes into her natural body only by virtue of its being so designated—having been appropriated—by the larger body politic? Or that the natural body "means" only in relation to its construction by or utility for the body politic. In another sense, if the natural body is so appropriated and designated, it cannot be said to be a "living" body since it cannot "die," there being no separation of it and the body politic to which its value and use have been conveyed and which can transfer its use to another natural body. The body politic, inhabiting the natural body, is a tenant (and succubus) for a given time, such that we could regard the handmaid "role" in the HMT as the body politic inhabiting each handmaid's body for the duration of its useful life. In this sense, the handmaid is both tenant of and landlord over the body politic, for she is both a womb within its body and the body that houses and expresses it as incubus.

At the point where the body politic and the natural body are disidentified, the handmaid becomes disposable, as when she is infertile or past optimal birthing age. Knowing this, she is resistant to emptying the house within her house, resistant to "wasting" lest she "want." In this sense, she both resists being a refuser, that is, she resists identifying with her emotional body, and she refuses autonomous control over her physical body. The handmaid behaves very much as a landlord here. She does not chose to be liable for the loss of her tenant/fetus even if to do so is to gain herself. She wants the right to regain what she has lost (her personal self) as well as the claim to the right of resistance, but not at the cost of wasting or "eating her own," emptying the tenant that cannibalizes her from within. Nor does the handmaid wish to risk being outlawed from the society that has given her the construction she herself inhabits, a construction that has "denatured" her in the process of "politicizing" her to reproduce Gilead (through its population plan). Her denaturing has, paradoxically, wasted her ability to produce her own identity by developing a meaningful sense of child-mother/mother-child relations that would reconnect her to her own lost mother and pre-Gilead child. The handmaid's paradox is that she must lose that which is herself (the fetus she is carrying) to gain herself (her sense of self). Unlike Toni Morrison's *Beloved*, in which the child-ghost of what might have been is embodied externally to be faced, embraced, and expelled, in the HMT Offred cannot escape the social constraints within which she is expected to act and so must be rescued by a man.

The handmaid struggles against a construction of herself that to be a good handmaid she must be a good caretaker, that she must govern her "house" well; but she cannot make a meaningful choice to do so as long as she is herself the ward of medicine and law which have the authority, first, to represent and, second, to judge her. As in *Doe v. Bolton* 410 U.S. 179 (1973), "the physician's medical judgment may be exercised in the light of all factors—physical, emotional, psychological, familial, and the woman's age—relevant to the well-being of the patient" (198). Woman, once pregnant, is well and fully taken, boarded and occupied by medical authority. By this argument, the doctor becomes intrinsic to the woman's privacy, invading not only her body but her very sense of self and her personhood; truly the physician "inhabits" her. If a woman ever plays a Samaritan role (a question raised regarding the pregnant woman's responsibility to support an unwelcome fetus; [Thomson; Foot]), it is here where the physician, coextensive with the patient, derives through her rights his substance and his sustenance.[22]

So long as the reproductive woman is "inhabited" by medical and legal authority, she is not able to give body to her own construction of self. Neither legal (the judge) nor medical (the physician) representation of the pregnant woman tries to create a likeness of her voice based on the values or attitudes of that which it mirrors. A second option, representing by coopting, seems a more appropriate description, insofar as these "authorities" endorse what the representor thinks "best" for the represented based on how well the "best" coincides with their own interests. In neither case does the represented speak for herself or in her own voice. Rather, she is placed in the position of hearing the other speak, whether she "listens" or not. Thus, the question arises, "What kind of knowledge of the pregnant woman is incorporated in her representation?" The only answer is knowledge relevant to the interpretive community of the representor. Legitimacy, by this argument, cannot be regarded as based in consensus but, rather, in coercion. The risk run by such representation is that it breaks the connection between different possible communities as well as the prospect of generating a larger understood community in which the diversity of interpretive communities might productively co-exist. Being judged by those unlike themselves renders a group essentially unrepresented in the larger scope of things, for such representation is neither characteristic of the group, adequate, nor to be confused with having the group's interest at heart. In effect, there is no "resemblance" (Minow). For the target group, its distinctive set of experiences are thereby not accounted for in the larger community, with all the problems in law, medicine, and politics such exclusion implies.

Because she cannot inhabit herself as herself, the handmaid is infertile; she has lost the ability to act as a proper landlord to her own property and by so doing forfeits ownership to it. Denied her right to "birth" herself, Offred is deprived of the only aspect of herself that is autonomously "productive." She can "reproduce" Gilead, but she cannot "produce" herself. Offred has no recourse once Gilead claims her offspring, which, like her pre-Gilead child, can be taken from her. That is, society has an action against her if she aborts, but she has none against society if it commandeers her produce, the same dilemma faced by the escaped slave Sethe in *Beloved*. In this sense, the handmaid can only be truly understood if she is seen as tenant of her own body in her handmaid role, which she inhabits but cannot be said either to own or to "represent" (since law, medicine, and politics have already coopted representation of it).[23] Coming full circle, she can be held liable for "waste" of property as a tenant to which the responsibility for care of the "house" has been, in effect, sublet. Judged incapable of being consigned full responsibility, she must be surveilled and punished.

By the same argument, women in present law can be regarded as liable for taking drugs or alcohol during pregnancy (*Johnson v. State* 602 So. 2d 1288 [Fla. 1992]; see Ikemoto 1265ff; Tobin 244ff), required to undergo a forced cesarean (*In re* A.C. 533 A. 2d 611 [D.C. 1987]; see Ikemoto 1240ff; Ehrenreich, "Colonization" 553ff), proscribed from a late-term abortion (the proscription put in place by the trimester formula in *Roe v. Wade* 410 U.S. 113 [1973]), interdicted from an early abortion (by being denied a state-funded Medicaid abortion, *Maher v. Roe* 432 U.S. 464 [1977]), or influenced from making an abortion choice herself (under the terms of a waiting period, informed consent, or parental notification provisions, *Planned Parenthood v. Casey* 112 S.Ct. 2791 [1992]).

COMPOSING HER "TAIL"

The handmaid in her pre-Gileadean life had regarded her body as an "instrument of pleasure, a means of transportation, or an implement for the accomplishment of my will" (95), no less an objectified entity than that to which she was reduced by those who defined her in Gilead. Where she had previously used her body as her instrument, she is now completely identified with and through it. What is missing in both views (her early view and Gilead's present view) is the idea of her body as a way of discovering a sense of her self. But even that self and the process of uncovering it is objectified: "my self is a thing I must now compose, as one composes a speech. What I must present is a made thing, not something born" (86). The handmaid must find her agency by composing her own body, even if she never completely loses her sense of being alienated from it. Indeed, her role as a Gileadean handmaid separates her from that which fills her; her body is "a cloud congealed around a central object, the shape of a pear, which is hard and more real than I am" (95). Should that object pass on, as a monthly omen, she is left empty again; "I see despair, Offred says, "coming towards me like famine" (95). Nevertheless, the handmaid owns both intellectual and property rights over that which she composes; once her body becomes her construction, she is removed that much further from the false consciusness and hegemonic domination of the other two views under which she nevertheless still struggles. Her compostion yields her an emergent "place" of her own, however constrained and informed by residual (past) and dominant (present) constructions.

The time of composing is night and the space her bedroom. Night not only opens and closes the tale, but it surfaces in alternate chapters throughout as that time of self that envelopes the handmaid inside her "room." By means of the night she can, as in an out-of-body experience, "step sideways out of my own time. Out of time. Though this is time, nor am I out of it. But the night is my time out. Where should I go? Somewhere good" (49). A concretized body within the amorphousness of night, she is set free in shapeless time. The handmaid reiterates the image of the fetal object within her that fills her "space [which is] huge as the sky at night and dark and curved like that, though black-red rather than black" (95). Free-falling in space, the handmaid embraces night as the time to "compose" herself in the story she tells and whose ending she controls (52). She makes it up as she goes along, trying on what she chooses to believe in alternate versions. Her missing husband Luke is reconstituted in four alternate storylines, any one of which might be true; all of which might be untrue (132-35). When the commander's wife Serena Joy delivers the handmaid to be impregnated by her chauffeur Nick, Offred offers three versions to access the possible ways the event could have happened (337-40). Waiting for the black van that will take her off to an unknown fate, the handmaid considers the number of things she could do—seven in all—of which she does none (374-75).

What is critical is that the ability to reconstrue reality is opened to the handmaid once she "recomposes" herself. She remembers the sign her mother had held at a protest march: "Take back the night" (154). She becomes embryonic in the night sky, floating in timeless time, in an emptied space that houses her as she is herself a house for an embryonic future Gilead. Night falls, it doesn't rise, because it is heavy and presses down on us like a stone, pressing like the fetus from within, but externally, the tension of the two holding her in place even as she falls. The Fall itself "was a fall from innocence to knowledge" (252), into something she could not bear to know. Night, after all, was not without its dangers, just as a woman in red endangers a man, both as forms and ways of "knowing." The woman in the night is, in the end, but one ring of a concentric set: she is recapitulated in the embryo within the space that is within the womb, which is itself housed in the woman encased in a cloak of the bloodied egg; the woman in the cloak is herself freed in space emptied of time under cover of the night. The handmaid escapes her body even as she remains connected. She crafts her meaning in fragments that are nonetheless related to other pieces in some larger understood whole. Overdetermined by medicine and law, economics and property, she both escapes and is captured by the Black Van that takes her away. She tries on a new construction in her own voice, of her own composing, but not in a vacuum. The handmaid is part of everything that made her re-made by the maid's hand.

NOTES

[1] Indeed, we find since *Roe v. Wade*, 410 U.S. 113 (1973), that women are referred to as that without which the fetus must be able to do. That is, to have, in Justice Blackmun's majority opinion, "the capability of meaningful life outside the womb" (Shapiro 67; quotes from all Supreme Court abortion decisions except *Planned Parenthood of Southeastern Pennsylvania v. Casey* are taken from this source) determines both the "'compelling point . . . at viability" (67) for the fetus and the "lack" of the pregnant woman's presence as a defining point for new life. In *Planned Parenthood of Kansas City v. Ashcroft*, 462 U.S. 476 (1983), (in a move that pits physician—the pregnant woman's decision-making "representative"—against physician, splitting the cultural authority of medicine from within), the state can require a second physician at the abortion of a viable fetus "to preserve the life and health of the viable unborn child" (167). The separation of a pregnant woman from her fetus is accomplished; two patients, two doctors. The fetus which was rarely referred to as "her fetus" is now formally disassociated as a separated entity. The woman, separated as host, is formally revealed, her interest severed from that of her fetus. The self-same separation is experienced once obstacles are put between the pregnant woman and her doctor by the informational requirement (by means of which the physician is "required" to counsel continuation of the pregnancy—see Justice Blackmun's part concurrence/part dissent in *Panned Parenthood of Southeastern Pennsylvania v. Casey*, 112 S. Ct. 2791 [1992]; all quotes and references from this Supreme Court decision are taken from Friedman 1993). The woman who could not be conceived of as "isolated" physiologically in her pregnancy is now separated legally from those with whom she would share it: the fetus within and the physician without. No longer private, she is no longer whole.

[2] Terms that arise to make such a futuristic vision more tangible include the "ectogenetic" and "cyborg" fetus. Terroristic scenarios arise in such culture products as the film *Terminator 2: Judgment Day* of terminating bodies that are historically problematic by "back to the future" technologies that erase them as embryos (Mason).

[3] The original position is an initial status quo that guarantees agreements will be fair; it is a position in which we suppose that all parties are equal, that is, that all have the same rights and ability to make a choice. It is the position that presumably will ensure "justice as fairness" (Rawls 17–22).

[4] In abortion law the "conceptually incommensurable premises" (Shapiro 19) represented by fetal as opposed to women's rights positions (the state interest position as against that of individual rights or the pro-life vs. the pro-choice positions) present us with oppositional narratives. The "bright line" provided by *Roe v. Wade*'s trimester analysis that presumes the promise of

reasonable territorial imperatives and a certain respect commensurate with those imperatives is replaced by contesting claims that overlap, as in *Planned Parenthood v. Casey*'s second trimester analysis, and parallel and nonconvergent interests throughout pregnancy, the new standard under *Casey*. To repair a judgment on a collision course with itself (Justice O'Connor's view of *Roe v. Wade*; see her dissent in *City of Akron v. Akron Center for Reproductive Health*, 462 U.S. 416, [1983] 160), Solomon the judge might have offered one of two alternatives: forced commensurability under the superordinate eye of a transcendent judge or a legal judgment for co-parenting. The joint opinion of Justices O'Connor, Souter, and Kennedy in *Planned Parenthood v. Casey* gives us the stalemate logic of a fetus constrained by harm to the health of the pregnant woman and a pregnant woman constrained by the potential viability of the fetus.

5 Justice Blackmun's concurrence in part/dissent in part in *Planned Parenthood v. Casey* is clear about the "physical invasiveness" of restrictive abortion laws. He contends that the government's reach into personal decisions that affect bodily integrity itself impermissibly invades an area of the human mind (417). Justice Rehnquist's concurrence in part/dissent in part refuses the construction of a woman as uninvadable; rather, her space incorporates the space of another such that both it and she have no existence outside of each other. The gun she discharges, he analogizes, is discharged into another's body (439). He goes on, indicatively, to expand the state's interest in the fetus to the state's interest in the husband's interest in the fetus (that is, in his own procreation) as well as the state's interest not only in the marriage but, presumptively, in the family that is to be.

6 It is not until the joint opinion of Justices O'Connor, Souter, and Kennedy in *Planned Parenthood v. Casey* that woman takes on an autonomous presence. Ennobled, sacrificing, bonded to her infant by love, "Her suffering is too intimate and personal for the State to insist, without more, upon its own vision of the woman's role, however dominant that vision has been in the course of our history and our culture" (349). Representing a construction shift from a century ago when "woman had no legal existence separate from her husband" (388) and was considered the heart of home and family, this view sees the woman exercising her right to abortion (presumably a balance to "the wonder of creation" [349]) based on her inability to provide for and nurture an infant "which is cruelty to the child and an anguish to the parent" (349). The joint opinion does not fail to raise issues (though it judges them *de minimus*) related to property and contract in the commercial context as they relate to abortion being "customarily chosen as an unplanned response to the consequence of unplanned activity" (352) and the consideration "that the abortion right invites some reliance prior to its actual exercise" (352). Nevertheless, the joint opinion constructs the emptied women as hav-

ing the ability "to participate equally in the economic and social life of the Nation," a human value served by the Constitution and facilitated by "the ability to control their reproductive lives" (353). Representing this ability as a component of liberty, the opinion concedes that "it might be said that a woman who fails to act before viability has consented to the State's intervention on behalf of the developing child" (365) and the State is free to establish a "reasonable framework" (367) within which a decision can be made even if the kind of interest it retains in a woman's "protected liberty" (370) cannot place "a substantial obstacle" (370) in the way of her terminating a nonviable fetus.

[7] In abortion law, the judge is constructed as struggling between the possibility of narrative collapse and the consequent necessity of legal compromise or violence; the physician is constructed as the figure who holds the cultural authority to dominate the choice decision in abortion law. The roles of both figures have implications for the legal construction of the pregnant woman; indeed, the constructions of judge and doctor both circumscribe and define the space left for women in the decision circle. Absent from the debate from the beginning, woman's place has been taken at the table by the physician with whom she must, if she is to be represented at all, share her seat. The debate from the outset was dominated by privacy law rather than equality law, which, until *Planned Parenthood v. Casey*, had little standing in abortion cases even as it would have permitted women their own voice with which to argue not merely women's health rights, as Condit argues (99–115), but fundamental freedom in the conduct of their lives.

[8] In one view, Solomon's judgment is said to describe a balance of rights (individual rights and impartial justice) with care (relationships and the moral life) (Allegretti). In another view, his judgment is a form of "folk wisdom" (the tale does possess characteristics of a traditional tale), the work of a clever trickster. Alternately, the judge can be understood as one whose action is the result of the kind of person he is, that is, a character-based decision whereby he does what his nature directs him to do. Where no code covers a case, judging is open to such variant readings. (See Allegretti; Ashe, "Abortion"; Althouse)

[9] Robert Cover (203–38) makes the point that law is itself inherently violent as it deals in fear, pain, and death. The legal system can be described as a mechanism to express, control, and limit the deliberate infliction of pain as part of an ideology of punishment. Legal interpretation thus takes place inside a system designed to generate violence, indeed, "legal interpretation is as a practice incomplete without violence . . . it depends upon the social practice of violence for its efficacy" (219).

[10] Atwood is clear in her intention to represent the present use of women's bodies, albeit in terms of a future dystopia (Bouson). She admits "I didn't invent a lot." Presenting her work as "a study of power" and "a logical exten-

sion of where we are now" (Davidson 26), she makes clear that "I transposed to a different time and place, but the motifs are all historical motifs" (24).

11 The argument made by Ehrenreich and MacKinnon is basically that both domains are state regulated so that if a state system puts its power behind (creates/reinforces) a given social structure or conditions, it bears responsibility for the inequities of those conditions or that structure as they are reflected in the private realm.

12 As it is presently constituted in the law, the use of women as surrogates is a form of sex work which, if not comparable to private economy prostitution, is its contract equivalent in selling one's body into slavery as a legitimized application of free market ideology. By such means, women profit from the commodification of their bodies, an option which (either out of false consciousness—largely white women—or economic necessity—largely poor and black women) is open only indirectly to the surrogate in the HMT who serves as the property of the State. (See here, Siegel; Tobin; Ehrenreich "Colonization," "Surrogacy"; Ikemoto.) The identification of woman with rights to "contract parenthood" in present law has at least the merit of moving the issue of surrogacy toward a social or economic definition of motherhood which to some extent frees pregnant women from biological determination and the double sex standard. Whereas it does so by means of a right to contract freely to sell a body part (so that, in effect, liberation enslaves), it puts us more in mind of legalized prostitution than contract law. (See here, Baldwin; Cooper; Radin.)

13 Its parallel in present-day law occurs as recently as the revised abortion law formula crafted by the joint opinion in *Planned Parenthood v. Casey*, whereby in Pennsylvania physicians must provide information to pregnant women that specifically dissuades them from choosing abortion. Extended to the metaphor of being housed and occupied, the notion of women as mothers, as Ehrenreich ("Colonization") contends, is a "colonized" concept "occupied and defined, given content and value" (492) by other than women themselves. A benevolent occupying force, the physician manages the property for women who accede to "good" motherhood (largely white middle class women) and surveills and punishes those "bad" mothers who rebel (largely black lower class women). Covert control through internalized false consciousness is reserved for women described by their private status as at-home mothers. They will have their care "managed" by a quasi-protective physician. Overt coercive control is reserved for "outsider" women, women who must support themselves through out-of-the-home labor or who are at the mercy of state support. These women are likely to experience drug testing, be denied abortion counseling and abortions, undergo court-ordered hospital detention, or be subject to the removal of the born child.

14 Blackmun in his concurrence in part/dissent in part in *Webster v. Reproductive Health Services*, 492 U.S. 490 (1989), regards the woman's con-

scripted body (Shapiro 193) as a central construction of the reproductive woman. His concurrence in part/dissent in part in *Planned Parenthood v. Casey* rejects a construction whereby women are conscripted into pregnancy as a labor without compensation to fulfill a duty owed as a matter of course, a duty held to be the "natural" condition of motherhood (Friedman 418).

[15] See on constructions of slavery as related to the use of women's bodies Katyal; Koppelman; Thomas; McConnell. One construction has the effect of placing the pregnant woman in the role of the slavemaster with legal control over her fetus/slave, which is thereby reduced to her chattel. This construction construes the fetus, like slaves in early American law, as only partial human beings not entitled to full human status or protection of the law (and therefore amenable to barter, trade, or sale). Moreover, it reverts to a perception of women prior to adoption of the thirteenth amendment (1865) as not entitled to be free before the law, under the presumption that Congress does not have the right to regulate "domestic" slavery. (See McConnell, 215ff.) Only men had the right to create and maintain families under an amendment that never "intended" to regulate marital relations. What was intended was the regulation of the master/slave relationship, but only that which was related to the institution of chattel slavery. A distinction was thereby made between slavery that was voluntary (as in marriage) and that which was institutional (as in chattel slavery).

[16] As in the surrogacy of Anna Johnson who carried both the ovum and sperm of a couple that wanted to conceive (Tobin 254ff). (See, on surrogacy, Ehrenreich "Surrogacy".)

[17] As with Mary Beth Whitehead who herself had a genetic claim to the fetus, having used her own ovum (Tobin 257ff).

[18] In line with this argument, the good mother through both her physical weakness relative to men and her maternal function is indelibly identified with child-rearing as the mainstay of the home. The bad mother, by contrast, is identified with women who vest themselves in the public sphere by working outside the home and those whose reproduction (the poor and those outside the dominant social cast by religion, racial, or ethnic group) society has no interest in encouraging (Ikemoto).

[19] She is not expected in the construction of the "good mother" to refuse society its "entitlement" or withhold her services unless, inversely, because she is poor and, usually, a minority she requires an entitlement herself to deliver one. Nor does she destroy or injure the product of her labor—a variation reserved in the construction for those, again poor and, usually, a minority, who deliver drugs or alcohol via the umbilical cord to the fetus within—without facing discipline and punishment (the fate of a Jennifer Johnson; Tobin 244ff). The good mother is no Medea, either, in the sense of overidentifying with her offspring (the error of a Mary Beth Whitehead; Tobin, 257ff). That

love which is "too thick" is not hers to give, even if to gain her own identity, as in *Planned Parenthood v. Casey*, she must merge her voice with that of the fetus and balance its interests with hers to claim her rights.

[20] In 1908, for example, *Muller v. Oregon* upheld restrictions on working hours for a woman (but not for men) to protect her health (see Goldstein, Leslie 19-22); women being valued for the well-being of the "race," their relative physical weakness, maternal and child-rearing attributes were given primary consideration. Indeed, as culturally defined, motherhood and the private sphere were seen as acting as a buffer against social disorder such that in *Bradwell v. Illinois* (1872) (Goldstein, Leslie 66-72), women were denied the right to practice law based on the State's interest in their domestic roles as wives and mothers (Ikemoto). The antithetical model to social order appears in "working" women, both those who work outside the home and those, in the outlaw sexual workplace of prostitution, who work outside the law. Outsiders, such women were more difficult to control and regulate through culturally defined motherhood, corrupted as they were by their access to the public sphere and their construction as outside the good mother ideology. Thus begins, with the Comstock Act of 1873 (which legislates a state preference for pregnancy—outlawing the distribution and advertisement of contraceptives as part of a social campaign to increase the middle class white birth rate in the face of growing immigration) through the next century (with some detours; for example, *Roe v. Wade*), a preference that results in 1992 (in *Planned Parenthood v. Casey*) in the Supreme Court upholding the requirement that physicians must provide information that specifically promotes carrying a pregnancy to term and dissuades women from choosing abortion. (On the legal history of women see Bartlett; Hoff; Otten.)

[21] The "reasonable man" standard essentially uses the perspective of a man (the burden of proof for demonstrating lack of consent falls on the female victim). The choice of a reasonable "man" is partially the result of generally prohibiting women from practicing law in the nineteenth and early twentieth centuries, as well as the presumption in rape law (emanating from as early as the sixteenth century and Chief Justice Mathew Hale) that a rape charge is easy for a woman to make and hard for a man to defend (Estrich 5, 31).

[22] The same is true of the physician under the doctrine of "informed consent," the intention of which was, in tort law, to protect a patient from assault and battery. In abortion law, informed consent becomes a physician-induced injection of information to activate a woman's "intelligent" choice in favor of continuing her pregnancy, an assault which the pregnant woman is required to endure. (See, on the physician's role in abortion decisions, Appleton.)

[23] Questions of representation (particularly pertinent to *Planned Parenthood of Central Missouri v. Danforth*, 428 U.S. 52 [1976], and *Planned Parenthood v. Casey* [1992], although in a new light; see Note 6) implicate prop-

erty rights over a woman's "childbearing potential" (*Planned Parenthood v. Danforth*, 84) and are compared to "an interest in real property" (84). Even if they deny the male parent "a veto power which the state itself is absolutely and totally prohibited from exercising" (85), it is clear that the woman is never left alone as a woman in her decision, for exclusive of the fetus itself, that very same state (through its interest in the marriage and the family) is present institutionally in its regulation of the physician whose co-decisional authority constitutes a woman's own "decisional autonomy." Moreover, the state need not, once it denies itself the right to "delegate to the husband the power to vindicate the State's interest" (88), take the position that, since the state's interest in the fetus is outweighed, the husband's interest "may not be protected by the State" (88). A male parent's interest is, by this argument, subject to the same analysis. Indeed, where the state argues in loco parentis, it may in effect double-dip representationally, that is, by representing itself representing the parent whose rights may be represented (protected) by the state, a tautology if ever there was one. The balance of rights or interests so fundamental to abortion law is undeniably confounded here as it is in *Planned Parenthood v. Casey*'s reassignment of interests whereby measures are taken to ensure that a woman's interest will include the fetal interest (367); the state is itself now represented as interested in both the fetus and the woman throughout the pregnancy; the woman's right thereby becoming confounded with state interest, the balance is unbalanced in what is represented as a "necessary reconciliation of the liberty of the woman and the interest of the State in promoting prenatal life" (367). The misconceiving of the pregnant woman's interest and the undervaluing of the state's interest have been corrected by conflation (367–68).

WORKS CITED

Allegretti, Joseph. "Rights, Roles, Relationships: The Wisdom of Solomon and the Ethics of Lawyers." *Cardozo Law Review* 25.4 (1992): 1119-139.

Althouse, Ann. "Beyond King Solomon's Harlots: Women in Evidence." *Southern California Law Review* 65 (1992):1265-278.

Appleton, Susan Frelich. "Doctors, Patients and the Constitution: A Theoretical Analysis of the Physician's Role in "Private" Reproductive Decisions." *Washington University Law Quarterly* 63.2 (1985): 183-236.

Ashe, Marie. "Abortion of Narrative: A Reading of the Judgment of Solomon." *Yale Journal of Law and Feminism* 4 (1991): 81-92.

———. "Law-Language of Maternity: Discourse Holding Nature in Contempt." *New England Law Review* 22 (1988): 521-59.

———. "Theoretics of Practice: The Integration of Progressive Thought and Action: The 'Bad Mother' in Law and Literature: A Problem of Represen-

tation." *Hastings Law Journal* 43 (1992): 1017-036.
Atwood, Margaret. *The Handmaid's Tale*. New York: Fawcett, 1985.
Baldwin, Margaret A. "Split at the Root: Prostitution and Feminist Discourses of Law Reform." *Yale Journal of Law and Feminism* 5 (1992): 47-120.
Barlett, Katharine T., and Rosanne Kennedy. *Feminist Legal Theory: Readings in Gender and Law*. Boulder: Westview P, 1991.
Bouson, J. Brooks. *Brutal Choreographies: Oppositional Strategies and Narrative Design in the Novels of Margaret Atwood*. Amherst: U of Massachusetts P, 1993.
Condit, Celeste Michelle. *Decoding Abortion Rhetoric: Communicating Social Change*. Urbana: U of Illinois P, 1990.
Cooper, Belinda. "Prostitution: A Feminist Analysis." *Women's Rights Law Reporter* 11.2 (1989): 99-119.
Cover, Robert. *Narrative, Violence and the Law: The Essays of Robert Cover*. Ed. Martha Minow, Michael Ryan, and Austin Sarat. Ann Arbor: U of Michigan P, 1992.
Daly, Brenda O., and Maureen T. Reddy, eds. Introduction. *Narrating Mothers: Theorizing Maternal Subjectivities*. Knoxville: U of Tennessee P, 1991.
Davidson, Arnold E. "Future Tense: Making History in *The Handmaid's Tale*." *Margaret Atwood: Vision and Forms*. Ed. Kathryn Van Spankeren and Jan Garden Castro. Carbondale: Southern Illinois UP, 1988.
Davidson, Cathy N. "A Feminist 1984." *Ms*. February 1986, 24-26.
Ehrenreich, Nancy. "The Colonization of the Womb." *Duke Law Journal* 43 (1993): 492-587.
———. "Surrogacy as Resistance? The Misplaced Focus on Choice in the Surrogacy and Abortion Funding Contexts." *DePaul Law Review* 41 (1992):1369-1406.
Estrich, Susan. *Real Rape*. Cambridge: Harvard UP, 1987.
Foot, Philippa. "Killing and Letting Die." *Abortion: Moral and Legal Perspectives*. Ed. Jay L. Garfield and Patricia Hennessey. Amherst: U of Massachusetts P, 1984.
Friedman, Leon, ed. *The Supreme Court Confronts Abortion: The Briefs, Argument, and Decision in Planned Parenthood v. Casey*. New York: Farrar, 1993.
Goldstein, Leslie Friedman. *The Constitutional Rights of Women: Cases in Law and Social Change*. Madison: U of Wisconsin P, 1989.
Goldstein, Robert D. *Mother-Love and Abortion: A Legal Interpretation*. Berkeley: U of California P, 1988.
Hammer, Stephanie Barbe. "The World As It Will Be? Female Satire and the Technology of Power in *The Handmaid's Tale*." *Modern Language Studies* 20.2 (1990): 39-49.

Hoff, Joan. *Law, Gender, and Injustice: A Legal History of Women*. New York: New York UP, 1991.
Holbrook, H. L. *Parturition Without Pain: A Code of Directions for Escaping from the Primal Curse*. New York: n.p., 1882
Holcombe, William H. *The Sexes Here and Hereafter*. Philadelphia, n.p., 1869
Ikemoto, Lisa C. "The Code of Perfect Pregnancy: At the Intersection of the Ideology of Motherhood, the Practice of Defaulting to Science, and the Interventionist Mindset of Law." *Ohio State Law Journal* 53 (1992): 1205-305.
Jordanova, Ludmilla J. *Sexual Visions: Images of Gender in Science and Medicine Between the Eighteenth and Twentieth Centuries*. Madison: U of Wisconsin P, 1989.
Katyal, Neal Kumar. "Men Who Own Women: A Thirteenth Amendment Critique of Forced Prostitution." *The Yale Law Journal* 103 (1993): 790-826.
Koppelman, Andrew. "Forced Labor: A Thirteenth Amendment Defense of Abortion." *Northwestern University Law Review* 84 (1990): 480-534.
MacKinnon, Catharine A. *Toward a Feminist Theory of the State*. Cambridge: Harvard UP, 1987.
Margolick, David. "Damages Rejected in Death of Fetus." *New York Times*, 16 June 1985, 26.
Mason, Carol. "Terminating Bodies: Toward a Cyborg History of Abortion." *Posthuman Bodies*. Ed. Judith Halberstam and Ira Livingston. Bloomington: Indiana UP, 1995.
McCombs, Judith, ed. *Critical Essays on Margaret Atwood*. Boston: Hall, 1988.
McConnell, Joyce E. "Beyond Metaphor: Battered Women, Involuntary Servitude and the Thirteenth Amendment." *Yale Journal of Law and Feminism* 4 (1992): 207-53.
Minow, Martha. "From Class Actions to 'Miss Saigon': The Concept of Representation in the Law." *Representing Women: Law, Literature, and Feminism*. Ed. Susan Sage Heinzelman and Zipporah Batshaw Wiseman. Durham: Duke UP, 1994.
Morrison, Toni. *Beloved*. New York: Penguin, 1987.
Otten, Laura A. *Women's Rights and the Law*. Westport: Praeger, 1993.
Petchesky, Rosalind Pollack. "Fetal Images: The Power of Visual Culture in the Politics of Reproduction." *Feminist Studies*13.2 (1987): 263-92.
Poovey, Mary. "The Abortion Question and the Death of Man." *Feminists Theorize the Political*. Ed. Judith Butler and Joan W.Scott. London: Routledge.1992.
Radin, Margaret Jane. "Market-Inalienability." *Harvard Law Review* 100 (1987): 1849-936.

Rawls, John. *A Theory of Justice*. Cambridge: Belknap, 1971.
Sandel, Michael. Introduction. *Liberalism and Its Critics*. Ed. Michael Sandel. New York: New York UP, 1984.
Savage, Gail. "'The Wilful Communication of a Loathsome Disease': Marital Conflict and Venereal Disease in Victorian England." *Victorian Studies* 34.1 (1990): 35-54.
Schneider, Carl. "Discretion, Rules, and Law: Child Custody and the UMDA's Best Interest Standard." *Michigan Law Review* 89 (1991): 2215-243.
Shapiro, Ian, ed. *Abortion: The Supreme Court Decisions*. Indianapolis: Hackett, 1995.
Siegel, Reva. "Reasoning from the Body: A Historical Perspective on Abortion Regulation and Questions on Equal Protection." *Stanford Law Review* 44 (1992): 261-380.
Smith-Rosenberg, Carroll, and Charles Rosenberg. "The Female Animal: Medical and Biological Views of Woman and Her Role in Nineteenth-Century America." *Concepts of Health and Disease: Interdisciplinary Perspectives*. Ed. Arthur L. Caplan, H. Tristram Engelhardt, Jr., and James J. McCartney. Reading: Addison-Wesley, 1981.
Sofia, Zoe. "Exterminating Fetuses: Abortion, Disarmament, and the Sexo-Semiotics of Extraterrestrialism." *Diacritics* 14 (1984): 47-59.
Squier, Susan M. "Reproducing the Posthuman Body: Ectogenetic Fetus, Surrogate Mother, Pregnant Man." *Posthuman Bodies*. Ed. Judith Halberstam and Ira Livingston. Bloomington: Indiana UP, 1995.
Thomas, Laurence. "Abortion, Slavery, and the Law: A Study in Moral Character." *Abortion: Moral and Legal Perspectives*. Ed. Jay L. Garfield and Patricia Hennessey. Amherst: U of Massachusetts P, 1984.
Thomson, Judith Jarvis. "A Defense of Abortion." *Philosophy and Public Affairs* 1 (1971): 44.
Tobin, Elizabeth. "Imagining the Mother's Text: Toni Morrison's *Beloved* and Contemporary Law." *Harvard Women's Law Journal* 16 (1993): 233-73.
Weisberg, Richard. *Poethics and Other Strategies of Law and Literature*. New York: Columbia UP, 1992.

CHAPTER TWELVE

Husbands, Wives, and Lawyers:
Gender Roles and Professional Representations
in Trollope and the Adelaide Bartlett Case
by Paula Jean Reiter

> There is, however, one subject which Mr. Trollope
> pursues with unremitting zeal. He cannot bear a lawyer.
> They are all rogues, not by nature, but by profession.
> Smalley 156[1]

The long list of memorable lawyers that grace Anthony Trollope's fiction attests to what one reviewer called his "unremitting zeal" on the subject of legal representatives. Trollope's obvious fascination with lawyers from all walks of life—from the outrageous Chaffenbrass to the impeccable Grey— has piqued the interest of modern scholars as well as his contemporary reviewers. Critics variously explain the presence of so many lawyers by reading them as part of the novelist's general theory of character, form, or morals; as evidence of his view of society; or as echoes of his biography.[2] In the first part of this article, I consider Trollope's lawyers in light of his concern with professional representation. In my discussion, I use the term "professional representation" in a dual fashion to mean the delineation of the professional character and role, and also to mean the task a legal professional undertakes in speaking for and advising a client. In other words, the term is both what a professional *is* and what he *does*. As I will argue, the two work in conjunction. As professionals labor to represent clients, they simultaneously argue for special privileges, authority, status, and an exclusive social role for themselves. To put it another way, nineteenth-century legal professionals argued on behalf of their clients while setting the boundaries and articulating the justifications for their own growing cultural authority.

Trollope made a particularly logical choice in selecting legal professionals for novelistic treatment. Legal men play central roles in highly dramatic situations, such as marriage settlements, wills, criminal cases, and parliamentary politics. Such tensions provide ideal plot lines, but plot did not fascinate Trollope to nearly the same degree as character did. Characterization was Trollope's forte, so it should come as no surprise that he lavishes attention upon his lawyers, whose calling (like that of novelists) required them to represent others. However, it is not the relationship between the lawyer and the novelist that I find so compelling in Trollope's fiction. Instead, I find the relationship between the Victorian professional and the Victorian husband to be a complex and significant one worthy of examination. In my examination, the role of the guilty female client serves as a lightning rod for myriad anxieties and opportunities for professional men. In fact, I posit the nineteenth-century woman as the pivotal symbolic figure in issues of professional representation. The lies and stories that Trollope's legal men must tell in defense of their guilty female clients trace the underlying currents in both heterosexual gender relations and professional development. To understand the confluence of the professional man with the role of husband, we need to consider the defining contrast the feminized Other offers each, especially in terms of the ability to speak and act publicly.

When representing a client in court, a barrister not only molded the version of his client that he wanted the court to believe, but he also literally spoke for his client. The representation provided by a barrister was thus two-fold: he constructed a narrative that he hoped would clear his client, and he physically stood in for his client and his client's voice. The value and believability of representations crafted by attorneys proceed at least in part from the privileged voice they have in a courtroom. Specialized legal discourse is *supposed* to produce truth. This leads directly to the second type of representation: providing a voice for the client and standing in for the client. The voice of the barrister presumably is "better," more authoritative, or more rational. As I will show, the stories barristers tell and the dynamics of the attorney-client relationship articulate and mimic the lines of conventional Victorian gender roles, particularly those within heterosexual marriage. In the professional relationship, the client plays the feminine role of the private, dependent, silent "wife" seeking public and legal representation. The professional plays the masculine role of the public, knowing, vocal "husband" providing this public, legal representation.

This pattern is most clearly visible when the male lawyer represents a female client or, in other words, when gender and biological sex characteristics line up. Although, technically, neither men nor women could speak in their own defense until 1898 (placing both in the feminized role vis-à-vis the professional), symbolically, proper women could not speak for themselves in any area of public life. As Susan Heinzelman and Zipporah Wiseman observe, "certain individuals and groups have come to be seen as able to speak for themselves, while others have been relegated to the category of those who must be spoken for" (2). Victorian women fell into the second category. When a woman defendant sought legal representation—to construct a believable story and to speak for her—she consciously reenacted the role she played outside the courtroom as a wife. "Good" women did not speak for themselves, but were represented by fathers, brothers, or husbands. Lady Mason, Trollope's most memorable female defendant, clearly understands these dynamics and uses them to her advantage in securing appropriate representation.

In speaking of the dynamics shared by heterosexual marriage and professional representation, I want to make clear the mutually defining and legitimizing implications they held for each other. Barristers, by modeling the attorney-client relationship along the lines of heterosexual marriage roles, helped to naturalize and legitimize those roles. Far from suggesting that the roles of "wife" and "husband" were somehow stable, ahistorical, or monolithic, my reading posits that heterosexual gender roles also experienced flux and development. The cultural logic that supported silence and dependence as appropriate characteristics for wives also proposed vocal and authoritative roles for male professionals. Because these roles were based on the same set of assumptions, they could circulate endlessly in a closed system that "proved" women were "naturally" dependent and men (especially male professionals) were "naturally" authoritative.

In the second part of this article, I examine these dynamics as played out in the historical 1886 trial of Adelaide Bartlett. By thus combining law and literature, I hope to better illustrate the shared cultural assumptions evident in the law courts, fiction, and professional development. Rather than examine a single legal issue or crime, I want to suggest how law and crime are part of a larger set of cultural assumptions about gender and responsibility. As such, my approach does not assume that law is somehow immune from or prior to cultural pressures; rather it begins with the contention that law is continuous with, complicit with, and contemporary with other social projects. This approach views law and literature as intricately embedded, not sequenced, projects. In other words, literature does not merely follow or mirror legal issues. They tell one story.

The story I wish to follow here considers the roles of husbands, wives, and professionals, the rewards of authority and responsibility, and the advantages of controlling or relinquishing self-representation. Trollope's novel, *Orley Farm*, and the trial of Adelaide Bartlett form part of this tale and illustrate the overlapping cultural dynamics shared by law and literature.

REPRESENTING PROFESSIONAL REPRESENTATION

> Would it be well that he should allow himself to feel the same interest in this case, to maintain respecting it the same personal anxiety, if he ceased to believe in it? He did ask himself this question, and he finally answered it in the affirmative. . . . Lady Mason was his client, and all the associations of his life taught him to be true to her as such. (Trollope I. 251)

Lady Mason is Mr. Furnival's client, and Furnival's fidelity to her during her second trial forms the centerpiece of Trollope's 1861 novel *Orley Farm*. During her first trial, which takes place 20 years before the opening of the novel, she was a young woman with an infant son. Her accuser, Mr. Mason of Groby Park, the eldest son of her husband by his first marriage and the presumed heir to Orley Farm, failed to produce any convincing evidence that the codicil (bequeathing Orley Farm to Lady Mason's son, Lucius) was a forgery.

For both the reader and the characters in the novel, the drama and tension of her second trial do not proceed from any doubt as to her guilt or innocence. The reader and Mason's barrister know early on that she is undoubtedly guilty of forging the codicil to her husband's will. Midway through the novel, Lady Mason confirms this knowledge by fully confessing to Sir Peregrine Orme.

> "Sir Peregrine, I am guilty."
> "Guilty! Guilty of what?" he said, startled rather than instructed by her words.
> "Guilty of all this with which they charge me." And she then threw herself at his feet, and wound her arms round his knees. (I. 42)

Many critics considered this a premature confession and a dramatic gaffe on Trollope's part. However, it is not doubt as to Mason's guilt or innocence that propels this plot but the question of what to do with knowledge of her guilt. Sir Peregrine's difficulty in acknowledging the truth of this confession, and his subsequent struggles with what his conduct toward a guilty Lady Mason should be, dramatize acutely the dilemma that other characters face as well. Rather than asking "Did she do it?," the novel asks the more subtle question "What will be the effect of her guilt?" The effect of that guilt on those who desire to represent her is particularly important. We see three men vie for this role: Mr. Furnival wishes to be her barrister; Sir Peregrine wants to be her husband; and her son, Lucius Mason, wants to act as head of the household.

Mr. Furnival's conduct, as emblematic of professional conduct in general and England's legal system in particular, comes under close scrutiny in the novel. His conduct will also come under close scrutiny here in an effort to analyze what kind of a defense Furnival plans for Mason and what kind of role he forges for himself. During the course of *Orley Farm*, characters from all walks of life debate the role of the barrister and the law courts. The highest ranking character in the novel, Sir Peregrine, issues an idealistic defense of the integrity of England's law courts and legal practitioners: "My love, what is the purport of law if it be not to discover the truth, and make it plain to the light of day?" Even the narrator finds such sentiments to be "perhaps beautiful, but . . . very simple" (II. 161). Mr. Moulder, traveling salesman, occupies the lowest social level of any character in the novel and proffers a correspondingly low opinion of the law. His opinion, blunt as it is, provides a more clear-sighted if less attractive vision of the role of a legal advocate.

> "They're paid for it; it's their duties; just as it's my duty to sell Hubbles and Grease's sugar. It's not for me to say the sugar's bad, or the samples not equal to the last. My duty is to sell, and I sell;—and it's their duty to get a verdict." . . .
>
> "But it aint justice," said Mrs. Smiley.
>
> "Why not? I say it is justice. You can have it if you choose to pay for it, and so can I." (II. 213)

Mr. Moulder understands professional advocacy strictly in terms of a business exchange.

It is not just those outside the legal profession, like Sir Peregrine or Mr. Moulder, who question the responsibility of paid legal representation. Perhaps the most damning statement of all comes from within the profession when Mr. Round drops all pretenses and names Mr. Dockwrath's motivating force. "Oh, of course! I suppose the real fact is, that it is a matter of money. You want to be paid for what information you have got. That is about the long and the short of it; eh, Mr. Dockwrath" (I. 161). Dockwrath attempts to soften these bald terms, but only succeeds in implicating Mr. Round in the comparison between blackmail and professional earnings. "As a professional man, of course I expect to be paid for my work;—and I have no doubt that you expect the same" (I. 161). Trollope further highlights this issue by inserting scenes from the Birmingham conference on legal reform. There, it is clear that "no amount of eloquence will make an English Lawyer think that loyalty to truth should come before loyalty to his client" (I. 165). Among the strongest supporters of this point of view is Mr. Furnival (I. 116).

Yet Mr. Furnival's loyalty to and representation of Lady Mason is more complicated than the bare bones commercial transaction suggested by Mr. Moulder. His decision to represent her even though he knows she is guilty stems not from his greed, but from his sense of what claims a beautiful, refined, unprotected, classed woman has on a man, and the pleasures that fulfilling those claims promise in return. Lady Mason claims his aid with her money, with her status, but most of all with her femininity. "I shall have your aid?" (I. 122) may be written as a question, but it actually functions as a declaration. In fact, Furnival never thinks of his fee, but he reflects continually on Lady Mason:

> How beautiful she looked while she stood in Sir Peregrine's library, leaning on the old man's arm—how beautiful and how innocent! That was the form which his thoughts chiefly took. And then she had given him her hand, and he still felt the soft silken touch of her cool fingers. He would not be a man if he could desert a woman in such a strait. And such a woman!. . . He would still bring her through! Yes; in spite of her guilt, if she were guilty; on the strength of her innocence, if she were innocent; but on account of her beauty, and soft hand, and deep liquid eye. So at least he would have owned, could he have been honest enough to tell himself the whole truth. (I. 341)

Furnival is determined, of course, to "be a man" by not deserting "such a woman." And although he never tells himself the whole truth nor explains his views on his masculine duty and her feminine charms to Lady Mason, they nonetheless completely understand one another. The narrator comments on Lady Mason's recognition of her powers, "Had she given way to dowdiness . . . Mr. Furnival, we may say, would not have been there to meet her;—of which fact Lady Mason was perhaps aware" (I. 117). The unspoken compromise they reach stipulates not a fee to be paid, but roles to be played. Lady Mason must not openly tell Mr. Furnival of her guilt; she must court "countenance" with neighboring dignitaries. Above all, she must continue to be soft, cool, and beautiful (i.e., "such a woman"). For his part, Mr. Furnival must pretend not to know that she is guilty, and in exchange for enjoying Lady Mason's femininity, he must champion, protect, and speak for her in court (i.e., "be a man").

This unspoken arrangement was so readily understood by Lady Mason and Mr. Furnival because his representation of her in court is modeled on male representation of women in general. Lady Mason's status of dependence and fragility, or her performance of typical feminine traits, calls forth from Mr. Furnival a corresponding activity and strength, or a performance of typical masculine traits. Mr. Furnival's wife is rightfully jealous of this arrangement. She recognizes and explicitly identifies that the dynamics of Furnival's relationship with his client look like the dynamics between a man and his wife. When Furnival lies to his wife about his meetings with Lady Mason, the narrator comments:

> The reader will of course observe that this deceit was practiced, not as between husband and wife with reference to an assignation with a lady, but between the lawyer and the outer world with reference to a private meeting with a client. But then it is sometimes so difficult to make wives look at such matters in the right light. (I. 111-12)

The light that illuminates this relationship for Mrs. Furnival causes her to view Lady Mason as a rival for the feminine role, not as a client who occupies too much of Mr. Furnival's time. The terms "husband" and "lawyer," and "lady" and "client," and "assignation" and "meeting" continually collapse into one another in *Orley Farm*. R. D. McMaster, in *Trollope and the Law*, comments on the inappropriateness of Lady Mason ever going to see Mr. Furnival in person. He points out that etiquette demanded that Lady Mason employ a solicitor, who would in turn seek out a barrister. Technically speaking, the solicitor is the barrister's client.[3] McMaster's chapter on *Orley Farm* (entitled "Sex in the Barrister's Chambers") reads the meetings between the Lady and the barrister in the same light that Mrs. Furnival reads them: "Lady Mason arrives dressed with fetching and studied plainness. An almost Pumblechookian degree of hand holding takes place (six times during the interview by my count) with dashes in the text to make us linger on their interpretation" (36). Lady Mason knows how to use her femininity and sexuality to attain appropriate male representation—both legal and social. Much of her grief in *Orley Farm* comes as a result of too many men in too many different roles wanting to act as her representative, not from any lack of volunteers. Her second would-be-representative, Sir Peregrine, makes explicit the connections between protection, representation, and marriage.

FLEXING HER WEAKNESS

The Ormes and the Furnivals would support her. They and such-like persons would acknowledge her weakness. . . . She had calculated the strength of her own weakness, and thought that she might still be supported by that,—if only her son would so permit. (I. 203)

Like her request for Mr. Furnival's help ("I shall have your aid?"), Lady Mason's appeal to Sir Peregrine Orme for his social countenance is more properly a claim: "Oh, Sir Peregrine, say that you will not desert me if all this trouble is coming on me again!" (I. 44). Although Lady Mason is described as "a woman of high character, of great talent, and of repute," her claim proceeds less from these positive virtues and more from her weakness, silence, and dependence (I. 5). What she lacks—strength, voice, and independence—demands compensation. Put more directly, her willingness to perform the upper-class feminine draws with it a claim from her male acquaintances to perform the masculine role of protector: "there was a soft meekness about her, an air of feminine dependence, a proneness to lean and almost to cling as she leaned, which might have been felt as irresistible by any man" (I. 260). Resistance would be futile; what is more, in the case of Lady Mason, surrender to the role of male protector promises to be highly gratifying.

Sir Peregrine Orme, venerable, old, rich, and "by general repute the greatest man in these parts," puts up no resistance to Lady Mason's clinging feminine dependence (I. 9). So strong is his feeling of *noblesse oblige* toward women of his class and so devoted is his view of a gendered equation of privileges and responsibilities, that it results in Lady Mason's overshooting her mark. Having underestimated Orme's devotion to traditional gender roles and the allure of championing a beautiful younger woman, she goes beyond simply guaranteeing his social backing to inspiring such fidelity in his breast that he claims complete responsibility for her representation.

This complete responsibility for her representation would come through marriage. Orme determines to change her name and social place, to give her shelter under his name and status:

> He resolved from that moment that Lady Mason should no longer be regarded as the widow of a city knight, but as the wife elect of a country baronet. . . . Men and women had dared to speak of her cruelly, and they should now learn that any such future speech would be spoken of one who was exclusively his property. . . . He had devoted himself to her that he might be her knight and bear her scatheless through the fury of this battle. . . . As soon as might be she should bear his name; but all the world should know at once what was her right to claim his protection. (I. 358)

Now, in her "time of trouble" (a euphemism, not incidentally often used in association with pregnancy), Orme offers marriage and protection—in exchange for complete ownership. The language of chivalric protection and ownership mingled in this passage make the terms of exchange clear. He would be her knight; she would be his property. The payment may not be so overt as in her first marriage (when her father gave her to Mason as part of a bankruptcy settlement), but it is nonetheless carefully calculated. In Sir William Blackstone's famous dictum explaining the legal non-existence of married women, the protection marriage offers a woman comes at the cost of total self-annihilation: "By marriage the husband and wife are one person in law, that is, the very being, or legal existence of a woman is suspended during marriage, or at least incorporated and consolidated into that of the husband, under whose wing, protection, and cover she performs everything" (Perkins 1-2). Becoming a *femme covert*, a hidden person, would appeal to Lady Mason as she faces charges of perjury and forgery.

Unwilling to shame the venerable Orme, and perhaps more to the point, doubting Orme's ability to effectively hide her under his name, Mason ultimately refuses this offer. She stepped out of the place of a *femme covert*—a woman politically, economically, and socially "covered" by her husband's name—when she forged the codicil to her husband's will. In this novel so centrally concerned with the representation of women, her crime is fittingly one specifically of representation. After failing to cajole her husband into leaving Orley Farm to her son, she determined to help herself. In the middle of the night, she forged a codicil, and the signatures of her husband, his lawyer, and two witnesses, and then lied about it while under oath, claiming that the codicil was dictated to her by the lawyer in her husband's presence (I. 3). She did not serve as a helpmate or an amanuensis, but took the proverbial pen(is) in hand, displacing both her husband and his lawyer and violating England's tradition of primogeniture. She made her own mark in the world. Additionally, the nature of her crime, forging a will, directly trespasses on the right to own property, bequeath property, and create an heir. Having dared to question the propriety of leaving all his property to his first son, Lady Mason dares further to usurp the rights of the father and the law. She not only reclaims her own voice by objecting to her husband's plans, but she drowns out the voices of her husband and his lawyer, literally stealing their will. She does so by making her own representation, by writing a codicil that will determine the direction of the rest of the story.

Lady Mason falters seriously as a wife by acting independently of, and even at odds with, her husband's representation of her. Instead of letting her husband be her legal representative, controlling her property, she insists on being his legal representative and dictating the fate of his property. By resisting economic and legal self-effacement in her first marriage, she stepped outside the pale of Sir Peregrine's ability to erase her past and shelter her as an extension of himself in a second marriage. Much smaller faults of independence can also make a woman ineligible for marriage in *Orley Farm*. The Miss Tristrams, for example, hunt marvelously, but their independence and courage foster the general opinion that they would not make appropriate wives.

Lady Mason must add another knight to her ranks if she expects to win her legal battle. Sir Peregrine's social backing can do much, but the old man is incapable of fighting effectively with legal weapons. His advice assumes Lady Mason to be innocent. Only her barrister and pseudo-husband, Mr. Furnival, is capable of advising and representing her in her guilt.[4] Even Mason's own son (who wants to assume the responsibility of supporting his mother and garner all the attendant privileges of acting as the male head of the house) is rejected in favor of a professional. Furnival knows she is guilty, but he can construct a defense that will (mis)represent her as innocent. As we shall see, the lies he chooses to utter are telling indeed. His representation is professional, temporary, and for hire. The temporary nature of his representation gives Lady Mason the flexibility to rely on him during the trial without relinquishing her self-representation permanently. Theirs is very much a temporary "marriage" of convenience, not surprisingly misconstrued by Mrs. Furnival as an extramarital affair. In fact, a jealous rivalry springs up between Lady Mason's son, her suitor, and her barrister, each claiming the right to be her lone representative. Lady Mason correctly estimates the usefulness of each would-be-representative: "Sir Peregrine's friendship was more valuable to her than that of Mr. Furnival, but a word of advice from Mr. Furnival was worth all the spoken wisdom of the baronet ten times over" (I. 115). She carefully flatters Orme but listens to Furnival. Although her guilt, and more precisely her unfeminine guilt of self-representation, necessitates that she abandon any hope of a marriage with Sir Peregrine Orme, that abandonment secures Mr. Furnival's undivided devotion, which is much more valuable.

MR. FURNIVAL AT WORK

All his old fire came back upon him, and before he had done he had almost brought himself again to believe Lady Mason to be that victim of persecution as which he did not hesitate to represent her to the jury. (II. 325)

Mr. Furnival's near self-conviction perfectly expresses the power of representations. First he constructs a narrative in which Lady Mason figures as an innocent victim, and then forgets the fictional, constructed nature of that image. Part of this believability or forgetting of fictionality stems from Mr. Furnival's desire to believe Lady Mason is innocent. That same desire in others aids him in his defense. Mr. Furnival's task of acquitting Lady Mason is two-pronged: he must first forcefully remind the jury of gender and class norms and then represent his client as a paragon of those norms. In other words, Mr. Furnival's job requires him to perform gender in Judith Butler's sense of performance as both actively constituting an identity and then "doing" that identity.[5] Focusing on gender norms, rather than any other sort of defense, points to the kind of story Furnival (and Trollope) considers to be most believable. Furnival, of course, does not start from scratch. The legal stage aids him tremendously, already assuming major gender divisions. Small choreographed steps are all that are necessary to crystallize the outlines of general Victorian gender norms. Lady Mason's silence, for example, and Mr. Furnival's voice speaking for her mimic a husband's right to be his wife's legal voice:

She was not called upon during the whole proceeding to utter one audible word. A single question was put to her by the presiding magistrate before the committal was signed, and it was understood that some answer was made to it; but this answer reached the ears of those in the room by means of Mr. Furnival's voice. (II. 126)

Allowing Furnival's voice to drown out or replace her own voice in this legal setting implies her approval of the transference of a whole range of legal powers that men claim in women's names—most pointedly in her case the right to own and bequeath property. Lady Mason knows that in addition to demonstrating her relinquishment of her legal voice, she must also give a performance of her dignity, innocence, and femininity. She plans her dress, carriage, and facial expressions accordingly. Even a matter as small as timing the lifting of her veil is not left to chance.

Lady Mason's twenty exemplary years of patience, modesty, refinement, and self-sacrifice, and her fulfillment of all that is expected of a woman of her standing, prepare the way for Mr. Furnival's defense and the public's acceptance of her claim to innocence. Sir Peregrine Orme, for example, cannot at first believe that she is guilty. Those twenty years speak more clearly to him than her own confession:

> Could this be possible? Could it be that she forged that will. . . . And then he thought of her pure life, of her womanly dignified repose, of her devotion to her son. . . of her sweet, pale face and soft voice! He thought of all this, and of his own love and friendship for her,—of Edith's love for her! He thought of it all, and he could not believe she was guilty. (II. 44)

Orme concludes that her confession is incompatible with her known conduct, and, more importantly, incompatible with his own and Edith's love for her. Believing that feminine traits are natural rather than prescribed and that a woman's conduct expresses innate femininity rather than complying with socially constructed norms, Orme cannot comprehend how Lady Mason could win his love and be guilty. In his understanding she *is* innocent, not merely acting in an innocent manner.

Furnival's defense rests on reinforcing in the jury's mind what Orme assumes, that gender is inescapable, natural, undefiable. Twenty years of exemplary performance of her womanly duties strongly support Furnival's contention that Lady Mason *is* an innocent woman and as such incapable of forgery. There can be no momentary slips out of character if you contend that her character is a natural expression of her being. The fiery speech in which he spells this out is worth quoting at length:

> During the incidents of this trial the nature of the life she had led during these twenty years . . . has been proved before you. I may fearlessly ask you whether so fair a life is compatible with the idea of guilt so foul?. . . Look at her, as she sits there! That she, at the age of twenty, or not much more,—she who had so well performed the duties of her young life, that she should have forged a will,—have traced one signature after another in such a manner as to have deceived all those lawyers who were on her track immediately after her husband's death! For, mark you, if this be true, with her own hand she must have done it!. . . Look at her! Was she a forger? Was she a woman to deceive the sharp blood-hounds of the law? (II. 329)

Furnival stresses the incompatibility of her guilt and her successful performance of the duties of life, repeatedly directing the jury to "look" at Lady Mason and resolve, if they can, her beauty and her guilt. In the second half of this line of defense, he challenges the absurd notion that a wee slip of a girl could possibly have outwitted the vigilance of legal men. Here he expresses his assumption about superior masculine intellect (especially legal intellect) as part and parcel of his defense resting on the impossibility of feminine guilt.

The logic behind this line of defense challenges the jury to consider the basis of character, especially feminine character. In order to find Lady Mason guilty, they would have to admit that she lived twenty blameless years, committed a premeditated crime, and then lived another twenty spotless years. Such a conclusion would deny the innate naturalness of gendered behavior or even the consistency of character. One resulting corollary to this "inescapable" femininity is a naturalizing of the roles played within heterosexual marriage. Furnival borrows from the heterosexual model of marriage both for Mason's defense and for defining his own role as a masculine and thus vocal, authoritative, and knowledgeable professional man. His assumptions in court help erase the constructed nature of those roles: women are *naturally* silent, and barristers *necessarily* speak for those who cannot.[6] Cultural assumptions about "wifely" behavior and his line of defense thus mutually constitute one another.

Defending a woman against charges of forgery hardly seems like a privilege to be hotly contested, but representing a woman also has its rewards. Although Lady Mason's trial causes Mr. Furnival much turmoil, he still refuses to yield the field to either her son or her suitor. Furnival receives approval from the legal community for his able defense or, in other words, he loses no professional ground from championing her cause (II. 331). The case also receives wide notoriety, and the participants become mini-celebrities. Yet I would suggest that Furnival, Lucius, and Orme take interest in the case for reasons that go beyond, while overlapping, professional or public notice. Their contest to represent Lady Mason turns on their desire to perform their own masculinity and garner the attendant privileges and power.

Lucius Mason is a young man, eager to prove his ability to represent a woman and to be the legal and economic head of the house. He boasts, "I would take the burden from her shoulders" (I. 273). He takes deep offense at his mother's decision to place her trust elsewhere. His campaign to take over the public representation of his mother occurs simultaneously with his courting of Mr. Furnival's daughter. He fails in both. Sir Peregrine Orme is in his twilight years and anxious to exercise his virility and gallantry one more time. He asks, "Will you give me the right to stand there with you. . . . There I may boast that I should be strong" (I. 356). Orme wishes to validate the privileges he already enjoys by playing knight, but he cannot fight in court. Mr. Furnival is middle-aged, unchallenged by work, and seeking excitement by "running after strange goddesses" (I. 99). As Mason's legal representative, Furnival plays pseudo-husband, taking pleasure in her beauty and sexuality and justifying his professional powers. Lady Mason is a goddess for all three men because her endangered womanhood and her attacked purity provide them with the opening to be correspondingly masculine and protective. The chance to represent her—as a mother, wife, or client—offers the opportunity to play with the mirror in which they are reflected, to exercise a kind of wish fulfillment and to justify the privileges they enjoy as men. The binary opposition between masculine and feminine qualities ensures that a manipulation of Lady Mason's representation will be reflected onto the men in her life. By making characters, or representing people, they can more effectively shape a world and amass the power that accompanies representing another person, whether it be legally, politically, economically, or socially. Rather than in marriages where we normally expect to see men exchange credible representation for control of women's property and persons, in *Orley Farm* that exchange of power is exercised most visibly in the courtroom by professional men.

Turning now to a historical court case, we can see a defense built on similar assumptions about what it means to be a "wife" and what responsibilities a "husband" incurs when he takes command of a woman's fortune and conduct. By juxtaposing Trollope's fiction with one of the most notorious and widely reported criminal trials of the century, I hope to highlight their shared assumptions and projects. The Bartlett case, like *Orley Farm*, grapples with problems of legal representation, particularly the representation of a woman who has lacked male representation most of her life.

The trial of Adelaide Bartlett for the murder of her husband raises questions similar to those about character and representation that Trollope explores in his fiction. The strategy Bartlett's barrister employs to defend her in the face of overwhelming evidence of her guilt mirrors the strategy used by Mr. Furnival. Adelaide must agree to be silent and abandon self-direction to secure the aid of counsel and to play convincingly the role that her defense demands of her—the same sacrifices Mason found so difficult to make in her first marriage. Finally, as in the case of Lady Mason, the marital exchange(s) involving Adelaide Bartlett brings to the fore the question of a woman's self-possession—of who owned Adelaide and who was responsible for her, and the costs and benefits of claiming the right to represent her. By placing a parallel discussion of this 1886 historical trial after my discussion of Trollope's 1861 novel, I am not proposing that the Bartlett case consciously borrowed from Trollope's work. Instead, I argue that both proceed from a shared cultural context and a similar professional-client dynamic.

THE PIMLICO MYSTERY

In the spring of 1886, Londoners were intrigued by an extraordinary tale of marriage, sex, poison, and murder that the papers came to dub "The Pimlico Mystery." The inquest provided great copy, and the trial itself turned into public entertainment, complete with fashionable ladies, smelling salts, and temporary hustings to provide additional seating.[7] Londoners crowded the courtroom and eagerly snatched up evening papers to see and read about Adelaide Bartlett, accused of poisoning her husband on New Year's Eve. While critics often note the extraordinarily "real" quality to Trollope's fiction, this "real-life" crime and subsequent trial took on the qualities of fiction—commanding a large audience, serializing information, and exposing extraordinary events. But most striking, a reading of the Bartlett trial breaks down the distinctions between "life" and "fiction" by revealing the extent to which legal representation, and by extension all representation, is constructed, motivated, narrated, and interlocked with broader cultural assumptions.

The Bartlett drama opened on April 9, 1875, with the marriage of Adelaide Blanche de la Tremoille and Thomas Edwin Bartlett. Adelaide's father arranged the marriage of his illegitimate daughter to Bartlett, ten years her senior, after only one meeting.[8] Historians surmise that although likely from distinguished circles himself, Adelaide's father arranged this middle-class marriage as the best compromise he could make: trading a sum of money (which Bartlett invested in his business) for a legitimizing family name for his daughter.[9] Bartlett was to take responsibility for Adelaide—give her a name and a social place, and manage her money and conduct. How well Mr. Bartlett fulfilled this role as the man responsible for Adelaide's social, legal, and economic representation became an issue after his death. During the trial, Mr. Bartlett compares unfavorably with the able representation of Mrs. Bartlett's barrister.

Early in their marriage, Mrs. Bartlett's new home was made uncomfortable and Mr. Bartlett's ability to guide his wife put to the test by accusations voiced by old Mr. Bartlett. Bartlett, Sr., later signed an apology, but during the trial claimed to have done so merely to make peace with his son and daughter-in-law. When pressed to elaborate on what kind of accusations he had made, Edwin Bartlett, Sr., replied, "Well, Adelaide ran away, and was away for some week or more, and Edwin and me thought she had gone along—we almost knew she had gone with Fred Bartlett, the brother, and we were after her" (Hall 101-14).[10] He added that she had run away on other occasions, and that he could produce witnesses to prove it. This breach in family peace was repaired by old Mr. Bartlett's apology, but the damage had been done, and he and Adelaide watched one another with suspicion.[11] On January 1, 1886, when summoned to the home of his son by the news that he had died, Mr.

Bartlett's first action was to smell his son's breath for traces of poison. His second action was to demand an inquest.

His suspicions seem well founded. His son was a robust man who, following a physical examination, was "passed as a first class life" and insured for £400 by the British Equitable Life Association (*Pall Mall Gazette* 13 April 1886). According to his business partner, he had never missed a day of work until December of 1885, when he began to complain of fatigue.[12] Dr. Leach examined Bartlett December 10, observed a distinctive blue streak around the patient's gum line (a common symptom of mercury poisoning), and assumed Bartlett was secretly taking the substance to combat syphilis, although he showed no signs of the disease.[13]

Bartlett recovered slowly, his convalescence hampered by problems with his teeth. By December 24, Bartlett had recovered from the mercurial/lead poisoning so far that Dr. Leach suggested a trip to the seaside. On the 30th, he was well enough that the doctor declared it unnecessary for him to visit again (*Pall Mall Gazette* 12 April 1886). But he was destined to visit one more time. In the early hours of the new year, Dr. Leach was called to the Bartlett home to find his patient had passed away with the dying of the old year.

EVIDENCE FOR THE PROSECUTION[14]

The bulk of the evidence for the prosecution focused on the classic questions of motive and opportunity. Opportunity was easily established as Mrs. Bartlett was the only person with Mr. Bartlett on the night he died. To establish Mrs. Bartlett's motive, the Attorney-General closely examined the Bartletts' marriage, which was anything but conventional. He asked Bartlett's father, "Did you know of your son's having any exceptional ideas on the subject of married life?" The father reluctantly replied, "He said one ought to have two wives, one to take out and one to do the work." Several other witnesses corroborated this response; Edwin Bartlett had told them that he thought one should have one wife for "companionship" and another for "use" (Bart 102). That, however, was not exactly the arrangement in the Bartlett household. Instead, as Dr. Leach testified, the Bartletts had begun a *ménage à trois* not with another woman, but with a man—the Reverend George Dyson. Adelaide had spoken to Dr. Leach about this arrangement, and he in turn described it to the jury, often quoting Adelaide's words:

> No female friends or relations were ever invited to the house, but he had always liked to surround her with male acquaintances. She said, "He thought me clever; he wished to make me more clever; and the more attention and admiration I gained from these male acquaintances the more delighted did he appear. Their attention to me gave him pleasure, or seemed to give him pleasure. . . . We became acquainted with Mr. Dyson. My husband threw us together. He

requested us to kiss in his presence, and he seemed to enjoy it." She gave me to understand—in fact, she used these words, "He had given me to Mr. Dyson." (Bart 206)

At no time previous to or during the trial do we hear Adelaide's voice unfiltered by either Dr. Leach or Mr. Clarke, her barrister. This ventriloquism is most apparent when private information that only Adelaide could possess (or invent) must be relayed via a male representative.

The daily papers were full of the intimate details of the Bartlett-Dyson-Bartlett affair. Witnesses testified to how Dyson arrived as early as nine o'clock in the morning, stayed all day while Mr. Bartlett was at work, and kept a coat and slippers at their home. A domestic servant reported seeing the defendant and Dyson sitting on the sofa together, discovering the curtains pinned together, and finding Adelaide sitting on the floor with her head in Dyson's lap (*Pall Mall Gazette* 12 April 1886). These details formed part of the Attorney-General's contention that Adelaide murdered Edwin so she could marry George Dyson. In response to questions posed by the Attorney-General, the nervous Reverend Dyson told the court that he kissed Adelaide both in front of her husband and when he was away from home, that all three of them referred to each other by their Christian names, and that Edwin Bartlett had paid for him to accompany them on vacation. According to Dyson, he discussed his growing fondness for Adelaide with her husband. In response, Mr. Bartlett seemed pleased and eager for the friendship to continue and deepen. He even asked Dyson to write his wife letters. These letters were not entered as evidence, but Dyson did produce a letter Bartlett had written to him, and the affectionate, even passionate tone suggests that Edwin enjoyed his relationship with George as much as he enjoyed George's relationship with Adelaide (Bart 135).[15] As further evidence of his confidence in Dyson, Edwin changed his will, leaving everything to his wife, making George the executor, and removing a clause that would have prevented Adelaide from inheriting if she ever remarried (*Times* 17 April 1886).[16] The motive that the Attorney-General sought to establish was nearly complete. He had one final and damning question to pose. When asked, "Did he [Mr. Bartlett] ever make reference to marriage between you and Mrs. Bartlett after he should be dead?" Dyson responded, "He has made statements which left no doubt on my mind but that he contemplated Mrs. Bartlett and myself being ultimately married" (Bart 155).

An autopsy clearly established that Edwin Bartlett died from ingesting chloroform sometime between midnight and two a.m., but how the chloroform got in his stomach remained to be answered. Several witnesses testified to the fact that Adelaide had chloroform in her possession and had asked questions about its effects. Dr. Leach asked her how she had intended to use the chloroform, and she told him it was to subdue her husband's sexual urges. According to Adelaide Bartlett, she and her husband did not have sexual intercourse. On one occasion only, after she begged for a child, did they engage in sex. In 1881, she gave birth to a stillborn child after a long and painful labor. Mrs. Bartlett claimed that after subsequently deciding never to have children, she and her husband maintained pleasant but platonic relations. Dr. Leach further recounted his conversation with Mrs. Bartlett, saying that she told him her husband "manifested some desire to renew sexual intercourse with her; that she did not desire this . . . . She considered that she had been made over in the future to Dyson." She planned to wave the chloroform under his nose, "lulling him into a kind of a stupor, and so prevent him giving effect to his sexual passion. That is the story she tells" (Bart 88).[17] Here, as we saw earlier, this is the story that Dr. Leach tells the court, serving again as an authoritative mouthpiece for the defendant.

Justice Wills then summed up.[18] He spent considerable time dwelling on a book found in the Bartlett home that discussed birth control and suggesting its dangerous effects on women, referring to it as "reading which helped to unsex them" (*Times* 17 April 1886).[19] He further stated that the jury ought to pity a woman whose husband "could throw such literature her way, and encourage her to read it. . . . One has learned to-day what is the natural and to be expected consequence of indulgence in literature of that kind." (Bart 372). Clearly, Judge Wills was referring to the belief that books and the information in them were potentially dangerous to the minds of women readers and that husbands ought to protect wives from such dangers. Mr. Bartlett failed decidedly in his duty to protect his wife from corrupting literature.[20] Finally, the Judge pointed out that the "French Letters" (condoms) found in Mr. Bartlett's pocket contradicted the defendant's story of a platonic relationship, and thus her reasons for wanting to obtain chloroform. Dropping even the appearance of objectivity, the judge concluded:

> When a young wife and a younger male friend get discussing, in or out of the presence of the husband, the possibilities of his decease within measurable time and of the friend succeeding to the husband's place, according to all experience of human life, the life of the husband was one that an insurance office would not like to take. (*Times* 17 April 1886)

Justice Wills clearly leaned heavily toward prosecution, finding marriage with Dyson to be a convincing motive for murder. The jury returned to the courtroom after two hours of deliberation:

> The Clerk of the Court— "Gentlemen, have you agreed upon your verdict?"
> The Foreman— "We have."
> The Clerk of the Court— "Do you find the prisoner, Adelaide Bartlett, guilty or not guilty?"

The Foreman— "We have well considered the evidence, and, although we think grave suspicion is attached to the prisoner, we do not think there is sufficient evidence to show how or by whom the chloroform was administered."

The Clerk of the Court— "Then you say that the prisoner is not guilty?"

The Foreman— "Not guilty."

At the announcement of the verdict there was immense cheering in the Court and outside. (Bart 402)

Incensed at the disturbance and, no doubt, by a verdict so obviously contrary to his summation, Judge Wills roared: "This conduct is an outrage. A court of justice is not to be turned into a theatre" (*Times* 17 April 1886).

In this, however, he was manifestly mistaken. Every trial is a performance, with the most convincing, or the most popular, or the most palatable rendition prevailing. Despite ample evidence, the jury could not or would not believe that Mrs. Bartlett murdered her husband. Mr. Clarke's rendition, as we shall see, proved to be much more palatable and extremely popular. The prosecution failed to anticipate the degree of responsibility popularly held to be attached to the role of husband and the degree of passivity popularly held to be attached to the role of wife. In the explanation proffered by the prosecution, Mrs. Bartlett actively cheated on her husband, withheld sex, and then poisoned him in order to marry Dyson and inherit the family money. In the rendition articulated by the defense, Mr. Bartlett seems woefully inadequate as a guiding force: he failed to keep Adelaide at home, failed to enforce family peace, failed to maintain a "normal" sexual relationship with his wife, and failed to produce children. Further, he led her into a corrupting situation with Dyson, and then wrote himself out of the picture by changing his will and "giving" her to Dyson. The evidence the prosecution used to establish Adelaide's guilt, when viewed through the lenses of Victorian gender conventions, was instead used by the defense to condemn the deceased Mr. Bartlett.

THE DEFENSE'S RENDITION

Adelaide Bartlett offered no statement. She put forth no account of the poisoning, gave no interviews, and remained silent at the inquest. According to the *Times*, "On the death of her husband the prisoner gave no explanation, at the inquest she did not tender herself to be examined, and even in her statement to Dr. Leach she made no suggestion of how her husband's death had been brought about" (17 April 1886). Adelaide's defense counsel, Mr. Clarke, likewise called no witnesses and produced no evidence. They did not have to. Adelaide and her counsel found it unnecessary to construct an explanation by stepping into a fully developed and popularly embraced rendition of middle-class womanhood and heterosexual marriage. As we saw in the fictional trial of Lady

Mason, part of such a defense reinforced and further defined the very terms it borrowed. Consequently, while Barrister Clarke used heterosexual marriage ideals to defend Adelaide, his own "appropriate" modeling of a male representative simultaneously condemned Mr. Bartlett and affirmed his own authority.

Clarke's basic contention was that a woman like Adelaide was incapable of murder. Nothing she could have said and no evidence Mr. Clarke could have presented would have carried the same, deeply ingrained message or would have rung so true to the ears of the jury. But more important, her silence allowed Dr. Leach and Mr. Clarke to tell her story, to lend her credibility by mouthing her words, to take her representation on their own backs, thereby elevating her believability by dint of their own trustworthy positions and reputations. However convincing Mrs. Bartlett's testimony might be, her silence would be more convincing because it dovetailed with the image of a perfect middle-class wife whose silence allowed her "husband" to speak for her.

I do not mean to suggest that Mr. Clarke did nothing. On the contrary, he labored for six hours in his closing comments to ensure that the jury recognized Adelaide as that fantasy of middle-class wife that they so revered. Part of his labor involved re-orientating the responsibility for unconventional behavior brought forth earlier in the trial, such as Adelaide's relationship with Dyson, but Clarke's greatest efforts went to reiterating the values and traits of the feminine ideal that Adelaide could claim—silence, passivity, tenderness, and reliance on male judgment. The inconsistency of Adelaide's role as a wife and as a murderess formed the crux of his argument. In addition to her silence and reliance on Clarke, Dr. Leach testified to Adelaide's patience and tenderness in nursing her often difficult husband. Her complete dependence on her barrister and doctor further solidified Adelaide's image as obedient to and leaning on male authority. How could this image be resolved with the prosecution's contention that she deliberately poisoned her husband, a most disobedient and aggressive act? Mr. Clarke argued:

> It is a marvelous thing that you are asked by the prosecution to accept—you are asked—and when I use that phrase I do not mean that you will be urged, but what I do mean is, that this is what you must accept if you accept the idea of guilt or the contention of guilt—you are asked to believe that a woman who, for years, had lived in friendship and affection with her husband; who, during the whole time of his illness, had striven to tend him, to nurse him, and to help him; who had tended him by day, who had sacrificed her own rest to watch over him at night, had spent night after night without going to restful bed, simply giving to herself sleep at the bottom of his couch that she might be ready by him to comfort him by her presence; who had called doctors, who had taken all the pains that the most tender and affectionate nurse possibly could. . . you are asked to imagine that

that woman on New Year's Eve was *suddenly transformed into a murderess*, committing crime, not only without excuse, but without any object. (Bart 294-95)

Mr. Clarke's strongest point lies in his insistence on the necessity of choosing a package deal. If the jury votes for conviction, then they *must* be able to resolve Adelaide's guilty, murderous action with her role as wife, nurse, and dependent woman. Mr. Clarke suggests rhetorically that this is not possible by selecting the phrase "suddenly transformed." Adelaide could not be wife and murderess simultaneously; no, she had to be *transformed* from the one to the other, and such a radical transformation, if ever possible, certainly would not be possible in the space of a few minutes, days, or even weeks. According to this line of thought, "wife" was an unalloyed property, certainly with no room for "murderess." Would the jury contend otherwise? Could Mrs. Adelaide Bartlett be both wife and murderess? To do so would be to destroy an idol, to admit to the fall of the angel in the house. It would also open the door for the suggestion that not all wives are "naturally" passive and in need of, desiring in fact, male representation. The jury could save the image of "wife" inviolate and keep their own role as "natural" leaders intact only by acquitting a murderess. It took the all-male jury two hours to make that choice.

While this is the outright challenge that Mr. Clarke presented to the jury, he argued in more subtle ways as well. Perhaps even more effective than his explicit argument was his shifting of attention from Adelaide to himself and his implicit case against Mr. Bartlett. While it would be unwise to malign the deceased, the tactful Clarke posed as a marked contrast to Mr. Bartlett. Mr. Clarke championed the silent Adelaide and become the revised focus of the press. The heroic tone used to describe Mr. Clarke increased in pitch until the day following the trial, when the *Daily News* declared: "From the position of *grave peril* in which, ever since the coroner's inquest, she had undoubtedly stood, she was *rescued* by the skill and eloquence of her counsel" 19 April 1886, my italics). Rescuing his client from *grave peril* dovetails nicely with the version of gender roles that Mr. Clarke needed to exploit in order to win. In such a script, Adelaide's silent passivity and reliance on male representation contrast with the determination and murderous energy presumably needed to poison one's husband. The "man" who would correspond to this feminine ideal would be active, commanding, authoritative, and protective—like Mr. Clarke. The *Penny Illustrated Paper* painted a touching picture of Adelaide and Clarke: "her eyes were drooping, and she stood motionless . . . stupefied by grief or pain, and only half conscious of what was going on around—except when the able speech of MR. EDWARD CLARKE, Q.C., M.P. FOR THE DEFENSE raised her hopes. Then colour mantled in her cheeks" (17 April 1886). Mr. Clarke's masculinity provided a backdrop to show off Adelaide's femininity. In a dynamic similar to what we saw in the Furnival/Mason relationship, Mr. Clarke performs as a pseudo-husband, making Adelaide's performance of the ideal (i.e., innocent) wife plausible. The version of Mr. Bartlett offered by the defense, by contrast, shows him entirely failing to protect Adelaide, instead using his authority to entangle her in a relationship with Dyson. Adelaide's supposed passivity not only disqualifies her as a murderess, but also suggests that the Dyson affair was instigated by her husband. Even the defendant's fantastic story of a platonic relationship, a desire to forego intercourse for years, and a plan to use chloroform to subdue her husband's passions accords with this version of womanhood. Pure and passionless—albeit with an unusual twist—Adelaide appears to be a girl without a family, grievously misled by a sexually knowledgeable husband and a corrupt clergyman, and now, finally, rescued by appropriate male representation in the guise of her barrister. The representation that her illegitimate father would not give her and that Bartlett failed to provide for her is delivered by a barrister who fashions an image of Adelaide that is at once popular, convincing, and respectable. The success of his defense hinges on the desire to believe that such an image of Adelaide is natural and to forget its constructed and strategic nature.

The personal and cultural costs and benefits of strategically invoking standard gender assumptions become clear when we read Trollope's fiction in conjunction with Bartlett's trial. Mason and Bartlett are clear-sighted about both their need for male representation and the loss of autonomy that it necessitates. Two guilty women escape punishment by acquiescing to a role that strips them of legal, social, economic, and political rights—the role of a wife. By doing so, they gave male juries what they desired to find. Mason's and Bartlett's defense depends upon the jury being invested in perpetuating gender divisions that view women as fundamentally different, as innately feminine, and as inescapably gentle. Once qualities such as gentleness, innocence, and passivity have been denoted as essentially "wifely" or "feminine," the constructive dimension of the representation of "wife" or "woman" is obscured and conveniently forgotten. If, on the other hand, the juries decided these women were not essentially feminine, then, in Mary Poovey's words, "It might also have become possible to think what was equally inconceivable—that one's reproductive nature did not necessarily dictate the social position of every man and woman—that, in other words, other differences might hold sway, and men and women could therefore be equal under the law, in social responsibilities and privileges, in relation to property and sexuality, and even in terms of political rights" (79). The juries avoided such issues by finding the women essentially "innocent." Arguments such as those made in the Mason and Bartlett cases draw upon and reinforce conventional divisions of rights and powers. Male juries and the professional legal men constructing these defenses benefited from protecting the status quo, which aligned enormous privileges with men.

The constructed nature of all representations (between book covers, within the walls of courtrooms, and beyond) becomes clear when reading fiction and trial transcripts together—both forms that openly acknowledge that representation is *made*, that they *do* representation. The transference of representational responsibility and the power derived from such duties from father to husband failed in the Bartlett and Mason marriages. The lies and crimes of these two women are telling: they are part of a struggle to represent their own interests. The lies told in their defenses deny their ability or desire to represent themselves by realigning the power to represent with men, and specifically with professional men. To escape punishment, Mason and Bartlett play the role of a wife as part of their legal defense and, one suspects, as part of their rehabilitation. They buy their acquittals, but the price is embracing the very stereotypes and roles that would continue to cripple them and that would perpetuate the very conditions against which their crimes rebelled. At the same moment and with the same "evidence" used to find these women essentially innocent, the growing power and authority of the Victorian professional was confirmed as necessary. My method of reading law and literature pieces together clues to larger, often obscured, cultural dynamics, such as the shared projects of professional self-definition and the reification of gender roles within heterosexual marriage.

NOTES

[1] "Mr. Trollope and the Lawyers," *London Review* 8 November 1862, 5. 405-7 as quoted in Smalley.

[2] On Trollope and character, see Wall. Lansbury's study of Trollope's legal fiction argues that Trollope adapted the format of Post Office reports that were modeled on legal declarations and used them as a pattern for his novels. Roberts's work reads Trollope's "virtuoso display of a variety of lawyers in action" as "a significant aspect of his Situation Ethics" (52). Epperly views the recurrence of lawyers as part of a pervasive pattern of repetition necessary for rapid, clear writing.

[3] Trollope would be well aware of the division in duties because his own childhood poverty was due to a large extent to his father's inability to foster ties with solicitors. Mr. Trollope senior was so querulous that he drove solicitors, and thus business, away. For more on the division between barristers and solicitors, see Kirk.

[4] Both old Sir Peregrine and young Perry Orme fail to win their lady-loves. Their aristocratic, traditional carriage is rejected in favor of new professional men. In fact, professional ambition and power generally seem to overshadow older, aristocratic privilege in *Orley Farm*.

[5] Butler succinctly expresses her idea of the performative when she writes: "gender is in no way a stable identity, or locus of agency from which various acts proceed; rather, it is an identity tenuously constituted in time— an identity instituted through a *stylized repetition of acts*" (270). Extending this logic, Butler continues, "If gender attributes, however, are not expressive but performative, then these attributes effectively constitute the identity they are said to express or reveal" (279).

[6] In this novel gender and sex characteristics are aligned in the figure of Mason. She is feminine and a woman. In terms of legal situations, all clients— both male and female—are feminized in their roles as clients who are incapable of self-representation.

[7] Both papers expressed their sense of the inappropriateness of ladies attending a trial where such shocking and sordid details were exposed: "How is it that women will crowd a criminal court to see another of their sex in such a painful position? The details of the case are by no means delicate, and yet alike on the floor of the court and in the public gallery all the best seats were occupied by women." *The Pall Mall Gazette* 12 April 1886. Such comments provide an additional indication as to what kind of gender assumptions were at play during the trial.

[8] Adelaide's age at the time of her marriage became an important and contested issue after her husband's death. She claimed that she was 16 when she married, but Mr. Bartlett senior claimed she was "twenty years and six months old." How much sexual knowledge she had when she married is crucial to the defense's claims. See the U.K., Public Records Office, CRIM 1/23/7 handwritten memo by Dr. Leach dated 4 February 1886, which records Adelaide's claim that she was 16 and Metropolitan Police District officer Marshall's examination of Mr. Bartlett, in which he claims she was older.

[9] See Bridges and Hartman.

[10] Testimony of Edwin Bartlett, Sr., Evidence for Prosecution in Bart 101-14. Original trial notes also part of CRIM 1/23/7.

[11] See prosecution exhibit CRIM 1/23/7, a letter dated 27 December Sunday night in which Adelaide tells Bartlett that she has "neither forgotten nor forgiven the past."

[12] See prosecution exhibit CRIM 1/23/7, a letter dated 9 December 1885 from Edwin to his partner, Mr. Edwards.

[13] In fact, Leach misdiagnosed Edwin. The coroner's report shows lead, not mercury, to be the cause of his initial illness. There would be no reason for Edwin to take lead, but Police Constable Tom Ralph found a bottle in Adelaide's possession at the time of her arrest.

[14] The Attorney-General, Mr. Poland, Mr. R. S. Wright, and Mr. Moloney were counsel for the prosecution on the part of the Crown. Mr. Edward Clarke, Q. C., Mr. Mead, and Mr. Beal appeared for the defense.

[15] Letter from Edwin Bartlett to George Dyson quoted in Bart 135. The original is preserved as part of CRIM 1/23/7.

[16] This new will was drawn up 3 September 1885.

[17] We never hear Adelaide's voice at the trial. Her words are always reported or quoted by someone else. In part this is due to her refusal to cooperate at the inquest when she could have offered an explanation. At the trial, she could not have spoken in her defense. For more on English criminal law see Emsley.

[18] If the name Justice Wills seems familiar, it is because he was the judge at the Oscar Wilde-Alfred Taylor trial ten years later. He sentenced Wilde to two years of hard labor and was booed by the courtroom spectators. His puritanical intolerance is evident in both cases.

[19] The book was *Esoteric Anthropology (The Mysteries of Man): A Comprehensive and Confidential Treatise on the Structure, Functions, Passional Attractions and Perversions, True and False Physical and Social Conditions, and the Most Intimate Relations of Men and Women* by Thomas Low Nicholas, MD, F.A.S.

[20] Here, Adelaide's age at the time of her marriage is particularly important. If she was 16, Bartlett would seem to be more responsible for her guidance than if she was almost 21.

WORKS CITED

Bart, John Hall, ed. *Trial of Adelaide Bartlett*. Edinburgh: William Hodge, 1927.

Bridges, Yseult. *Poison and Adelaide Bartlett: The Pimlico Poisoning Case*. London: Hutchinson, 1962.

Butler, Judith. "Performative Acts and Gender Constitution: An Essay in Phenomenology and Feminist Theory." *Performing Feminisms: Feminist Critical Theory and Theatre*. Ed. Sue-Ellen Case. Baltimore: The Johns Hopkins UP, 1990.

Daily News. 19 April 1886.

Emsley, Clive. *Crime and Society in England: 1750-1900*. London: Longman, 1987.

Epperly, Elizabeth R. *Patterns of Repetition in Trollope*. Washington, DC: The Catholic U of America P, 1989.

Hartman, Mary S. *Victorian Murderesses: A True History of Thirteen Respectable French and English Women Accused of Unspeakable Crimes*. New York: Schocken, 1977.

Heinzelman, Susan, and Zipporah Wiseman, eds. *Representing Women: Law, Literature, and Feminism*. Durham: Duke UP, 1994.

Kirk, Harry. *Portrait of a Profession: A History of the Solicitor's Profession, 1900 to the Present Day*. London: Lyez, 1976.

Lansbury, Coral. *The Reasonable Man: Trollope's Legal Fiction*. Princeton: Princeton UP, 1981.

McMaster, R. D. *Trollope and the Law*. London: Macmillan, 1986

Pall Mall Gazette. 12 April 1886.

Pall Mall Gazette. 13 April 1886.

Penny Illustrated Paper. 17 April 1886.

Perkins, Joan. *Women and Marriage in Nineteenth-Century England*. London: Routledge, 1989.

Poovey, Mary. *Uneven Developments: The Ideological Work of Gender in Mid-Victorian England*. Chicago: Chicago UP, 1988.

Roberts, Ruth. *Trollope: Artist and Moralist*. London: Chatto and Windus, 1971.

Smalley, Donald, ed. *Trollope: The Critical Heritage*. London: Routledge and Kegan Paul, 1969.

Times. 17 April 1886.

Times. 19 April 1886.

Trollope, Anthony. *Orley Farm*. Oxford: Oxford UP, 1985.

U.K. Public Records Office. *Adelaide Bartlett and George Dyson*. CRIM. 28 January 1997.

Wall, Stephen. *Trollope and Character*. London: Faber and Faber, 1988.

CHAPTER THIRTEEN

Fictive Tales, Real Lives:
Problems With Reading Law as Literature
by Patrick Colm Hogan

In literature, we deal habitually with fictions. We re-imagine them with students in isolated classrooms and, more solipsistically still, through essays for journals read, if at all, only by other academics. Human beings always have a tendency to separate speculation from real material life, to devise theories that break away from human activity and experience to exist in the rarefied air of the Idea. The concrete circumstances of literary study exacerbate this tendency. This is unfortunate enough when it is merely a matter of literature. Still, nobody dies or lives due to what we say about the signifier in Chaucer; nobody starves or is fed; nobody is locked in prison or set free. It is worse when extended to such politically and humanly consequential disciplines as law. As writers such as Robert Cover have suggested, this imperviousness to real consequence seems to be a particular danger of "reading law as literature," one of the main components in discussions of law and literature today (see chapter 5 of Cover; on reading law as literature, see Ward 15-22).

In the following pages, I should like to consider three problems with this common idea of reading law as literature, focusing particularly on the use of narrative study as a model for legal study, of understanding legal interpretation and adjudication as a form or function of storytelling. These problems suggest that the narrative analogy most often adds little to our understanding of law *per se*, and in many cases even impedes that understanding. Though I will draw on the work of several theorists of law and literature and touch on cases from a number of different writers, it is clearly impossible to discuss all of this material in sufficient detail. I will therefore focus particularly on Richard Delgado's highly influential essay, "Storytelling for Oppositionists and Others: A Plea for Narrative."

THEORIES AS INCITEMENTS TO REFLECTION AND AS RESEARCH PROJECTS

In practice, it may well be that the synthesis of law and literature has had salutary effects. Advocates of law and literature sometimes paint a picture of law schools as filled with unimaginative drones who somehow managed to believe that laws and legal decisions were the direct manifestation of an abstract and objective justice, and that all legal cases were decidable with the precision and certainty of mathematical proofs. In this view, law and literature, as well as Critical Legal Studies (CLS), woke at least some of the legally brain-dead from their dogmatic slumbers. One does not have to accept this rather extreme characterization of legal studies before law and literature (or CLS) to believe that the sudden influx of different texts and theories and methods served to make professors, lawyers, judges, more aware of some common and unquestioned assumptions in their work, challenging them to re-consider, criticize, re-formulate, or discard these assumptions.

But to grant that law and literature has done this is to say relatively little about the intrinsic value of law and literature. Almost any idea radically at odds with the status quo can serve to bring unquestioned assumptions to light, to challenge standard ways of thinking and acting. That is why it is important to foster such alternative views—in hiring, tenure and promotion, publication, etc. (a point to which I shall return in the final section). But this has no consequences whatsoever regarding our evaluation of the "challenging" idea *per se*. The fact that an idea leads us to re-think our beliefs says nothing about the intrinsic validity of that idea.

Suppose I discover a study comparing marriages determined by astrological charts with marriages determined by standard American methods of dating. Suppose further that, marriages of the former type turn out to be no less satisfactory to either party. A study of this sort would give me good reason to reflect on my assumptions about American dating practices as appropriate means for determining marriage. But this does not mean that it would give me any reason to accept astrology. I can assume that astrology is entirely baseless and still recognize that it serves to challenge common views about marriage and about the choice of marriage partners in the United States.

Put more technically, the fact that a given theory, practice, or whatever, has value in inciting reflection about standard ideas and practices tells us nothing about its potential value for initiating a research program (in, roughly, the Lakatosian sense). The fact that astrology might lead us to question our beliefs about courtship practices tells us nothing about whether it would be worthwhile to pursue a research program in astrology. To take an example from law, the existence of racist jurisprudence in Vichy has led Richard Weisberg to valuable insights about communal standards in legal interpretation. But no one would say that this shows anything valuable about racist jurisprudence or that it serves as an appropriate initiator of a research program.

My general contention in the following sections, then, is that, while the pairing of law and literature in general, and the invocation of law as narrative in particular, may well—probably does—have value for inciting reflection, it has not thus far demonstrated that it has value for initiating a research program, except in very limited areas, primarily those extending rhetorical analysis through the use of narratological concepts. I do not eliminate the possibility that law and literature will in the future give rise to theoretical achievements that merit pursuit in a research program. But, at present, that is only a possibility. Moreover, treating it as more than a possibility has deleterious effects, for it turns our attention away from other areas of theory and practice that are just as likely to provoke reflection or self-criticism, and far more likely to prove fruitful in initiating research programs—especially areas, such as cognitive science, that are widely viewed as incompatible with a literary and narrative orientation.

ROMANTICISM AND FORMALIST POLITICS

The first problem I should like to consider follows directly from this last point. There is a broad Romantic tendency implicit in literary study today that is likely to be extended to any project reading law as literature. Indeed, this tendency is particularly apparent in the most widely celebrated literary theories (such as Deconstruction), and it has been incorporated into the mainstream of law and literature as well—the tendency to divide all human thought and action into two categories, one good (ethically admirable, politically progressive), the other evil (ethically reprehensible, politically reactionary). The evil category is mechanistic, rational, scientific, robotic, unfeeling, objective, static, hierarchical. The good category is organic, imaginative, artistic, human, emotive, personal, dynamic, disruptive of hierarchies. This division pervades Romantic thought, as can be seen in the writings of Schiller, Coleridge, Wordsworth, Shelley, and others. More significantly, most post-Romantic theories that have appealed to students of literature are founded upon some variant of this division. In Nietzsche, it becomes the Socratic and the Dionysian. (The Apollonian is a complication of the model.) In Bakhtin, it is the monological and the dialogical. In Derrida, it is the logocentric and the deconstructive. In different versions of legal theory, it becomes intentionalism and indeterminacy, or "linear, coercive discourse" and "storytelling," as Delgado puts it (2415). There would be nothing wrong with operating within this division, if it were at all accurate. But it is not. And it is inaccurate at two levels. First of all, it is mistaken in presuming that these widely different properties cluster together into two opposed groups. For instance, science and art are *both* logical and imaginative, *both* creative and mechanistic. The objective is not opposed to the personal, but to the biased—which may be personal (as when someone favors relatives) or impersonal (as when someone hates unknown members of another ethnic group). Moreover, bias is, in principle, eschewed by both scientists and artists. Indeed, as a conceptual division, this Romantic dichotomy is so faulty that its longevity is difficult to understand. In part, it lasts because it simplifies difficult ethico-political dilemmas. Most real-world political situations are messy. I believe that the U.S. bombings during the Gulf War were inexcusable war crimes, and I actively opposed the war. But this was a real political issue and involved real people, with no good guys. In opposing the war, I left myself open to the accusation of supporting Iraq's invasion of Kuwait, or Saddam Hussein's rule more generally, of being insensitive to the history of the Jewish people and the consequent security needs of Israel, etc. One reason for the appeal of the great Romantic division is that it allows us to be political, to take an ethical stance, upon the basis of purely formal criteria. This formalism allows us to evaluate politics based on such issues as whether it is narratively based or logically based. It frees us from the messiness of real-world issues, where moral conflicts arise at almost every step.

This brings us to the second problem with the Romantic dichotomy. The political associations assigned to these properties are no more plausible than the clustering of the properties. Neither science nor art has, as a discipline, an intrinsic morality (or immorality). If one's aim is to kill a lot of people, then scientific pursuit of this goal is indeed bad. But if one's aim is to find a cure for AIDS, then it is not so bad. Conversely, consider the claim of Martha Nussbaum that "the genre [of the novel] itself, on account of some general features of its structure, generally constructs empathy and compassion in ways highly relevant to citizenship" (10; cf. O'Donovan and West) or Richard Delgado's assertion that "Stories humanize us," a common view in law and literature studies. It probably is the case that any sort of imbalance in education and experience limits our thought and feeling in humanly consequential ways. Thus, someone who spends all his/her time in a laboratory or a court may indeed benefit from reading literature; it may have a humanizing effect. (See also Friedrichs 58 for a related, though more limited, claim regarding students' conception of law.) But does it have a humanizing effect as literature *per se*, rather than as one manifestation of human spirit, important in contexts of imbalance (after all, lots of things might have a humanizing effect, in an appropriate context, as van Roermund has noted [8])?

One would have thought that claims about the humanizing effects of literature would have been put to rest long ago, at the very least following the Holocaust. As George Steiner has noted, "Not only did the general dissemination of literary, cultural values prove no barrier to totalitarianism; but in notable instances the high places of humanistic learning and art actually welcomed and aided the new terror. . . . We know that some of the men who devised and administered Auschwitz had been taught to read Shakespeare or Goethe, and continued to do so" (5). Indeed, Steiner wonders if the development of literary empathy might have an *inhibitory* effect on empathy in the real world (5)—precisely the contrary of Nussbaum's claim (or O'Donovan's or West's). This may be too extreme a judgment. But it seems clear that, in any case, empathy is not a good in and of itself. Everyone has empathy. Hitler had empathy. Goebels had empathy. Indeed, all Nazis had empathy—for "Aryans." The problem is that, for rather too many people, empathy appears to be a function of one's group identifications (see Duckitt 83). To take a current example, opponents of affirmative action have empathy for the "victims" of reverse discrimination. This victimage is largely imaginary—whereas discrimination against minorities is largely real. But that only re-inforces the main point—that empathy *per se* is, like science or art, morally neutral.

In addition to these problems with art and empathy, numerous Marxist analysis have explored class ideology in a wide range of literary works, feminist critics have explored sexism, and post-colonial writers have examined colonialism in that literature. Perhaps writing that involves misogyny, racism, and class bias, writing that appears to co-exist quite easily with worst sorts of brutality, writing that may or may not foster empathy—empathy which, in any case, is likely to be empathy with one's "own kind"—perhaps such writing is intrinsically humanizing, due to "some general features of its structure." But this hardly seems likely.

Of course, many writers recognize and accept all this, including many writers in law and literature. Indeed, I imagine that almost all of them, and almost all the literary theorists on whom they rely, would reject the Romantic dichotomy, admitting many of the objections raised above. But the problem with this dichotomy is not that it operates as what might be called an "assent belief," a belief with which one would concur if asked. Rather, it operates as a structure of thought, a presupposition of argument and analysis, even when it is explicitly denied.

Consider Delgado's essay. It treats several different accounts or "stories" about why a particular minority candidate was not hired at a major law school. We will discuss the substance of the essay in the following sections. Here I merely wish to note Delgado's characterization of storytelling as such. Delgado acknowledges that storytelling is not a good in and of itself. On the second page of his article, he states that "The dominant group creates its own stories" (2412), the implication being that, in this case, the stories are oppressive, not liberatory. Moreover, the fact that the entire article treats stories about the minority candidate's non-hiring—at least one of which is complicit with racism—would seem to suggest a rejection of a Romantic and formalist politics of storytelling.

But Delgado continually slips into the Romantic view. In the first paragraph, he clearly comes out in favor of those who have rebelled against mechanical conventions of legal writing and "have been daring to become more personal," to express "feeling," to use "narrative" (2411). Having thus established that he is on the "human" side of the Romantic division, he goes on to express the formalist politics of that division, insisting that "Many . . . who have been telling legal stories are members of what could be loosely described as outgroups, groups whose marginality defines the boundaries of the mainstream, whose voice and perspective—whose consciousness—has been suppressed, devalued, and abnormalized" (2412). He does qualify the "many" by adding "but by no means all," but the qualification does not appear to affect his argument or presuppositions. Stories told by the dominant groups are tacitly treated as exceptions to the generally progressive thrust of storytelling. In standard Romantic fashion, Delgado presents stories as "subvert[ing]" the dominant order (2413) and providing a "powerful means for destroying mindset" (2413). Indeed, he goes so far as to assert that society is pervaded by hierarchy and "oppression" and "The cure is storytelling" (2414; parenthetically, Delgado adds, "or as I shall sometimes call it, counter-storytelling," thereby again acknowledging that it is not storytelling *per se* that is progressive—an acknowledgment he, again, immediately sets aside). Delgado goes on to say that "stories . . . can show that what we believe is ridiculous, self-serving, or cruel" and that they "offer a respite from the linear, coercive discourse that characterizes much legal writing" (2415). The Romantic division is almost explicit in this final opposition.

But, again, even by Delgado's own principles, stories are just as likely to lead us to believe "ridiculous, self-serving, or cruel" things as to undermine such beliefs. In Delgado's essay, the account of relevant events given by the radical and—I agree entirely with Delgado here—largely correct Al-Hammar is vastly superior to Professor Vernier's (racist) account. But it is not superior because one is narrative and the other is something else. What Vernier does is as much a matter of storytelling as what Al-Hammar does. Indeed, insofar as we are concerned with storytelling *per se*, as opposed to empirical investigation, then Vernier is more the storyteller, because his account is less involved with or constrained by the facts. It is purer fabulation, less bound up with "linear, coercive discourse." In this way, Vernier's case should serve to show that a stress on storytelling is more likely to do harm than good, insofar as it is separated from (or, worse still, opposed to) a stress on the empirical determination of facts and on explanatory rigor and plausibility, a stress on storytelling is more likely to do harm than good. (Coughlin makes a similar point, referring, in this case, to the subjective impressions on which personal narratives are often based, rather than to the narratives themselves; see 1279.)

Indeed, the possible harm of storytelling should be particularly obvious with respect to racism. As Teun van Dijk has pointed out, personal anecdotes—precisely the sort of storytelling celebrated by Delgado—are particularly common in white racist speech (157). White racists repeatedly rely on stories about brilliant white men who got cheated out of jobs because of some third-rate black woman or about a black "welfare queen" who drove around in her Cadillac to collect fifteen welfare checks. Storytelling—creative, organic, etc., and deeply opposed to scientific rationality—is absolutely central to maintaining and furthering racist belief.

Finally, if any sort of discourse is "coercive," it is not logical and empirical argument (presumably what Delgado means by "linear"), which proceeds from premises to conclusions on the basis of standard inferential principles and statistically significant evidence. One can always respond to such an argument, by pointing out inferential errors, by introducing contravening evidence, by challenging premises. To take Delgado's own example, it is only through a range of empirical and logical studies (e.g., those on in-group/out-group bias, to which we will return below) that we can defend Al-Hammar's view against Vernier's. Indeed, we particularly require such studies in this case *because Vernier is storytelling*. In this way, Delgado has it exactly backwards. The one truly coercive discourse is, precisely, the sort of personal storytelling that Delgado characterizes as a "respite from . . . linear, coercive discourse" (2415). All such stories, including the anecdotes that circulate in racist discourse, are undisputable. Whether the speaker is a white man who is in no sense a genuine victim or a black woman who has suffered genuine brutality at the hands of white racists, the personal story is absolutely coercive: You cannot respond; you were not there; you do not feel my pain.

It is true that, when faced with a racist personal story, a good response, perhaps the only response, is another personal story that opposes that racism. Personal stories have their value and Delgado is right to emphasize that. But they are not intrinsically valuable simply because they are personal stories. The Romantic presuppositions that underlie such a view are mistaken, and thus are likely to distort our understanding of law, our theorization of legal principles, our interpretation of legal texts, our adjudication of legal issues.

THE MEANING OF "NARRATIVE"

This disagreement over the formal politics of storytelling leads to, and in some ways derives from, a second problem. Part of the reason Delgado can make claims for the political value of narrative is that he has never said precisely what he means by "narrative." Moreover, Delgado is not alone in this. One of the most common themes in law and literature is the putative "narrative construction" of legal meaning. But theorists who put forth this claim rarely define the term "narrative" in such a way as to prevent the claim from being vacuous.

Consider, for example, Robert Cover. He repeatedly insists that law is enmeshed in "narratives that locate it and give it meaning" (95-96). And he argues that law is "not merely a system of rules to be observed, but a world in which we live," a world structured by "narratives" (96). But it is never clear what exactly he has in mind. In these particular instances, he seems to be speaking of some sort of grand narratives of national history or social life. But what might those narratives be? For example, what are these narratives in the U.S. today? One might conceive of the common view of the American revolution in these terms—a story in which freedom-loving colonials rebel against imperial despotism. But it is hard to see how this sort of narrative works its way into legal decisions. Of course, one might claim that this story embodies a principle—the principle of preserving individual freedom—and that this principle has an important judicial function. But, insofar as this is true, it is the principle, not the story that has that function. One can imagine an argument that principles embedded in narratives have greater saliency or greater emotional force and thus have greater effect on judicial decisions, or that narratives inflect the uses of principles in particular ways. But Cover has not made any such argument.

Cover does give some examples of his own. But these do not really clarify the matter. For instance, he quotes the following passage from Chief Justice Burger's judgment in the Bob Jones University case: "it cannot be said that educational institutions that . . . practice racial discrimination, are institutions exercising 'beneficial and stabilizing influences in community life' . . . or should be encouraged by having all tax payers share in their support by way of special tax status." This seems a fairly straightforward instance of evaluation by reference to principles (e.g., that concerning "beneficial and stabilizing influences in community life"). There is no obvious narrative involved. But Cover considers the judgment to be based on "a narrative of redemption" (169). Perhaps it is—but in what way? And, with what consequences for our understanding of the case or of judicial decisions more generally? (The preceding two paragraphs are drawn from my "Review.")

Delgado's essay suffers from much the same vagueness, for he too never clarifies precisely what he intends by "narrative." This absence of definition is particularly striking when one considers Delgado's essay in conjunction with the Cover's work. For, while Cover seems to have in mind first of all the sort of "master narratives" discussed by, say, Lyotard (see also Papke, "Discharge" 207-08), Delgado first of all has in mind something individual, experiential, as we have already seen. Indeed, Delgado appears to use "narrative" at least in part to refer to simple personal testimony. Moreover, his argument does suggest the importance of greater diversity of testimony, especially testimony of oppressed people. But, again, Delgado does not discuss law, politics, oppression in terms of diversity in personal testimony—a valuable, if necessarily limited approach. Rather, he treats it in terms of storytelling versus "linear, coercive discourse." (In a later essay, Delgado takes up something more like "master narratives" in his discussion of "dominant stories" ["Shadowboxing" 818]. Interestingly, this does not affect his tacit Romanticism, for he tends to associate oppression with abstract and common stories—despite the fact that these are as often liberatory as oppressive—treating personal anecdotes as liberatory. Thus the politics remain romantic and formal.)

As already mentioned, Delgado centers his essay on a case in which a black candidate, John Henry, is rejected after interviewing for a position at a major law school. Delgado gives us four versions of the events. For instance, one is "the stock story" presented by Professor Blas Vernier. Delgado does an excellent job re-creating the smug tone, the mendacious arguments, the moral evasions of a secure white professor defending the rejection of yet another minority candidate. Vernier insists that he cannot give the full arguments against Henry because of "confidentiality" (2420)—a standard excuse for concealing bias in hiring, tenure, and promotion decisions regarding women and minorities—but he can say that Henry "didn't measure up" (2419). He explains how "there is nothing that would please me more" than hiring a qualified minority (2421), but we must retain our standards. (I will not outline the other versions, but they are equally well-crafted and plausible. The entire presentation is of great illustrative value, and demonstrates Delgado's sensitivity to and knowledge of the insidious racism of hiring decisions.)

One of the first questions that might arise in this context is—why are these versions of events, these alternative explanations for the negative hiring decision, most importantly construed as "stories"? What narrative characteristics do they have? And what are the consequences of this? It is true that, in a general sense of the word, they are stories, for they purport to include a causal account of human action. They say—the members of the hiring committee acted this way, because they thought these things. But, at that level, it is inconsequential to call these versions "narratives." It is to say only that they are putative explanations—which is precisely how they are understood in the jurisprudence Delgado is opposing. The only obvious difference here is that the word "explanation" is unlikely to carry romantic and political formalist presuppositions.

Delgado does say that each version "picks and chooses from among the available facts to present a picture of what happened" (2421). This is a widely remarked property of storytelling and thus may provide one reason for Delgado's characterization of these versions as "narratives." We will return to the issue of selectivity in the next section, but here we need only remark that selectivity characterizes all causal accounts, whether we would ordinarily consider these to be stories or not. Indeed, to a great extent, scientific research is a matter of determining, not only causal sequences, but the proper descriptions for understanding these sequences. Clearly, then, selectivity does not distinguish these accounts as narrative in any consequential way.

Before turning to the third, and most encompassing, problem with law and literature, we might ask whether there is anything that can be done to avoid the vacuity of the concept of narrative as applied to law and make such application fruitful. The current vogue of applying narrative theory to other disciplines appears to have begun with Hayden White's *Metahistory*, in which White put forth the view that historiography is a form of emplotment. Whether valid or invalid, White's claims were not perniciously vague. He drew on specific ideas of tragedy and comedy and argued that historians take up particular patterns to shape their histories. In other words, when they examine the complex of individual and collective actions and passions that tumble together to make an historical event, they begin to organize those events according to standard narrative structures, inferring causal connections, overall evaluations, implications for future political action, on the basis of those narrative structures.

In principle, a similar idea could be applied to law. Of course, it might turn out to be false. Perhaps this sort of thing is not terribly important in law. But it seems likely that it has at least some importance. We could think about it this way. Each of us learns how to tell stories, not only by learning the very general structures of storytelling (causal sequence involving human agency, etc.), but by learning a series of more specific structures governing narrative organization, character typology, etc. For example, we are likely to have internalized tragedy and comedy as two "basic" genres. In tragedy, we may have internalized the Aristotelian notion of a tragic hero who is better than most of us, but marred by a single flaw. We may have a series of other narrative and character schemas that serve to guide our storytelling. Thus, when recounting, say, life experiences, we may spontaneously reformulate those experiences to fit standard plot and character types.

The question then would be—to what extent are legal narratives shaped by these sorts of internalized schemas? To what extent do judges or juries structure causal accounts of the events of a case in accordance with character typologies, genre conventions, etc.? To what extent do judges and juries reach conclusions about guilt or innocence based, not on principles of law and the evidence of the case, but on an assimilation of that evidence, a re-organization of that evidence according to stereotyped plot structures or standard character prototypes?

Advocates of narrative jurisprudence do not seem to have undertaken this sort of study in general. However, Robin West has considered legal theories in this way, arguing that they embody particular narrative structures, specifically, the narrative structures isolated by Northrop Frye in his "theory of myths" (see chapter 8 of West). West's thesis here is not at all trivial. She takes up details of narrative structure in a way that is substantive and consequential and, in that respect, can serve as a model for the sort of narrativist analysis that could in principle be valuable in legal study. Unfortunately, West's specific analysis is not, in my view, convincing. In fact, despite her admirable attempt to focus on narrative specifics, the actual connections she draws between Frye's myths and legal theories are very general. In consequence, her work ultimately suffers from much the same faults as other narrativist analysis in law. Frye's typology of myths necessarily instantiates more general typological oppositions, such as idealism vs. materialism or religious devotion vs. secularism. When West finds links with legal theories, they are almost invariably links only at this more general level—a level at which the specificity of narrative is lost.

In sum, a more highly specified concept of narrative could possibly lead to a worthwhile research program in law and literature. But, thus far, influential discussions of "narrative jurisprudence" have suffered from pernicious vagueness. Moreover, they have most often been put forth in the context of Romantic presuppositions that are likely to discourage the rigorous analysis required for this approach, and the systematic empirical research which such an approach presupposes (e.g., research in cognitive psychology treating our internal schemas, the operation of these schemas in perception, interpretation, and explanation, etc.).

TELLING FICTIONS, CONSTRUING FACTS

This point about empirical research leads us to the final, and most significant problem with reading law as literature. We might refer to this as the problem of reference and selection principles. Legal adjudication is largely a matter of determining factual plausibility and the relevance of (factually plausible) specifics to governing laws. There is no clear parallel to either practice in literary study in general or storytelling and narratology in particular.

Before going on to elaborate this point, I should perhaps immediately respond to the idea that this statement presupposes a sort of realism that has been discredited since we all realized that reality is socially constructed. I do not wish to discuss this issue at length, primarily because no one really believes that reality is socially constructed in any significant sense. Delgado asserts that "We participate in creating what we see in the very act of describing it" (2416), but he does not for a moment believe we create Henry's not getting the job by saying that he didn't get the job, that Vernier creates a non-racist law school by saying that his school is non-racist, etc. Indeed, elsewhere in the same essay, Delgado objects to Vernier for considering certain things to be "'facts' without examining their truth" (2421-22). For this reason, the thesis does not merit detailed refutation.

Rather than showing where it is false, then, let me point out what is true in this "constructivist" view: it is true that the categories in which we discuss the world are social categories. They could have been different. ("Socially constructed" is, in these cases, simply an obscure way of saying "social.") This is an important and consequential point, especially in relation to legal study. For in law, the categories through which we define proscribed behavior should be open to debate. It is important to recognize that, say, "murder," as used in the U.S. penal code, is not an unalterable essence. We decide what counts as murder. Typically, we have decided that it is street crime, a particular type of "causing to die" that is most often committed by the poor. By our decision, murder does not, most often, encompass the more devastating array of industrial crimes, the "causing to die" committed by the rich against the poor. (Mokhiber notes that, according to government estimates, there are about 24,000 street homicides each year, but about 56,000 job-related deaths [14].)

Again, this is an extremely important point. But, as far as I can tell, has nothing to do with literature in general or narrative in particular. Nor is it appropriately referred to as "creating what we see in the very act of describing it" (2416). As Donald Davidson has argued, even if our concepts are not immutable or absolute, that does not in any way affect the truth or falsity of our claims. "Snow is white" is as absolutely true as anyone could wish, despite the fact that we could have divided the color spectrum differently. For, given the way the color spectrum is divided, snow is, in fact, white. This is not a fact that we have in any way "created."

And that returns us to the issues of factual plausibility and the completeness of descriptive and explanatory accounts relative to governing laws. Again, there is no parallel for this in literature, or in narrative *per se*. But these are absolutely crucial to any legal adjudication. Moreover, advocacy of storytelling draws our attention away from this crucial issue, especially when that advocacy is based on Romantic presuppositions which tacitly set narrative in opposition to empirical study.

Consider, again, Delgado and Vernier. As we noted above, Delgado does not give any clear indication as to why Vernier's discussion of Henry's non-hiring should be considered in terms of narrative rather than in terms of explanatory plausibility. As a causal account, Vernier's statements set out the reasons for the hiring committee's actions. Once we think of this account in terms of storytelling, we are likely to look at narratology and related disciplines for help in understanding and evaluating Vernier's discussion. This is not entirely irrelevant. Most obviously, it may have some bearing on the rhetorical effectiveness or ineffectiveness of Vernier's version of events. But narratology cannot deal with the issues of greatest consequence—which concern precisely facts about human actions and the causes of or reasons for those actions, facts and actions and reasons that are not in any way "created" by those stories.

It seems likely that this focus on narrative, and the associated ignoring of explanatory issues relating to cognition, etc., explain why Delgado's response to Vernier is so timid. Delgado notes that Vernier's story "emphasizes the school's benevolent motivation . . . and good faith" and "it purports to be scrupulously meritocratic and fair." Here, the most obvious objection to Vernier's account, considered as a causal explanation, is that it is false or implausible, that the facts or explanations are other than those asserted by Vernier, that the evaluation was *not* scrupulously meritocratic and fair. But Delgado's major objection to Vernier is not that Vernier is, in all likelihood, violating his own avowed principles. Rather, his objection is that "the merit criteria employed in judging Henry are themselves debatable, *chosen*—not inevitable" (2421). The implication seems to be that Delgado accepts the committee's judgments relative to that committee's own criteria, though he questions the inevitability of the criteria. In and of itself, there is nothing wrong in this. If Vernier's criterion were "being white," then, yes, the problem would be the criterion. But Vernier objected that Henry was "vague and diffuse about his research interests" and "had nothing new to say" about the areas in which he wished to work. Thus precision, clarity, and new insight constitute the explicit criteria. Delgado implicitly accepts the claims that Henry lacked precision, clarity, and new insight. He objects only that these criteria are not "inevitable." If I were Henry, I suspect I would be repeating the adage, "With friends like this . . . ."

The problem here seems to be that Delgado is indeed following his own principles and thinking of what Vernier says as a story—to which we might respond only by offering other stories, with different (here unspecified) criteria. But, suppose that, instead, we think of it as an explanatory and justificatory account of an evaluation. This leads us to at least two issues. The first is the validity of the evaluation in this particular case. One crucial element of evaluative validity in any particular case is consistency. Something is a criterion of evaluation only if it is employed consistently across cases. So, in this instance, we might ask to what extent the rest of the law faculty at this university can reasonably be said to have new ideas about their areas of expertise. Moreover, we might ask what counts as new—for "novelty" is as perniciously vague in Vernier's usage as "narrative" is in Delgado's. And, in cases such as this, vagueness allows latitude for bias. More concretely, we might ask to what extent is novelty actually invoked in evaluating other faculty—is it a standard evaluative criterion, or has it been invoked unusually in this case? For example, does it routinely enter into determinations of merit pay?

The second issue to arise when we consider Vernier's account not as a story (open to narratological analysis), but as an explanatory and justificatory account of actual events, concerns the general validity of evaluations of this sort, the problems with and possibilities for any such account: How valid are such evaluations, on the whole? In fact, there is massive evidence that almost all evaluations of this type are grossly biased. It would require another essay to overview all the relevant work (for a summary of some of this research, see my "Teaching" and "Ethics"). However, two points can serve to illustrate.

The first point concerns the specific criteria invoked by Vernier—novelty, precision, and clarity. Do we, in fact, generally prize work that has something "new to say"? In fact, we do not do this at all. Research in the evaluation of work for publication in academic outlets indicates clearly that conformity to standard disciplinary doctrine, which is to say, lack of novelty, is one of the most important positive factors in predicting publication. In a famous study, Michael Mahoney ("Publication") took a research article and switched the data tables, revising the conclusion to fit the reversed data. In one version, the data strongly confirmed standard disciplinary views. In the other version, the data strongly disconfirmed such views. Clearly, the second version was the "new" version, the one that brought fresh ideas, the one that was more intellectually valuable, because it did not simply repeat what was already known. But this second version was far less likely to be published than the first version. Unless Professor Vernier was radically different from most of his fellow academics, then his objection to Henry's originality was almost certainly irrelevant and part of an implicit double standard. In keeping with this, other empirical research indicates that opacity too is a positive factor in predicting academic publication (see Mahoney "Open," summarizing research by Armstrong). Thus the objections to Henry as "vague and diffuse" were almost certainly irrelevant and part of an implicit double standard as well.

So, why then did Vernier and the others reject Henry? If it was not a matter of his vagueness and lack of originality—points which would ordinarily count in his favor, given actually prevailing academic practices—what was it? The second body of research I should like to consider concerns in-group/out-group relations. Once an in-group/out-group division is created, members of one group systematically evaluate other members of their own group more favorably than members of the other group (see Duckitt 68, 81). Note that this is true even in "minimal" groups, groups defined by some trivial factor, such as whether the fifth digit of one's social security number is odd or even (Duckitt 83, Hirschfeld 1). In other words, if people are asked to divide into groups according to this criterion, they will consistently evaluate members of their own group as more intelligent, friendly, etc., than members of the other group (Duckitt 69). And they do this evidently without any sense that they are favoring their own group. The situation only becomes worse as the group division becomes more salient (Duckitt 69, Hirschfeld 24). Race is obviously one of the most salient differentiae of groups in America today. In Henry's case, the regular teaching faculty of this law school was entirely white, except for one untenured Asian professor (Delgado, "Storytelling" 2419). Given general human cognitive tendencies, it would be bizarre if in-group/out-group biases did not assert themselves and lead to strongly unfavorable evaluations of Henry, evaluations which were then justified by an appeal to supposedly standard criteria.

In sum, if Delgado had thought of the situation in terms of explanatory accounts and justificatory principles and practices, rather than as a matter of rival stories, he may have been led to question, not the stated criteria, but the evaluative process as a whole. He may have been led to research that allows us to see how this probably was a racist hiring decision—racist because the precision, rigor, and insight of blacks are commonly overlooked by whites, not because we need to establish another standard for blacks, who are, by implication, imprecise, lax, and dull.

A similar point could be made about Richard Weisberg's analysis of two judicial opinions by Benjamin Cardozo. Weisberg does an excellent job of drawing out the rhetorical differences between the two opinions. As Weisberg points out, in one opinion, Cardozo personalizes the plaintiff, as "a lad of 16" (18). He develops the situation with considerable human sympathy, and concludes in the plaintiff's favor. In the second case, there is no such personalization. The woman in question "is referred to throughout by the impersonal term 'plaintiff'" (18). Unsurprisingly, Cardozo finds against this woman. Weisberg analyzes the rhetoric of these opinions in an illuminating manner and thereby shows that "reading law as literature" has value in rhetorical analysis. (The general point is fairly widely accepted; see, for example, chapter 6 of Posner. Other work demonstrating this value would include that of O'Barr and Conley, Maynard, and, especially, Goodwin.) Nonetheless, it is difficult to say just what this analysis demonstrates. Rhetorical analysis on its own does not seem to tell us much of legal importance. Perhaps Cardozo made up his mind about the case, then adopted a style that fit the conclusion. Indeed, this rather inconsequential point seems to be implied by Weisberg's analysis.

But drawing on the research in evaluation just discussed, one worries that the precise opposite might be the case. One worries that Cardozo was able to empathize with the boy as a member of his (gender-based) in-group, but not with the woman, and that this important in-group/out-group division affected both the style of his opinions and, more importantly, the decisions themselves. This, the most crucial consideration, is entirely absent from a narratively focused analysis. Indeed, it is, once again, likely to be occluded by an advocacy of narrative, if that advocacy is based on the romantic dichotomy discussed above.

In conclusion, I should like to consider one particular legal case in relation to these issues—*Regents of the University of California v. Bakke* (438 U.S. 265, 98 S. Ct. 2733, 57 L.Ed.2d 750 [1978]). I choose this case for two reasons. First of all, as an historically important decision on affirmative action, it has direct bearing on current issues of great consequence. Second, it was mythologized almost immediately and established as a prototypical case of "reverse discrimination." In connection with the latter point, one could say that the case defined a "narrative" of "reverse discrimination," a narrative that goes something like this: A good, hard-working white man with excellent qualifications—high grades, high test scores, etc.—was cheated out of a place in medical school, because he is white, and his spot was given to an underqualified minority. Moreover, this way of speaking (in terms of narrative) makes some sense here. This is indeed a sort of "story line" and the Bakke case was an early, influential instance of that sort of tale telling. Indeed, this even involves a lone hero (the white man), who has been tragically excluded from his rightful place in society (the U.C./Davis Medical School) by a nemesis (the minority) and is battling an unjust system (affirmative action). Thus it is narrative in a non-trivial sense. (Though, of course, it does not at all conform to the Romantic political formalism discussed above.)

But does speaking of the case in terms of narrative aid our understanding of what happened in the case, what it meant, what its consequences were? Does it highlight what should be criticized or investigated or accepted or thought through in the case? Does it provide us with a valuable way of considering and understanding the case—intellectually, politically, or in any other way? I think not. Once again, we need to understand this "narrative" as an explanatory account, referring to specific and real events, an account that must be evaluated relative to those factual events, to more general principles of explanatory plausibility, and to governing legal principles.

The Bakke case concerned admissions to the Medical School of the University of California at Davis. Bakke sued the university, claiming that he was denied admission unfairly because 16 of the 100 entering slots were reserved for minorities and the average test scores, grades, etc., of the minorities were well below Bakke's. In fact, Bakke was right about his test scores and those of minority admittees. What is most striking to me about the case, however, is the way in which the entire debate surrounded these minority spaces. Though it is a matter of selection, this narrowing of relevance and causal analysis is not highlighted or clarified by reading the case as literature— because the problem with the selectivity in this case has to do not with narrative *per se*, but with real causal sequences and with governing laws, which is to say, precisely what is missing in the literary/narratological model. Specifically, if we consider the facts of the case, we find that, in 1974, Bakke's qualifications were not only much higher than those of entering minority students; they were also substantially higher than those of entering *white* students. More exactly, his qualifications were superior to at least 42 *regular* admittees, but he sued the university on the grounds that his qualifications were superior to those of, at most, 16 *minority* admittees.

Bakke's rejection by the Davis Medical School appears, in fact, to have been a matter of ideological disagreement with the chairman of the admissions committee—specifically, a disagreement over affirmative action. Indeed, it seems to have been a case for the ACLU, and a case with considerable merit from that perspective. Though I disagree with Bakke's views on affirmative action, he should not suffer disability in employment or education because of his political beliefs. That appears to be precisely what happened. However, what is crucial here is that he did not see the problem in terms of freedom of political expression, but in terms of race. He did not respond by urging freedom of speech, but by demanding that something be taken away from non-white people. If anything, this case shows the great need for affirmative action programs. Roughly three times as many white students as non-white students were "underqualified" relative to Bakke, but only the non-white students were viewed as "taking" Bakke's spot. It is precisely this continuing double standard that makes affirmative action programs necessary. And we cannot discover this by "reading the case as a literary text." We can discover this only by taking into account whatever evidence we have about the real world.

CONCLUSION: RESEARCH PROGRAM EVALUATION VS. INSTITUTIONAL EVALUATION

In the preceding pages, I have suggested some ways in which the study of law and literature in general, and law and narrative in particular, could have positive value, primarily in the area of rhetorical analysis. Moreover, I have noted that both projects are likely to have salutary effects in challenging previously unquestioned assumptions in legal theory and practice. Nonetheless, it should be clear that, in my view, these possible benefits are few and limited. I do not see a great deal of promise for an extensive development of this field in an autonomous research program. Indeed, so long as law and literature studies develop tacitly within the context of Romantic presuppositions and formalist politics, they are likely to do more harm than good, diverting attention from other, far more promising areas of research, which happen not to fall on the correct side of the Romantic dichotomy.

However, having said all that, I should conclude by stressing that none of this has any institutional consequences whatsoever. Just as I have distinguished theories as incitements to reflection from theories as initiators of research programs, I should like to distinguish two very different sorts of evaluation—evaluation relative to research programs and evaluation relative to the rewards and punishments distributed by institutions. Evaluation relative to research programs should, most often, be rigorously critical. Though I would not go so far as Karl Popper, advocating an evaluative practice oriented entirely toward falsification, it seems clear that a central part of any evaluative response to an active or potential research program is an analysis of its flaws. This is the sort of evaluation I have undertaken in the preceding pages.

It is obvious that, in my evaluation of law and literature as a research program, I share certain views with prominent critics of narrative jurisprudence, such as Farber and Sherry. (Though even here I should note that I disagree with some of their specific points—for example, they significantly misrepresent Patricia Williams's work, which is, in my view, sensitive, insightful, and illuminating, with respect to law, human life, and the pervasive racism of this country.) However, Farber and Sherry evidently wish to extend their evaluation to such areas as hiring, tenure and promotion, publication, etc. Put differently, they implicitly identify research program evaluation with institutional evaluation. I strongly disagree with this identification.

It would take too long to go into the details. But, simply put, my view is that institutional evaluation has to be almost the precise opposite of research program evaluation. If the latter emphasizes the negative, the former must emphasize the positive. More precisely, in publication, in hiring, tenure, and promotion, in all institutional structures and outlets, it is both intellectually crucial and politically just to foster a range of theoretical approaches, a range of ways in which problems can be formulated and considered—prominently including those professional approaches which we ourselves might find entirely unpromising as research programs.

I say that such systematic institutional pluralism is intellectually crucial for a million reasons. It is necessary to have a range of views in order to stimulate criticism and development of even the best theories. I say it is politically just because, however well-formulated our arguments, they are likely to express certain types of prejudice, certain biases that, collectively, are likely to harm minorities (not only racial minorities, but intellectual minorities—"heretics"—as well), to deprive them of social goods in unjust ways. (For fuller discussion, see my "Ethics.")

In short, I believe that law and literature is highly problematic as a research program. But even those of us who feel this way should welcome its appearance as a critical challenge to entrenched doctrines—themselves often no less problematic as research programs. Moreover, we must welcome this new, challenging work, not only in the profession at large, but in journals and curricula and law faculties as well.

WORKS CITED

Coughlin, Anne M. "Regulating the Self: Autobiographical Performances in Outsider Scholarship." *Virginia Law Review* 45 (1993): 807-55.

Cover, Robert. *Narrative, Violence, and the Law: The Essays of Robert Cover.* Ed., Martha Minow, Michael Ryan, and Austin Sarat. Ann Arbor: U of Michigan P, 1995.

Davidson, Donald. "On the Very Idea of a Conceptual Scheme." *Inquiries Into Truth and Interpretation.* Oxford: Oxford UP, 1984.

Delgado, Richard. "Shadowboxing: An Essay on Power." *Cornell Law Review* 77 (1992): 813-24.

———. "Storytelling for Oppositionists and Others: A Plea for Narrative." *Michigan Law Review* 87 (1989): 2411-441.

Duckitt, John. *The Social Psychology of Prejudice.* New York: Praeger, 1992.

Farber, Daniel A., and Suzanna Sherry. "Telling Stories Out of School: An Essay on Legal Narratives." *Stanford Law Review* 45 (1993): 807-55.

Friedrichs, David O. "Narrative Jurisprudence and Other Heresies: Legal Education at the Margin." *Narrative and the Legal Discourse: A Reader in Storytelling and the Law.* Ed. David Ray Papke. Liverpool, UK: Deborah Charles, 1991.

Goodwin, Jill Thomasson. "Trial Advocacy Handbooks: Narratology and Opening Statements." *Mosaic* 27 (1994): 215-30.

Hirschfeld, Lawrence A. *Race in the Making: Cognition, Culture, and the Child's Construction of Human Kinds.* Cambridge: MIT P, 1996.

Hogan, Patrick Colm. "The Ethics of Tenure Decisions." *Higher Education Review* 30.3 (1998): 23-41.

———. *On Interpretation: Meaning and Inference in Law, Psychoanalysis, and Literature.* Athens: U of Georgia P, 1996.

———. Rev. of *Narrative, Violence, and the Law: The Essays of Robert Cover,* ed. Martha Minow, Michael Ryan, and Austin Sarat, and *Law's Violence,* ed. Austin Sarat and Thomas Kearns. *Arachne* 19.1 (1997): 117-28.

———. "Teaching and Research as Economic Problems." *Education and Society* 11.1 (1993): 15-25.

Lakatos, Imre. "Falsification and the Methodology of Scientific Research Programs." *Criticism and the Growth of Knowledge.* Ed. Imre Lakatos and Alan Musgrave. Cambridge: Cambridge UP, 1970.

Lyotard, Jean Francois. *The Postmodern Condition: A Report on Knowledge.* Trans. Geoff Bennington and Brian Massumi. Minneapolis: U of Minnesota P, 1985.

Mahoney, Michael. "Open Exchange and Epistemic Progress." *American Psychologist* 40 (1985): 29-39.

———. "Publication Prejudices: An Experimental Study of Confirmatory Bias in the Peer Review System." *Cognitive Therapy and Research* 1: (1977) 161-75.

Maynard, Douglas W. "Narratives and Narrative Structure in Plea Bargaining." *Narrative and the Legal Discourse: A Reader in Storytelling and the Law*. Ed. David Ray Papke. Liverpool: Deborah Charles, 1991.

Mill, John Stuart. *On Liberty. Essential Works of John Stuart Mill*. Ed. Max Lerner. New York: Bantam, 1961.

Mokhiber, Russell. "Underworld, U.S.A." *In These Times* 1 April 1996, 14–16.

Nussbaum, Martha C. *Poetic Justice: The Literary Imagination and Public Life*. Boston: Beacon P, 1995.

O'Barr, William M., and John M. Conley. "Litigant Satisfaction Versus Legal Adequacy in Small Claims Court Narratives." *Narrative and the Legal Discourse: A Reader in Storytelling and the Law*. Ed. David Ray Papke. Liverpool: Deborah Charles, 1991.

O'Donovan, Katherine. "Identification With Whom?" *Tall Stories? Reading Law and Literature*. Ed. John Morison and Christine Bell. Aldershot: Dartmouth, 1996.

Papke, David Ray. "Discharge as Denouement: Appreciating the Storytelling of Appellate Opinions." *Narrative and the Legal Discourse: A Reader in Storytelling and the Law*. Ed. David Ray Papke. Liverpool: Deborah Charles, 1991.

———. *Narrative and the Legal Discourse: A Reader in Storytelling and the Law*. Liverpool: Deborah Charles, 1991.

Popper, Karl. *The Logic of Scientific Discovery*. New York: Harper and Row, 1968.

Posner, Richard A. *Law and Literature: A Misunderstood Relation*. Cambridge: Harvard UP, 1988.

Steiner, George. *Language and Silence: Essays on Language, Literature, and the Inhuman*. New York: Atheneum, 1977.

van Dijk, Teun. *Communicating Racism: Ethnic Prejudice in Thought and Talk*. Newbury Park: Sage, 1987.

van Roermund, Bert. *Law, Narrative and Reality: An Essay in Intercepting Politics*. Dordrecht: Kluwer Academic Publishers, 1997.

Ward, Ian. *Law and Literature: Possibilities and Perspectives*. Cambridge: Cambridge UP, 1995.

Weisberg, Richard. *Poethics and Other Strategies of Law and Literature*. New York: Columbia UP, 1992.

West, Robin. *Narrative, Authority, and Law*. Ann Arbor: U of Michigan P, 1993.

White, Hayden. *Metahistory*. Baltimore: Johns Hopkins UP, 1973.

CONTRIBUTORS

Jane B. Baron
Peter J. Liacouras professor of law at Temple University and the author of articles on narrative and law in such journals as *Duke Law Journal* and *Southern California Law Review*.

Theron Britt
Associate professor of English at the University of Memphis. He has published essays on medical discourse, law and literature, and contemporary fiction and is currently finishing a book on the relation of indeterminacy and legitimization in contemporary American narratives.

Michael Brooks
Professor of English at West Chester University and the author of *John Ruskin and Victorian Architecture* (1987) and *Subway City: Riding the Trains, Reading New York* (1997).

Lesley Higgins
Associate professor of English at York University, Toronto. She has published articles on modernist literary culture, textual studies, and gender, with emphasis on the works of Gerard Manley Hopkins and Walter Pater.

Patrick Colm Hogan
Associate professor of English and comparative literature at the University of Connecticut and author of *The Politics of Interpretations, Joyce, Milton, and the Theory of Influence,* and *On Interpretation: Meaning and Influence in Law, Psychoanalysis, and Literature.*

Contributors

Dennis R. Klinck
Professor of law at McGill University and the author of *The Word of the Law* (1992); he also holds a doctorate in English literature with specialization in Renaissance drama.

Marie-Christine Leps
Associate professor of English and social and political thought at York University and the author of *Apprehending the Criminal: The Production of Deviance in Nineteenth-Century Discourse*.

Kostas Myrsiades
Professor of comparative literature and English at West Chester University, and editor of *College Literature*. He is the author/editor/translator of fifteen books on modern Greek literature and culture and the teaching of literature.

Linda Myrsiades
Associate professor of English at West Chester University and associate editor of *College Literature*. She has authored two studies on Greek folk theater and one on guerrilla theater, *Cultural Representation in Historical Resistance* (1999).

Frances J. Ranney
Visiting instructor of English at Miami University. She is the author of several articles on judicial rhetoric and the integration of writing in business courses.

Paula Jean Reiter
Lecturer at Marquette University and the author of *Popular Fiction and the Weldon Trial* (1996).

Anne E. Shaw
MFA candidate in English at George Mason University.

Alane C. Spinney
Assistant professor of art at Carthage College.

Richard Clarke Sterne
Professor of English, Emeritus, Simmons College and the author of *Dark Mirror: The Sense of Injustice in Modern European and American Literature*.

Richard H. Weisberg
Professor of law at Benamin N. Cardozo Law School, general editor of *Cardozo Studies in Law and Literature*, and the author of *The Failure of the Word* (1984), *Poethics* (1992), and *Vichy Law and the Holocaust in France* (1996).

Jennifer K. Wood
Doctoral candidate in the Department of Communication at the University of Pittsburgh where she is completing her dissertation on "Codes of Innocence: The Rhetoric of Victims' Rights."

INDEX

A
ABA Journal 105
abortion law 238, 241
abortion-related violence 47-71
abortion rights 47-68, 219-35
Abraham 226
Act to Regulate the Issue and Validity of Passports 122
adoption law 2
Agee, Phillip 139-42, 150
Alienage 121-26
Aliens Act 124, 125
Aliens Restriction (Amendment) Act 125-26
Allen, Barry Allen 29
Ambedkar, Bhimrao Kamji 217
Anglo-Indians 206-16
Anselm 121
antiabortion movement 49-50
antiabortion movement in Milwaukee 50-52
antiabortion oratory 64-65
antiabortion spectacle 60-65
antifoundational stories 21-20
Aristotle 173
Atwood, Margaret 8, 219-45

Handmaid's Tale, The 8, 219-45
Auschwitz 275

B
Baby Girl Clausen. See Baby Jessica case
Baby Jessica case 3, 14-16, 22-27
Baby Richard case 23-24
Bailey v. Alabama 228
Bakhtin 273
Bakke case. See Regents of the University of California v. Bakke
Baldwin, Stanley 124
Baron, Jane B. 73
Bartlett, Adelaide Case 246-70
Beccaria, Cesare 91
Benjamin, Paul 35, 37
Bennett, W. Lance 74
Berger, Vivian 88
Bhabha, Homi 146
Birmingham conference on legal reform 250
Blackstone, William 193-194, 200, 202
Blanche de la Tremoille, Adelaide.

See Bartlett, Adelaide Case
Blackmun, Harry A. 236, 237
Bob Jones University case 278
Bolton, W. F. 190-191, 193-194, 202-203
Booth v. Maryland 72-73, 78-79, 89-90
Boucher, Christopher 44
Boucher, Jack 42
Bourdieu, Pierre 73, 80-81
Bradwell v. Illinois 241
Braver, Susan 40, 41
Bray, Michael 66
Brennan, William J., Jr. 89, 90, 142
Breslin, Jimmy 38, 44
Britain's Joint Council for the Welfare of Immigrants: 145
British Nationality Act 134
British raj 206-08
Bronson, Charles 35-36, 41
Brown, Wesley 32
Buck v. Bell 99
Bunting, Basil 122
    "The Passport Officer" 122
Burger, Warren E. 278
Burson, Charles 82

C

Cabey, Darrell 44
Cabey, Darrell 29, 38, 39, 42
Canty, Troy 29
Cardenas, Juan 91
Cardozo, Benjamin 90, 285
Carr v. Allison 5
Carr v. Allison Gas Turbine Division 94-96, 102, 104-16
Case of the Duchy of Lancaster 191-92
Cashinahua Indians 172, 178
Chaudhuri, Nirad C. 206
Christensen, Diana 91
Christopher, Charisse 76-77, 79, 83-84, 87
Christopher, Lacie 77, 79-80, 83-84, 87
Christopher, Nicholas 77-89
CIA 141
City of Akron v. Akron Center for Reproductive Health 237
Civil Rights Act of 1964 107
Clarke, Edward 261, 263-66
clinic violence 69
Clint Eastwood 41
Coke, Sir Edward 193-94, 196-97, 199-201, 204
    First Part of the Institutes 194
colonial justice 206-16
Commonwealth Immigrants Act 134
community 143-49
comprehending contraries 111
Comstock Act of 1873 241
Condit, Celeste 48, 52-53, 63, 68
Constitutions of Clarendon 121
contract parenthood 239
Cover, Robert 9, 271, 278
Cox, Darrius 34
Crane, Stephen 29
crime 30-36
Critical Legal Studies (CLS) 272
critical legal theory 273-85

D

Death Wish 4, 28, 35-36, 41-42, 44
DeBoer v. Schmidt 22-23
Deconstruction 273
Defense of the Realm Act 122
Delgado, Richard 3, 9, 18-19, 272-83, 285
    "Storytelling for Oppositionists and Others: A Plea for Narrative." 9, 272
Deltejo, Jose 39
Derrida, Jacques 155, 174, 178, 273
    "Economimesis." 178

"Force of Law" 178
Dickens, Charles 156
   Our Mutual Friend 156
Doctorow, E. L. 155
   Ragtime 155
Doe v. Bolton 232
domestic violence 17
Domian, Christopher 40
Donis, Miles 30
   The Fall of New York 30
Douglas, William O. 141
Dyson, Reverend George 260-61, 264

E
economic theory of sexuality 96-98
Edmund v. Florida 76
Eliot, T. S. 6, 119-20, 128-33, 149-50, 154-56
   After Strange Gods 129
   For Lancelot Andrewes 155
   "Gerontion" 129
   "Love Song of J. Alfred Prufrock, The" 128
   Prufrock and Other Observations 155
   Queen Mary's Book for India 130
   "Song for Simeon, A" 154
   "To the Indians who Died in Africa." 130
   Waste Land, The 6, 119-20, 130-32, 155, 156, 160
Equal Employment Opportunity Commission (EEOC) 107
equality law 238
Estrich, Susan 3, 16-17
ethics 107, 109-13
Ettema, James S. 74-75
European Union (EU) 121, 146, 150, 159

F
FACE 51, 68
Feiffer, Jules 30
   Little Murders 30
feminist difference theory 229
Feminist Majority Foundation 47
femme covert 253
fetus 220-22, 228, 231, 236-37, 240-42
fiction and fact 281-87
Fish, Stanley 96
Fiske, John 72, 76, 85
Fletcher, George P. 29, 42
   Crime of Self Defense; Bernhard Goetz and the Law on Trial, A 29
Foreman, Joseph 50-51
Formalist Politics 273
Forster, E. M. 7, 206-18
   Passage to India, A 7, 206-218
   Chandrapore 215
   Marabar 210, 212, 213, 217
   Sweepers 209, 215
Foucault, Michel 5, 118, 120, 126, 134-36, 145-146, 150-52, 154-59, 225
foundationalist stories 20-21
Frederick, Andy 38
Freedom of Access to Clinic Entrances Act. See FACE
Freemen standoff 43
Frye, Northrop 281
Furman v. Georgia 89

G
Garfield, Brian 4, 35-36, 41
General Motors (GM) 94, 105, 109-10, 112-114
Glasser, Theodore L. 74-75
Goethe, Johan Wolfgang von 275
Goetz case 28-46, 86
Goetz, Bernhard. See Goetz case

good mother 228-29, 240, 241
governmentality 133-43, 149-52
Gregg v. Georgia 89, 91
Gulf War 274

H
Habermas 171, 178
Haig v. Agee 141, 142
Hale, Matthew 241
Hanauer, Joan 30-31
Harvard Law Review 16
Haynes, Richard 89
Heaney, Seamus 151
   "From the Republic of Conscience" 151
Henry III 121
Henson v. City of Dundee 110-112
Herodotus 149, 160
   Histories 149, 160
Hill v. Grange 202
Hill, Paul 66
Hindus 209, 213-15
Hinton, Harold 118
Hirschfeld, Gerald 32
Hitler/Gandhi situation 174
Hoffman, Darnay 44
Holliday, George 72, 84-85
Holmes, Oliver Wendell 96, 99, 101
Horton, Willie 84
House Un-American Activities Committee (HUAC) 140
Hunter, William 220
   Gravid Uterus 220
Huxley 222
   Brave New World 222

I
indentured servitude 230
innocent victims 83-89
institutional analysis 287-88
interdisciplinarity 1-3, 9-10, 180-87
   linear interdisciplinarity 2
   Restrictive interdisciplinarity 3
   supplemental interdisciplinarity 3
Internal Security Act 139
International Committee Against Piracy 151
interpretation 2, 107-08, 271
Iowa Supreme Court 16, 22

J
James, Henry 6, 120, 126-28, 150
   American Scene, The 6, 120, 126-128
Joyce, William 158
judgment 172-76
justice 170-71, 173

K
Kafka, Franz 96
Kaminsky, Alice 39-40, 41
   The Victim's Song 39
Kant, Immanuel 6, 175-176, 178
   Critique of Judgment 175-176
   genius 176
Kantorowicz, Ernst 191-193, 199, 201
Kennedy, Anthony M. 90
Kennedy, Randall 83
Kenney, Dennis Jay Kenney 33
   Crime, Fear, and the New York City Subways 33
Kent v. Dulles 141
King George V 125
King John 121
King Solomon. See Solomon
King William I 121
King, Rodney 5, 72, 84, 86
Kipling, Rudyard 160-161
   Kim 160-161
Kramer, Lawrence 35
Krishna celebration 216
Kuby, Ron 44

L

landlords 190-201, 233
law and control 229-231
law and literature 1-2, 9-10
law and narrative 287
law as translation 102-104
lawyers 246-48
Leach, Dr. 260-64
League of Nations' Passport Conferences, The 124, 143
Lee, Lop B. 34
legalism 180-87
legal representation 223-26, 237-38, 249-52 255-58, 263-66
legal rituals and symbolic violence 72-89
Lesly, Mark 43
liability issues 190-201
literary perspectives 104
Lochner v. New York 99, 100
Lord Darcy v. Askwith 195
Lord Haw-Haw 150
Lord Wilmot 142-143
Luker, Kristen 51-52
Lyotard, Jean-Francois 2, 3, 6, 151, 169-179, 278
   Au Juste 170
   Differend, The 170
   discours, figure 78
   economie libidinale 178
   Just Gaming 6, 169-179
   metanarratives 171
   modernity 172
   narrative pragmatics 172-173, 174, 175, 176, 177
   Postmodern Condition, The 151, 171
   Postmodern Explained, The 178

M

Maastricht Treaty, The 144
Magna Carta 121

Maher v. Roe 234
Mahoney, Michael 284
"many realities" storytelling 18-20
Marshall, John 90, 96
Marshall, Thurgood 113
matriarchal systems 224
Matthew Trewhella 50-51
McCleskey v. Kemp 75-76, 89
McGee, Michael Calvin 74
Medea 240
Melville, Herman 7, 180
   Billy Budd 7, 180
Christian legalism 181-84
Meritor Savings Bank v. Vinson 111, 114
Michigan Supreme Court 22-23
Miller, J. Hillis 169-71, 176, 177
   "Laying Down the Law: The Example of Kleist" 169
Miller, Monica Migliorino 50-51
Missionaries to the Preborn (MTP) 51
Monroe, Harriet 155
Mormile, Andrew 31
Morrison, Toni 232
   Beloved 232, 233
mother-child relation 223
Motola, Nunzio 37
Mr. T 14
Muller v. Oregon 241

N

N.O.W. et al. v. Scheidler et al 69
narrative 9, 277-81, 283, 286, 288
narrative and justice 169-71
narrative identity 127-33
narrative methodology 73-75
narrative pragmatics 2, 169-77
narrative study 271-290
narrative theory 280
narratology 282-283

National Abortion Federation (NAF) 47
nationalism 124-26
national identity 127-33
natural body 232
natural vs.officialized law 224
Ne Exeat Regno 121, 142
Nelson, John S. 74
New York city 29-36
Nicholas Christopher v. Payne 83
Nichols, Bill 84-85
Nietzsche, Friedrich Wilhelm 126, 273
Nightline 88
nineteenth-century woman 247
Nixon, Richard 140
Noganz, Julia 35
Nussbaum, Martha C. 106

O
O'Connor, Sandra Day 87, 237
Ondaatje, Michael 6, 121, 146-149, 150, 155, 160
   English Patient, The 6, 121, 146-149, 160
   In the Skin of a Lion 155, 160
   Truman, Truman 148
Operation Rescue (OR) 50, 51, 53, 69
Orwell, George 206
Oscar Wilde-Alfred Taylor trial 269
Oster, Jerry 34
   Sweet Justice 34

P
passports 2, 5, 117-68
patriarchal systems 224
Payne v. Tennessee 5, 72-73, 76-89, 90-91
Payne, Pervis Tyrone 76-79, 80, 83-85, 89
Peerce, Larry 4, 31-32

Incident, The 4, 31-32
Pimlico Case 8, 259-66
Planned Parenthood 63-65
Planned Parenthood of Central Missouri v. Danforth, 241-42
Planned Parenthood of Kansas City v. Ashcroft 236
Planned Parenthood of Southeastern Pennsylvania v. Casey 234, 236-42
Planned Parenthood v. Danforth 242
Poetry 155
Pope Urban II 121
Posner, Richard 5, 94-116
   "Judicial Opinion and the Poem, The" 103
   Law and Literature: A Misunderstood Relation 98
   "Law and Literature: A Relation Reargued." 98-102
   literary theory 98-102
   Sex and Reason 96, 97
post-abortion syndrome 56
Pound, Ezra 128, 155, 156
Powell, Lewis F. 90
pregnant woman 221-22, 228, 230-31, 233, 236, 23-42
primer seisin 203
primogeniture 254
privacy law 238
private harms 190-201
Pro-Life Action Network (PLAN) 50, 69
property law 190-201, 231-34
propiska 157
public harms 190-201

R
race and law 3, 17-18, 20-21, 86
Racketeer and Corrupt Organizations Act (RICO) 69
Ramseur, James 29, 43

rape law 3, 16-17
Read, Herbert 128
Reed v. Shepard 113, 114
reference and selection principles 281
Regents of the University of California v. Bakke 9, 286-87
Rehnquist Court 73
Rehnquist, William H. 78-81, 83-86, 90 237
relationships 108-09
religious hostility 206, 209, 213-15
Report on the Operation of the Treaty on European Union 143-44
representation 234-35, 248-58, 267
reproduction 221, 223
reproductive woman 8, 219-20, 224, 233
resistance to power 225
rhetoric and reason 105-06
rhetoric and sexuality 96-98
rhetoric in law 100-101
rhetoric of antiabortion demonstrators 48-71
rhetorical analysis 2, 287
Riverside Shakespeare, The 195
Robeson, Paul 139-140, 142, 150
Roe v. Wade 4, 49, 65, 234-37, 241
Rolling Stone 34-35
Romanticism 273-77
Ron Kuby 28
Ronny and the Urban Watchdogs 29
"Subway Vigilante" 29
Rosary Society 60-62
Rube Goldberg device 31
Rubin, Lillian 39
   Quiet Rage: Bernie Goetz in a Time of Madness 39

S
Said, Edward W. 216-17
Salvi, John 66
Scheidler, Joseph 50, 51, 69
   Closed: 99 Ways to Stop Abortion 50
Schmidt, Daniel 22
Schwanberg, Sidney 38
sexual harassment law 2, 5, 94-115
sexual market 109-10
Shakespeare 6-7, 13, 96, 180-189, 190-205, 275
   Merchant of Venice, The 6, 180-189
      "ring plot" 188
      "Shylock Trust" 184-85
      "Shylock Will" 185-86
   Richard II 7, 190-205
      "Body politic" of King 196-97
      Dignity royal 191
      doctrine of "the king's two bodies." 191-92
      law of waste 193
      property law 190-05
Shelley, Mary 222
   Frankenstein 222
Shelley, Percy Bysshe 169, 177
   "Defense of Poetry" 169
Shipley, Ruth B. 118, 150
Sidewalk Counseling 4, 53-57, 64-70
Simpson, O. J. 13, 43
Sliwa, Curtis 33-34
   "The Magnificent Thirteen Subway Safety Patrol," 33
Slotnick, Barry 28, 42, 44
Smeal, Eleanor 47
Solomon 2-3, 14-16, 22, 25, 219, 223-26, 237-38
Souter, David H. 90
South Carolina v. Gathers 72-73, 78-79, 89, 90
Southern Christian Leadership Con-

ference (SCLC) 91
Soviet passport 157
Spencer, Herbert 99-100
  Social Statics 99-100
State v. Payne 77-78
Statute of Gloucester 193-94, 197, 200
Statute of Marlbridge 193-94, 197-98
Statute of Wills 202
Steiner, Bradley J. 34
  Subway Survival! 34
Steiner, George 274-275
Stevens, John Paul 16, 82
storying methodology 2-3, 13-25, 28-44
story-telling 16-22, 24-25, 271
Subversive Activities Control Act 139
subway 29-43
Supreme Court 2, 6, 75-76, 78-80, 83, 140, 142, 241
surrogacy 228-29, 239
symbolic violence 80-87

T
Taft, William Howard 107
Tailhook scandal 106
tenants 190-201, 234
Terminator 2: Judgment Day 236
Terry, Randall 50
theory 272-73
Thomas of Woodstock 198
Tiresias 156
Travel Control Act 122
trial 72-89, 102-04, 181-84, 208-14, 255-58, 260-66
Trollope, Anthony 8, 246-70
  Orley Farm 8, 248-50, 252-58

U
Unibomber 43
United Nations 143

Universal Declaration of Human Rights 143
Untouchables 209
Urena, Furman 39

V
values 108-09
VCY/America, 52, 65
Vichy 225, 273
victim impact statements (VIS) 2, 75-76
victim's rights 72-89
Victorian husband 247
Victorian professional 247
Victorian women 248
von Kleist, Heinrich 169
  "Michael Kohlhaas" 169

W
Wachs, Eleanor 30
Waples, Gregory 42-44
Webster v. Reproductive Health Services 239
Weisberg, Richard 5, 273, 285
welcome harassment 105, 108, 110-12
West, Robin 5, 9, 79, 96-97, 102-03, 113
Whalen, Richard 30
"what really happened" stories 20
White, Hayden 280
  Metahistory 280
White, James Boyd 5, 96, 102-04, 107, 111-13
  Justice As Translation 107
Whitehead, Mary Beth 240
Williams, Patricia 3, 17-18, 20-21, 86
Willion v. Berkley 192
Wills, Justice 262, 263, 269
Winner, Michael 36
Wisconsin Women's Health Center in Brown Deer 60-61

Wolfe, Thomas 4, 34-35, 44
    The Bonfire of the Vanities 4, 34
woman and autonomy 237-38
woman and representation 234-35, 242, 249-52
woman and separation 220-23, 236-37
woman and slavery 228-29, 240
woman as economic commodity 227-31, 240-41
woman as property 231-34, 239
woman's function as a business transaction 230-231
womb 223, 232
Woolf, Virginia 6, 120, 136-139, 150, 157-158
    Mrs. Dalloway 6, 120, 136-38, 157-58
    Three Guineas 138-139
Wrotesley v. Adams 197

Y
Youth For America 51

Z
Zant v. Stephens 76
Zvolanek, Mary 76-77, 84-85, 87

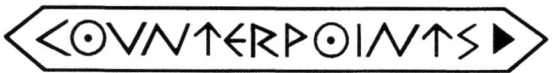

Studies in the Postmodern Theory of Education

General Editors
Joe L. Kincheloe & Shirley R. Steinberg

Counterpoints publishes the most compelling and imaginative books being written in education today. Grounded on the theoretical advances in criticalism, feminism, and postmodernism in the last two decades of the twentieth century, Counterpoints engages the meaning of these innovations in various forms of educational expression. Committed to the proposition that theoretical literature should be accessible to a variety of audiences, the series insists that its authors avoid esoteric and jargonistic languages that transform educational scholarship into an elite discourse for the initiated. Scholarly work matters only to the degree it affects consciousness and practice at multiple sites. Counterpoints' editorial policy is based on these principles and the ability of scholars to break new ground, to open new conversations, to go where educators have never gone before.

For additional information about this series or for the submission of manuscripts, please contact:

> Joe L. Kincheloe & Shirley R. Steinberg
> 637 West Foster Avenue
> State College, PA 16801

To order other books in this series, please contact our Customer Service Department at:

> (800) 770-LANG (within the U.S.)
> (212) 647-7706 (outside the U.S.)
> (212) 647-7707 FAX

or browse online by series at:
> www.peterlang.com